SO-BAI-711

This coupon entitles you to special discounts
when you book your trip through the

TRAVEL NETWORK®
RESERVATION SERVICE

**Hotels ♦ Airlines ♦ Car Rentals ♦ Cruises
All Your Travel Needs**

Here's what you get: *

♦ A discount of $50 on a booking of $1,000** or more
for two or more people!

♦ A discount of $25 on a booking of $500** or more
for one person!

♦ Free membership for three years, and 1,000 free miles
on enrollment in the unique Miles-to-Go™ frequent-
traveler program. Earn one mile for every dollar spent
through the program. Earn free hotel stays starting at
5,000 miles. Earn free roundtrip airline tickets starting
at 25,000 miles.

♦ Personal help in planning your own, customized trip.

♦ Fast, confirmed reservations at any property
recommended in this guide, subject to availability.***

♦ Special discounts on bookings in the U.S. and around
the world.

♦ Low-cost visa and passport service.

♦ Reduced-rate cruise packages.

Call us toll-free in the U.S. at 1-888-940-5000, or fax
us at 201-567-1832. In Canada, call us toll-free at
1-800-883-9959, or fax us at 416-922-6053.

* To qualify for these travel discounts, at least a portion of your trip must
  include destinations covered in this guide. No more than one coupon discount
  may be used in any 12-month period, for destinations covered in this guide.
  Cannot be combined with any other discount or program.
**These are U.S. dollars spent on commissionable bookings.
***A $10 fee, plus fax and/or phone charges, will be added to the cost of
  bookings at each hotel not linked to the reservation service. Customers
  must approve these fees in advance.

Valid until December 31, 1997. Terms and conditions of the Miles-to-
Go™ program are available on request by calling 201-567-8500, ext 55.

Frommer's 97

Cancún, Cozumel & The Yucatán

by Marita Adair

Macmillan • USA

ABOUT THE AUTHOR

Marita Adair's lifelong passion for Mexico's culture, people, and history began at age 11 on her first trip across the border to Nogales. An award-winning travel writer, she logs about 10,000 miles a year traveling in Mexico—by all means of conveyance. Her freelance photographs and articles about Mexico have appeared in numerous newspapers and magazines.

MACMILLAN TRAVEL

A Simon & Schuster Macmillan Company
1633 Broadway
New York, NY 10019

Find us online at **http://www.mgr.com/travel** or
on America Online at **Keyword: Frommer's**.

ISBN 0-02-861246-9
ISSN 1064-1416

Editor: Ian Wilker
Production Editor: Carol Sheehan
Design by Michele Laseau
Map Editor: Douglas Stallings
Digital Cartography by Ortelius Design and Raffaele DeGennaro
Maps copyright © by Simon & Schuster, Inc.

SPECIAL SALES

Bulk purchases (10+ copies) of Frommer's and selected Macmillan travel guides are available to corporations, organizations, mail-order catalogs, institutions, and charities at special discounts, and can be customized to suit individual needs. For more information write to Special Sales, Macmillan General Reference, 1633 Broadway, New York, NY 10019.

Manufactured in the United States of America

Contents

Appendix 232

Index 239

List of Maps

AN INVITATION TO THE READER

In researching this book, I discovered many wonderful places—resorts, inns, restaurants, shops, and more. I'm sure you'll find others. Please tell me about them, so I can share the information with your fellow travelers in upcoming editions. If you were disappointed with a recommendation, I'd love to know that, too. Please write to:

Marita Adair
Frommer's Cancún, Cozumel & the Yucatán
Macmillan Travel
1633 Broadway
New York, NY 10019

AN ADDITIONAL NOTE

Please be advised that travel information is subject to change at any time—and this is especially true of prices. We therefore suggest that you write or call ahead for confirmation when making your travel plans. The authors, editors, and publisher cannot be held responsible for the experiences of readers while traveling. Your safety is important to us, however, so we encourage you to stay alert and be aware of your surroundings. Keep a close eye on cameras, purses, and wallets, all favorite targets of thieves and pickpockets.

A FEW WORDS ABOUT PRICES

In December 1994, the Mexican government devalued its currency, the peso. Over the ensuing months, the peso's value against the dollar plummeted from 3.35 pesos against U.S. $1 to nearly 7 pesos against U.S. $1. The peso's value continues to fluctuate—at press time it was around 7.5 pesos to the dollar. Therefore, to allow for inflation, prices in this book (which are always given in U.S. dollars) have been converted to U.S. dollars at a rate of 7 pesos to the dollar, with 15 percent added for inflation. Inflation for 1996/1997 is forecast at around 36%. Many moderate-priced and expensive hotels, which often have U.S. toll-free reservation numbers and have many expenses in U.S. dollars, do not lower rates in keeping with the sinking peso.

Mexico has a Value-Added Tax of 15% (Impuesto de Valor Agregado, or IVA, pronounced "ee-bah") on almost everything, including restaurant meals, bus tickets, and souvenirs. (Exceptions are Cancún, Cozumel, and Los Cabos, where the IVA is 10%.) Hotel taxes are 17% everywhere except Cancún, Cozumel, and Los Cabos where they are 12%. The IVA will not necessarily be included in the prices quoted by hotels and restaurants. In addition, prices charged by hotels and restaurants have been deregulated. Mexico's new pricing freedom may cause some price variations from those quoted in this book; always ask to see a printed price sheet and always ask if the tax is included.

WHAT THE SYMBOLS MEAN

✪ Frommer's Favorites

Hotels, restaurants, attractions, and entertainment you should not miss.

⑤ Super-Special Values

Hotels and restaurants that offer great value for your money.

Getting to Know Mexico's Yucatán Peninsula

When I finally wrested myself from the bed and shuffled to the coffeemaker in my *casita* at Rancho Encantado, at Lake Bacalar in the southeastern Yucatán, I had already been awake in the darkness for some time listening to the sounds of the natural outdoor aviary. Eagerly I awaited daylight—I had to see the birds. But first coffee.

Then, with the Rancho's bird list in one hand and a coffee cup in the other, I strolled the tranquil tree-filled grounds beside Lago Bacalar, stealing quietly through the grass while gazing upward. There were so many chattering parrots that it was easy to dismiss them in search of something *more* exotic. Then I stopped. Above me in the broad canopy of a tall tree, sitting so quietly that his existence would have been undetected had I not been craning my neck upward, sat a toucan with an enormous bright green bill, yellow chest, and splash of red under its black tail. The sight of this resplendent bird in the wild, a common part of Mexico's Caribbean coast landscape, became memorable in a year of many such "ah ha, this is Mexico" moments: so much nature, so much history, so many newly discovered ruins, and so much progress—despite all we read to the contrary.

Traveling in Mexico is akin to walking through history, and in many places it's a walk in an exotic natural landscape as well. At Rancho Encantado I was within a few miles of newly excavated Maya ruins—just one site in an area so overgrown with newly discovered ruins that archaeologists expect further study of it will transform our knowledge of the Mesoamerican world. Tropical birds and other wildlife were so visible that they became commonplace.

The worthiness of Rancho Encantado and its location so close to Mexico's rich past was but one of the many satisfying rediscoveries I made this year. Others included inflation's failure to soar prices as I had expected; bargains were—and still are—everywhere.

In the aftermath of *La Crisis* (as Mexicans call the 1994 peso devaluation) and Hurricane Roxanne's rampage across the Yucatán Peninsula, I began the year gloomily anticipating finding numerous boarded-up restaurants, hotels, and other businesses during my annual research travels. But my worst fears failed to take shape—instead, I found a frenzy of new construction and Mexicans rustling up business wherever it could be found.

Just a few weeks after Roxanne pounded the Yucatán, I sped along Highway 307 south of Cancún—it had been nearly impassable immediately after the storm, flooded and clotted with downed trees. The hurricane's winds blew out almost every window in its path, yet hotels stood proudly sporting new paint, mattresses, furniture, and roofs—and shiny replacement glass glistened everywhere. "The day after the hurricane a man came through selling fresh palm fronds," John Swartz of La Rana Cansada in Playa del Carmen chuckled, "and of course we all bought them," he said. Woven palm roofs *(palapas)* are a functional and handsome architectural staple in much of Mexico. Teams of *palaperos* (professional palapa weavers) worked at such a furious pace that everywhere I went for hundreds of miles, handsome new palapas appeared completed. I saw numerous young men peddling along the narrow highway with palm fronds tied to each side of their bicycles, bound to some construction project for which a sale of palm leaves was as-sured. Hurricane-downed palms thus became a source of fresh palm leaves. . . . All in all, there were innumerable examples of Mexican ingenuity, creating opportunity out of devastation.

Incredibly, almost everywhere I checked along the Caribbean coast, hoteliers were adding rooms—not because of the storm, but in readiness for a progressive future, for which this coast is poised. The Cabañas Paamul is gearing up for a major expan-sion on their pretty little bay; the abovementioned Rancho Encantado has added four gorgeous *casitas* with Maya-theme murals on the walls and more tours to the Río Bec ruin route; developers are staking out the undeveloped beaches just north of the Majahual/Xcalak Peninsula; in Xcalak proper, small hotels are appearing on the Río Bec ruin route; and lavish private beachfront homes are going up like mad south of Cancún. The owner of the Hotel Albatros in Playa del Carmen razed his funky old hotel and erected a smashingly handsome pueblo-style one—the Pelicano Inn—in its place. He and others explained the building frenzy: "We're taking advantage of the low cost of building materials and labor right now."

For those whose businesses earn payment in dollars, and those without debt with exorbitant interest, this was the year to invest in new construction—not at all bad for the Mexican economy.

Still, despite such prosperity, La Crisis is troubling for most Mexicans. Until only a few years ago, the middle class seldom made use of credit. But as Mexico's infla-tion spiraled upward, loans for homes and cars and use of credit cards increased. When the devaluation hit there was no ceiling on interest—ordinary people found themselves paying 80% to 150% interest on debts. These are the people we've seen profiled in our newspapers. The less affluent populace earned even fewer pesos after the devaluation, while the rising cost of transportation and food (which still seem relatively inexpensive to us because our dollar buys more) made purchasing basic com-modities very difficult.

The U.S. newspapers have picked up many stories of crisis-panicked Mexicans who've turned to thievery. I don't wish to diminish safety concerns or the terrible experience of being victimized, but I must say that average tourist meets far more kind, hardworking people than thieves and blackguards. To me, these working people with the smiling faces are Mexico's unpaid goodwill ambassadors, the ones who gen-erate warm memories when we're nestled once again in our homes far away. Of course, they don't make headlines. After a trip to South America this year, where ram-pant crime forced me to guard my possessions every minute, I returned home grateful for the relative safety of my own hometown, but more than that, I viewed Mexico with fresh, appreciative eyes.

In fact, my enthusiasm for Mexico was so keen this year that I spent Thanksgiv-ing on top of Temple II at Calakmul with ruins specialist Serge Riou, munching a chicken sandwich and musing over the mysteries of this site only 75 miles north of

Tikal in Guatemala. It was such a clear and beautiful day that from our lofty perch we could see El Mirador, another Guatemalan site 30 miles south, rising from an ocean of jungle.

This year, as always, it was difficult to leave Mexico and plunge into months of remembering and writing about the places I've been. But in just a few days I'll sally south again for a more slow-paced respite, drinking in more of Mexico City; after that, it's on to the soothing, slow-paced streets of 16th-century Pátzcuaro . . . and then who knows where else.

It's been such a pleasure to meet so many of you as we ramble through Mexico. I hope to cross paths with more of you and share travel tales about our journeys in the land of our southern neighbor. See you there.

—Marita Adair, May 16, 1996

1 The Land & Its People

For most of us, the image that comes to mind at the mention of the words "Cancún" or "Yucatán" is a beach. And not just any beach—we're talking about the proverbial drifting-powdery-white-sand-beach-fronting-a-turquoise-sea. And so Cancún's beaches really are—they're the best in Mexico and stretch down the coastline nearly to Belize.

But traveling in the Yucatán Peninsula provides an opportunity to witness several contrasting faces of Mexico—its ties to an ancient past, its giant leaps into an upscale, fast-moving future, and its timeless natural beauty. Within its confines, one can see pre-Hispanic ruins such as **Chichén-Itzá, Uxmal,** and **Tulum** and the living descendants of the cultures who built them, as well as the ultimate in resort Mexico— **Cancún.**

Edged by the rough deep-aquamarine Gulf of Mexico on the west and north and the clear cerulean-blue Caribbean Sea on the east, the peninsula covers almost 84,000 square miles, with nearly 1,000 miles of shoreline. Covered with dense jungle, the porous limestone peninsula is mostly flat, with thin soil supporting a low, scrubby jungle that contains almost no surface rivers. Rainwater is filtered by the limestone into underground rivers. *Cenotes*, or collapsed caves, are natural wells dotting the region. The only sense of height comes from the curvaceous terrain rising from the western shores of Campeche inland to the border with Yucatán state. This rise, called the Puuc hills, is the Maya "Alps," a staggering 980 feet high. Locally the hills are known as the Sierra de Ticul or Sierra Alta. The highways undulate a little as you go inland, and south of Ticul there's a rise in the highway that provides a marvelous view of the "valley" and misty Puuc hills lining the horizon. Ancient Maya near the Puuc hills developed a decorative style that incorporated geometric patterns and masks of Chaac (the Maya rain god), thus giving the style its name—Puuc.

The interior is dotted with lovely rock-walled villages inhabited by the kind, living Maya of today along with crumbling henequén haciendas surrounded by fields of maguey. Henequén, a yucca-like plant with tough fiber ideal for binder twine, was the king crop in the Yucatán in the 19th century. Though the industry has declined in the past century, the spiny plant is still used today to produce rope, packing material, shoes, and purses. Besides henequén, other crops grown on the mostly agricultural peninsula are corn, coconuts, oranges, mangoes, and bananas.

The western side of the peninsula fronts the Gulf coast and is the complete opposite of the Caribbean coast. The beaches, while good enough, don't compare to those on the Caribbean. But nowhere else can you see flocks of flamingos as you can at national parks near **Celestún** and **Río Lagartos.**

Mexico

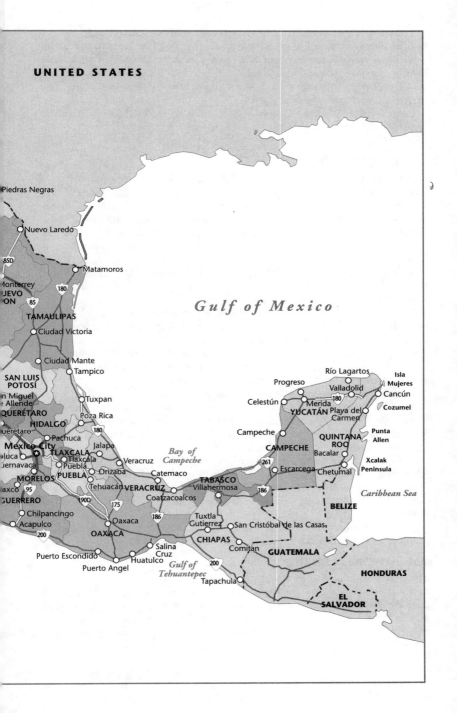

UNITED STATES

Piedras Negras

Nuevo Laredo

85D

Matamoros

Monterrey
NUEVO
LEON

85

180

TAMAULIPAS

Ciudad Victoria

Ciudad Mante

Tampico

SAN LUIS
POTOSÍ

San Miguel
de Allende

QUERÉTARO

Querétaro

HIDALGO

Poza Rica

Pachuca

180

Mexico City

Toluca

TLAXCALA

Jalapa

Cuernavaca

Tlaxcala

Puebla

Veracruz

MORELOS

PUEBLA

Orizaba

Catemaco

Taxco

Tehuacán

VERACRUZ

95

GUERRERO

190D

175

Coatzacoalcos

Chilpancingo

Oaxaca

186

Acapulco

200

OAXACA

Salina
Cruz

Puerto Escondido

Huatulco

Puerto Angel

*Gulf of
Tehuantepec*

Tuxtla
Gutierrez

CHIAPAS

Comitán

200

Tapachula

Gulf of Mexico

*Bay of
Campeche*

Tuxpan

Progreso

Río Lagartos

Isla
Mujeres

Valladolid

Cancún

Celestún

Merida

180

Cozumel

YUCATÁN

Playa del
Carmen

Campeche

QUINTANA
ROO

Punta
Allen

CAMPECHE

Bacalar

261

Xcalak
Peninsula

Escarcega

Chetumal

TABASCO

Villahermosa

186

Caribbean Sea

San Cristóbal de las Casas

BELIZE

GUATEMALA

HONDURAS

EL
SALVADOR

5

This peninsula is excellent for a driving trip, since roads are generally flat, well-kept, and not heavily trafficked. Outside the resorts, the Maya continue life as they did before the invasion of tourists began in 1974. Besides the friendly Maya faces you can meet in any village where you stop, you see men on bicycles with hunting rifles and cork-capped water gourds on their shoulders turning from the highway down bumpy, narrow dirt tracks into the thick jungle.

Even in Cancún you can plot an economical vacation, but your bucks will go much further on the islands of **Isla Mujeres** and **Cozumel** and farther still down the coast south of Cancún.

THE MEXICAN PEOPLE

The population of Mexico is 85 million; 15% are ethnically European (most are of Spanish descent, but a French presence lingers on from the time of Maximilian's abortive empire, and other European nationalities are represented), 60% are *mestizo* (mixed Spanish and Indian), and 25% are pure Indian (descendants of the Maya, Aztecs, Huastecs, Otomies, Totonacs, and other peoples). Added to this ethnic mix are Africans brought as slaves (this group has been so thoroughly assimilated that it is barely discernable).

Although Spanish is the official language, about 50 Indian languages are still spoken, mostly in the Yucatán Peninsula, Oaxaca, Chiapas, Chihuahua, Nayarit, Puebla, Sonora and Veracruz, Michoacán, and Guerrero.

Modern Mexico clings to its identity while embracing outside cultures—Mexicans enjoy the Bolshoi Ballet as easily as a family picnic or village festival. Mexicans have a knack for knowing how to enjoy life, and families, weekends, holidays, and festivities are given priority. They also enjoy stretching a weekend holiday into four days called a *puente* (bridge) and, with the whole family in tow, fleeing the cities en masse to visit relatives in the country, picnic, or relax at resorts.

The Mexican workday is a long one: Laborers begin around 7am and get off at dusk; office workers go in around 9am and, not counting the two- to three-hour lunch, get off at 7 or 8pm. Once a working career is started, there is little time for additional study. School is supposedly mandatory and free through the sixth grade, but many youngsters quit long before that or never go at all.

Sociologists and others have written volumes trying to explain the Mexican's special relationship with death. Death and the dead are at once mocked and mourned. The Days of the Dead, November 1 and 2, a cross between Halloween and All Saints' Day, is a good opportunity to observe Mexico's relationship with the concept of death.

Mexico's social complexity is such that it's difficult to characterize the Mexican people as a whole, but some broad generalizations can be drawn.

CLASS DIVISIONS IN MEXICO

There are vast differences in the culture and values of Mexico's various economic classes, and these gulfs have grown even wider over the last 10 years. On the one hand there are the fabulously rich; before the devaluation, according to *Forbes* magazine, Mexico had the fourth-most billionaires in the world, with at least 24. Upper-class Mexicans are extremely well-educated and well-mannered; they are very culturally sophisticated and often speak several languages. Many of Mexico's recent presidents have been educated in the United States.

The Mexican middle class—merchants, small restaurant and souvenir-shop owners, taxi drivers, tour guides, etc.—swelled from the 1950s through the 1980s. Now, however, it's struggling to stay afloat after a decade of incredible inflation that was

Impressions

Considering the variety of nations, tongues, cultures, and artistic styles, the unity of these peoples comes as a surprise. They all share certain ideas and beliefs. Thus it is not inaccurate to call this group of nations and cultures a Mexoamerican civilization. Unity in space and continuity in time; from the first millennium before Christ to the sixteenth century, these distinct Mexoamerican peoples evolve, reelaborate, and re-create a nucleus of basic concepts as well as social and political techniques and institutions. There were changes and variation . . . but never was the continuity broken.

—Octavio Paz, 1990

punctuated by the 1994 devaluation—the latter cut the value of an average Mexican's earnings in half. And yet these middle-class Mexicans are educating their children to higher standards—many young people now complete technical school or university. The middle-class standard of living includes trappings of life many take for granted in the States—maybe a phone in the home (a luxury that costs the equivalent of U.S. $600 to install), fancy tennis shoes for the children, occasional vacations, an economy car, and a tiny home or even smaller apartment in a modest neighborhood or high-rise.

Mexico's poorer classes have expanded. Their hopes for a decent future are dim and the daily goal for many is simply survival.

Machismo & Machisma

Sorting through the world of machismo and machisma in Mexico is fraught with subtleties better suited to sociological studies. Suffice it to say that in Mexico, and especially Mexico City, the roles of men and women are changing both slowly and rapidly. Both sexes cling to old sex roles—women in the home and men in the workplace—but they are relinquishing traditional ideas too. More women are being educated and working than ever before. And men are learning to work side-by-side with women of equal education and power.

Though women function in many professional positions, they encounter what they call the "adobe ceiling" (as opposed to the see-through "glass ceiling" in the United States): The male grip on upper-level positions in Mexico is so firm that women aren't able to even glimpse the top. Strong-willed women opt for setting up their own businesses as a result. Anyone used to a more liberated world may be frustrated by the extent to which Mexico is still a man's world—not uncommon are provocatively dressed women who pander to old-fashioned negative stereotypes, and flirtatious Mexican men who have difficulty sticking to business when dealing with a woman, even a serious businessperson who is dressed accordingly. Typically the Mexican man is charmingly polite, and affronted or embarrassed by the woman who won't permit him to open doors, seat her, and in every way put her on a respectful pedestal.

The Family

As a rule, Mexicans are very family-oriented. Family takes priority over work. Whole extended families routinely spend weekends and holidays together, filling parks and recreational spots until the last minute of the holiday. During those times men are often seen playing with, tending to, and enjoying the children as readily as women. In the home, girls are supervised closely until they are married. But the untethering of boys begins around age 15, when they are given more freedom than their sisters. It's customary, however, for all children to remain in the home until they marry, although there are more young people breaking the mold nowadays.

The Yucatán Peninsula

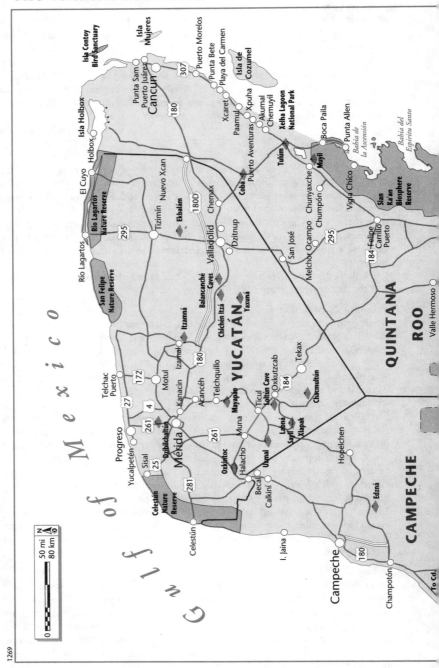

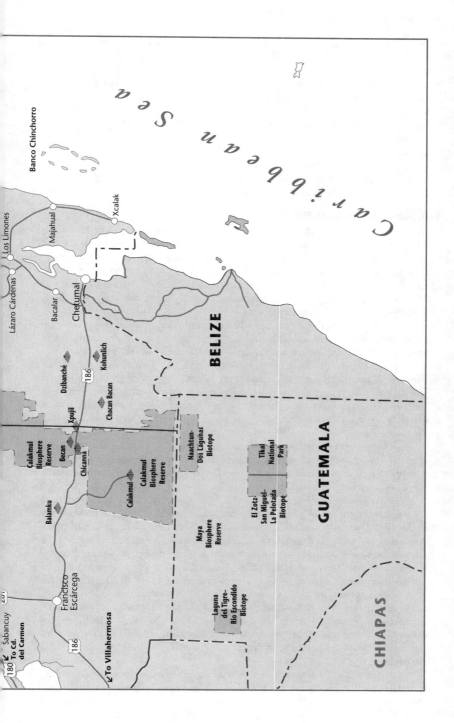

Caribbean Sea

Banco Chinchorro

Los Limones

Lázaro Cárdenas

Majahual

Xcalak

Bacalar

Chetumal

BELIZE

Dzibanché

Kohunlich

186

Chacán Bacán

Xpujil

Calakmul
Biosphere
Reserve

Becán

Chicanná

Calakmul

Calakmul
Biosphere
Reserve

Naachtun-
Dos Lagunas
Biotope

Tikal
National
Park

Balamku

Maya
Biosphere
Reserve

El Zotz-
San Miguel-
La Pelotada
Biotope

GUATEMALA

Francisco
Escárcega

¿To Villahermosa

Laguna
del Tigre-
Rio Escondido
Biotope

180 Sabancuy
To Cd.
del Carmen

186

CHIAPAS

9

Family roles among indigenous people are clear-cut. Women tend the babies, the home, the hearth, and often the fields. Men do the heavy work, tilling the soil, but women often join them for planting and harvesting. Theirs is a joint life focused on survival. Though not so much an unbendable custom now among these cultures, it's common to see women walking behind her spouse, carrying a child on her back and heavy bundles on her shoulders. When these people reach Mexico City, these roles shift somewhat; for example, a husband and wife will take turns tending their street stall with a child sleeping in a box or playing nearby. But always she will prepare the food.

Generally speaking, children are coddled and loved and are very obedient. Misbehaving children are seldom rebuked in public, since Mexican parenting style seems to favor gentle prodding, comforting, or nurturing instead.

THE MEXICAN CHARACTER

Describing the Mexican character is at least as complex as trying to describe the difference between New Englanders and Southerners in the United States. At the risk of offending some, I'll try to describe the values of the average Mexican. He or she is generous, honest, and loyal, and accepts acquaintances at face value. Visitors are far more likely to have something returned than to discover it stolen. But just as Mexicans are accepting, they can become unreasonably suspicious, and nothing will divert them from suspecting ill will.

The fierce Mexican dignity doesn't allow for insult. An insulting shopper, for example, may discover that suddenly nothing in the store is for sale, or that the prices have suddenly become ridiculously high for the duration of the shopper's visit.

Longtime friendships can fall apart instantly over a real or imagined wrong. Once wronged, Mexicans seldom forgive and never forget. The expression of indifference and distrust a Mexican wears when taking exception can appear to have been set in concrete. The more you try to right a wrong, or correct a wrong impression, the more entrenched it can become. This goes for personal friendships as well as dealings with the government.

Their long memories harbor the bad and the good. A Mexican will remember a kind deed or a fond, but brief, acquaintance until death. They will never forget the number of times the United States has invaded Mexico, or the government massacre of peaceful demonstrators at Tlatelolco Square in the capital in 1968.

Mexicans seem to thrive on gossip. And it runs the gamut from what government is doing behind the public's back to neighborhood squabbles. It figures prominently in the breakdown of personal and business relationships as well as the lack of confidence the public has in the government. During Mexico's recent investigation of the assassinations of two prominent government leaders, newspapers published the intrigue and conspiracy the public believed caused both events, alongside different official government reports. Mexicans often express the belief that their president takes his orders from the U.S. president.

No matter how poor or opulent their lives may be, all Mexicans love festivities, whether simple family affairs or the citywide parades on Revolution and Independence days. Often this celebratory spirit is just as evident at lunch in a festive place such as the Fonda del Recuerdo in the capital, known for its lively music and jovial atmosphere.

When it comes to foreigners, Mexicans want visitors to know, love, and enjoy their country and will extend many thoughtful courtesies just to see pleasure spread across the face of a visitor. They'll invite them to share a table in a crowded restaurant, go out of their way to give directions, help with luggage, and see stranded travelers safely on their way. An entire trip can be joyously colored by the many serendipitous en-counters with the people of this nation, whose efficiency and concern will be as memorable as their warmth and good humor.

2 A Look at the Past

Mexico is undergoing fast-paced and far-reaching change, as are most countries touched by modern technology. Some changes are astounding in their rapidity—for example, the country's gone literally straight from manual typewriters to computers. Modern turnpikes are proliferating; though the tolls can be eye-popping, they've made getting from one place to another something of (dare I say it) a luxurious breeze. These new roads and the level of service provided by Mexico's luxury bus lines have made using public transportation worthy of anticipation.

On the other hand, many villages and most rural communities don't have electricity, running water, or a public sewer system; there's no natural gas pipeline servicing the country either.

And unreliable phone service is still one of the country's greatest obstacles to progress. But here as elsewhere progress is being made: The lofty aim of recent efforts to modernize the telephone system was to install at least one telephone in 70% of the villages without such service—and 1995 saw that goal achieved. Toll-free telephone numbers and fax phones, almost unheard of as little as three or four years ago, are common nowadays.

Despite Mexico's immense technological advances, some customs die hard: A handmade tortilla is still preferred over one made by machine; a housewife may have a tiny washing machine, but the maid is instructed to give the whole wash a thorough scrubbing *again* by hand on the cement washboard; clothes dryers are a rarity, never having won approval over line-drying in the open air—usually on the rooftop; orange juice—which most of us grew up drinking from the carton, heedless of the difference between pasteurized and fresh juice—is usually freshly squeezed while you watch; and prepackaged and frozen foods haven't yet overtaken dishes made from fresh ingredients bought at a colorful open-air market.

Whether small-scale traditions like these, or carefully observed manners and mores, or the ritualized pomp and circumstance of the country's many religious fiestas, Mexicans stubbornly cling to their traditional ways of doing things. And the country's traditions arise out of its long history—it's Mexican

Mexico Dateline

- **10,000–2300** B.C. Prehistoric period.
- **1500** Preclassic period begins: Olmec culture develops and spreads.
- **1000–900** Olmec San Lorenzo center destroyed; Olmecs regroup at La Venta.
- **600** La Venta Olmec cultural zenith; Cholula begins 2,000-year history as ceremonial center.
- **500–100** B.C. Zapotecs flourish; Olmec culture disintegrates.
- **A.D. 100** Building begins on Sun and Moon pyramids at Teotihuacán; Palenque dynasty emerges in Yucatán.
- **300** Classic period begins: Xochicalco established; Maya civilization develops in Yucatán and Chiapas.
- **650** Teotihuacán burns and by 700 is deserted. Cacaxtla begins to flourish.
- **750** Zapotecs conquer valley of Oaxaca; Casas Grandes culture begins on northern desert.
- **900** Postclassic period begins: Toltec culture emerges at Tula. Cacaxtla begins to decline.
- **978** Toltec culture spreads to Chichén-Itzá.
- **1156–1230** Tula and El Tajín are abandoned. Aztecs trickle in to the Valley of Mexico.
- **1290** Zapotecs decline and Mixtecs emerge at Monte Albán; Mitla becomes refuge of Zapotecs.
- **1325–45** Aztec capital Tenochtitlán founded. Aztecs

continues

dominate Mexico until 1521, when they are defeated by Spaniards.

- **1519–21** Conquest of Mexico: Hernán Cortés and troops arrive near present-day Veracruz; Spanish gain final victory over Aztecs at Tlaltelolco near Tenochtitlán in 1521. Diseases brought by Spaniards begin to decimate native population.

- **1521–24** Cortés organizes Spanish empire in Mexico and begins building Mexico City atop ruins of Tenochtitlán; Spanish bring first cattle to Mexico.

- **1524** First Franciscan friars arrive from Spain.

- **1525–35** Cortés removed from leadership; Spanish king sends officials, judges, and finally an *audiencia* to govern.

- **1530** King Charles V of Spain declares Mexico City the capital of New Spain.

- **1535–1821** Viceregal period: Mexico governed by 61 viceroys appointed by king of Spain. Landed aristocracy, a small elite owning huge portions of land (haciendas) emerges.

- **1562** Friar Diego de Landa destroys 5,000 Maya religious stone figures and burns 27 hieroglyphic painted manuscripts at Maní, Yucatán.

- **1571** The Inquisition is established in Mexico.

- **1767** Jesuits expelled from New Spain.

- **1810–21** Independence War: Miguel Hidalgo's *grito* starts independence movement; after a decade of war, Augustín Iturbide achieves compromise between monarchy and a republic. Mexico becomes independent nation.

continues

history, in large part, that makes the country so rich for visitors.

PREHISPANIC CIVILIZATIONS

The earliest "Mexicans" were Stone Age men and women, descendants of a people who had crossed the Bering Strait and reached North America before 10,000 B.C. These were *Homo sapiens* who hunted mastodons and bison and gathered other food as they could. Later, during the **Archaic period** (5200–1500 B.C.), signs of agriculture and domestication appeared: baskets were woven; corn, beans, squash, and tomatoes were grown; turkeys and dogs were kept for food. By 2400 B.C., the art of making pottery had been discovered, a significant advance. Though life in these times was still very primitive, there were "artists" who made clay figurines for use as votive offerings or household deities. Many symbolized Mother Earth or Fertility. Use of these figurines predates any belief in well-defined gods.

It was in the **Preclassic period** (1500 B.C.–A.D. 300) that the area known by archaeologists as Mesoamerica (running from the northern Mexico Valley to Costa Rica) began to show signs of a farming culture. The inhabitants farmed either by the "slash-and-burn" method of cutting grass and trees and then setting fire to the area to clear it for planting, or by constructing terraces and irrigation ducts. The latter method was used principally in the highlands around Mexico City, where the first large towns developed. At some time during this period, religion became an institution as certain men took the role of shaman, or guardian of magical and religious secrets. These were the predecessors of the folk healers and nature priests still found in modern Mexico.

The most highly developed culture of the Preclassic period was that of the Olmecs, which flourished from 1500 to 100 B.C. They lived in what are today the states of Veracruz and Tabasco, where they used river rafts to transport the colossal multiton blocks of basalt out of which they carved roundish heads that are the best-known legacy of their culture. These sculptures still present problems to archaeologists: What do they signify? The heads seem infantile in their roundness, but all have the peculiar "jaguar mouth" with a high-arched upper lip. Those with open eyes are slightly cross-eyed. The artists seemed obsessed with deformity, and many smaller carved or clay figures represent monstrosities or misshapen forms. Besides their achievements in sculpture, the Olmecs were the first in Mexico to use a calendar and to develop a written language, both of which were later perfected by the Maya.

The link between the Olmecs and the Maya has not been clearly established, but Izapa (400 B.C.–A.D. 400), a ceremonial site in the Chiapan cacao-growing region near the Pacific coast, appears to be one of several places where transition between the two cultures took place. When discovered, its monuments and stelae were intact, having escaped the destruction wrought on so many sites. El Pital, a large site being excavated in northern Veracruz state, may illuminate more links between the Olmec and other cultures.

Most of pre-Columbian Mexico's artistic and cultural achievement came during the **Classic period** (A.D. 300–900), when life centered in cities. Class distinctions arose as a military and religious aristocracy took control; a class of merchants and artisans grew, with the independent farmer falling under a landlord's control. The cultural centers of the Classic period were Yucatán and Guatemala (also home of the Maya), the Mexican Highlands at Teotihuacán, the Zapotec cities of Monte Albán and Mitla (near Oaxaca), and the cities of El Tajín and Zempoala on the Gulf coast.

The Maya represented the apex of pre-Columbian cultures. Besides their superior artistic achievements, the Maya made significant discoveries in science, including the use of the zero in mathematics and a complex calendar with which priests were able to predict eclipses and the movements of the stars for centuries to come. The Maya were warlike, raiding their neighbors to gain land and subjects as well as to take captives for their many blood-centered rituals. Recent studies, notably *Blood of Kings* (Braziller, 1986) by Linda Schele and Mary Ellen Miller, debunked the long-held theory that the Maya were a peaceful people. Scholars continue to decipher the Maya hieroglyphs, murals, and relief carvings, revealing a world tied to the belief that blood sacrifice was necessary to communicate with celestial gods and ancestors and to revere the dynasties of earthly blood kin. Through bloodletting and sacrifice the Maya nourished their gods and ancestors and honored royal births, deaths, marriages, and accessions during a calendar full of special occasions. Numerous carvings and murals show that members of the

- **1822–24** First Empire: Iturbide enjoys brief reign as emperor; is expelled; returns; and is executed by firing squad.
- **1824–55** Federal Republic period: In 1824, Guadalupe Victoria elected first president of Mexico; 26 presidents and interim presidents follow during next three decades, among them José Antonio Lopez de Santa Anna, who is president of Mexico off and on 11 times.
- **1835** Texas declares independence from Mexico.
- **1838** France invades Mexico at Veracruz.
- **1845** United States annexes Texas.
- **1846–48** War with United States concludes with U.S. paying Mexico $15 million for half of its national territory under terms of Treaty of Guadalupe Hidalgo.
- **1855–72** Era of Benito Juárez, literal or de facto president through Reform Wars and usurpation of Mexican leadership by foreign Emperor Maximilian. Juárez nationalizes church property and declares separation of church and state.
- **1864–67** Second Empire: Interim period; Maximilian of Hapsburg is emperor of Mexico; Juárez orders execution of Maximilian and resumes presidency until his death in 1872.
- **1872–84** Post-Reform period: Only four presidents hold office but country is nearly bankrupt.
- **1880** Electric lights go on in Mexico City for the first time.

continues

- **1876–1911** Porfiriato: With one four-year exception, Porfirio Díaz is president/dictator of Mexico for 35 years, leading country through rapid modernization.
- **1911** Mexican Revolution begins; Díaz resigns; Francisco Madero becomes president.
- **1913** Madero assassinated.
- **1914, 1916** United States invades Mexico.
- **1917–40** Reconstruction: Present constitution of Mexico signed in 1917. Land and education reforms are initiated and labor unions strengthened. Mexico expels U.S. oil companies and nationalizes all natural resources and railroads. Presidential term limited to one term of six years. Presidents Obregón and Carranza are assassinated as are Pancho Villa and Emiliano Zapata.
- **1940** President Lázaro Cárdenas leaves office; Mexico enters period of political stability, tremendous economic progress, and rising quality of life that continues to this day, though not without many continuing problems.
- **1942** Mexico enters World War II when Germans sink two Mexican oil tankers in the Caribbean.
- **1949** 10,000-year-old "Tepexpan Man" (really a woman) is unearthed near Mexico City.
- **1955** Women given full voting rights.
- **1957** Major earthquake rocks the capital.
- **1960** Mexico nationalizes electrical industry.
- **1968** President Díaz Ordaz orders army to fire on protesters at Tlaltelolco Plaza

continues

ruling class, too, ritualistically mutilated themselves to draw sacrificial blood.

The identity of the people of Teotihuacán (100 B.C.–A.D. 700—near present-day Mexico City) isn't known, but it is thought to have been a city of 200,000 or more inhabitants covering 9 square miles. At its height, Teotihuacán was the greatest cultural center in Mexico; its influence extended as far southeast as Guatemala. Its layout has religious significance: High priests' rituals occurred on the tops of pyramids consecrated to the sun and moon, and these were attended, but not observed, by the masses of people at the foot of the pyramid. Some of the magnificent reliefs and frescoes that decorated the religious monuments can be seen in Mexico City's museums.

The Zapotecs, influenced by the Olmecs, raised an impressive culture in the region of Oaxaca. Their two principal cities were Monte Albán (500 B.C.–A.D. 800), inhabited by an elite of merchants and artisans, and Mitla, reserved for the high priests. Both cities exhibit the artistic and mathematical genius of the people; highlights include characteristic geometric designs, long-nosed gods with feathered masks, hieroglyph stelae, a bar-and-dot numerical system, and a 52-cycle calendar. Like the Olmecs, the Zapotecs favored grotesque art, of which the frieze of the "Danzantes" at Monte Albán—naked figures of distorted form and contorted position—is an outstanding example.

El Tajín (A.D. 300–1100), covering at least 2,600 acres on the upper Gulf coast of Veracruz, continues to stump scholars. The Pyramid of the Niches there is unique, and recent excavations have uncovered a total of 17 ball courts and Teotihuacán-influenced murals. Although Huastec Indians inhabited the region, the identity of those who built the site and occupied it remains a mystery. Death and sacrifice are recurring themes depicted in relief carvings. Pulque (pre-Hispanic fermented drink), cacao (chocolate) growing, and the ball game figured heavily into Tajín society.

In the **Postclassic period** (A.D. 900–1500), warlike cultures developed impressive societies of their own, although they never surpassed the Classic peoples. All paintings and hieroglyphs of this period show war, migration, and disruption. Somehow the glue of society became unstuck; people wandered from their homes, and the religious hierarchy lost influence. Finally, in the 1300s, the warlike Aztecs settled in the Mexico Valley on Lake Texcoco (site of Mexico City), with the island city of Tenochtitlán as their capital. Legend has it that as the wandering Aztecs were passing the lake, they saw a sign predicted by their prophets: an eagle perched on a cactus plant with a snake in its mouth. They built their city there, and it became a huge (pop. 300,000) and impressive capital. The Aztec empire was a more or less loosely united territory of great size. The high lords of the capital became fabulously rich in gold, stores of food, cotton, and perfumes; skilled artisans were prosperous; state events were elaborately ceremonial. Victorious Aztecs returning from battle sacrificed thousands of captives on the altars atop the pyramids, cutting their chests open with stone knives and ripping out their still-beating hearts to offer to the gods.

The legend of **Quetzalcoatl,** a holy man who appeared during the time of troubles at the end of the Classic period, is one of the most important tales in Mexican history and folklore and contributed to the overthrow of the Aztec empire by the Spaniards. Quetzalcoatl means "feathered serpent." Learned beyond his years, he became the high priest and leader of the Toltecs at Tula and put an end to human sacrifice. His influence completely changed the Toltecs from a group of warriors to peaceful and productive farmers, artisans, and craftsmen. But his successes upset the old priests, and they called on their ancient god of darkness, Texcatlipoca, to degrade Quetzalcoatl in the eyes of the people. One night the priests conspired to dress Quetzalcoatl in ridiculous garb, get him drunk, and tempt him to break his vow of chastity. The next morning the shame of this night of debauchery drove him out of his own land and into the wilderness, where he lived for 20 years. He emerged in Coatzacoalcos, in the Isthmus of Tehuantepec, bade his few followers farewell, and sailed away, having promised to return in a future age. Toltec artistic influences noted at Chichén-Itzá in the Yucatán seem to suggest that he in fact landed there and, among the Maya, began his "ministry" again, this time called Kukulkán. He supposedly died there, but the legend of his return in a future age remained.

THE CONQUEST OF MEXICO

When Hernán Cortés and his fellow conquistadors landed in 1519, in what would become Veracruz, the enormous Aztec empire was ruled by Moctezuma (a name often misspelled Montezuma) in great splendor. It was thought that these strange

meeting, killing hundreds of spectators and participants. Olympic Games are held in the capital.

- **1982** President Echeverria nationalizes the country's banks.

- **1985** Deadly earthquake crumbles buildings in the capital and takes thousands of lives.

- **1988** Mexico enters the General Agreement on Tariffs and Trade (GATT).

- **1992** Sale of *ejido* land (peasant communal property) to private citizens is allowed. Mexico and the Vatican establish diplomatic relations after an interruption of 100 years.

- **1993** Mexico deregulates hotel and restaurant prices; New Peso currency begins circulation.

- **1994** Mexico, Canada, and the United States sign the North American Free Trade Agreement (NAFTA). An Indian uprising in Chiapas sparks protests countrywide over government policies concerning land distribution, bank loans, health, education, and voting and human rights. In an unrelated incident, PRI candidate Luis Donaldo Colossio is assassinated five months before the election; replacement candidate Ernesto Zedillo Ponce de Leon is elected and inaugurated as president in December. Within weeks, the peso is devalued, throwing the nation into turmoil.

- **1995** The peso loses half its value within the first three months of the year. The government raises prices on oil and utilities. Interest on debt soars to 140%;

continues

businesses begin to fail; unemployment rises. The Chiapan rebels threaten another rebellion, which is quickly quashed by the government. Former president Carlos Salinas de Gortari, with the devaluation having left his reputation for economic leadership in a shambles, leaves Mexico for the United States. And Salinas's brother is accused of plotting the assassination of their brother-in-law, the head of the PRI. The United States extends Mexico $40 billion in loans to stabilize the economy following the peso crisis.

■ **1996** Effects of the devaluation continue as in 1995, but many businesses without debt expand and prosper. Mexico begins repaying the loan from the United States extended in 1995; the wife of the president's brother is arrested attempting to remove millions of dollars from a Swiss bank—drug ties are alleged; former president Salinas's whereabouts are unknown, though he speaks out on occasion; the Chiapan crisis remains unsettled.

visitors might be Quetzalcoatl and his followers, returning at last. Moctezuma was not certain what course to pursue; if this was in fact the god returning, no resistance must be offered; on the other hand, if the leader was not Quetzalcoatl, he and his men might be a threat to his empire. Moctezuma tried to bribe them with gold to go away, but this only whetted the Spaniards' appetites. Along the way from Veracruz to Tenochtitlán, Cortés made allies of Moctezuma's enemies, most notably the Tlaxcaltecans.

Though the Spaniards were outnumbered by the hundreds of thousands of Aztecs, they skillfully kept things under their control (with the help of their Tlaxcalan allies) until a revolt threatened Cortés's entire enterprise. He retreated to the countryside, made alliances with non-Aztec tribes, and finally marched on the empire when it was governed by the last Aztec emperor, Cuauhtémoc. Cuauhtémoc defended himself and his people valiantly for almost three months, but was finally captured, tortured, and ultimately executed.

What began as an adventure by Cortés and his men, unauthorized by the Spanish Crown or its governor in Cuba, turned out to be the undoing of a continent's worth of people and cultures. Soon Christianity was being spread through "New Spain." Guatemala and Honduras were explored and conquered, and by 1540 the territory of New Spain included Spanish possessions from Vancouver to Panama. In the two centuries that followed, Franciscan, Augustinian, and Dominican friars converted great numbers of Indians to Christianity, and the Spanish lords built up huge feudal estates on which the Indian farmers were little more than serfs. The silver and gold that Cortés had sought and found made Spain the richest country in Europe.

THE VICEREGAL ERA

Hernán Cortés set about building a new city and the seat of government of New Spain upon the ruins of the old Aztec capital. Spain's influence was immediate. For indigenous peoples (besides the Tlaxcaltecans, Cortés's Indian allies), heavy tributes once paid to the Aztecs were now rendered in forced labor to the Spanish. In many cases they were made to provide the materials for the building of New Spain as well. Diseases carried by the Spaniards, against which the Indian populations had no natural immunity, killed millions.

Over the three centuries of the Viceregal period (1535–1821), Mexico was governed by 61 viceroys appointed by the king of Spain. From the beginning, more Spaniards arrived as overseers, merchants, craftsmen, architects, silversmiths, etc., and eventually African slaves were brought in as well. Spain became rich from New World gold and silver, chiseled out by backbreaking Indian labor. The colonial elite built lavish homes both in Mexico City and in the countryside. They filled their homes

When we [Cortés and Moctezuma] met I dismounted and stepped forward to embrace him, but the two lords who were with him stopped me with their hands so that I should not touch him.... When at last I came to speak to Mutezuma himself I took off a necklace of pearls and cut glass that I was wearing and placed it around his neck; after we had walked a little way up the street a servant of his came with two necklaces, wrapped in a cloth, made from red snails' shells, which they hold in great esteem; and from each necklace hung eight shrimps of refined gold almost a span in length.

—Hernán Cortés, *Letters from Mexico* (1519)

When they arrived at the treasure house called Teucalco, the riches of gold and feathers were brought out to them: ornaments made of quetzal feathers, richly worked shields, disks of gold, the necklaces of the idols, gold nose plugs, gold greaves and bracelets and crowns.... The Spaniards ... gathered all the gold into a great mound and set fire to everything else.... Then they melted down the gold into ingots.

—The Broken Spears: The Aztec Account of the Conquest of Mexico (1528)

with ornate furniture, had many servants, and adorned themselves in velvets, satins, and jewels imported from abroad. A new class system developed: the *gauchupines* (Spaniard born in Spain), considered themselves superior to the *criollos* (Spaniard born in Mexico). Those of other races, the *castas* or castes, the pure Indians and Africans, and mixtures of Spanish and Indian, Spanish and African, and Indian and African, all took the last place in society.

It took great cunning to stay a step ahead of the money-hungry Spanish Crown, which demanded increasingly higher taxes and contributions from its well-endowed faraway colony. Still, the wealthy prospered grandly enough to develop an extravagant society.

However, discontent with the mother country simmered for years over issues such as the Spanish-born citizen's advantages over a Mexican-born subject, taxes, the Spanish bureaucracy, and restrictions on commerce with Spain and other countries. Dissatisfaction with Spain boiled to the surface in 1808 when, under the weak leadership of King Charles IV, Spain was invaded by Napoléon Bonaparte of France, who placed his brother Joseph on the Spanish throne. To many in Mexico, allegiance to France was out of the question—after nearly 300 years of restrictive Spanish rule, Mexico revolted.

INDEPENDENCE

The independence movement began in 1810 when a priest, Father Miguel Hidalgo, gave the cry for independence from his pulpit in the town of Dolores, Guanajuato. The uprising soon became a revolution, and Hidalgo, Ignacio Allende, and another priest, José María Morelos, gathered an "army" of citizens and threatened Mexico City. Battle lines were drawn between those who sided with the Spanish Crown and those who wanted Mexico to be a free and sovereign nation. Ultimately Hidalgo was executed, but he is honored as "the Father of Mexican Independence." Morelos kept the revolt alive until 1815, when he too was executed.

The nation endured a decade of upheaval (1810 until 1821), and then the warring factions finally agreed on a compromise, Augustín Iturbide's *Plan de Iguala*. It made three guarantees: Mexico would be a constitutional monarchy headed by a European prince; the Catholic Church would have a monopoly on religion; and Mexican-born citizens would have the same rights as those born in Spain. He

Impressions

Without more chin than Maximilian ever had, one can be neither handsome nor a successful emperor.

—Charles Flandrau, *Viva Mexico* (1908)

thoughtfully tagged on another proviso allowing for a Mexican emperor, should no European prince step forward to take the role of king. When the agreement was signed, Iturbide was positioned to take over. No suitable European monarch was located and the new Mexican congress named him emperor. His empire proved short-lived: The very next year his administration fell. The new nation became a republic, but endured a succession of presidents and military dictators, as well as invasions, a war, and devastating losses of territory to its neighbor to the north, the United States.

Characteristic of the Republic's turbulent history during the half-century following independence was the French Intervention, in which three old colonial powers—England, France, and Spain—and the United States demonstrated continued interest in meddling with Mexico's internal affairs. Together they sent troops and warships to Veracruz to pressure the Mexican government for payment of debts. The English and Spanish withdrew before long, but the French remained and declared war on Mexico.

The Mexicans enjoyed a glorious victory over the French at Puebla (the event that birthed the nation's Cinco de Mayo celebrations), yet the victory proved hollow. The French marched on Mexico City, and the Mexican president, Benito Juárez, was forced to retreat to the countryside to bide his time. With the help of anti-Juárez factions, a naive young Austrian, Archduke Maximilian of Hapsburg, was installed by the French as king of Mexico. For three years Maximilian tried to "rule" a country effectively in the midst of civil war, only to be left in the lurch when the French troops that supported him withdrew at the behest of the United States. Upon his triumphant return, Juárez summarily executed the Austrian interloper. Juárez, who would be remembered as one of the nation's great heroes, did his best to strengthen and unify the country before dying of a heart attack in 1872.

THE PORFIRIATO & THE REVOLUTION

From 1877 to 1911, a period now called the "Porfiriato," center stage in Mexico was occupied by Porfirio Díaz, a Juárez general who was president for 30 years and lived in the Castillo de (Castle of) Chapultepec in Mexico City. He was a terror to his enemies—that is, anyone who dared challenge his absolute power. Nevertheless, he is credited with bringing Mexico into the industrial age and for his patronage of architecture and the arts, the fruits of which are still enjoyed today. Public opinion forced him from office in 1911; he was succeeded by Francisco Madero.

After the fall of the Porfiriato, several factions split the country, including those led by "Pancho Villa" (whose real name was Doroteo Arango), Alvaro Obregón, Venustiano Carranza, and Emiliano Zapata. A famous photograph shows Zapata and Villa taking turns trying out Díaz's presidential chair in Mexico City. The decade that followed is referred to as the Mexican Revolution. Around two million Mexicans died for the cause. Drastic reforms occurred in this period, and the surge of vitality and progress from this exciting, if turbulent, time has inspired Mexicans to the present. Succeeding presidents have invoked the spirit of the Revolution, which lives in the hearts and minds of Mexicans as though it happened yesterday.

BEYOND THE REVOLUTION

The decades from the beginning of the revolution in 1911 to stabilization in the 1940s and 1950s were tumultuous. Great strides were made during these years in distributing land to the peasant populations, irrigation, development of mineral resources, and the establishment of education, health, and sanitation programs. However, the tremendous economic pressure Mexico faced from its own internal problems and the world depression of the 1930s did little for political stability. From 1911 to 1940, 16 men were president of Mexico. Some stayed in power a year or less.

One of the most significant leaders of the period, and the longest-lasting, was Lázaro Cárdenas (1934–40). He helped diminish the role of Mexico's military in national politics by dismantling the machine of General Plutarco Calles and exiling him from the country. He is remembered fondly as a president who listened to and cared about commoners. He made good on a number of the revolution's promises, distributing nearly 50 million acres of land, primarily to *ejidos*, or communal farming groups; pouring money into education; and encouraging organized labor. And in one of his most memorable and controversial decisions, he nationalized Mexico's oil industry in 1938, sending foreign oil companies packing. Although Mexicans still view this act with great pride—the government stood up for Mexican labor—it did considerable damage to Mexico's standing with the international business community.

Despite many steps foward during the Cárdenas era, jobs could not keep pace with population growth, and with foreign investors shy of Mexico and the world mired in the Great Depression, the Cárdenas era ended in 1940 with the nation in dark economic circumstances.

From the 1930s through the 1970s, socialism had a strong voice in Mexico; its impact was most marked in the state's attempts to run the country's businesses—not just oil, but railroads, mining, utilities, hotels, motion pictures, the telephone company, supermarkets, etc.

Miguel Aleman, president from 1946 to 1958, continued progress by building dams, improving highways and railways, encouraging trade, and building the Ciudad Universitario (University City) in Mexico City, home of Mexico's national university. Americans began to invest in Mexico again. Yet problems remained, many of which still plague the country today: The country's booming population created unemployment, wages of the common people were appallingly low, and Aleman's administration was plagued by corruption and graft.

In 1970, Luis Echeverria came to power, followed in 1976 by José López Portillo. During their presidencies there emerged a studied coolness in relations with the United States and an activist role in international affairs. This period also saw an increase in charges of large-scale corruption in the upper echelons of Mexican society. The corruption, though endemic to the system, was encouraged by the river of money from the rise in oil prices. When oil income skyrocketed, Mexican borrowing and

Impressions

[Porfirio Díaz] looks what he is—a Man of Iron, the most forceful character in Mexico. Whatever was done in the sixteenth century was the work of Cortez . . . who was responsible for everything but the climate. Whatever is effected in Mexico to-day is the work of Porfirio Díaz.

—Stanton Davis Kirkham, *Mexican Trails* (1909)

spending did likewise. The reduction of oil prices in the 1980s left Mexico with an enormous foreign bank debt and serious infrastructure deficiencies.

The country inherited by President Miguel de la Madríd Hurtado in 1982 was one without King Oil, and with new challenges to build agriculture, cut expenditures, tame corruption, and keep creditors at bay. He began the process of privatizing government-held businesses (airlines, hotels, banks, etc.) and led the country into membership in GATT (the General Agreement on Tariffs and Trade), an important preparation for entering NAFTA (the North American Free Trade Agreement), which was accomplished during his successor's presidency. Nevertheless, soaring inflation of 200% faced Carlos Salinas de Gortari as he took office in 1989. Salinas's accomplishments included decreasing inflation to 15% annually by adeptly gaining the necessary agreement of industry and labor leaders to hold wages and prices; continuing the privatization of government-held businesses called the *pacto*; and leading the country into NAFTA, which over a 15-year period would reduce trade barriers and allow business to flourish more freely between Mexico, the United States, and Canada. During Salinas's six-year term Mexico's world position as a country poised for great prosperity strengthened, and Mexican public opinion held his administration in high esteem. But a cloud arose over the country toward the end of the Salinas era when disgruntled Maya Indians staged an armed uprising after the NAFTA agreement was signed, and assassins' bullets felled both the PRI presidential candidate and the head of the PRI Party. The presidential elections, while automated for the first time and more honest than previous ones, were still marred by allegations of corruption. Still, these incidents failed to dampen Mexico's hope for continued progress when Ernesto Zedillo assumed office in December 1994.

TOWARD THE FUTURE

From the time of the revolution to the present, political parties and their roles have changed tremendously in Mexico. Although one political party, the **Partido Revolucionario Institucional** (PRI, called "el pree") has been in control under that name since 1946, opposition to it has become increasingly vocal and effective in recent years. In the beginning, the forerunner of the PRI, the Partido Revolucionario Mexicano, established by Lázaro Cárdenas, had four equal constituent groups—popular, agrarian, labor, and the military. At the risk of greatly oversimplifying a complex history and attendant issues, the widespread perception that the party is out of touch with the common Mexican, and its current problems retaining leadership, are the result of a change in focus away from those groups. The PRI today is heavily backed by, and in turn run by, business and industry leaders.

The crisis in Chiapas has become a focal point for many of the nation's problems. Opposition parties such as the **Partido Accion Nacional** (PAN) had taken up the cause of the seemingly disenfranchised masses, but no one had spoken for or paid much attention to Mexico's millions of poor indigenous people for some time. And on New Year's Day in 1994, when militant Maya Indians attacked Chiapan towns, killing many, attention was drawn to the plight of neglected indigenous groups and others in rural society, which the PRI-led government seemed to relegate to the bottom of the agenda. These groups are still clamoring for land they never received after the Revolution. That population growth has outstripped the availability of distributable land, that Mexico needs large-scale, modern agribusiness to keep up with the country's food needs—these are realities not understood by the millions of rural Mexicans who depend on their small family fields to feed the family. President Carlos Salinas de Gortari's bold, controversial decision in the early 1990s to allow sale of *ejido* land may reflect Mexico's 21st-century needs, but it is at odds with firmly entrenched farm- and land-use traditions born before the 16th-century conquest. These issues of agrarian reform and the lack of other basics of life (roads, electricity, running water, education, health care, etc.) are being raised in areas besides Chiapas, most notably Oaxaca, Chihuahua, Guerrero, and Michoacán. This is a grave and festering problem, made all the more serious now that Mexico is reeling from the devaluation of the peso.

The surprise decision to devalue the currency threw domestic and international confidence in Mexico into turmoil. The peso had already been in a fairly rapid, but controlled, daily devaluation process just prior to the government intervention, and it had been obvious for at least three years that a devaluation was overdue. But the Zedillo government erred in not involving industry and labor in the decision, in shocking the population with an overnight devaluation, and in not anticipating national and international repercussions. Within three months of the devaluation the peso lost half its value, reducing Mexico's buying power by 50%. After the government issued its harsh economic recovery program, interest rates on credit cards and loans (which have variable, not fixed rates in Mexico), soared 80% to 140%. Overnight the cost of gasoline increased 35%, and gas and electricity 20%. As a partial solution, a $40 million loan package offered by the United States to ease the peso crisis uses Mexico's sacred petroleum revenue as collateral—a staggering blow to Mexico's national pride. The effect so far has been a loudly expressed lack of confidence in Zedillo and in the PRI, a dramatically slowed and cautious international investment climate, and a feeling among the citizenry of betrayal by the government. Responsibility for paying for governmental mismanagement of the economy has been shifted to ordinary Mexican citizens who were blindsided by this unexpected financial burden. Ordinary costs of daily living exceed the ability of average people to pay; businesses are closing and jobs are being eliminated.

Meanwhile, as the effects of the peso crisis worsened, the Chiapan rebels threatened another uprising, the volcano Popocatepetl began spitting smoke and flames, and inflation predictions of 45% to 60% were heard. Former president Carlos Salinas de Gortari's brother was jailed and accused of involvement in the assassination of their brother-in-law, the head of the PRI Party. Carlos Salinas de Gortari and his family left Mexico quickly for the United States, after Salinas threatened a hunger strike unless his name was cleared regarding the assassination of his brother-in-law, and after he spoke publicly (an unheard-of breach of conduct by a past president) against the present government's handling of the peso crisis.

It seems incredulous that a country so poised for prosperity should career backward so rapidly, and that such an admired and trusted president should so quickly fall from grace—because the people's trust and hopes in government under Salinas were so high, the betrayal is particularly bitter. However, as grim as all this seems, using Mexico's history just this century as a rule, the country bounces back from adversity to become even stronger. A strong popular will to progress undergirds the Mexican spirit, and despite recent sobering events, the country still bustles with commercial activity. Meanwhile, as long as inflation doesn't outpace the effect of the devaluation, the country is quite a bargain; even a year after the devaluation, prices are still better than they've been since 1985.

Economically, Mexico, though still a Third World country, is by no means a poor country. Only about a sixth of the economy is in agriculture. Mining is still fairly important. Gold, silver, and many other important minerals are still mined, but the big industry today is oil. Mexico is also well industrialized, manufacturing everything from textiles and food products to cassette tapes and automobiles.

3 Margaritas, Tortillas & *Poc-Chuc*: Food & Drink in Mexico

Mexican food served in the United States or almost anywhere else in the world is almost never truly Mexican. The farther you get from the source the more the authenticity is lost in translation. True Mexican food usually isn't fiery hot, for example; hot spices are added from sauces and garnishes at the table.

While there are certain staples like tortillas and beans that appear almost universally around the country, Mexican food and drink varies considerably from region to region; even the beans and tortillas will sidestep the usual in different locales.

MEALS & RESTAURANTS *A LA MEXICANA*

BREAKFAST

Traditionally, businesspeople in Mexico may start their day with a cup of coffee or *atole* and a piece of sweet bread just before heading for work around 8am; they won't sit down for a real breakfast until around 10 or 11am, when restaurants fill with men (usually) eating hearty breakfasts that may look more like lunch with steak, eggs, beans, and tortillas. Things are slowly changing as some executives are beginning to favor an earlier breakfast hour, beginning between 7 and 8am, during which business and the morning meal are combined.

Foreigners searching for an early breakfast will often find that nothing gets going in restaurants until around 9am; however, markets are bustling by 7am (they are a great place to get an early breakfast) and the capital's hotel restaurants often open as early as 7am to accommodate business travelers and those leaving on early flights. If you like to stoke the fires first thing, you might also bring your own portable coffeepot and coffee and buy bakery goodies the night before and make breakfast yourself.

LUNCH

The main meal of the day, lunch, has traditionally been a two- to three-hour break, occurring between 1 and 5pm. But in the capital at least, an abbreviated midday break is beginning to take hold. Short or long, the typical Mexican lunch begins with soup, then rice, then a main course with beans and tortillas and a bit of vegetable, and lastly dessert and coffee. But here too you'll see one-plate meals and fast food beginning to encroach on the multicourse meal. Workers return to their jobs until 7 or 8pm.

DINNER

The evening meal is taken late, usually around 9 or 10pm. Although you may see many Mexicans eating in restaurants at night, big evening meals aren't traditional; a typical meal at home would be a light one with leftovers from breakfast or lunch, perhaps soup or tortillas and jam, or a little meat and rice.

RESTAURANT TIPS & ETIQUETTE

Some of the foreigner's greatest frustrations in Mexico occur in restaurants, when they need to hail and retain the waiter or get their check. To summon the waiter, wave or raise your hand, but don't motion with your index finger, a demeaning gesture that may even cause the waiter to ignore you. To gesture someone to them, Mexicans will stand up, extend an arm straight out at shoulder level, and make a straight-armed, downward, diving motion with their hand cupped. A more discreet version, good to use when seated, has the elbow bent and perpendicular to the shoulder; with hand cupped, make a quick, diving motion out a bit from the arm-pit. (Both of these motions may make you feel silly until you practice. The latter one looks rather like the motion Americans make to signify "be still" or "shut up.")

If the waiter arrives to take your order before you are ready, you may have trouble getting him again. Once an order is in, however, the food usually arrives in steady sequence. Frequently, just before you've finished, when your plate is nearly empty, the waiter appears out of nowhere to whisk it away—unwary diners have seen their plates disappear mid-bite.

Finding your waiter when you're ready for the check can also be difficult. While waiters may hover too much while you're dining, they tend to disappear entirely by meal's end. It's considered rude for the waiter to bring the check before it's requested, so you have to ask for it, sometimes more than once. (To find a missing waiter, get up as if to leave and scrape the chairs loudly; if that fails, you'll probably find him chat-ting in the kitchen.) If you want the check and the waiter is simply across the room, a smile and a scribbling motion into the palm of your hand will send the message. In many budget restaurants, waiters don't clear the table of finished plates or soft drink bottles because they use them to figure the tab. Always double-check the addition.

FOOD AROUND THE COUNTRY

You won't have to confine yourself to Mexican food during a visit to Mexico—you'll find restaurants that prepare world-class French, Italian, Swiss, German, and other international cuisines. But you can also delve into the variety of Mexico's traditional foods, which derive from pre-Hispanic, Spanish, and French cuisines. At its best Mexican food is among the most delicious in the world. Visitors can fairly easily find hearty, filling meals on a budget, but finding truly delicious food is not so easy—one positive is that some of the country's best food is found in small inexpensive restau-rants where regional specialties are made to please discerning locals. Explanations of specific dishes are found in the appendix.

Recipes such as mole poblano—developed by nuns during colonial times to please priests and visiting dignitaries—have become part of the national patrimony, but the basics of Mexico's cuisine have endured since pre-Hispanic times. Corn, considered holy, was the foundation staple food of pre-Hispanic peoples. These people used corn leaves to bake and wrap food and ground corn to make the *atole* drink in many fla-vors (bitter, picante, or sweet) as well as tortillas and tamales (stuffed with meat).

When the Spanish arrived they found a bounty of edibles never seen in the Old World, including turkey, chocolate, tomatoes, squash, beans, avocados, peanuts, and vanilla (in addition to corn). All of these ingredients were integral parts of pre-Hispanic foods, and remain at the heart of today's Mexican cooking. Also central to the Indian peoples' cuisines were chiles, nopal cactus, amaranth, eggs of ants, turtles and iguanas, corn and maguey worms, bee and fly larvae, flowers of the maguey and squash, grasshoppers, jumiles (similar to stinkbugs), armadillos, rattlesnake, hairless dogs, deer, squirrels, monkeys, rats, frogs, ducks, parrots, quail, shrimp, fish, crabs, and crawfish. Exotic fruits such as sapodilla, guava, mamey, chirimoya, and pitahuayas rounded out the diet. Some of these are mainstream foods today, and others are considered delicacies and may be seen on specialty menus.

But much of what we consider Mexican food wouldn't exist without the contri-butions of the Spanish. They introduced sugarcane, cattle, sheep, wheat, grapes, barley, and rice. The French influence is best seen in the extensive variety of baked goods available in the capital.

Tequila!!!

Perhaps looking to distract themselves from the cares of conquest, the first waves of Spanish colonists in Mexico fiddled around with *pulque* (*pool*-kay), a mildly intoxicating drink popular among indigenous peoples. They hit upon a stronger drink in the late 16th century when Cenobio Sauza distilled his first bottle of a special hooch in Tequila, Jalisco—thus was born an 80-proof potation now consumed the world over, which can truly be called the "spirit" of Mexico.

True tequila is made only from the sweet sap at the heart of the blue *agave* (ah-*gah*-veh) plant, grown in the states of Jalisco, Nayarit, and Michoacán. The laborious process by which tequila is produced involves roasting the enormous agave heart (it can weigh 100 pounds or more) in a pit; the cooked heart is then pulped and the juice distilled. It is double distilled before it is bottled.

The basic tequila is *blanco*, or white. Many "gold" tequilas are just *blanco* with a little artificial coloring; the true golds are always *reposado*, or "rested" at least six months. The aging process does lend tequilas a light-gold tint. Also available, at the super-premium end of the market, are *añejo* tequilas, which must be aged at least two years.

A similar but less-refined drink is *mescal*; it is made from one of the other 400 varieties of agave. It's mescal, not tequila, that comes with a worm in the bottom of the bottle. Pulque, which comes from yet another agave, is still produced.

The hoary old ritual for drinking tequila, dating back long before margaritas began hogging the spotlight, is to put a dash of salt in your left hand, a shot glass of tequila before you in the middle, and a nice fresh slice of lime on your right—consume them from left to right, in bang-bang-bang fashion. This is a bracing combination—I dare you to do it without falling into unconscious mimicry of Jack Nicholson having a snort in *Easy Rider*. (It should be noted that reckless repetition of this procedure has felled many a tourist onto barroom floors.)

In the 1940s, when Margarita Sames concocted the original tequila-based "margarita" drink, she entertained friends with it in her Acapulco home. She never imagined that sunsets from Anchorage to Argentina would one day be celebrated with the tasty lime-laden cocktail, and sipped from big, long-stemmed glasses named especially for her drink. The concoction became so popular that bartenders far and wide laid claim to its creation, but Sames's story is the most believable. Sames made her drink with tequila, fresh-squeezed lime juice, and Cointreau, a French liqueur made with the skins of both bitter and sweet oranges. The particulars can change, but these three categories of ingredient—real tequila, lime juice, and orange-flavored liqueur—are the holy trinity of margarita making.

Here are a few variations you can work into your bartending. There are a lot of tequilas available beyond the usual Cuervo and Sauza varieties. Herradura is another big-name brand, perhaps the best of these. If your liquor store is enlightened they may be able to procure lesser-known brands; you can also, of course, add a special bottle of tequila to your shopping list for each trip you make south of the border. As far as liqueur goes, these days most people use triple sec instead of Cointreau—both are orange-based liqueurs, but Cointreau is considerably more expensive. If you're using an expensive premium tequila, try the Cointreau—it's delicious. If you're using triple sec, don't buy one of the bargain-basement varieties—it's just not the real stuff. Marie Brizard, Bols, and DeKuyper all make good triple secs. Another substitute for triple sec is Grand Marnier, a top-shelf orange- and cognac-flavored liqueur—it may sound odd, but the cognac flavor lends an interesting character to a margarita. And finally, while traditionalists will tell you there's no substitute for fresh-squeezed lime juice, it can be nearly impossible to procure a decent supply of juicy, ripe limes—the fruit is notorious for inconsistent quality. One solution is to use fresh-squeezed lemon juice; the flavors are nearly indistinguishable in the context of the cocktail, and lemons are much more consistent. Another is to use a bottled lime juice, but if you do, get Rose's Lime Juice— it's just better than any of the other brands.

The proportions of the cocktail are 2 parts tequila, 1 part liqueur, and 1 1/2 part lime juice. Purists will tell you that there's only one way to mix a margarita (in a shaker with fairly coarse chunks of ice) and only two ways to serve it (either "on the rocks" into a kosher salt–rimmed hurricane glass or "straight up" strained from the shaker into a salt-rimmed martini- or champagne-style glass). But why let an ideologue impinge on your fun? If you want to use a blender for frozen margaritas, knock yourself out—just use less expensive brands of tequila and triple sec, as the Slurpee effect will dilute the flavors of the spirits. Or add some fresh fruit—strawberries, raspberries, ripe peaches, and kiwis all are delicious additions to a frozen margarita.

All the squabbles over minor additives, salt or no salt, or who actually created the drink aside, three cheers to the margarita itself: so refreshingly smooth it goes down as agreeably as lemonade on a summer day…just watch out for that sneaky wallop—Mike Tyson's got nothing on it for knockout power.

In Chapala, Jalisco, a widow (in Spanish, *viuda*) invented a spicy orange juice–based drink as a tequila chaser and bottled it under the La Viuda label, which is made in Chapala and sold countrywide. Along came bloody mary–style tequila drinks and many more, including the tequila sunrise, which blends tequila, orange juice, and a splash of grenadine into a cocktail that looks as promising as a tropical sunrise.

Tequila is making inroads into new territory these days—as a flavoring in food in everything from banana nut bread, cookies, and jalapeño jelly, to salsa, pot roast, baked chicken, and stuffed peppers. If this revolution takes hold the way margaritas did, we could soon see tequila beside wine on the cook's list of pantry staples. Tequila-flavored dishes are already beginning to appear on menus of fine restaurants in Mexico.

At least four books are available that expound at length the versatility of Mexico's most famous liquor: *Tequila: The Spirit of Mexico* by Lucinda Hutson (Ten Speed Press, 1994); *The Tequila Cook Book* by Lynn Nusom (Golden West Publishers, 1994); *Tomás' Tequila Book* by Don and Alice Hutson and Dianne Goss (Pasquale Publishing, 1992); and *The Tequila Book* by Ann Walker (Chronicle Books, 1994).

MEXICO'S REGIONAL CUISINES

Tamales are a traditional food all around Mexico, but there are many regional differences. In Mexico City you can often find the traditional Oaxaca tamales, which are steamed in a banana leaf. The *zacahuil* of coastal Veracruz is the size of a pig's leg (that's what's in the center) and is pit-baked in a banana leaf; it can be sampled from street vendors on Sunday at the Lagunilla market.

Tortillas, another Mexican basic, are also not made or used equally. In northern Mexico, flour tortillas are served more often than corn tortillas. Blue corn tortillas, once a market food, have found their way to gourmet tables throughout the country. Tortillas are fried and used as a garnish in tortilla and Tarascan soup. Filled with meat they become, of course, tacos. A tortilla stuffed, rolled, or covered in a sauce and garnished results in an enchilada. A tortilla filled with cheese and lightly fried is a quesadilla. Rolled into a narrow tube stuffed with chicken, then deep fried, it becomes a flauta. Leftover tortillas cut in wedges and crispy fried are called totopos and used to scoop beans and guacamole salad. Yesterday's tortillas mixed with eggs, chicken, peppers, and other spices are called chilaquiles. Small fried corn tortillas are delicious with ceviche, or when topped with fresh lettuce, tomatoes, sauce, onions, and chicken they become tostadas. Each region has a variation of these tortilla-based dishes and most can be found in Mexico City.

Since a variety of Mexico's cuisines appear on menus all over the country, it's useful to know some of the best to try.

Puebla is known for the many dishes created by colonial-era nuns, among them traditional *mole poblano* (a rich sauce with more than 20 ingredients served over turkey), the eggnog-like *rompope,* and *bunuelos* (a kind of puff pastry dipped in sugar). Puebla is also known for its Mexican-style barbeque, lamb *mixiotes* (cooked in spicy sauce and wrapped in maguey paper), and *tinga* (a delicious beef stew). *Chiles enogada,* the national dish of Mexico, was created in Puebla in honor of Emperor Augustín Iturbide. The national colors of red, white, and green appear in this dish, in which large green poblano peppers are stuffed with spicy beef, topped with white almond sauce, and sprinkled with red pomegranate seeds. It's served around Independence Day in September.

Tamales wrapped in banana leaves and a number of different mole sauces are hallmarks of **Oaxacan** cuisine.

The **Yucatán** is noted for its rich (but not *picante*) sauces and pit-baked meat. Mild but flavorful achiote-based paste is one of the main flavorings for Yucatecan sauces.

The states of **Guerrero, Nayarit,** and **Jalisco** produce *pozole,* a soup of hominy and chicken or pork made in a clear broth or one from tomatoes or green chiles (depending on the state), and topped with a variety of garnishes.

Michoacán comes forth with a triangular-shaped tamal called *corunda,* and *uchepo,* a rectangular tamal that is either sweet or has meat inside. The state is also known for its soups, among them the delicious *Tarascan* soup, made with a bean-broth base.

And **Veracruz,** of course, is famous for seafood dishes, especially red snapper Veracruz-style, smothered in tomatoes, onions, garlic, and olives.

DISTINCTIVE MEXICAN DRINKS

Though Mexico grows flavorful **coffee** in Chiapas, Veracruz, and Oaxaca, a jar of instant coffee is often all that's offered, especially in budget restaurants. Decaffeinated coffee appears on some menus, but often it's the instant variety, even in the best restaurants.

Specialty drinks are almost as varied as the food in Mexico. **Tequila** comes from the blue agave grown near Guadalajara and it's the intoxicating ingredient in the famed margarita. Hot **ponche** (punch) is found often at festivals and is usually made with fresh fruit and spiked with tequila or rum.

Domestic wine and beer are excellent choices in Mexico, and in the past have been cheaper than any imported variety. However, NAFTA has lowered trade barriers against U.S.–made alcoholic drinks, and prices for them are becoming lower as well.

Baja California and the region around Querétaro is prime grape growing land for Mexico's **wine** production. Excellent **beer** is produced in Monterrey, the Yucatán, and Veracruz. The best **pulque,** a pre-Hispanic drink derived from the juice of the maguey plant, supposedly comes from Hidalgo state. Mexicans prefer freshly fermented pulque and generally avoid the canned variety, saying it's just not the real thing. Visitors to the capital can sample it at restaurants around Garibaldi Square. Delicious **fruit-flavored waters** appear on tables countrywide; they are made from hibiscus flowers, ground rice and melon seeds, watermelon, and other fresh fruits. Be sure to ask if they are made with purified water. **Sangria** is a spicy tomato-, orange juice-, and pepper-based chaser for tequila shots—not the sweet red wine with fruit in it that Americans are used to.

Though the rich, eggnog-like **rompope** was invented in Puebla, now other regions such as San Juan de los Lagos, Jalisco, produce it. It's sold in liquor and grocery stores countrywide.

4 Recommended Books

There are an endless number of books written on the history, culture, and archaeology of Mexico and Central America. I have listed those I especially enjoyed.

HISTORY

Dennis Tedlock produced an elegant translation of the *Popul Vuh,* a collection of ancient Maya mythological tales (Simon & Schuster, 1985). *A Short History of Mexico* (Doubleday, 1962) by J. Patrick McHenry is a concise historical account. A remarkably readable and thorough college textbook is *The Course of Mexican History* (Oxford University Press, 1987) by Michael C. Meyer and William L. Sherman. Bernal Díaz's *The Conquest of New Spain* (Shoe String, 1988) is the famous story of the Mexican Conquest written by Cortés's lieutenant. *The Crown of Mexico* (Holt, Rinehart & Winston, 1971) by Joan Haslip, a biography of Maximilian and Carlota, reads like a novel. Eric Wolf's *Sons of the Shaking Earth* (University of Chicago Press) is the best single-volume introduction to Mexican history and culture that I know. *Ancient Mexico; An Overview* (University of New Mexico Press, 1985) by Jaime Litvak, is a short, very readable history of pre-Hispanic Mexico.

The Wind That Swept Mexico (University of Texas Press, 1971) by Anita Brenner, is a classic illustrated account of the Mexican Revolution. Early this century Charles Flandrau wrote the classic *Viva Mexico: A Traveller's Account of Life in Mexico* (Eland Books, 1985), a blunt and humorous description of Mexico. Jonathan Kandell's *La Capital, Biography of Mexico City* (Random House, 1988) is assiduously researched, yet wonderfully readable.

Life in Mexico: Letters of Fanny Calderón de la Barca (Doubleday, 1966), edited and annotated by Howard T. Fisher and Marion Hall Fisher, is as lively and entertaining today as when it first appeared in 1843, but the editor's illustrated and annotated update makes it even more contemporary. Scottish-born Fanny was married to the Spanish ambassador to Mexico, and the letters are the accounts of her experiences. *My Heart Lies South* by Elizabeth Borton de Treviño (1953) is a humorous, tender, and insightful autobiographical account of the life of an American woman married to a Mexican in Monterrey; it begins in the 1930s.

Several modern writers have attempted to view Mexican culture through the lens of history. Harry A. Franck's *Trailing Cortés Through Mexico* (Frederick A. Stokes, 1935) and Mathew J. Bruccoli's *Reconquest of Mexico* (Vanguard Press, 1974) pursue the Conquest route of Cortés, interweaving history with customs of rural and city life of this century.

CONTEMPORARY MEXICAN LIFE

Five Families (Basic Books, 1979) and *Children of Sanchez* (Random House, 1979), both by Oscar Lewis, are sociological studies written in the late 1950s about typical Mexican families. Irene Nicholson's *Mexican and Central American Mythology* (Peter Bedrick Books, 1983) is a concise illustrated book that simplifies the subject.

A good but controversial all-around introduction to contemporary Mexico and its people is *Distant Neighbors: A Portrait of the Mexicans* (Random House, 1984) by Alan Riding. In a more personal vein is Patrick Oster's *The Mexicans: A Personal Portrait of the Mexican People* (HarperCollins, 1989), a reporter's insightful account of ordinary Mexican people. A book with valuable insights into the Mexican character is *The Labyrinth of Solitude* (Grove Press, 1985) by Octavio Paz. The best single source of information on Mexican music, dance, and mythology is Frances Toor's *A Treasury of Mexican Folkways* (Crown, 1967).

Anyone going to San Cristóbal de las Casas, Chiapas, should first read *Living Maya* (Harry N. Abrams, 1987) by Walter F. Morris, with excellent photographs by Jeffrey J. Foxx, all about the Maya living today in the state of Chiapas. Peter Canby's *The Heart of the Sky: Travels Among the Maya* (Kodansha International, 1994) takes readers on a rare but rugged journey as he searches to understand the real issues facing the Maya of Mexico and Guatemala today. For some fascinating background on northern Mexico and the Copper Canyon, read *Unknown Mexico* (Dover Press, 1987) by Carl Lumholtz, an intrepid writer and photographer around the turn of the century.

PRE-HISPANIC MEXICO

Anyone heading for Yucatán should first read the wonderfully entertaining accounts of travel in that region by the 19th-century traveler, New York lawyer, and amateur archaeologist John L. Stephens. His book *Incidents of Travel in Central America, Chiapas and Yucatán*, and also the account of his second trip, *Incidents of Travel in Yucatán*, have been reprinted by Dover complete with Frederick Catherwood's original illustrations. Dover has also released Diego de Landa's *Yucatán Before and After the Conquest* (Dover, 1978), written in the 1560s. Friar Diego's account is a detailed description of Maya daily life, much of which has remained the same from his time until today. Another must is *The Maya* (Thames and Hudson, 1987) by Michael Coe, which is helpful in relating to the different Maya periods. *A Forest of Kings: The Untold Story of the Ancient Maya* (William Morrow, 1990) by Linda Schele and David Freidel, uses the written history of Maya hieroglyphs to tell the dynastic history of selected Maya sites. You'll never view the sky the same after reading *Maya Cosmos: Three Thousand Years on the Shaman's Path* (William Morrow, 1993) by David Freidel, Linda Schele, and Joy Parker, whose personal insights and scholarly work take us along a very readable path into the amazing sky-centered world of the Maya. *The Blood of Kings: Dynasty and Ritual in Maya Art* (George Braziller, 1986) by Linda Schele and Mary Ellen Miller, is a pioneer work and unlocks the bloody history of the Maya. The most comprehensive guide to Maya ruins is Joyce Kelly's *An Archeological Guide to Mexico's Yucatán Peninsula* (University of Oklahoma Press, 1993).

Michael Coe's *Mexico: From the Olmecs to the Aztecs* (Thames and Hudson, 1994), takes us through the latest discoveries and theories regarding Mexico's ancient Indian

Cultures (but excludes the Maya which are covered in his other book *The Maya,* mentioned above). For the latest on the mysterious Olmec culture don't miss *The Olmec World: Ritual and Rulership* (The Art Museum, Princeton University and Harry N. Abrams, 1996), the splendid catalog of a major exhibition of privately owned Olmec art in the United States. Major Olmec scholars in the United States provided essays on current theories about Mexico's little-studied "mother culture."

Several fictionalized accounts of Aztec life have been written. These include Gary Jenning's *Aztec* (Avon, 1981), a superbly researched and colorfully written account of Aztec life before and after the Conquest. Equally revealing is *The Luck of Huemac,* by Daniel Peters (Random House, 1981), a compelling novel about four generations of an Aztec family between the years 1428 and 1520.

ART & ARCHITECTURE

A book that tells the story of the Indians' "painted books" is *The Mexican Codices and Their Extraordinary History* (Ediciones Lara, 1985) by María Sten. *Mexico Splendors of Thirty Centuries* (Metropolitan Museum of Art, 1990), the catalog of the 1991 traveling exhibition, is a wonderful resource on Mexico's art from 1500 B.C. through the 1950s. Another superb catalog, *Images of Mexico: The Contribution of Mexico to 20th Century Art* (Dallas Museum of Art, 1987) is a fabulously illustrated and detailed account of Mexican art gathered from collections around the world. Elizabeth Wilder Weismann's *Art and Time in Mexico: From the Conquest to the Revolution* (HarperCollins, 1985), illustrated with 351 photographs, covers Mexican religious, public, and private architecture with excellent photos and text. *Casa Mexicana* (Stewart, Tabori & Chang, 1989) by Tim Street-Porter, takes readers through the interiors of some of Mexico's finest homes-turned-museums or public buildings and private homes using color photographs. *Mexican Interiors* (Architectural Book Publishing Co., 1962) by Verna Cook Shipway and Warren Shipway, uses black-and-white photographs to highlight architectural details from homes all over Mexico.

FOLK ART

Chloè Sayer's *Costumes of Mexico* (University of Texas Press, 1985) is a beautifully illustrated and written work. *Mexican Masks* (University of Texas Press, 1980) by Donald Cordry, based on the author's collection and travels, remains the definitive work on Mexican masks. Cordry's *Mexican Indian Costumes* (University of Texas Press, 1968) is another classic on the subject. Carlos Espejel wrote both *Mexican Folk Ceramics* and *Mexican Folk Crafts* (Editorial Blume, 1975 and 1978), two comprehensive books that explore crafts state by state. *Folk Treasures of Mexico* (Harry N. Abrams, 1990) by Marion Oettinger, curator of Folk and Latin American Art at the San Antonio Museum of Art, is the fascinating illustrated story behind the 3,000-piece Mexican folk-art collection amassed by Nelson Rockefeller over a 50-year period, and also includes much information about individual folk artists. The fantastically colorful sculpted animals and figures of Oaxaca's wood-carvers is the subject of *Oaxacan Woodcarving* (Chronicle Books, 1993), by Shepard Barbash and photographed by Vicki Ragan, a finely illustrated exposition of colorful work from wood-carvers in Oaxaca and an insightful glimpse of the rural communities where the artists live.

NATURE

A Naturalist's Mexico (Texas A&M University Press, 1992), by Roland H. Wauer, is a fabulous guide to birding in Mexico. *A Hiker's Guide to Mexico's Natural History* (Mountaineers, 1995), by Jim Conrad, covers Mexican flora and fauna and tells how to find the easy-to-reach and out-of-the-way spots he describes. Most comprehensive of all the birding guide books is *A Guide to the Birds of Mexico and North Central America* (Oxford University Press, 1995), by Steve N. Ottowell and Sophie Webb, an encyclopedic volume with hundreds of color illustrations. *Peterson Field Guides: Mexican Birds* (Houghton Mifflin), by Roger Tory Peterson and Edward L. Chalif, is an excellent guide to the country's birds. *Birds of the Yucatán* (Amigos de Sian Ka'an) has color illustrations and descriptions of 100 birds found primarily in the Yucatán peninsula. *A Guide to Mexican Mammals and Reptiles* (Minutiae Mexicana), by Norman Pelham Wright and Dr. Bernardo Villa Ramírez, is a small but useful guide to some of the country's wildlife.

Planning a Trip to the Yucatán

Before any trip, you need to do a bit of advance planning. When should I go? What's the best way to get there? How much will this trip cost me? And can I catch a festival during my visit? I'll answer these and other questions for you in this chapter.

1 Visitor Information, Entry Requirements & Money

SOURCES OF INFORMATION

The **Mexico Hotline** (☎ 800/44-MEXICO in the U.S.) is a good source for very general informational brochures on the country and for answers to the most commonly asked questions. If you have a fax, Mexico's Ministry of Tourism also offers **FaxMeMexico** (☎ 5̶0̶3̶/ 541 385-9282). Call, provide them with a fax number, and select from a variety of topics—from accommodations (the service lists 400 hotels) to shopping, dining, sports, sightseeing, festivals, and nightlife. They'll then fax you the materials you're interested in.

The **U.S. Department of State** (☎ 202/647-5225 for travel information, ☎ 202/647-9225 for bulletin board information), offers a **Consular Information Sheet** on Mexico, with a compilation of safety, medical, driving, and general travel information gleaned from reports by official U.S. State Department offices in Mexico. You can also request the Consular Information Sheet (☎ 202/647-2000) by fax. The **Center for Disease Control hotline** (☎ 404/ 332-4559), is another source for medical information affecting travelers to Mexico and elsewhere.

MEXICAN GOVERNMENT TOURIST OFFICES   Mexico has tourist offices throughout the world, including the following:

United States: 70 E. Lake St., Suite 1413, Chicago, IL 60601 (☎ 3̶1̶2̶/̶5̶6̶5̶-̶2̶7̶7̶8̶)̶, 5075 Westheimer, Suite 975, West Houston, TX 77056 (☎ 713/629-1611); 10100 Santa Monica Blvd., Suite 224, Los Angeles, CA 90067 (☎ 310/203-8191); 2333 Ponce de Leon Blvd., Suite 710, Coral Gables, FL 33134 (☎ 305/443-9160); 405 Park Ave., Suite 1401, New York, NY 10022 (☎ 212/ 838-2947); and the Mexican Embassy Tourism Delegate, 1911 Pennsylvania Ave. NW, Washington, DC 20006 (☎ 202/ 728-1750).

Canada: One Place Ville-Marie, Suite 1526, Montréal, PQ H3B 2B5 (☎ 514/871-1052); 2 Bloor St. W., Suite 1801, Toronto, ON M4W 3E2 (☎ 416/925-1876). 99 W. Hastings #1610, Vancouver, British Columbia V6C 2W2 (☎ 604/669-3498).

Europe: Weisenhüttenplatz 26, D 6000 Frankfurt-am-Main 1, Germany (☎ 49/69-25-3413); 60-61 Trafalgar Sq., London WC2 N5DS, United Kingdom (☎ 171/734-1058); Calle de Velázquez 126, 28006 Madrid, Spain (☎ 341/261-1827); 4 rue Notre-Dame-des-Victoires, 75002 Paris, France (☎ 331/4020-0734); and via Barberini 3, 00187 Rome, Italy (☎ 396/482-7160).

Asia: 2.15.1 Nagato-Cho, Chiyoda-Ku, Tokyo 100, Japan (☎ 813/580-2962).

STATE TOURISM DEVELOPMENT OFFICES   Two Mexican states have tourism and trade development offices in the United States: **Casa Guerrero State Promotion Office,** 5075 Westheimer, Suite 980 W., Houston, TX 77056 (☎ 713/552-0930; fax 713/552-0207); **Casa Nuevo León State Promotion Office,** 100 W. Houston St., Suite 1400, San Antonio, TX 78205 (☎ 210/225-0732; fax 210/225-0736).

OTHER SOURCES   The following newsletters may be of interest to readers: *Mexico Meanderings,* P.O. Box 33057, Austin, TX 78764, aimed at readers who travel to off-the-beaten-track destinations by car, bus, or train (six to eight pages, photographs, published six times annually, subscription $18); *Travel Mexico,* Apdo. Postal 6-1007, 06600 Mexico, D.F., from the publishers of the *Traveler's Guide to Mexico,* the book frequently found in hotel rooms in Mexico, covers a variety of topics from archaeology news to hotel packages, new resorts and hotels, and the economy (six times annually, subscription $18).

ENTRY REQUIREMENTS

DOCUMENTS   All travelers to Mexico are required to present **proof of citizenship,** such as an original birth certificate with a raised seal, a valid passport, or naturalization papers. Those using a birth certificate should also have a current photo identification such as a driver's license. And those whose last name on the birth certificate is different from their current name (women using a married name, for example) should also bring a photo identification card *and* legal proof of the name change such as the *original* marriage license or certificate (I'm not kidding). This proof of citizenship may also be requested when you want to reenter either the United States or Mexico. Note that photocopies are *not* acceptable.

You must also carry a **Mexican Tourist Permit,** which is issued free of charge by Mexican border officials after proof of citizenship is accepted. The Tourist Permit is more important than a passport in Mexico, so guard it carefully. If you lose it, you may not be permitted to leave the country until you can replace it—a bureaucratic hassle that takes several days to a week at least. (If you do lose your Tourist Permit, get a police report from local authorities indicating that your documents were stolen; having one *might* lessen the hassle of exiting the country without all your identification.)

A Tourist Permit can be issued for up to 180 days, and although your stay south of the border may be shorter than that, you should ask for the maximum time, just in case. Sometimes officials don't ask—they just stamp a time limit, so be sure to say "six months" (or at least twice as long as you intend to stay). If you should decide to extend your stay, you'll eliminate hassle by not needing to renew your papers.

This is especially important for people who take a car into Mexico. Additional documentation is required for driving a personal vehicle in Mexico (see "By Car" under "Getting There," below).

Puenta Maroma
   owner Jose Louise
   wife (Chicagoan) Kathy

   phone (52) 987-31213

Sacbe Cultura Mija
(Ecological Park)

Snorkeling in caves
(7 people only) at a time
underwater candle lit
caverns. 3 mi from
Playa del Carmen

Note that children under age 18 traveling without parents or with only one parent must have a notarized letter from the absent parent or parents authorizing the travel.

Lost Documents   To replace a **lost passport,** contact your embassy or nearest consular agent (see "Fast Facts: Mexico," below). You must establish a record of your citizenship and also fill out a form requesting another Mexican Tourist Permit. Without the **Tourist Permit** you can't leave the country, and without an affidavit affirming your passport request and citizenship, you may have hassles at Customs when you get home. So it's important to clear everything up *before* trying to leave. Mexican Customs may, however, accept the police report of the loss of the Tourist Permit and allow you to leave.

CUSTOMS ALLOWANCES   When you enter Mexico, Customs officials will be tolerant as long as you have no illegal drugs or firearms. You're allowed to bring in two cartons of cigarettes, or 50 cigars, plus a kilogram (2.2 lb.) of smoking tobacco; the liquor allowance is two bottles of anything, wine or hard liquor; you are also allowed 12 rolls of film.

When you're reentering the United States, federal law allows you to bring in duty free up to $400 in purchases every 30 days. The first $1,000 over the $400 allowance is taxed at 10%. You may bring in a carton (200) of cigarettes or 50 cigars or 2kg (4.4 lb.) of smoking tobacco, plus 1 liter of an alcoholic beverage (wine, beer, or spirits).

Canadian citizens are allowed $20 in purchases after a 24-hour absence from the country or $100 after a stay of 48 hours or more.

Going through Customs   Mexican customs inspection has been streamlined. At most points of entry tourists are requested to punch a button in front of what looks like a traffic signal, which alternates on touch between red and green signals. Green light and you go through without inspection; red light and your luggage or car may be inspected briefly or thoroughly. I've been seeing more red lights these days; seems the government is stepping up their inspections.

MONEY
CASH/CURRENCY

In 1993, the Mexican government dropped three zeroes from its currency. The new currency is called the *Nuevo Peso,* or New Peso. The purpose was to simplify accounting; all those zeroes were becoming too difficult to manage. Old Peso notes were valid through 1996. Paper currency comes in denominations of 10, 20, 50, and 100 New Pesos. Coins come in denominations of 1, 2, 5, and 10 pesos and 20 and 50 *centavos* (100 centavos make one New Peso). The coins are somewhat confusing because different denominations have a similar appearance. You may still see some prices written with *N* or *NP* beside them, which refer to New Pesos. Currently the U.S. dollar equals around NP$7.50; at that rate an item costing NP$5, for example, would be equivalent to U.S. 67¢.

These changes are likely to cause confusion among U.S. and Canadian travelers to Mexico in several ways. Before the New Peso was instituted, merchants and others skipped the small change; now they don't. Small change (a peso or less than a peso) is often unavailable, so cashiers often offer gum or candy to make up the difference. Centavos will appear on restaurant bills and credit cards, but are paid differently depending on if you pay in cash or by credit card. On restaurant bills that you pay in cash, for example, the centavos will be rounded up or down to the nearest five centavos. Credit-card bills, however, will show the exact amount (not rounded), and will have *N* written before the amount to denote that the bill is in New Pesos. Be sure to double-check any credit-card vouchers to be sure the *N* or *NP* appears on the total line.

Getting change continues to be a problem in Mexico. Small-denomination bills and coins are hard to come by, so start collecting them early in your trip and continue as you travel. Shopkeepers everywhere seem to always be out of change and small bills; that's doubly true in a market.

Note: The dollar sign ($) is used to indicate pesos in Mexico. To avoid confusion, I will use the dollar sign in this book *only* to denote U.S. currency.

Only dollar prices are listed in this book; they are a more reliable indication than peso prices. Many establishments dealing with tourists quote prices in dollars. To avoid confusion, they use the abbreviations "Dlls." for dollars and "m.n." (*moneda nacional*—national currency) for pesos.

Every effort has been made to provide the most accurate and up-to-date information in this guide, but price changes are inevitable.

EXCHANGING MONEY

The December 1994 devaluation of the peso has had varied meanings for tourists. First, the rate of exchange fluctuates daily, so be careful not to exchange too much of your currency at once. Don't forget, however, to allow enough to carry you over a weekend or Mexican holiday, when banks are closed. Cash can sometimes be difficult to exchange because counterfeit U.S. dollars have been circulating recently in Mexico; merchants and banks are wary, and many, especially in small towns, refuse to accept dollars in cash. In general, avoid carrying the U.S. $100 bill, the one most commonly counterfeited. Since small bills and coins in pesos are hard to come by in Mexico, the U.S. $1 bill is very useful for tipping.

Bottom line on exchanging money of all kinds: It pays to ask first and shop around. Banks in Mexico often give a less favorable rate of exchange than the official daily rate, and hotels usually exchange less favorably than do banks. Exchange houses are generally more convenient than banks since they have more locations and longer hours, and the rate of exchange may be the same as a bank or slightly lower. Personal checks may be cashed but not without weeks of delay—a bank will wait for your check to clear before giving you your money. Canadian dollars seem to be most easily exchanged for pesos at branches of Banamex and Bancomer. *Before leaving a bank or exchange house window, always count your change in front of the teller before the next client steps up.*

Banks are open Monday through Friday from 9am to 1:30pm; a few banks in large cities offer extended afternoon hours. Most banks won't exchange money until 10am, when they receive the day's official rate. Large airports have currency-exchange counters that often stay open whenever flights are arriving or departing. Don't go for the first one you see in an airport—there's usually more than one and you'll often find a better exchange rate farther along the concourse.

TRAVELER'S CHECKS

Traveler's checks are readily accepted nearly everywhere, but they can be difficult to cash on a weekend or holiday or in an out-of-the-way place. Their best value is in replacement in case of theft. I usually arrive in Mexico with half of my money in cash (in $1, $20, and $50 bills) and half in traveler's checks ($20 and $50 denominations). Mexican banks sometimes pay more for traveler's checks than for dollars in cash, but in some places *casas de cambio* (exchange houses) pay more for cash than for traveler's checks. Additionally, some but not all banks charge a service fee to exchange either traveler's checks or dollars.

CREDIT CARDS & ATMS

You'll be able to charge some hotel and restaurant bills, almost all airline tickets, and many store purchases on your credit cards. You can get cash advances of several hundred dollars on your card, but there may be a wait of 20 minutes to two hours. You can't charge gasoline purchases in Mexico.

VISA ("Bancomer" in Mexico), MasterCard ("Carnet" in Mexico), and, less widely, American Express are the most accepted cards. The Bancomer bank, with branches throughout the country, has inaugurated a system of **automatic-teller machines (ATMs)** linked to VISA International's network. If you are a VISA customer, you may be able to get peso cash from one of the Bancomer ATMs.

ATM machines are also associated with other banks and may work with your own bank ATM. There's usually a $200 limit per transaction. Two cautions about using automatic teller machines are in order: first, though ATMs are located next to banks, or in a bank lobby, use the same precautions you would at home—don't use one at night, or on a lonely street, etc.; second, don't depend on them totally for your extra cash—you might not always have access to one, and you'll be out of luck if the machine eats your card.

FOR TRAVELERS ON A BUDGET

I love budget travel because it puts me close to the sights and sounds of Mexico, to its culture and people. Traveling on a budget in Mexico is anything but a hardship. You can stay at charming inns, eat well and in fine surroundings, and enjoy low-cost or free entertainment almost everywhere, as well as low-cost transportation. Even otherwise expensive resort cities such as Puerto Vallarta or Cancún offer rich, culture-filled experiences for cost-conscious travelers, and this book will tell you where to find them.

Because of the devaluation of the peso and inflation running as high as 25% to 50%, there may be some surprises when it comes to deciding how much money travel in Mexico will cost. Before the devaluation it was possible to travel comfortably on our budget. Even now, two years after the devaluation, Mexico is still a travel bargain.

Below are some tips that will help you to enjoy a first-class experience of the Yucatán without draining your wallet:

Air Travel

- "Low season" in Mexico runs from Easter Sunday through approximately December 20, and airlines often offer discounted airfares. Many of these fares are unadvertised, especially during the slowest months mentioned above (mid-summer), and again in January, when the Christmas travelers have dispersed and hotel and airline occupancies are low.
- Charter flights from cold-weather cities in the United States—most run only in winter—often offer a considerable savings over scheduled airlines because they go direct to the destination (avoiding the necessity of overnighting en route) and they usually include low airfare and hotel. However, these same charters often offer round-trip airfare only, allowing more independent travelers to choose a less expensive hotel, and the option of staying longer and returning on a later charter flight.
- Regional airlines affiliated with Mexicana and Aeromexico cost much more to book from the United States than if booked in Mexico and paid in pesos. Of course if a connection is critical you'll want to book from the United States, but if you can wait, or want to take a chance that seats will be available, you can save at least one-third or sometimes even one-half of the fare.

Accommodations

- "Low season" yields even greater discounts in hotel rates than airfares—prices are 20% to 50% lower than during high season. There's often a lull after New Year's in Cancún and Cozumel—prices can fall to somewhere between high- and low-season norms.
- In most of Mexico, July and August are very slow, but there are some exceptions. Mexicans and Europeans take vacations in those months, and some hotels in Isla Mujeres and Playa del Carmen thus raise their prices.
- Rooms with air-conditioning are almost always more expensive than those with only fans. Rooms with a view of the street may be more expensive (not to mention noisier) than those with windows opening onto an airshaft. Sea views cost more than garden or street views at the same resort. A room with a balcony or patio, however, will cost the same as one without.
- Hotels a block or two from the beach cost 50% to 100% less than those right on the sand.
- Fewer and fewer hotels in Mexico have rooms without private baths. The few bathless rooms listed in this book will be somewhat cheaper, but not necessarily by very much, than those with baths.
- It is generally cheaper for two people to share a room with one bed than for them to share a room with two beds.
- If you ask a desk clerk to price a room, the quote he gives you may not be for the cheapest room available. Ask to see a cheaper room by saying *"quiero ver un cuarto más barato, por favor"*—it can't hurt.
- Package vacations that include the cost of air transportation and hotel will usually save you money—except right after a currency devaluation, as 1995 proved. Package prices may have been negotiated at predevaluation rates.
- To check out package deals, look for hotels listed in this book with toll-free reservation numbers in the United States; they may be a part of a package offered by a scheduled or charter airline or wholesale package dealer. (Most hotels in this book are not included in package vacations.) To evaluate the value of a package, call the airline to determine the cost of round-trip airfare and if possible call the hotel for their per-day rack (public), promotional, and discount rates. This will give you some idea of the actual cost as compared to the package cost. Take into consideration that round-trip transportation from the airport to your hotel is often included in package rates and can save you $20 to $30 in such places as Cancún.
- In Cozumel, you can save money by purchasing diving packages, which include the price of the hotel and usually two dives. If the dive operates from the hotel, you will also save on transportation costs. Many divers, however, save more money by staying in a cheaper hotel and booking dives directly with a diving concession. This method may be particularly practical in the fall, when stormy seas often preclude diving, and you therefore won't have to pay for unused dives.
- By law, hotel rates should be posted within view of the reception desk, but often they are not. If a hotel's quoted rate seems too high, ask to see their official rate sheet and ask about discounts and promotional rates. Walk away if the price seems too high.

    Additionally, budget quality hotels may charge you 10% to 15% more if you want a receipt. Since it isn't wise to pay a desk clerk for a room without getting a receipt for your payment—for example, readers have reported paying an evening clerk on check-in, only to discover upon checkout that the day clerk has no record of the transaction—I carry a pad of receipts, so they won't have to use their official ones. As an alternative, I've asked them to write, sign, and date an informal receipt in my notebook.

- If you're traveling in the off-season (and not during a Mexican holiday), it is not necessary to make reservations. Arrive at your destination early in the day and target your choice of hotel. This will save you the price of a long-distance call to reserve a room and the uncertainty of knowing if your reservation deposit has been received. Mexican hotels often do not respond to reservation requests made by mail, even though they will honor such requests.

- When calling from outside Mexico for a reservation, you'll almost always be asked from where you are calling. If you say you're from the United States or some other country, the price may go up. Instead, say you're calling from a nearby Mexican city and you're more likely to get good rates.

- If you have reserved a room, ask the going rate for a room on arrival. If it is less than the rate you reserved, register as a new client and take a room at the lower cost. If you've paid a deposit, ask that it be applied to your new account. You may have to debate the point, but it will be worth it. Only if you've used the hotel's U.S. toll-free reservation number can the hotel logically justify a higher rate for your reservations.

- If you arrive in a city without a hotel reservation, call a hotel from the public telephone/fax office in most bus stations and airports. For only the cost of a local call, you'll be assured of a room when you arrive. In addition, you will not incur hefty taxi fares. If you don't speak Spanish and if the person at the telephone office isn't busy, ask him or her to make the call for you.

- Most hotels allow children under age 12 to stay for free in their parents' room. Many hotels will accommodate kids with a roll-away bed. When making your reservation, always verify that the hotel has this service and take down the name of the person with whom you spoke.

- Although Mexican campsites are not of the same quality as those in the United States, most beach destinations have designated camping areas; in this book, you'll find campgrounds at Playa del Carmen and at Tulum.

- In Mexico, hotels on the main square are often slightly higher priced than hotels a block or two away.

- Finally, some destinations *do* have cheaper places to stay than those I've written up for this book. But I purposely have not listed rock-bottom hotels in this guide because of frequent reports of thefts at such places—especially of cameras and money from backpackers. While nothing can guarantee complete security, I have chosen hotels that feel safe.

Dining and Drinking

- Generally the least expensive, most filling items on Mexican menus are local specialties such as enchiladas, tacos, chilaquiles, carne tampiqueña, and milanesa.

- Other inexpensive meals (which come in a bowl) include sopa tlalpeño—a hearty vegetable soup—and pozole soup, in its different regional varieties.

- Free coffee refills are rare in Mexico, so you pay by the cup at 75¢ to $1.25 a shot. To make your own coffee or tea, pack a travel-size coffeepot (or an immersion coil), a heat-resistant plastic cup, instant coffee or a tea bag, and powdered milk. (Having a coil or a hot pot is also very handy if you are ill and can stomach only chamomile tea or bouillon.)

- Trail mix, granola bars, and fruit from the market are great to bring along for snacks. You can also prepare instant soup (not easily found in Mexico) with your own hot-water maker in your room and save $1 to $4 on the cost of a bowl of soup in a restaurant.

- Mexico's abundant fresh-fruit markets and bakeries are ideal for concocting inexpensive breakfasts.
- The *comida corrida*, Mexico's traditional noon-time fixed-price menu, often includes an entire meal, from soup to dessert. It can be a good value if portions are large and if a beverage and dessert are included. If the comida corrida is over $4, you're probably better off ordering from the a la carte menu.
- Although eating in American-style restaurants such as Denny's, Vips, and Lyni's surely isn't classic Mexican dining, these places offer value and dependable food. They are especially good deals in Mexico City and Guadalajara, where there are fewer economical restaurants.
- Since Mexico has a value-added tax (IVA) of 10% in Cancún, Cozumel, and Los Cabos, and 15% in the rest of the country, determine the amount of your tip from the cost of your meal *before* the tax has been included. For meals costing under $3, leave loose change; for meals costing $4 to $5, leave 6% to 10%, depending on the quality of service. For meals above $5, include a 10% to 15% tip.
- Avoid buying a beverage with each meal by drinking water—yes, water. Most restaurants serving tourists (and many serving primarily Mexicans) use purified water from large commercial jars. To get free water and not bottled water (for which you pay), ask if they have *agua purificada natural de la garrafon* (noncarbonated, purified water from the big bottle dispenser) *sin hielo* (without ice). The garrafon (big bottle of purified water) is often within view in the dining room and you can point to it if you don't speak Spanish. If the waiter puts a small bottle of commercially produced purified water on the table, it'll cost $1.50 to $3 extra.
- At 75¢ to $2 each, soft drink or beer costs can add up as you travel, especially in hot-weather destinations. To quench thirst more economically, carry a small water jug and replenish it with bottled water purchased at a grocery store for around 75¢ to $1 per gallon.
- Mexico produces excellent wine, beer, and rum which are considerably less expensive than imported spirits.
- If your craving for beer, soft drinks, and liquor is acute, save money by buying them at a grocery store and have drinks in your room, patio, or balcony rather than at a restaurant or bar. A soft drink, for example, can cost as little as 25¢ at a corner grocery and as much as 75¢ to $2 at a restaurant.
- Mexicans recycle soft drink bottles, and you'll be charged more if you take bottles with you from a grocery store or *abarote* (neighborhood store). Usually, clerks will ask if your drink is to go *(para llevar)* or to drink there. Often, though, they pour the whole bottled drink into a fresh plastic bag, stick a straw in it, and send you off clasping the loose neck of your portable container at no extra charge.
- Happy hours, when drinks are two for the price of one, proliferate, especially in resort areas. Often there are also happy hours at lobby bars in major cities.
- Sports bars offer TV or video sports entertainment without a cover charge.

Sightseeing, Outdoor Activities & Nightlife

- Bring your own snorkeling gear to beach destinations and save $5 to $10 on the cost of daily rental.
- For a leisurely and inexpensive orientation to the spread-out city and resort of Cancún, take a city bus along the main thoroughfares for 25¢ to 50¢.
- If you're female, look for ladies' nights, when women pay no cover charge at discos.
- Free weekend concerts are often presented in central parks and plazas all over Mexico. For example, Mérida has free entertainment in city parks almost nightly.

- Almost all museums and archaeological sites are free to the public on Sunday and Mexican holidays—a savings of $1.50 to $7.

- Most archaeological sites charge visitors $5.50 to $8.50 for using their personal video cameras. If you are visiting many sites, you'll save a lot of money by not using your video camera or by saving it for the most important sites. A few sites charge visitors for using still cameras, so consider whether the lighting conditions and site are worth this expense.

Money Matters

- At the Cancún airport you can lose substantial amounts of money by using the first exchange booth you see—compare exchanging $100 at seven pesos to the dollar (700 pesos) and at 6.5 pesos (650 pesos) to the dollar. There's a 50 peso ($7.15) difference. As a general rule, take a few minutes to scout the exchange houses for the best rate and then change only enough to tide you over until you can go to a bank, which usually offer better deals.

- Try not to carry U.S. $100 bills, which may not be exchangeable; there's a surfeit of counterfeit bills circulating in that denomination, and banks, exchange houses, and others are wary of accepting them.

- Carry at least $50 in U.S. one-dollar bills to avoid overtipping in pesos. For example, a 10-peso tip ($1.43 at seven pesos to the dollar) may be too much, but five pesos (about 71¢) might not be enough. Using one-dollar bills helps conserve small-denomination peso bills and coins, which are in short supply.

- Carry enough cash to cover a weekend or holiday, since travelers checks and credit cards may be difficult to use at those times.

- Do not rely on your credit card in out-of-the-way places or in many budget hotels and restaurants. Such places often do not accept credit cards, and you will waste time looking for a bank and could pay dearly for a cash advance.

- Some establishments charge an additional 3% for use of a credit card, but they usually tell you first.

- If credit cards are accepted and incur no additional fees, use them whenever possible. The exchange rate may be in your favor when the peso-to-dollar rate is determined later during billing. Such savings can be considerable.

- Always count your change, especially at taxi ticket booths, where shortchanging is common. One reader wrote me about having saved money equivalent to the cost of this book by following this tip at the Mexico City airport.

- Most hotel and restaurant prices you'll see posted in Mexico include the 10% to 15% IVA tax. Look at the bottom of menus for information about whether the tax is included in meals; ask *before* you rent a room or order a meal.

- A 10% to 15% tip is sometimes, though not often, included in bills, most often in the Yucatán. Restaurants which serve many visitors from Europe (where the tip is customarily included in the cost of food) may tack it onto the bill when it is presented to you.

Transportation

- Inner-city bus service in Cancún is so good and inexpensive (50¢ per ride) that there's little need for a taxi.

- Most airports and bus stations in large cities have *colectivo* (shared) or fixed-rate taxis to town. The colectivo is always the least expensive way to go.

- Except for Mexico City, taxis in Mexico aren't metered. In other cities, you must agree on a price before you get in. Taxi prices to the most common destinations are usually posted inside the front door of most hotels. Use these prices as guides to taxi costs, since taxi drivers are notorious for bargaining high.

- A Volkswagen Beetle (which are made in Puebla, Mexico) with manual transmission and without air-conditioning, is the least expensive car you can rent in Mexico. Save money by reserving a rental car before you leave the United States. Avis's prepay rental deal is a substantial cost saver. Weekly rentals and those with mileage included are the best deals, but watch out for high deductibles.
- During high season and Mexican holidays, rates for car rentals are inflated. Rentals also cost more during weekends at resorts and weekdays in business-oriented cities.

Shopping

- Bargaining is expected in markets. Start at half the price first quoted to you and agree finally on something in between. You'll get a cheaper per-item price if you buy more than one of the same item. If the vendor senses that you're prepared to walk away, the price will often come down. Even in stores with fixed prices, discounts are often available if you are buying many things, but you'll have to ask for them.
- In resort areas, resort clothing is often a bargain, especially when there's a sale. Be careful about Mexican-made zippers; sometimes they aren't up to the task.

Last, But Not Least

- Pack plenty of insect repellant and suntan lotion. When available, these commodities cost at least triple what they do in the States. Lotions with an SPF rating are almost impossible to find.
- Although prices have risen recently, prescription drugs are often less expensive in Mexico than in the States and can be purchased without a prescription. Drugstores, however, won't sell drugs that are controlled in the States—tranquilizers for instance. High-priced antibiotics cost about the same in Mexico as they do in the United States. Aspirin and over-the-counter sinus medications are difficult, if not impossible, to find in Mexico.
- Save money on long-distance calls by calling collect. If that's not possible, then the least expensive option is to use a *larga distancia* office, found in most towns. Generally there's a service charge of about $2.50 to $3.50 in addition to the cost of the call. Using the phone in your hotel room can be the most expensive way to call; a hefty service charge is often added to the price of the call—even if you are calling a toll-free number. Many budget hotels, however, charge the same rates as those at a larga distancia office; ask before you call.
- Save money on laundry by doing it yourself. Bring a self-sealing plastic bag of powdered detergent; as an extra, it keeps your suitcase smelling fresh. Budget hotels often also offer very inexpensive laundry service. For a small tip, you can usually have everything ironed as well. Be wary of getting delicate items laundered at hotels.
- If the copy of *War and Peace* you brought along didn't last the trip, you can exchange it for a different book at one of the many hotels listed in the book that have an honor book exchange. Novels from the United States for sale at Sanborn's and other outlets in Mexico often cost at least twice the U.S. cover price.
- Hotels will store guests' luggage free in a locked closet set aside especially for this purpose. There's usually no limit on the length of time luggage can be stored.

BRIBES & SCAMS

You will probably find yourself in situations in Mexico where bribes—called *propinas* (tips) or *mordidas* (bites)—are expected, or where con artists are working their trade. Here's how to deal with them.

BRIBES

Extortion, of course, exists everywhere in the world, but in Mexico as in other developing countries, the tolls are smaller and collected more often.

Border officials appear to be slipping back into the petty-extortion habit they largely shed during the administration of President Salinas de Gortari. Just so you're prepared, here are a few hints based on my experiences.

First rule: Even if you speak Spanish, don't say a word of it to Mexican officials. This allows you to appear to be innocent, even dumb, all the while understanding every word. Some border officials will do what they're supposed to do (stamp your passport or birth certificate and perhaps lightly inspect your luggage) and then wave you on through. If you don't offer a tip of a few dollars to the man who inspects your car (if you're driving), he may ask for it, as in "Give me a tip *(propina).*" I usually ignore this request, but you'll have to decide for yourself based on your circumstances at the time, especially if the official decides a complete search of your belongings is suddenly in order. If you're charged for the stamping or inspection (for example, the inspector says, "One dollar," followed by an outstretched hand), ask for a receipt (*recibo;* "ray-*see*-bow"). If he says there's no receipt, don't pay the bribe. By then he's probably already nonchalantly waved you ahead anyway, the quicker to hit up the next unsuspecting victim. You can also simply ignore the request or pretend not to understand it and walk on.

Officials don't ask for bribes from everybody. Travelers dressed in a formal suit and tie, wearing pitch-black sunglasses and a scowl, are rarely asked to pay a bribe. Those who are dressed for vacation fun or seem good-natured and accommodating are targets. Whatever you do, avoid impoliteness, and absolutely *never* insult a Latin American official! When an official's sense of machismo is roused, he can and will throw the book at you, and you may be in trouble. Stand your ground, but do it politely.

How do I know when paying a bribe would be better than fighting it? Here are a couple of scenarios: A driving rain is drenching the world outside and the scowling border guard orders everyone out of the vehicle to unpack belongings for inspection—in the rain. Cut your losses and offer a bribe. You're stopped for a traffic infraction that you did or didn't commit, and the policeman keeps inspecting your car documents, your driver's license, or your Tourist Permit, finding things "wrong." If you're in a hurry, offer a bribe. If you're not, offer to follow him to the station. He'll probably not want to do that, and will find some way to save face—your credentials are all right after all—and move on. You must allow him to save face.

How much should I offer? Usually $3 to $5 or the equivalent in pesos will do the trick. There's supposedly a number to report irregularities with customs officials (☎ toll-free **91-800-00148** in Mexico). Your call will go to the office of the Comptroller and Administrative Development Secretariat (SECODAM). It's worth a try. But be sure you have some basic information, such as the name of the person who wanted a bribe or was rude, and the place, time, and day of the event.

SCAMS

As you travel in Mexico, you may encounter several types of scams. The **distraction scam** is found frequently on the Mexico City subway, or on crowded buses, but it can happen on a busy city street, market, or festival, anywhere. Someone in front of you on the subway or street drops to the ground searching for something. You're mildly distracted as you manage to get around the person in the way, probably with people crowding you from behind. By the time you're beyond the distraction, a hand has already found its way to your wallet—even when it's stowed in a front-facing fanny pack or your front pants pocket. As a variation, an impeccably dressed man or woman tells you that you've got a foreign substance, like white powder or a wet paintlike substance, on the back of your nice jacket. He (usually it's a male, but sometimes it's a "married couple") spends a long time helping you remove the stain with his nicely pressed handkerchief. Your thanks are so profuse for this kind assistance to you, the foreigner, that you don't realize until later that your wallet is missing. A variation of this one, starring the impeccably dressed local again, occurs in hotel lobbies: He or she strikes up a conversation with you, and while your head is turned your purse, bag, or packages disappear. Or the lobby is filled with well-dressed people and you turn your attention away from your belongings for a second, and the next thing you know a well-dressed someone with straight-faced aplomb has disappeared with your purse or valise on his or her arm. If you catch the villain, he or she will feign mortification switching quickly to indignant anger while proclaiming that the object looked just like his or hers. Another variation is the unaccompanied, frightened or perhaps lost child, who takes your hand for safety on the subway. Who would deny a child a hand—right? Meanwhile the child, or an accomplice, manages to plunder your pockets. Needless to say, these people are really slick and outwardly unsuspicious-looking.

More and more in Mexico City I'm confronted with the **"I've just been robbed and lost everything" scam.** A distraught person appearing to be in wide-eyed shock and on the verge of tears approaches you and says, "Someone just stole my purse! (Or vehicle, or wallet, etc., etc.) Can you give me money to take a bus home?" Then it turns out he or she lives in Tijuana or some other distant city and the pesos required for the trip are substantial. Often the perpetrator of this one has hungry, poorly dressed children in tow, and maybe a hopeless-faced or teary-eyed wife as well. Or well-dressed, innocent-looking teenagers accompany the truthful-sounding con artist, and you think, "These people are middle class and educated—how can this be a scam?" And of course, they'll need food money, because the trip takes several days. Then, naturally they've got to pay for transportation to the bus station. It really tugs at your heartstrings. I usually say I've just run out of money myself and they quickly move on to the next target.

Because hotel desk clerks are usually so helpful, I hesitate to mention the **lost objects scam** for fear of tainting them all. But here's how it works. You "lose" your wallet after cashing money at the desk, or you leave something valuable such as a purse or camera in the lobby. You report it. The clerk has it, but instead of telling you he does, he says he will see what he can do; meanwhile, he suggests you offer a high reward. This scam has all kinds of variations. In one story a reader wrote about, a desk clerk in Los Mochis was in cahoots with a bystander in the lobby who lifted the reader's wallet in the elevator.

Another scam readers have mentioned might be called the **infraction scam.** Officials, or men presenting themselves as officials, demand money for some supposed infraction. Never get into a car with them. I avoided one begun by a bona fide policeman-on-the-take in Chetumal when my traveling companion feigned illness and began writhing, moaning, and pretending to have the dry heaves. It was more than the policeman could handle.

Legal and necessary car searches by military personnel looking for drugs are mentioned elsewhere in this book. Every now and then, however, there are police-controlled illegal roadblocks where motorists are forced to pay before continuing on their way.

Along these lines, if you are stopped by the police, I also suggest you avoid handing your driver's license to a policeman. Hold it so that it can be read but don't give it up.

Then there's the **taxi ticket scam.** This usually happens at taxi ticket booths in airports and bus stations. You're vulnerable because you may be a new arrival to the country and not yet have your peso legs, your Spanish may not be up to par, or you're preoccupied with getting where you're going. You give the ticket seller a 50-peso bill and the seller returns change for 20 pesos. I'll say this elsewhere: *Count your change before leaving the booth!* Better yet, when you hand the seller the bill, say out loud the amount of the ticket and the amount of the bill and say *cambio* (*kahm*-bee-oh) which means change.

The **shoeshine scam** is an old trick, used most often in Mexico City. Here's how it works. A tourist agrees to a shine for, say, 15 pesos. When the work is complete, the vendor says "That'll be 50 pesos" or $15 dollars, and insists that the shocked tourist misunderstood. A big brouhaha ensues involving bystanders who side with the shoeshine vendor. The object is to get the bewildered tourist to succumb to the howling crowd and embarrassing scene and fork over the money. A variation of the scam has the vendor saying the price quoted is per shoe. To avoid this scam, ask around about the price of a shine, and when the vendor quotes his price, write it down and show it to him *before* the shine.

Similar to the shoeshine scam because of the pronunciation of numbers is the ***dos*** **(two) and** ***doce*** **(twelve) scam.** Usually taxi drivers work this one. You ask how much and he holds up two fingers or says "dos." You think the ride costs two pesos. At drop off he says "That'll be two U.S. dollars," looking at you as though you're especially stupid to think he'd ever accept 2 pesos. Or he says "dos" (pronounced "dohs") pesos but when you get to your destination he says "doce" (pronounced "*doh*-say") pesos. Or he says "doce," which you understand to refer to pesos, and then he wants 20 *dollars* before you depart. The same confusion can cause an uproar over *tres* ("trays") which means three, and *trece* ("*tray*-say"), meaning thirteen, *quince* ("*keen*-say"), which means fifteen, and *quinientos* ("*keen*-ee-ehn-tohs"), the word for 500, or *cuatro* ("*kwah*-troh"), which means four, and *catorce* ("kah-*tohr*-say"), which means 14.

Tourists are suckered daily into the **iguana scam,** especially in Puerto Vallarta and nearby Yelapa Beach. Someone, often a child, strolls by carrying a huge iguana and says, "Wanna take my peekchur?" Photo-happy tourists seize the opportunity. Just as the camera is angled properly, the holder of the iguana says (more like mumbles) "One dollar." That means a dollar per shot! Sometimes they wait until the shutter clicks to mention money.

Although you should be aware of such hazards and how to deal with them, I log thousands of miles and many months in Mexico each year without serious incident, and I feel safer there than at home in the United States. So I must reiterate that you are more likely to meet kind and helpful Mexicans than you are to encounter those who've mastered thievery and deceit. And as you can see by these scams, Mexicans with bad intentions prefer to use stealth and wit more than an outright holdup to take your possessions. (See also "Emergencies" under "Fast Facts: Mexico" later in this chapter).

2 When to Go

High season in the Yucatán—from just before Christmas through Easter Sunday—is certainly the best time to be in the Yucatán if you're here for calm, warm weather, for snorkeling, diving, and fishing (the calmer weather means clearer and more predictable seas), or for the ruins that dot the interior of the peninsula. Book well in advance if you're planning on being in Cancún around the holidays.

Low season in Mexico runs from Easter Sunday through approximately December 20, and airlines often offer discounted airfares. Many of these fares are unadvertised, especially during the slowest months mentioned above (mid-summer), and again in January, when the Christmas travelers have dispersed and hotel and airline occupancies are low.

Low season yields even greater discounts in hotel rates than airfares—prices are 20% to 50% lower than during high season. There's often a lull after New Year's in Cancún and Cozumel—prices can fall to somewhere between high- and low-season norms.

In most of Mexico, July and August are very slow, but there are some exceptions. Mexicans and Europeans take vacations in those months, and some hotels in Isla Mujeres and Playa del Carmen thus raise their prices.

Generally speaking, Mexico's dry season runs from November through April, with the rainy season stretching from May through October. It isn't a problem if you're staying close to the beaches, but for those bent on road-tripping to Chichén-Itzá, Uxmal, or other sites, temperatures and humidity in the interior can be downright stifling from May through July. Later in the rainy season the frequency of tropical storms and hurricanes increases; such storms, of course, can put a crimp in your vacation.

3 Active Vacations in the Yucatán

Cancún has several **golf** courses and ample opportunity for other such leisure sports (**tennis, racquetball, squash, waterskiing, jet-skiing, powerboating,** and the like).

If adventure sports, wilderness trips, and eco-tours are more your bag, you'll find most of Mexico strangely behind the times—which can be a good or bad thing, depending on your perspective. The natural wonders are there in overwhelming abundance, but the problem is that outdoor adventure sports and activities haven't caught fire the way they have in the States or even in nearby Costa Rica, which draws huge numbers of adventure travelers. There aren't very many expert Mexican adventure-tour leaders, and Mexican companies specializing in natural history are few. As a result, most of the national parks and nature reserves are understaffed and/or not staffed by knowledgeable people. Most companies offering this kind of travel are U.S.–operated, with trips led by specialists. If you're an experienced backcountry traveler, there are many lonely places awaiting you in Mexico. If, on the other hand, you're trying your hand at something new, the Mexican outback is not the place to be testing your independence, and you should definitely work with one of the outfitters or tour operators listed below.

Some adventure sports are thoroughly established in the Yucatán and in Chiapas state: deep-water sportfishing, fly-fishing the shallow saltwater flats for bonefish, rafting the Usumacinta River; and snorkeling and scuba diving anywhere along the Caribbean coast—but most famously at Cozumel's Palancar Reef and Xcalak's

Chinchorro Banks—are all trips run by various adventure-tour operators. The following companies offer a variety of off-the-beaten-path travel experiences:

- **ATC Tours and Travel,** Calle 5 de Febrero no. 15, 29200 San Cristóbal de las Casas, Chiapas (☎ 967/8-2550; fax 967/8-3145), a Mexico-based tour operator with an excellent reputation, offers specialist-led trips primarily in southern Mexico. In addition to trips to the ruins of Palenque and Yaxchilán (extending into Belize and Guatemala by river, plane, and bus if desired), they also offer horseback tours and day trips to the ruins of Toniná around San Cristóbal de las Casas, Chiapas; birding in the rain forests of Chiapas and Guatemala (including in the El Triunfo Reserve of Chiapas where you can see the rare quetzal bird and orchids); hikes out to the shops and homes of native textile artists of the Chiapas highlands; and walks from the Lagos de Montebello in the Montes Azules Biosphere Reserve, with camping and canoeing.

- **Columbus Travel,** 900 Rich Creek Lane, Bulverde, TX 78163-2872 (☎ 210/885-2000 or 800/843-1060 in the U.S. and Canada), has a variety of easy to challenging adventures, primarily in Copper Canyon and Michoacán. They can design trips for special-interest groups of agriculturists, geologists, rockhounds, and birdwatchers. The company also arranges trips to see the monarch butterflies in Michoacán.

- **Mexico Sportsman,** 202 Milam Building, San Antonio, TX 78205 (☎ 210/212-4567 or fax 210/212-4568), is sport-fishing central for anyone interested in advance arrangements for fishing in Cancún, Cozumel, Puerto Vallarta, Ixtapa/Zihuatanejo, Cabo San Lucas and Mazatlán. The company offers complete information from the cost (nothing hidden) to the length of a fishing trip, kind of boat, line and tackle used, and whether or not bait, drinks, and lunch are included. Prices are as good as you'll get on-site in Mexico.

- **Mountain Travel · Sobek,** 6420 Fairmount Ave., El Cerrito, CA 94530 (☎ 510/527-8100 or 800/227-2384), the granddaddy of adventure outfitters, leads groups into Copper Canyon and kayaking in the Sea of Cortez.

- **PanAngling Travel Service,** 180 North Michigan Ave., Chicago, IL 60601 (☎ 312/263-5246) focuses on fishing off the Yucatán Peninsula and the Baja Peninsula near East Cape and Cabo San Lucas. Yucatán fishing includes bonefish and tarpon fishing, and stays at some remote and unique lodges.

- **Trek America,** P.O. Box 189 Rockaway, NJ 07866 (☎ 201/983-1144 or 800/221-0596 in the U.S.; fax 201/983-8551) organizes lengthy, active trips that combine trekking and hiking (with van transportation) with camping in the Yucatán, Chiapas, Oaxaca, Copper Canyon, and Mexico's Pacific coast, and touching on Mexico City and Guadalajara.

- **Victor Emanuel Tours,** P.O. Box 33008, Austin, TX 78764 (☎ 512/328-5221 or 800/328-VENT), is an established leader in birding and natural history tours.

- **Zapotec Tours,** 2334 W. Lawrence Ave., Suite 219, Chicago, IL 60625 (☎ 312/973-2444 or, outside Illinois, **800/44-Oaxaca** in the U.S.), offers a variety of tours to Oaxaca City and the Oaxaca coast (including Puerto Escondido and Huatulco), and two specialty trips—for Day of the Dead in Oaxaca, and the "chocolate route" in the states of Tabasco and Oaxaca. Coastal trips emphasize nature. In Oaxaca City tours focus on the immediate area with visits to weavers, potters, and markets. They are also the U.S. contact for several hotels in Oaxaca City and for the Oaxaca state route of AeroMorelos airlines (serving the Oaxaca coast and Oaxaca City). Call them for information, but all reservations must be made through a travel agent.

4 Health, Safety & Insurance

STAYING HEALTHY

Of course, the very best way to avoid illness or to mitigate its effects is to make sure you're in top health when you travel and that you don't overdo it.

Important note: Antibiotics and other drugs that you'd need a prescription to buy in the States are sold over-the-counter in Mexican pharmacies, but Mexican pharmacies don't have the common over-the-counter sinus or allergy remedies we're accustomed to finding easily. If you're prone to this trouble, bring your own supply of pills.

COMMON AILMENTS

It's a rare person indeed who doesn't experience some degree of gastric upheaval when traveling; see the box on Moctezuma's Revenge for tips on preventing and dealing with **traveler's diarrhea.**

Altitude Sickness is another problem travelers experience; Mexico City is at an elevation of more than 7,000 feet, as are a number of other central Mexican cities. At high elevations it takes about 10 days to acquire the extra red blood corpuscles you need to adjust to the scarcity of oxygen. At very high elevations, such as Ixta-Popo Park outside Mexico City (13,000 ft.), you may not sleep well at night.

Altitude sickness results from the relative lack of oxygen and the decrease in barometric pressure that characterizes high elevations (over 5,000 ft./1,500m). Symptoms include shortness of breath, fatigue, headache, and even nausea.

Take it easy for the first few days after you arrive at a high elevation. Drink extra fluids but avoid alcohol. If you have heart or lung problems, talk to your doctor before going above 8,000 feet.

Mosquitoes and gnats are prevalent along the coast and in the Yucatán lowlands. Insect repellent *(rapellante contra insectos)* is a must, and it's not always available in Mexico. If you're sensitive to bites, pick up some antihistamine cream from a drugstore at home. Rubbed on a fresh mosquito bite, the cream keeps the swelling down and reduces the itch.

Though they proliferate in the deserts, most readers won't ever see a scorpion *(alacrán)*. If you're stung, go to a doctor.

MORE SERIOUS DISEASES

You shouldn't be overly concerned about tropical diseases if you stay on the normal tourist routes and don't eat street food. However, both dengue fever and cholera have appeared in Mexico in recent years. Talk to your doctor, or a medical specialist in tropical diseases, about any precautions you should take. You can also get medical bulletins from the U.S. State Department and the Center for Disease Control (see "Sources of Information," above). You can protect yourself by taking some simple precautions. Watch what you eat and drink; don't swim in stagnant water (ponds, slow-moving rivers, and Yucatecan *cenotes,* or wells; avoid mosquito bites by covering up, using powerful repellent, sleeping under mosquito netting, and staying away from places that seem to have a lot of mosquitoes. The most dangerous areas seem to be on Mexico's west coast, away from the big resorts (which are relatively safe).

Ay Carumba! Moctezuma's Revenge

Turista, or Moctezuma's Revenge, are the names given to the persistent diarrhea, often accompanied by fever, nausea, and vomiting, that attacks so many travelers to Mexico. Doctors, who call it travelers' diarrhea, say it's not caused by just one "bug," or factor, but by a combination of consuming different food and water, upsetting your schedule, being overtired, and experiencing the stresses of travel. Being tired and careless about food and drink is a sure ticket to turista. A good high-potency (or "therapeutic") vitamin supplement, and even extra vitamin C, is a help; yogurt is good for healthy digestion and is becoming much more available in Mexico than in the past.

Preventing Turista: The U.S. Public Health Service recommends the following measures for prevention of travelers' diarrhea:

• *Drink only purified water.* This means tea, coffee, and other beverages made with boiled water; canned or bottled carbonated beverages and water; beer and wine; or water you yourself have brought to a rolling boil or otherwise purified. Avoid ice, which may be made with untreated water. However, most restaurants with a large tourist clientele use only purified water and ice.

• *Choose food carefully.* In general, avoid salads, uncooked vegetables, and unpasteurized milk or milk products (including cheese). Choose food that is freshly cooked and still hot. Peel fruit yourself. Don't eat undercooked meat, fish, or shellfish.

The Public Health Service does not recommend you take any medicines as preventives. All the applicable medicines can have nasty side effects if taken for several weeks. In addition, something so simple as clean hands can go a long way toward preventing turista. I carry packages of antiseptic towelettes for those times when wash facilities aren't available and to avoid using a communal bar of soap—a real germ carrier.

How to Get Well: If you get sick, there are lots of medicines available in Mexico that can harm more than help. Ask your doctor before you leave home what medicine he or she recommends for travelers' diarrhea.

The Public Health Service guidelines are the following: If there are three or more loose stools in an eight-hour period, especially with other symptoms (such as nausea, vomiting, abdominal cramps, and fever), see a doctor.

The first thing to do is go to bed and don't move until the condition runs its course. Traveling makes it last longer. Drink lots of liquids: Tea without milk or sugar or the Mexican *té de manzanilla* (chamomile tea) is best. Eat only *pan tostada* (dry toast). Keep to this diet for at least 24 hours, and you'll be well over the worst of it. If you fool yourself into thinking a plate of enchiladas can't hurt or beer or liquor will kill the germs, you'll have a total relapse.

The Public Health Service advises that you be especially careful to replace fluids and electrolytes (potassium, sodium, and the like) during a bout of diarrhea. Do this by drinking Pedialyte, a rehydration solution available at most Mexican pharmacies, or glasses of fruit juice (high in potassium) with honey and a pinch of salt added, or you can also try a glass of boiled pure water with a quarter teaspoon of sodium bicarbonate (baking soda) added.

EMERGENCY EVACUATION

For extreme medical emergencies there's a service from the United States that will fly people to American hospitals: **Air-Evac,** a 24-hour air ambulance (☎ **800/ 854-2569** in the U.S. or call collect: ☎ **510/786-1592.** You can also contact the service in Guadalajara (☎ **3/616-9616** or **91-800/90345**).

SAFETY

Boisterous drunks aside, I've never had trouble of any kind in Mexico, and seldom feel suspicious of anyone or any situation. You will probably feel physically safer in most Mexican cities and villages than in any comparable place at home.

Crime, however, is more of a problem in Mexico than it used to be. Be smart, be careful, take all the normal precautions you'd take to deter pickpockets and muggers traveling to any large American city, for example.

Keep a photocopy of your credit cards, driver's license, and passport or birth certificate in a separate place from where you're keeping the originals. (In case you lose, or are relieved of, the originals, these copies will make replacement easier). Use hotel security boxes or in-room safes for your passport and other valuables.

Keep your things with you on the less responsible village buses and some second-class buses on country routes.

And, of course, *never* carry a package back to the States for an acquaintance or a stranger.

See "Sources of Information" at the beginning of this chapter for how to contact the U.S. Department of State for their latest advisories. At press time their crime cautions included warnings about bold highway holdups in the Yucatecan state of Campeche (including robbery of buses on Highway 186 heading east from Escarcega, and between Escarcega and Candalaria); about criminals representing themselves as police or official authorities in the northwestern state of Sinaloa; and particularly about robberies and murders on Highway 15 and the adjacent toll highway, from the U.S. border and on down the Pacific Coast. They urge travelers to contact them for security information before traveling to Chiapas.

Lastly I urge you not to let these cautionary statements deter you from traveling in Mexico. Were I to write a similar section about travel in the United States, it would take several pages. Mexico is a wonderful country, and your good experiences with

---

The Traveler's Toolbox

There are a few miscellaneous gadgets and sundries that come in handy time and again in Mexico: a rain poncho for those seasonal and unseasonal rains; arm, waist, or leg money pouches; a washcloth, or better yet, a face sponge (which dries quickly)—you'll rarely find washcloths in a budget-category hotel room, and many first-class hotels don't furnish washcloths either; a basin plug (it's packaged by that name), for all those plugless sinks; a small plastic bag can double as a plug in a pinch; inflatable hangers and a stretch clothesline; a luggage cart saves much effort and tip money—buy a sturdy, steel one with at least 4-inch wheels that can take the beating of cobblestone streets, stairs, and curbs; a heat immersion coil, plastic cup, and spoon for preparing coffee, tea, and instant soup; a small flashlight for those generator-operated places with no lights after 10pm and archaeological sites with dark interiors; and a combination pocketknife for peeling fruit, fixing cameras and eyeglasses, and opening *cervezas* and bottles of wine.

its people and culture will far outweigh any negative incidents. I eagerly return there year after year.

INSURANCE

HEALTH/ACCIDENT/LOSS   Even the most careful of us can experience the Murphy's Law of travel—you discover you've lost your wallet, your passport, your airline ticket, or your Tourist Permit. Always keep a photocopy of these documents in your luggage—it makes replacing them easier. To be reimbursed for insured items once you return, you'll need to report the loss to the Mexican police and get a written report. If you don't speak Spanish, take along someone who does. If you lose official documents, you'll need to contact both Mexican and U.S. officials in Mexico before you leave the country.

Health Care Abroad, Wallach and Co. Inc., 107 W. Federal St. (P.O. Box 480), Middleburg, VA 22117 (☎ **540/687-3166** or **800/237-6615**), and **World Access,** 6600 W. Broad St., Richmond, VA 23230 (☎ **804/285-3300** or **800/628-4908**), offer medical and accident insurance as well as coverage for luggage loss and trip cancellation. Always read the fine print on the policy to be sure that you're getting the coverage you want.

5 Tips for Travelers with Special Needs

FOR SINGLES

Mexico may be an old favorite for romantic honeymoons, but it's also a great place to travel on your own without really being or feeling alone. Although offering an identical room rate regardless of single or double occupancy is slowly becoming a trend in Mexico, most of the hotels mentioned in this book still offer singles at lower rates.

Mexicans are very friendly, and it's easy to meet other foreigners. Isla Mujeres, Playa del Carmen, Celestún, and Cancún are great places to go to on your own.

If you don't like the idea of traveling alone, then try **Travel Companion Exchange,** P.O. Box 833, Amityville, NY 11701 (☎ **516/454-0880;** fax 516/454-0170), which brings prospective travelers together. Members complete a profile, then place an anonymous listing of their travel interests in the newsletter. Prospective traveling companions then make contact through the exchange. Membership costs $99 for six months or $159 for a year.

FOR WOMEN

As a frequent female visitor to Mexico, mostly traveling alone, I can tell you firsthand that I feel safer traveling in Mexico than in the United States. Mexicans are very warm and welcoming people, and I'm not afraid to be friendly wherever I go. But I use the same common-sense precautions I use traveling anywhere else in the world—I'm alert to what's going on around me.

Mexicans in general, and men in particular, are nosy about single travelers, especially women. They want to know with whom you're traveling, whether you're married or have a boyfriend, and how many children you have. My advice to anyone asked these details by taxi drivers or other people with whom you don't want to become friendly is to make up a set of answers (regardless of the truth): "I'm married, traveling with friends, and I have three children."

If you're a divorcée, revealing such may send out the wrong message about availability. Drunks are a particular nuisance to the lone female traveler. Don't try to be polite—just leave or duck into a public place.

Generally lone women will feel comfortable going to a hotel lobby bar, yet are asking for trouble by going into a pulquería or cantina. In restaurants, as a general rule, single women are offered the worst table and service. You'll have to be vocal about your preference and insist on service. Don't tip if service is bad.

FOR MEN

I'm not sure why, but non-Spanish-speaking foreign men seem to be special targets for scams and pickpockets. So if you fit this description, whether traveling alone or in a pair, exercise special vigilance.

FOR FAMILIES

Mexicans travel extensively in their country with their families, so your child will feel very welcome. Hotels will often arrange for a baby-sitter. Several hotels in the middle-to-luxury range have small playgrounds and pools for children and hire caretakers on weekends to oversee them. Few budget hotels offer these amenities.

Before leaving, you should check with your doctor to get advice on medications to take along. Bring along a supply just to be sure. Disposable diapers cost about the same in Mexico but are of poorer quality. Gerber's baby foods are sold in many stores. Dry cereals, powdered formulas, baby bottles, and purified water are all easily available in midsize and large cities.

Cribs, however, may present a problem. Except for the largest and most luxurious hotels, few Mexican hotels provide cribs. However, rollaway beds to accommodate children staying in the room with parents are often available. Likewise, child seats or high chairs at restaurants are rare.

Many of the hotels I mention, even in noncoastal regions, have swimming pools, which can be a treat at the end of a day of traveling with a child who has had it with sightseeing.

FOR PEOPLE WITH DISABILITIES

Travelers who are unable to walk or who are in wheelchairs or on crutches discover quickly that Mexico is one giant obstacle course. Beginning at the airport on arrival, you may encounter steep stairs before finding a well-hidden elevator or escalator—if one exists. Airlines will often arrange wheelchair assistance for passengers to the baggage area. Porters are generally available to help with luggage at airports and large bus stations, once you've cleared baggage claim.

In addition, escalators (there aren't many in the country) are often not operating. Few handicapped-equipped rest rooms exist, or when one is available, access to it may be via a narrow passage that won't accommodate a wheelchair or someone on crutches. Many deluxe hotels (the most expensive) now have rooms with baths for the handicapped and handicapped access to the hotel. Those traveling on a budget should stick with one-story hotels or those with elevators. Even so, there will probably still be obstacles somewhere. Stairs without handrails abound in Mexico. Intracity bus drivers generally don't bother with the courtesy step on boarding or disembarking. On city buses, the height between the street and the bus step can require considerable force to board. Generally speaking, no matter where you are, someone will lend a hand, although you may have to ask for it.

Few airports offer the luxury of boarding an airplane from the waiting room. You either descend stairs to a bus that ferries you to the waiting plane that's boarded by climbing stairs, or you walk across the airport tarmac to your plane and ascend the stairs. Deplaning offers the same in reverse.

6 Getting There

BY PLANE

The airline situation in Mexico is changing rapidly, with many new regional carriers offering scheduled service to areas previously not served. In addition to regularly scheduled service, charter service direct from U.S. cities to resorts is making Mexico more accessible from the United States.

THE MAJOR INTERNATIONAL AIRLINES   The main airlines operating direct or nonstop flights from the United States to Cancún, Cozumel, and Mérida include **Aero California** (☎ 800/237-6225), **Aeroméxico** (☎ 800/237-6639), **Air France** (☎ 800/237-2747), **American** (☎ 800/433-7300), **Continental** (☎ 800/231-0856), **Lacsa** (☎ 800/225-2272), **Mexicana** (☎ 800/531-7921), **Northwest** (☎ 800/225-2525), **United** (☎ 800/241-6522), and **USAir** (☎ 800/428-4322).

Excursion and package plans proliferate, especially in the off-season. A good travel agent will be able to give you all the latest schedules, details, and prices, but you may have to investigate the details of the plans to see if they are real deals. You'll also have to sleuth regional airlines for yourself (see "By Plane" under "Getting Around," below), since most travel agents don't have that information.

CHARTERS   Charter service is growing, especially during winter months and usually is sold as a package combination of air and hotel. Charter airlines, however, may sell air packages only, without hotel. Check your local paper for seasonal charters.

Well-known **tour companies** operating charters include **Club America Vacations, Apple Vacations,** and **Friendly Holidays.** You can make arrangements with these companies through your travel agent.

BY CAR

Driving is certainly not the cheapest way to get to Mexico, but it is the best way to see the country. Even so, you may think twice about taking your own car south of the border once you've pondered Mexico's many bureaucratic requirements for doing so.

In 1994, Mexico's Ministry of Tourism published its own *Official Guide: Traveling to Mexico by Car.* Unfortunately its information can be inconsistent, unclear, or inaccurate. Of possible use, however, is the list it includes of the times at which you'll find government officials on duty at border crossings to review your car documents and issue Temporary Car Importation Permits. To get a copy, inquire at a branch of the regional Mexican Government Tourism Office.

It's wise to check and double-check all the requirements before setting out for a driving tour of Mexico. Read through the rest of this section, and then address any additional questions you have or confirm the current rules by calling your nearest Mexican consulate, Mexican Government Tourist Office, AAA, or Sanborn's (☎ 800/222-0185 in the U.S.). To check on road conditions, or to get help with any travel emergency while in the country, there's a 24-hour number (toll-free 91-800/9-0329 in Mexico) that you can call. Another 24-hour help number (☎ 5/250-0123 or 5/250-0151) is in Mexico City. Both numbers are supposed to be staffed by English-speaking operators.

In addition, check with the U.S. Department of State (see "Sources of Information" at the beginning of this chapter) for their warnings about areas where driving the highways can be dangerous. Their current warnings regarding crime and highway travel are in "Safety," above.

CAR DOCUMENTS

To drive a personal car into Mexico, you'll need a Temporary Car Importation Permit, granted upon completion of a long and strictly required list of documents (see below). The permit can be obtained either through Banco del Ejército *(Banjercito)* officials, who have a desk, booth, or office at the Mexican Customs *(Aduana)* building after you cross the border into Mexico. You can obtain the permit before you travel through Sanborn's Insurance and the American Automobile Association (AAA), each of which maintains border offices in Texas, New Mexico, Arizona, and California. These companies may charge a fee for this service, but it will be worth it to avoid the uncertain prospect of traveling all the way to the border without proper documents for crossing. However, even if you go through Sanborn's or AAA, your credentials *may* be reviewed again by Mexican officials at the border—you must have them all with you since they are still subject to questions of validity.

The following requirements for border crossing were accurate at press time:

- *A valid driver's license,* issued outside of Mexico.
- *Current, original car registration and a copy of the original car title.* If the registration or title is in more than one name and not all the named people are traveling with you, then a notarized letter from the absent person(s) authorizing use of the vehicle for the trip is required; have it ready just in case. The car registration and your credit card (see below) must be in the same name.
- *An original notarized letter from the lien or lease holder,* if your registration shows a lien or lease, giving you permission to take the vehicle into Mexico.
- *A valid international major credit card.* Using only your credit card, you are required to pay a $12 car-importation fee. The credit card must be in the same name as the car registration.

  Note: Those without credit cards will forego the $12 importation fee and instead will be required to post a cash bond based on the value of the car. The rules and procedures are complicated (and expensive), so contact AAA or Sanborn's for details.
- *A signed declaration promising to return to your country of origin with the vehicle.* This form is provided by AAA or Sanborn's before you go or by Banjercito officials at the border. There's no charge. The form does not stipulate that you return through the same border entry you came through on your way south.

You must carry your Temporary Car Importation Permit, Tourist Permit, and, if you purchased it, your proof of Mexican car insurance in the car at all times.

Important reminder: Someone else may drive the car, but the person (or relative of the person) whose name appears on the Car Importation Permit must *always* be in the car at the same time. (If stopped by police, a nonregistered family member driver, driving without the registered driver, must be prepared to prove familial relationship to the registered driver.) Violation of this rule makes the car subject to impoundment and the driver to imprisonment and/or a fine.

Only under certain circumstances will the driver of the car be allowed to leave the country without the car. If it's undrivable, you can leave it at a mechanic's shop if you get a letter to that effect from the mechanic and present it to the nearest Secretaria de Hacienda y Credito Público (a treasury department official) for further documentation, which you then present to a Banjercito official upon leaving the country. Then you must return personally to retrieve the car. If the driver of the car has to leave the country without the car due to an emergency, the car must be put under Customs seal at the airport and the driver's Tourist Permit must be stamped to that effect.

There may be storage fees. If the car is wrecked or stolen, your Mexican insurance adjuster will provide the necessary paperwork for presentation to Hacienda officials.

If you receive your documentation at the border (rather than through Sanborn's or AAA), Mexican border officials will make two copies of everything and charge you for the copies.

The Temporary Car Importation Permit papers will be issued for six months and the Tourist Permit is usually issued for 180 days, but they might stamp it for half that, so check. It's a good idea also to overestimate the time you'll spend in Mexico, so that if something unforeseen happens and you have to—or want to—stay longer, you'll have avoided the long hassle of getting your papers renewed.

Important note: Whatever you do, don't overstay either permit. Doing so invites heavy fines and/or confiscation of your vehicle, which will not be returned. Remember also that six months does not necessarily work out to be 180 days—be sure that you return before whichever expiration date comes first.

Other documentation is required for an individual's permit to enter Mexico—see "Entry Requirements," above.

MEXICAN AUTO INSURANCE

Although auto insurance is not legally required in Mexico, driving without it is foolish. U.S. insurance is invalid in Mexico; to be insured there, you must purchase Mexican insurance. Any party involved in an accident who has no insurance is automatically sent to jail and his or her car is impounded until all claims are settled. This is true even if you just drive across the border to spend the day, and it may be true even if you're injured.

I always buy my car insurance through **Sanborn's Mexico Insurance,** P.O. Box 310, Dept. FR, 2009 S. 10th, McAllen, TX 78505-0310 (☎ **210/686-0711;** fax 210/686-0732 in Texas, or 800/222-0158 in the U.S.). The company has offices at all of the border crossings in the United States. Their policies cost the same as the competition's do, but you get legal coverage (attorney and bail bonds if needed) and a detailed mile-by-mile guide to your proposed route—to me, this last part is the kicker. With the ongoing changes in Mexico's highway system it's inevitable that your log will occasionally be a bit outdated, but for the most part having it is like having a knowledgeable friend in the car telling you how to get in and out of town, where to buy gas (and which stations to avoid), what the highway conditions are, and what scams you need to watch out for. It's especially helpful in remote places. Most of Sanborn's border offices are open Monday through Friday, and a few are staffed on Saturday and Sunday. You can purchase your auto liability and collision coverage by phone in advance and have it waiting at a 24-hour location if you are crossing when the office is closed. The annual insurance includes a type of evacuation assistance in case of emergency, and emergency evacuation insurance for shorter policies is available for a small daily fee. They also offer a medical policy.

AAA auto club also sells insurance.

All agencies selling Mexican insurance will show you a full table of current rates and recommend the coverage they think is adequate. The policies are written along lines similar to those north of the border, with the following exception: The contents of your vehicle aren't covered. It's no longer necessary to overestimate the amount of time you plan to be in Mexico because it's now possible to get your policy term lengthened by fax from the insurer. However, if you are staying longer than 48 days, it's more economical to buy a nonrefundable annual policy. For example, Sanborn's Insurance quotes a car (registered to an individual, not a business) with a value of $10,000 can be insured for $137.82 for two weeks or $73.91 for one week. An annual policy for a car valued between $10,000 and $15,000 would be a reduced rate of $519 which you get by joining Sanborn's Amigo Club for $40. (The Amigo Club membership offers hotel discounts, emergency air ambulance, and a newsletter.) Be sure the policy you buy will pay for repairs in either the United States or Mexico and will pay out in dollars, not pesos.

PREPARING YOUR CAR

Check the condition of your car thoroughly before you cross the border. Parts made in Mexico may be inferior, but service generally is quite good and relatively inexpensive. Carry a spare radiator hose and belts for the engine fan and air conditioner. Be sure your car is in tune to handle Mexican gasoline. Also, can your tires last a few thousand miles on Mexican roads?

Don't forget a flashlight and a tire gauge—Mexican filling stations generally have air to fill tires but no gauge to check the pressure. When I drive into Mexico, I always bring along a combination gauge/air compressor sold at U.S. automotive stores that plugs into the car cigarette lighter, making it a simple procedure to check the tires every morning and pump them up at the same time.

Not that many Mexican cars comply, but Mexican law requires that every car have **seat belts** and a **fire extinguisher.** Be prepared!

CROSSING THE BORDER WITH YOUR CAR

After you cross the border into Mexico from the United States and you've stopped to get your Tourist Card and Car Permit, somewhere between 12 and 16 miles down the road you'll come to a Mexican customs post. In the past, all motorists had to stop and present travel documents and possibly have their cars inspected. Now there is a new system under which some motorists are stopped at random for inspection. All car papers are examined, however, so you must stop. If the light is green, go on through; if it's red, stop for inspection. In the Baja Peninsula the procedures may differ slightly—first you get your Tourist Permit, then farther down the road you may or may not be stopped for the car inspection.

RETURNING TO THE UNITED STATES WITH YOUR CAR

The car papers you obtained when you entered Mexico *must* be returned when you cross back with your car or at some point within the time limit of 180 days. (You can cross as many times as you wish within the 180 days.) If the documents aren't returned, heavy fines are imposed ($250 for each 15 days late), and your car may be impounded and confiscated or you may be jailed if you return to Mexico. You can only return the car documents to a Banjercito official on duty at the Mexican Customs *(Aduana)* building *before* you cross back into the United States. Some border cities have Banjercito officials on duty 24 hours a day, but others do not; some also do not have Sunday hours. On the U.S. side Customs agents may or may not inspect your car from stem to stern.

BY SHIP

Numerous cruise lines serve the Mexican Caribbean. Possible trips might run from Miami to the Caribbean (which often includes stops in Cancún, Playa del Carmen, and Cozumel).

If you don't mind making last-minute arrangements, several cruise-tour specialists arrange substantial discounts on unsold cabins. One such company is **The Cruise Line, Inc.,** 4770 Biscayne Blvd., Penthouse 1–3, Miami FL 33137 (☎ **305/ 576-0036, 800/777-0707,** or **800/327-3021**).

PACKAGE TOURS

Package tours offer some of the best values to the coastal resorts, especially during high season—from December until after Easter. Off-season packages can be real bargains. However, to know for sure if the package will save you money, you must price the package yourself by calling the airline for round-trip flight costs and the hotel for rates. Add in the cost of transfers to and from the airport (which packages usually include) and see if it's a deal.

Packages are usually per person, and single travelers pay a supplement. In the high season a package may be the only way of getting to certain places in Mexico because wholesalers have all the airline seats. The cheapest package rates will be those in hotels in the lower range, always without as many amenities as higher-priced hotels. You can still use the public areas and beaches of more costly hotels without being a guest.

Travel agents have information on specific packages.

7 Getting Around

An important note: If your travel schedule depends on an important connection, say a plane trip between points, or a ferry or bus connection, use the telephone numbers in this book or other information resources mentioned here and find out if the connection you are depending on is still available. Although I've done my best to provide accurate information, transportation schedules can and do change.

BY PLANE

To fly from point to point within Mexico, you'll rely on Mexican airlines. Mexico has two privately owned large national carriers: **Mexicana** (☎ **800/531-7921** in the U.S.) and **Aeroméxico** (☎ **800/237-6639** in the U.S.), in addition to several up-and-coming regional carriers. Mexicana and Aeroméxico both offer extensive connections to the United States as well as within Mexico.

Several of the new regional carriers are operated by or can be booked through Mexicana or Aeroméxico. Regional carriers are **Aero Cancún** (see Mexicana), **Aero Caribe** (see Mexicana), and **Aerolitoral** (see Aeroméxico). The regional carriers are expensive, but they go to places that are difficult to reach. In each applicable section of this book, I've mentioned regional carriers with all pertinent telephone numbers. (For tips on saving money on regional carriers, see "For Travelers on a Budget" earlier in this chapter.

Because major airlines can book some regional carriers, read your ticket carefully to see if your connecting flight is on one of these smaller carriers—they may leave from a different airport or check in at a different counter.

AIRPORT TAXES

Mexico charges an airport tax on all departures. Passengers leaving the country on an international departure pay $12 in cash—dollars or the peso equivalent. (That tax is usually included in your ticket.) Each domestic departure you make within Mexico costs around $6, unless you're on a connecting flight and have already paid at the start of the flight; you shouldn't be charged again if you have to change planes for a connecting flight.

RECONFIRMING FLIGHTS

Although airlines in Mexico say it's not necessary to reconfirm a flight, I always do. Aeromexico seems particularly prone to canceling confirmed reservations. Also, be aware that airlines routinely overbook. To avoid getting bumped, check in for an international flight the required hour and a half in advance of travel.

BY BUS

Bus service in the Yucatán Peninsula is beginning to catch up to the high standard seen elsewhere in Mexico. Buses are frequent, readily accessible, and can get you to almost anywhere you want to go. Buses are an excellent way to get around, and they're often the only way to get from large cities to other nearby cities and small villages. Ticket agents can be quite brusque or indifferent, especially if there's a line; in general, however, people are willing to help, so never hesitate to ask questions if you're confused about anything. *Important Note:* There's little English spoken at bus stations, so come prepared with your destination written down, then double-check the departure several times just to make sure you get to the right departing lane on time.

Dozens of Mexican companies operate large, air-conditioned, Greyhound-type buses between most cities. Travel class is generally labeled first, second, and deluxe, referred to by a variety of names—*plus, de lujo, ejecutivo, primera plus,* and so on. The deluxe buses often have fewer seats than regular buses, show video movies en route, are air-conditioned, and have few stops; some have complimentary refreshments. Many run express from origin to the final destination. They are well worth the few dollars more you'll pay than you would for first-class buses. First-class buses may get there as fast as a deluxe bus, but without the comfort; they may also have many stops. Second-class buses have many stops and cost only slightly less than first-class or deluxe buses. In rural areas, buses are often of the schoolbus variety, with lots of local color.

Whenever possible, it's best to buy your reserved-seat ticket, often via a computerized system, a day in advance on many long-distance routes and especially before holidays. Schedules are fairly dependable, so be at the terminal on time for departure.

Many Mexican cities have replaced the bewildering array of tiny private company offices scattered all over town with new central bus stations, much like sophisticated airport terminals.

Keep in mind that routes and times change, and as there is no central directory of schedules for the whole country, current information must be obtained from local bus stations.

For long trips, *always* carry food, water, toilet paper, and a sweater (in case the air-conditioning is too strong).

A Safety Precaution: The U.S. State Department notes that bandits target long-distance buses traveling at night, but there have also been daylight robberies as well. I've always avoided overnight buses, primarily because they usually must negotiate mountain roads in the dark, which I prefer not to risk. (See "Sources of Information," above, for contact information, and "Safety," above, for specific areas of caution.)

See the Appendix for a list of helpful bus terms in Spanish.

BY CAR

Most Mexican roads are not up to U.S. standards of smoothness, hardness, width of curve, grade of hill, or safety marking. Never drive at night if you can avoid it—the roads aren't good enough; the trucks, carts, pedestrians, and bicycles usually have no lights; and you can hit potholes, animals, rocks, dead-ends, or bridges out with no warning. Enough said!

You will also have to get used to the "spirited" style of Mexican driving, which sometimes seems to ask superhuman vision and reflexes from drivers. Be prepared for new procedures, as when a truck driver flips on his left-turn signal when there's not a crossroad for miles. He's probably telling you the road's clear ahead for you to pass—after all, he's in a better position to see than you are. It's difficult to know, however, whether he really means that he intends to pull over on the left-hand shoulder. Another strange custom decides who crosses a one-lane bridge first when two cars approach from opposite directions—the first car to flash its headlights has right of way. Still another custom that's very important to respect is how to make a left turn. Never turn left by stopping in the middle of a highway with your left signal on. Instead, pull off the highway onto the right shoulder, wait for traffic to clear, then proceed across the road. Other driving exasperations include following trucks without mufflers and pollution-control devices for miles. Under these conditions, drop back and be patient, take a side road, or stop for a break when you feel tense or tired.

GASOLINE

There's one government-owned brand of gas and one gasoline station name throughout the country—**Pemex** (Petroleras Mexicanas). Each station has a franchise owner who buys everything from Pemex. There are two types of gas in Mexico: *nova,* an 82-octane leaded gas, and *magna sin,* an 87-octane unleaded gas. Magna sin is sold from brilliantly colored pumps and costs around $1.15 a gallon; nova costs slightly less. In Mexico, fuel and oil are sold by the liter, which is slightly more than a quart (40 liters equals about 10¹/₂ gallons). Nova is readily available. Magna sin is now available in most areas of Mexico, along major highways, and in the larger cities. Plan ahead; fill up every chance you get, and keep your tank topped off. *Important Note:* No credit cards are accepted for gas purchases.

Here's what to do when you have to fuel up. First rule is to keep your eyes on the pump meters as your tank is being filled. Check that the pump is turned back to zero, go to your fuel filler cap and unlock it yourself, and watch the pump and the attendant as the gas goes in. Though many service-station attendants are honest, many are not. It's better to ask for a specific peso amount rather than saying "full." This is because the attendants tend to overfill, splashing gas on the car and anything within range.

As there are always lines at the gas pumps, attendants often finish fueling one vehicle, turn the pump back quickly (or don't turn it back at all), and start on another vehicle. You've got to be looking at the pump when the fueling is finished because it may show the amount you owe for only a few seconds. This "quick draw" from car to car is another good reason to ask for a certain peso amount of gas. If you've asked for a certain amount, the attendant can't charge you more for it. (Just for convenience' sake, I'll note that, at the current exchange rate, the $10 fill-up you'd ask for at home would be approximately 70 ("say-*ten*-tah") pesos in Mexico. See the Appendix for pronunciation of other useful round numbers.)

Once the fueling is complete, let the attendant check the oil or radiator or put air in the tires. Do only one thing at a time, be with him as he does it, and don't let him rush you. Get into these habits, or it'll cost you.

If you get oil, make sure the can that is tipped into your engine is a full one. If in doubt, have the attendant check the dipstick again after the oil has supposedly been put in. Check your change and, again, don't let them rush you. Check that your locking gas cap is back in place.

DRIVING RULES

If you park illegally or commit some other infraction and are not around to discuss it, police are authorized to remove your license plates *(placas)*. You must then trundle over to the police station and pay a fine to get them back. Mexican car-rental agencies have begun to weld the license tag to the tag frame; you may want to devise a method of your own to make the tags more difficult to remove. Theoretically, this may encourage a policeman to move on to another set of tags, one easier to confiscate. On the other hand, he could get his hackles up and decide to have your car towed. To weld or not to weld is up to you.

Be attentive to road signs. A drawing of a row of little bumps means there are speed bumps *(topes)* across the road to force you to reduce speed while driving through towns or villages. Slow down when coming to a village whether you see the sign or not—sometimes they install the bumps but not the sign!

Mexican roads are never as well marked as you'd like—when you see a highway route sign, take note and make sure you're on the right road. Don't count on plenty of notice of where to turn, even on major interchanges; more often than not, the directional sign appears without prior notice exactly at the spot where you need to make a decision. Common road signs include these:

Camino en Reparación	Road repairs
Conserva Su Derecha	Keep right
Cuidado con el Ganado, el Tren	Watch out for cattle, trains
Curva Peligrosa	Dangerous curve
Derrumbes	Falling rocks
Deslave	Caved-in roadbed
Despacio	Slow
Desviación	Detour
Disminuya Su Velocidad	Slow down
Entronque	Highway junction
Escuela	School (zone)
Grava Suelta	Loose gravel
Hombres Trabajando	Men working
No Hay Paso	Road closed
Peligro	Danger
Puente Angosto	Narrow bridge
Raya Continua	Continuous (solid) white line
Tramo en Reparación	Road under construction
Un Solo Carril a 100 m.	One-lane road 100 meters ahead
Zone Escolar	School zone

TOLL ROADS

Mexico charges among the highest tolls in the world to use its network of new toll roads. As a result, they are comparatively little used. Generally speaking, using the toll roads will cut your travel time between destinations. The old roads, on which no tolls are charged, are generally in good condition but overall mean longer trips—they tend to be mountainous and clotted with slow-moving trucks.

MAPS

Guia Roji, AAA, and International Travel Map Productions have good maps to Mexico. In Mexico, maps are sold at large drugstores like Sanborn's, at bookstores, and in hotel gift shops.

BREAKDOWNS

Your best guide to repair shops is the Yellow Pages. For specific makes and shops that repair them, look under "Automoviles y Camiones: Talleres de Reparación y Servicio"; auto-parts stores are listed under "Refacciones y Accesorios para

Automoviles." On the road, often the sign of a mechanic simply says TALLER
MECÁNICO.

I've found that the Ford and Volkswagen dealerships in Mexico give prompt, courteous attention to my car problems, and prices for repairs are, in general, much lower
than those in the United States or Canada. I suspect other big-name dealerships give
similar satisfactory service. Often they will begin work on your car right away and
make repairs in just a few hours, sometimes minutes. Hondas are now manufactured
in Mexico, so those parts will become more available.

If your car breaks down on the road, help might already be on the way. Radio-
equipped green repair trucks manned by uniformed English-speaking officers patrol
the major highways during daylight hours to aid motorists in trouble. These **"Green
Angels"** will perform minor repairs and adjustments for free, but you pay for parts
and materials.

MINOR ACCIDENTS

When possible, many Mexicans drive away from minor accidents to avoid hassles with
police. If the police arrive while the involved persons are still at the scene, everyone
may be locked in jail until blame is assessed. In any case you have to settle up
immediately, which may take days of red tape. Foreigners who don't speak fluent
Spanish are at a distinct disadvantage when trying to explain their side of the event.
Three steps may help the foreigner who doesn't wish to do as the Mexicans do: If
you're in your own car, notify your Mexican insurance company, whose job it is to
intervene on your behalf. If you're in a rental car, notify the rental company immediately and ask how to contact the nearest adjuster. (You did buy insurance with the
rental—right?) Finally, if all else fails, ask to contact the nearest Green Angel, who
may be able to explain to officials that you are covered by insurance.

See also "Mexican Auto Insurance" in "By Car" under "Getting There," above.

PARKING

When you park your car on the street, lock it up and leave nothing within view
inside (day or night). I use guarded parking lots, especially at night, to avoid vandal-
ism and break-ins. This way you also avoid parking violations. When pay lots are not
available, small boys usually offer to watch your car for you—tip them well on your
return.

CAR RENTALS

With some trepidation I wander into the subject of car-rental rules, which change
often in Mexico. The best prices are obtained by reserving your car a week in advance
in the United States. Mexico City and most other large Mexican cities have rental
offices representing the various big firms and some local ones. You'll find rental desks
at airports, all major hotels, and many travel agencies. The large firms like Avis, Hertz,
National, and Budget have rental offices on main streets as well. Renting a car during a major holiday may prove difficult if all the cars are booked or not returned on
time. To avoid being stranded without a vehicle, if possible plan your arrival before
the anticipated rush of travelers.

I don't recommend renting a car in Mexico City for one-day excursions from the
city. It can be a real hassle, and parking is also a problem.

Cars are easy to rent if you have a charge or credit card (American Express, VISA,
MasterCard, and the like), are 25 or over, and have a valid driver's license and pass-
port with you. Without a credit card you must leave a cash deposit, usually a big one.
Rent-here/leave-there arrangements are usually simple to make but very costly.

Costs

Don't underestimate the cost of renting a car. And unfortunately, the devaluation of the peso has not resulted in lower car-rental costs in Mexico. When I checked recently for rental on May 15 (after Easter when rates go down) the basic cost of a one-day rental of a Volkswagen Beetle, with unlimited mileage (but before 15% tax and $15 daily insurance) was $44 in Cancún, $45 in Mexico City, $38 in Puerto Vallarta, $45 in Oaxaca, and $25 in Mérida. Renting by the week gives you a lower daily rate. Avis was offering a basic seven-day weekly rate for a VW Beetle (without tax or insurance) of $180 in Cancún and Puerto Vallarta, $150 in Mérida, and $216 in Mexico City.

So you can see that it makes a difference where you rent, for how long, and when. If you have a choice of renting in Mérida and driving to Cancún, you might save more money than if you rent in Cancún. Mileage-added rates can run the bill up considerably. Car-rental companies usually write up a credit card charge in U.S. dollars. *Important Tip:* Take advantage of Avis's prepay offer. You *prepay* the daily rental by credit card before you go and receive a considerable discount. Under this plan, you pay tax and insurance in Mexico. As an example, working through Avis here in the States, I recently prepaid a week's use of a VW Beetle in Cancún for $167 (before tax and insurance), which averages $23.86 daily. If I had chosen to pay in Cancún *after* using the car, the weekly rate would have been $267, or $38.14 daily (before tax and insurance).

Rental Confirmation

Make your reservation directly with the car-rental company. Write down your confirmation number and request that a copy of the confirmation be mailed to you (rent at least a week in advance so the confirmation has time to reach you). Present that confirmation slip when you appear to collect your car. If you're dealing with a U.S. company, the confirmation must be honored, even if the company has to upgrade you to another class of car—don't allow them to send you to another agency. The rental confirmation will also display the agreed-on price, which protects you from being charged more in case there is a price change before you arrive. Insist on the rate printed on the confirmation slip.

Deductibles

Be careful—deductibles vary greatly; some are as high as $2,500, which comes out of your pocket immediately in case of car damage. Hertz's deductible is $1,000 on a VW Beetle; Avis's deductible is $500 for the same car. You will be asked to sign two separate credit card vouchers, one for the insurance, which is torn up on your return if there's no damage to the car, and one for the rental. Don't fail to get information about deductibles.

Insurance

Many credit-card companies offer their cardholders free rental-car insurance. *Don't use it in Mexico,* for several reasons. Even though insurance policies that specifically cover rental cars are supposedly optional in Mexico, there may be major consequences if you don't have one. First, if you buy insurance, you pay only the deductible, which limits your liability. Second, if you have an accident or your car is vandalized or stolen and you don't have insurance, you'll have to pay for everything before you can leave the rental-car office. This includes the full value of the car if it is unrepairable—a determination made only by the rental-car company. While your credit card may eventually pay your costs, you will have to lay out the money in the meantime. Third, if an accident occurs, everyone may wind up in jail until guilt is determined, and if you are the guilty party, you may not be released from jail until restitution is paid in full to the rental-car owners and to injured persons—made doubly difficult if you have no rental-car insurance. Fourth, if you elect to use your credit-card insurance anyway, the rental company may ask you to leave them with a cash bond, or a credit-card voucher with a high amount filled in.

Insurance is offered in two parts. **Collision and damage** insurance covers your car and others if the accident is your fault, and **personal accident** insurance covers you and anyone in your car. I always take both.

Damage

Always inspect your car carefully, and mark all problem areas using this checklist:

- Hubcaps
- Windshield (for nicks and cracks)
- Tire tread
- Body (for dents, nicks, etc.)
- Fenders (for dents, etc.)
- Muffler (is it smashed?)
- Trim (loose or damaged?)
- Head and taillights
- Fire extinguisher (it should be under the driver's seat, as required by law)
- Spare tire and tools (in the trunk)
- Seat belts (required by law)
- Gas cap
- Outside mirror
- Floor mats

Note every damaged or missing area, no matter how minute, on your rental agreement or you will be charged for all missing or damaged parts, including missing car tags, should the police confiscate your tags for a parking infraction (which is very costly). I can't stress enough how important it is to check your car carefully. A tiny nick in a windshield can grow the length of the glass while in your care, and you'll be charged for the whole windshield if you didn't note the nick at the time of rental. Car companies have attempted to rent me cars with bald tires and tires with bulges; a car with a license plate that would expire before I returned the car; and cars with missing trim, floor mats, or fire extinguishers. They've also attempted to charge me for dings that were on the auto when I rented it, which they were unable to do because the dings were marked on the agreement.

Fine Print

Read the fine print on the back of your rental agreement and note that insurance is invalid if you have an accident while driving on an unpaved road.

Trouble Number

One last detail to see to before starting out with a rental car: Be sure you know the rental company's trouble number. Get the direct number to the agency where you rented the car and write down its office hours. The large firms have toll-free numbers, but they may not be well staffed on weekends.

Problems, Perils, Deals

At present, I find the best prices are through Avis, and that's the company I use; generally I am a satisfied customer, though I sometimes have to dig in my heels and insist on proper service. I have had even more difficult problems with other agencies. I have encountered certain kinds of situations within the past four years that could occur with any company. These problems have included an attempt to push me off to a no-name company rather than upgrade me to a more expensive car when a VW Beetle wasn't available; poorly staffed offices with no extra cars, parts, or mechanics in case of a breakdown. Since potential problems are varied, I'd rather deal with a company based in the States so at least I have recourse if I am not satisfied.

Signing the Rental Agreement

Once you've agreed on everything, the rental clerk will tally the bill before you leave and you will sign an open credit-card voucher that will be filled in when you return the car, and a credit-card voucher for the amount of the deductible which will be used only if there is damage. Read the agreement and double-check all the addition. The time to catch mistakes is before you leave, not when you return.

Picking Up/Returning the Car

When you rent the car, you agree to pick it up at a certain time and return it at a certain time. If you're late in picking it up or if you cancel the reservation, there are usually penalties—ask what they are when you make the reservation. If you return the car more than an hour late, an expensive hourly rate kicks in. Also, you must return the car with the same amount of gas in the tank it had when you drove out. If you don't, the charge added to your bill for the difference is much more than for gas bought at a public station.

BY RV

Touring Mexico by recreational vehicle (RV) is a popular way of seeing the country. Many hotels have hookups. RV parks, while not as plentiful as those in the United States, are available throughout the country.

BY FERRY

In the Yucatán, ferries take passengers between Puerto Juárez and Isla Mujeres, Playa Linda and Isla Mujeres, and Playa del Carmen and Cozumel.

BY HITCHHIKING

You see Mexicans hitching rides (for example, at crossroads after getting off a bus), but as a general rule hitchhiking isn't done. It's especially unwise for foreigners, who may be thought to carry large amounts of cash.

FAST FACTS: Mexico

Abbreviations   Dept. = apartments; Apdo. = post office box; Av. = Avenida; Calz. = Calzada (boulevard). "C" on faucets stands for *caliente* (hot), and "F" stands for *fría* (cold). PB *(planta baja)* means ground floor.

Business Hours   In general, Mexican businesses in larger cities are open between 9am and 7pm; in smaller towns many close between 2 and 4pm. Most are closed on Sunday. Bank hours are Monday through Friday from 9 or 9:30am to 1pm. A few banks in large cities have extended hours.

Camera/Film   Buying a camera can be inconvenient in Mexico, but there are cheap, imported models available. Film costs about the same as that in the United States. Take full advantage of your 12-roll film allowance by bringing 36-exposure rolls. Also bring extra batteries: AA batteries are generally available, but AAA and small disc batteries for cameras and watches are rare. A few places in resort areas advertise color film developing, but it might be cheaper to wait until you get home.

Important note about camera use: Tourists wishing to use a video or still camera at any archaeological site in Mexico and at many museums operated by the Instituto de Historia y Antropología (INAH) may be required to pay $8.50 per video camera and/or still camera in their possession at each site or museum visited. (In some museums camera use is not permitted.) If you want to use either kind of camera or both, the fee must be paid for each piece of equipment. When you pay the fee, your camera will be tagged and you are permitted to use the equipment. Watchmen are often posted to see that untagged cameras are not used. Such fees are noted in the listings for specific sites and museums.

It's courteous to ask permission before photographing anyone. In some areas, such as around San Cristóbal de las Casas, Chiapas, there are other restrictions on photographing people and villages. Such restrictions are noted in specific cities, towns, and sites.

Cigarettes   Cigarettes are much cheaper in Mexico than in the United States, even U.S. brands, if you buy them at a grocery or drugstore and not a hotel tobacco shop.

Doctors/Dentists   Every embassy and consulate is prepared to recommend local doctors and dentists with good training and modern equipment; some of the doctors and dentists even speak English. See the list of embassies and consulates under "Embassies/Consulates," below, and remember that at the larger ones, a duty officer is on call at all times. Hotels with a large foreign clientele are often prepared to recommend English-speaking doctors. Almost all first-class hotels in Mexico have a doctor on call.

Drug Laws   Briefly, don't use or possess illegal drugs in Mexico. Mexicans have no tolerance for drug users, and jail is their solution, with very little hope of getting out until the sentence (usually a long one) is completed or heavy fines or bribes are paid. (*Important Note:* It isn't uncommon to be befriended by a fellow user, only to be turned in by that "friend"—he's collected a bounty for turning you in. It's a no-win situation!) Bring prescription drugs in their original containers. If possible, pack a copy of the original prescription with the generic name of the drug.

I don't need to go into detail about the penalties for illegal drug possession upon return to the United States. Customs officials are also on the lookout for diet drugs sold in Mexico, possession of which could also land you in a U.S. jail because they are illegal here. If you buy antibiotics over the counter (which you can do in Mexico)—say, for a sinus infection—and still have some left, you probably won't be hassled by U.S. Customs.

Drugstores   Drugstores (*farmacías*) will sell you just about anything you want, with a prescription or without one. However, over-the-counter medicines such as aspirin, decongestants, or antihistamines are rarely sold. Most drugstores are open Monday through Saturday from 8am to 8pm. If you need to buy medicines after normal hours, ask for the *farmacía de turno*—pharmacies take turns staying open during off-hours. Find any drugstore, and in its window may be a card showing the schedule of which drugstore will be open at what time.

Electricity   The electrical system in Mexico is 110 volts, 60 cycles, as in the United States and Canada. However, in reality it may cycle more slowly and overheat your appliances. To compensate, select a medium or low speed for hair dryers and curling irons, though they may still overheat. Older hotels still have electrical outlets for flat two-prong plugs; you'll need an adapter for using any modern electrical apparatus that has an enlarged end on one prong or that has three prongs to insert. Many first-class and deluxe hotels have the three-holed outlets (*trifacicos* in Spanish). Those that don't may loan adapters, but to be sure, it's always better to carry your own.

Embassies/Consulates They provide valuable lists of doctors and lawyers, as well as regulations concerning marriages in Mexico. Contrary to popular belief, your embassy cannot get you out of a Mexican jail, provide postal or banking services, or fly you home when you run out of money. Consular officers can provide you with advice on most matters and problems, however. Most countries have a representative embassy in Mexico City and many have consular offices or representatives in the provinces.

The Embassy of **Australia** in Mexico City is at Jaime Balmes 11, Plaza Polanco, Torre B (☎ **5/395-9988** or **566-3053**); it's open Monday through Friday from 8am to 1pm.

The Embassy of **Canada** in Mexico City is at Schiller 529, in Polanco (☎ **5/724-7900**); it's open Monday through Friday from 9am to 1pm and 2 to 5pm (at other times the name of a duty officer is posted on the embassy door). In Acapulco, the Canadian consulate is in the Hotel Club del Sol, Costera Miguel Alemán, at the corner of Reyes Católicos (☎ **74/85-6621**); it's open Monday through Friday from 8am to 3pm.

The Embassy of **New Zealand** in Mexico City is at Homero 229, 8th floor (☎ **5/250-5999** or **250-5777**); it's open Monday through Thursday from 9am to 2pm and 3 to 5pm and Friday from 9am to 2pm.

The Embassy of the **United Kingdom** in Mexico City is at Lerma 71, at Río Sena (☎ **5/207-2569** or **207-2593**); it's open Monday through Friday from 9am to 2pm. There are honorary consuls in the following cities: Acapulco, Hotel Las Brisas, Carretera Escénica (☎ **74/84-6605** or **84-1580**); Ciudad Juárez, Calle Fresno 185 (☎ **16/7-5791**); Guadalajara, Paulino Navarro 1165 (☎ **3/611-1678**); Mérida, Calle 58 no. 450 (☎ **99/28-6152** or **28-3962**); Monterrey, Privada de Tamazunchale 104 (☎ **83/78-2565**); Oaxaca, Ev. Hidalgo 817 (☎ **951/6-5600**); Tampico, 2 de Enero 102-A-Sur (☎ **12/12-9784** or **12-9817**); Tijuana, Blv. Salinas 1500 (☎ **66/81-7323**); and Veracruz, Emparan 200 PB (☎ **29/31-0955**).

The Embassy of the **United States** in Mexico City is next to the Hotel María Isabel Sheraton at Paseo de la Reforma 305, at the corner of Río Danubio (☎ **5/211-0042**). There are U.S. Consulates General in Ciudad Juárez, López Mateos 924-N (☎ **16/13-4048**); Guadalajara, Progreso 175 (☎ **3/625-2998**); Monterrey, Av. Constitución 411 Poniente (☎ **83/45-2120**); and Tijuana, Tapachula 96 (☎ **66/81-7400**). There are U.S. Consulates in Hermosillo, Av Monterrey 141 (☎ **621/7-2375;** Matamoros, Av. Primera 2002 (☎ **88/12-4402**); Mérida, Paseo Montejo 453 (☎ **99/25-6366**); Nuevo Laredo, Calle Allende 3330 (☎ **871/4-0512**). In addition, Consular Agencies are in Acapulco (☎ **74/85-6600** or **5-7207**); Cabo San Lucas (☎ **114/3-3566**); Cancún (☎ **98/84-2411** or **84-6399**); Mazatlán (☎ **69/13-4444,** ext. 285); Oaxaca (☎ **951/4-3054**); Puerto Vallarta (☎ **322/2-0069**); San Luis Potosí (☎ **481/2-1528**); San Miguel de Allende (☎ **465/2-2357** or **2-0068**); Tampico (☎ **12/13-2217**); and Veracruz (☎ **29/31-5821**).

Emergencies The 24-hour Tourist Help Line in Mexico City is ☎ **5/250-0151.**

Legal Aid International Legal Defense Counsel, 111 S. 15th St., 24th Floor, Packard Building, Philadelphia, PA 19102 (☎ **215/977-9982**), is a law firm specializing in legal difficulties of Americans abroad. See also "Embassies/Consulates" and "Emergencies," above.

Mail Mail service south of the border tends to be slow and undependable—though it is improving. If you're on a two-week vacation, it's not a bad idea to buy and mail your postcards in the arrivals lounge at the airport to give them maximum time to get home before you do.

For the most reliable and convenient mail service, have your letters sent to you c/o the American Express offices in major cities, which will receive and forward mail for you if you are one of its clients (a travel-club card or an American Express traveler's check is proof). They charge a fee if you wish to have your mail forwarded.

If you don't use American Express, have your mail sent to you care of Lista de Correos (General Delivery), followed by the Mexican city, state, and country. In Mexican post offices there may actually be a "lista" posted near the Lista de Correos window bearing the names of all those for whom mail has been received. If there's no list, ask and show them your passport so they can riffle through and look for your letters. If the city has more than one office, you'll have to go to the central post office—not a branch—to get your mail. By the way, in many post offices they return mail to the sender if it has been there for more than 10 days. Make sure people don't send you letters too early.

In major Mexican cities there are also branches of such U.S. express mail companies as UPS, Federal Express, and DHL, as well as private mail boxes such as Mail Boxes Etc.

Newspapers/Magazines   Two English-language newspapers, the *News* and the *Times,* are published in Mexico City, and carry world news and commentaries, plus a calendar of the day's events including concerts, art shows, and plays. Newspaper kiosks in larger Mexican cities will carry a selection of English-language magazines.

Pets   Taking a pet into Mexico entails a lot of red tape. Consult the Mexican Government Tourist Office nearest you (see "Information, Entry Requirements & Money," earlier in this chapter).

Police   Police in general in Mexico are to be suspected rather than trusted; however, you'll find many who are quite honest, and helpful with directions, even going so far as to lead you where you want to go.

Rest rooms   The best bet in Mexico is to use rest rooms in restaurants and hotel public areas. Always carry your own toilet paper and hand soap, neither of which is in great supply in Mexican rest rooms. Public facilities, usually near the central market, vary in cleanliness and usually have an attendant who charges a few pesos for toilet use and a few squares of toilet paper. Pemex gas stations have improved the maintenance of their rest rooms along major highways. No matter where you are, even if the toilet flushes with paper, there'll be a wastebasket for paper disposal. Many people come from homes without plumbing and are not accustomed to toilets that will take paper, so they'll throw used paper on the floor rather than put it in the toilet; thus, you'll see the basket no matter what quality of place you are in. On the other hand, the water pressure in many establishments is so low that paper won't go down. Thus the disposal basket again—which can be a disgusting sight, but better that than on the floor. There's often a sign telling you whether or not to flush paper.

Taxes   There's a 15% IVA tax on goods and services in most of Mexico, and it's supposed to be included in the posted price. This tax is 10% in Cancun, Cozumel, and Los Cabos.

Telephone/Fax   Telephone area codes are gradually being changed all over the country. The change may affect the area code and first digit or only the area code. Some cities are even adding exchanges and changing whole numbers. Often a personal or business telephone number will be changed without notification to the subscriber. Telephone courtesy messages announcing a phone number change are nonexistent in Mexico. You can try operator assistance for difficult-to-reach numbers, but often the phone company doesn't inform its operators of recent changes. People who have fax machines often turn them off when their offices are closed. Many fax numbers are also regular telephone numbers; you have to ask whoever answers your call for the fax tone *(Por favor darme el tono por fax)*. Telephone etiquette in Mexico does not prompt the answerer to offer to take a message or to have someone return your call; you'll have to make these suggestions yourself. In addition, etiquette doesn't necessarily demand that a business answer its phone by saying its name; often you'll have to ask if you have the right place.

Time   Central standard time prevails throughout most of Mexico. The west coast states of Sonora, Sinaloa, and parts of Nayarit are on Mountain standard time. The state of Baja California Norte is on Pacific time, but Baja California Sur is on Mountain time. Though adoption of **Daylight Saving Time** was announced at least twice before, and didn't happen, beginning in October 1996, it will occur—by presidential decree.

Water   Most hotels have decanters or bottles of purified water in the rooms, and the better hotels have either purified water from regular taps or special taps marked AGUA PURIFICADA. In the resort areas, especially the Yucatán, hoteliers are beginning to charge for in-room bottled water. If the water in your room is an expensive imported variety such as Evian, for sure there's an extra charge for using it. Virtually any hotel, restaurant, or bar will bring you purified water if you specifically request it, but you'll usually be charged for it. Bottled purified water is sold widely at drugstores and grocery stores.

Cancún 3

Say the word "Cancún" to most people, and they'll think of fine sandy beaches, limpid, incredibly blue Caribbean waters, and expensive luxury resorts—these images are all true. Isla Cancún is lined with shopping centers and upscale resort hotels, many of which are luxurious by any world standard. Ciudad Cancún, on the mainland, grew up with hotels more for the budget-minded traveler and boasts a downtown area chockablock with restaurants, each trying to outdo the others to attract clientele. Many travelers who select an island hotel as a base never get to explore the more funky mainland establishments.

Twenty years ago, the name Cancún meant little to anyone, but these days Cancún is the magic word in Mexican vacations. A hook-shaped island on the Caribbean side of the Yucatecan coast, Cancún opened for business in 1974 with one hotel and a lot of promotion, after being judged the best spot in the country for a new jet-age resort. Meanwhile, Ciudad Cancún popped up to house the working populace that flocked to support the resort.

Cancún *is* a perfect resort site: the long island's powdery limestone sand beaches; air and water temperatures that are just right. Furthermore, Cancún can be a starting point for exploration of other Yucatecan lures. The older, less expensive island resorts of Isla Mujeres and Cozumel are close at hand. The Maya ruins at Tulum, Chichén-Itzá, and Cobá are within driving distance, as are the snorkeling reserves of Xcaret and Xel-Ha. And along the coast south of Cancún, in places such as Playa del Carmen, new resorts in all price ranges are popping up.

Cancún today is a city of 450,000 people and boasts more than 18,000 hotel rooms between the mainland city and the resort-filled island. The 14-mile-long island's resorts together make for quite a variegated display of modern architectural style; they seem to get grander and more lavish each year.

Fans of Cancún see its similarity to U.S. resorts as a plus—a foreign vacation without foreign inconveniences. Cancún is a good place to ease into Mexican culture, though it's not at all like the rest of the country. But if you like beaches, Cancún and the coast to its south have the best beaches in Mexico. Food and drinks are just one sybaritic step from your lounge chair.

If you're beginning your Yucatecan adventure in Cancún, you should read up on the history of the Yucatán in Chapter 5.

1 Orientation

ARRIVING & DEPARTING
BY PLANE

Several airlines connect Cancún with other Mexican and Central American cities. **Aeroméxico** (☎ **84-3571** or **84-1186**) offers service from Mexico City, Mérida, and Tijuana. **Mexicana** (☎ **87-4444** or **87-2769** in Cancún and toll-free **800/5-0220** for 24 hour reservations) flies in from Guadalajara, Mexico City, and Flores, Guatemala. Regional carriers **Aerocozumel** and **Aerocaribe** (☎ **84-2000,** both affiliated with Mexicana) fly from Cozumel, Havana, Mexico City, Tuxtla Gutiérrez, Villahermosa, Mérida, Oaxaca, Veracruz, and Cuidad del Carmen. The regional airline **Aviateca** (☎ **84-3938** or **87-1386**) flies from Cancún to Mérida, Villahermosa, Tuxtla Gutiérrez, Guatemala City, and Flores (near Tikal). **Avio Quintana** (☎ **86-0422**) flies a 19-passenger plane to and from Chetumal Monday through Saturday. **Taesa** (☎ **87-4314**) has flights from Tijuana, Chetumal, Mérida, and other cities within Mexico.

You'll want to confirm departure times for flights back to the States; here are the Cancún airport numbers of the major international carriers: **American** (☎ **98/86-0151**), **Continental** (☎ **98/86-0005** or **86-0006**), **Northwest** (☎ **98/86-0044** or **86-0046**), and **United** (☎ **98/86-0158**).

Special vans run from Cancún's international airport into town for $5 per person. Rates for a cab are double or triple the collectivo fare depending on your destination. From the airport there's no minibus transportation to the Puerto Juárez passenger ferry to Isla Mujeres. The least expensive way to get there is to take the minibus to the bus station in downtown Cancún and from there bargain for a taxi, which should cost around $5. Most major rental-car firms have outlets at the airport, so if you're renting a car, consider picking it up and dropping it off at the airport to save on airport-transportation prices.

There is no collectivo service returning to the airport from Ciudad Cancún or the Zona Hotelera, so you'll have to hire a taxi. From Ciudad Cancún the fare's around $9 to $10; from the Zona Hotelera it's around $10 to $15.

BY BUS

Cancún's bus terminal has been renovated and is divided into two parts: The air-conditioned ADO and Green Line ticket windows and waiting rooms occupy the right half of the building; the left half holds the unair-conditioned second-class ticket windows.

The difference between first- and second-class buses here is that first-class buses are usually air-conditioned, often have video movies, sometimes a snack area aboard, and have fewer, if any, stops en route to the destination. Second class buses may also be air-conditioned and often also offer limited stop service to the destination. Often, the price difference between the two is not great. *Bus Travel Note:* Bus travel in this region changes more than any I check on in the country. So services and buslines could be dramatically changed (usually improved) when you travel. This is what was in effect when I checked for this edition.

Autotransportes Playa Express runs buses from Cancún to Playa del Carmen and Tulum almost every 20 minutes between 6am and 9pm from their ticket counter opposite the bus station near the corner of Avenida Tulum and Pino. They also have frequent service to Xcaret, Tulum, the Capitan Lafitte resort, Puerto Aventuras, Xpuha, Akumal, and Felipe Carrillo Puerto. Check on their Tulum service that

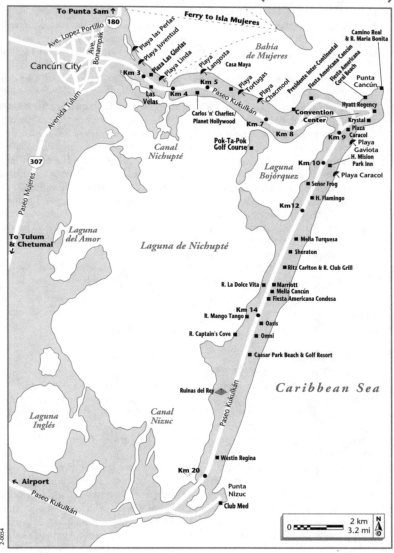

includes entry and transportation to the entrance to the ruins (as opposed to letting you off on the highway). In the second-class bus terminal section are: **ATS** (Autotransportes del Sureste) **and Autotransportes de Oriente (ADO) buses.** ATS buses have large ATS letters on the sides of its buses, which run every 20 minutes to Playa del Carmen. Other ATS buses travel to Palenque, San Cristóbal, Mérida, Valladolid, and Chetumal. Its buses leave from the left end of the bus terminal (if you're facing it). Autotransportes de Oriente buses go frequently to Mérida, on both the short route (via the toll road) and long route (via the free road), as well as to Chichén-Itzá, Izamal, and Tizimin. **Transportes de Lujo Linea Dorado,** despite its name, is a second-class line. Its buses go hourly to Playa del Carmen, Xcaret, Tulum, Lago Bacalar, Oxkutzcab, and Ticul. In the first class part of the station are **Greenline Paquete** and **ADO** buses with their separate air-conditioned waiting room on the far right. **ADO** buses go to Mérida and Valladolid almost twice hourly until 11:30pm; the company also has daily service to Mexico City, Veracruz, and Villahermosa. They have three classes of service: GL buses have air-conditioning, a small snack area, bathroom, spacious seating, and video. UNO buses are similarly equipped but some have 25 super reclining seats, and some have 40 seats. **Greenline Paquetes** offer packages *(paquetes)* to popular nearby destinations. To Chichén-Itzá the bus leaves at 9am and the round trip ticket includes the air-conditioned bus ride, with video, for the three-hour trip to Chichén-Itzá, entry to the ruins, two hours at the ruins, lunch, a brief stop for shopping, visit to a cenote, and return to Cancún by 5pm. The trip to Xcaret (which is much cheaper than the same trip offered at the Xcaret terminal office), includes round-trip transportation and entry to the park. Departures are at 9 and 10am daily with return at 5pm. To Cozumel, the departures leave at 8, 9, and 10am with return at 5pm, and include a bus and ferry escort, round trip, air-conditioned transportation to Playa del Carmen, and the ferry ticket to and from Cozumel. This takes the mystery out of getting to Cozumel, but you can do this simple trip on your own, by bus from this terminal, for half the price.

The bus station is in downtown Ciudad Cancún at the intersection of Avenidas Tulum and Uxmal, within walking distance of several of my hotel suggestions. All out-of-town buses arrive there.

BY FERRY

For ferry service to Cozumel or to Isla Mujeres, see Chapter 4.

VISITOR INFORMATION

The **State Tourism Office** (☎ 98/84-8073) is centrally located downtown on the east side of Avenida Tulum immediately left of the Ayuntamiento Benito Juárez building between Avenidas Cobá and Uxmal. It's open daily from 9am to 9pm. A second tourist information office (☎ **98/84-3238** or **84-3438**) is located on Avenidas Cobá at Avenida Tulum, next to Pizza Rolandi, and is open Monday through Friday from 9am to 9pm. Hotels and their rates are listed at each office, as well as ferry schedules.

A Warning: The friendliest people in town are often representatives of time-share real estate businesses who snag your attention by offering "information." However, their real mission is for you to attend a spiel about the wonders of a Cancún time-sharing or condo purchase. They'll go so far as to shout at you across a busy street, just to get your attention. You represent dollars, and they are paid a bounty for convincing you to attend one of their sales talks. If you get suckered in by these sales professionals you will spend no less than half a day of your vacation listening to them; you probably won't, however, receive the gift they'll promise.

Pick up free copies of the monthly *Cancún Tips* booklet and a seasonal tabloid of the same name. Both are useful and have fine maps. The publications are owned by the same people who own the Captain's Cove restaurants, a couple of sightseeing boats, and time-share hotels, so the information (though good) is not completely unbiased. Don't be surprised if, during your stay, one of their army of employees touts the joys of time-sharing, though more subtly than the others.

CITY LAYOUT

There are two Cancúns: **Isla Cancún** (Cancún Island) and **Ciudad Cancún** (Cancún City). The latter, on the mainland, has restaurants, shops, and less expensive hotels, as well as all the other establishments that make life function—pharmacies, dentists, automotive shops, banks, travel and airline agencies, car-rental firms—all within an area about nine blocks square. The city's main thoroughfare is **Avenida Tulum.** Heading south, Avenida Tulum becomes the highway to the airport, as well as to the south to Tulum and Chetumal; heading north, it intersects the highway to Mérida and the road to Puerto Juárez and the Isla Mujeres ferries.

The famed **Zona Hotelera** (alternately called the **Zona Turística**) stretches out along Isla Cancún, a sandy strip 14 miles long, shaped like a "7." It's now joined by bridges to the mainland at the north and south ends. **Avenida Cobá** from Cancún City becomes **Paseo Kukulkán,** the island's main traffic artery. Cancún's international airport is just inland from the south end of the island.

FINDING AN ADDRESS   The street-numbering system is left over from Cancún's early days. Addresses are still given by the number of the building lot and by the *manzana* (block) or *super-manzana* (group of city blocks). The city is still relatively small, and the downtown section can easily be covered on foot.

On the island, addresses are given by kilometer number on Paseo Kukulkán or by reference to some well-known location.

2 Getting Around

BY BUS

In town, almost everything is within walking distance. **Ruta 1** and **Ruta 2** ("Hoteles") city buses travel frequently from the mainland to the beaches along Avenida Tulum (the main street) and all the way to Punta Nizuc at the far end of the Zona Hotelera on Isla Cancún. **Ruta 8** buses go to Puerto Juárez/Punta Sam for ferries to Isla Mujeres. They stop on the east side of Avenida Tulum. Both these city buses operate between 6am and midnight daily. Beware of private buses plying the same route—they charge far more than the public ones! The public buses have the fare amount painted on the front; when last I checked it was 2.5 pesos.

BY TAXI

Settle on a price in advance. The trip from Ciudad Cancún to the Hotel Camino Real, for example, should cost $4; from Ciudad Cancún to the airport, $9 to $10; within Cancún proper, $3 to $5.

BY MOPED

Mopeds are a dangerous way to cruise around through the very congested traffic. Rentals start at $25 for a day. A credit-card voucher is required as security for the moped. You should receive a crash helmet (it's the law) and instructions on how to lock the wheels when you park. Read the fine print on the back of the rental agreement regarding liability for repairs or replacement in case of accident, theft, or vandalism. You rent at considerable risk.

BY RENTAL CAR

There's really no need to have a car in Cancún, since bus service is good, taxis on the mainland are relatively inexpensive, and most things in Ciudad Cancún are within walking distance. But if you do rent, the cheapest way is to arrange for the rental before you leave your home country. If you rent on the spot after arrival, the daily cost of a rental car will be around $65–$75 for a VW Beetle. For more details, see "Getting Around" in Chapter 2.

Important Note: Observe all speed zones on the island and the mainland. Police give tickets to speeders!

FAST FACTS: Cancún

American Express The local office is at Av. Tulum 208 and Agua (☎ **98/ 84-1999, 84-4243,** or **87-0831**), open Monday through Friday from 9am to 2pm and 4 to 6pm and Saturday from 9am to 1pm. It's one block past the Plaza México.

Area Code The telephone area code is 98.

Climate It's hot but not overwhelmingly humid. The rainy season is May through October. August through October is the hurricane season, which brings erratic weather. November through February can be cloudy, windy, somewhat rainy, and even cool, so a sweater is handy, as is rain protection.

Consulates The U.S. Consular Agent is in the Maruelos Building at Avenida Nader 40 (☎ **98/84-2411**). The office is open Monday through Friday from 9am to 2pm and 3 to 6pm. In an emergency, call the U.S. Consulate in Mérida (☎ **99/ 47-2285**).

Crime Car break-ins are just about the only crime, and they happen frequently, especially around the shopping centers in the Zona Hotelera. VW Beetles and Golfs are frequent targets. Don't leave valuables in plain sight.

Currency Exchange Most banks are downtown along Avenida Tulum and are usually open Monday through Friday from 9:30am to 1:30pm. In the hotel zone you'll find banks in the Plaza Kukulcán and next to the Convention Center. There are also many *casas de cambio* (exchange houses). Downtown merchants are eager to change cash dollars, but island stores don't offer good exchange rates. Avoid changing money at the airport as you arrive, especially at the first exchange you see—its rates are less favorable than any in town or others farther inside the airport concourse.

Drugstores Next to the Hotel Caribe Internacional, Farmacia Canto, at Avenida Yaxchilán 36, at Sunyaxchen (☎ **98/84-4083** or **84-9330**), is open 24 hours.

Emergencies To report an emergency dial **06,** which is supposed to be similar to 911 in the United States. For first aid, Cruz Roja (Red Cross; ☎ **98/ 84-1616**) is open 24 hours on Avenida Yaxchilán between Avenidas Xcaret and Labná, next to the Telemex building. Total Assist, a small nine-room emergency hospital with English-speaking doctors at Claveles 5, SM22, at Avenida Tulum (☎ **98/84-1058** or **84-1092**), is open 24 hours. Desk staff may have limited English. Clínica Quirurgica del Caribe, at SM63, Mz Q, Calle 3 inte. no. 36 (☎ **98/ 84-2516**), is open 24 hours. *Urgencias* means "Emergencies."

Luggage Storage/Lockers Hotels will generally tag and store excess luggage while you travel elsewhere.

Newspapers/Magazines For English-language newspapers and books, go to Fama on Avenida Tulum between Tulipanes and Claveles (☎ **98/84-6586**), open daily from 8am to 10pm. (Avoid filling out a contest flier here that will result in a call from a time-share promoter.)

Police To reach the police (Seguridad Pública), dial **98/84-1913** or **84-2342.**

Post Office The main post office is at the intersection of Avenidas Sunyaxchen and Xel-Ha (☎ **98/84-1418**). It's open Monday through Friday from 8am to 7pm and Saturday from 9am to 1pm.

Safety There is very little crime in Cancún. People in general are safe late at night in touristed areas; just use ordinary common sense. As at any other beach resort, don't take money or valuables to the beach. See "Crime," above.

Swimming on the Caribbean side presents real dangers from undertow. See "The Beaches" in "Beaches, Water Sports & Other Things to Do," below, for flag warnings.

Seasons   Technically, high season is December 15 through Easter, when prices are higher; low season is May through November, when prices are reduced 10% to 30%. Some hotels are starting to charge high-season rates between July and September when travel is high for European and school-holiday visitors. There's a mini-low season in January just after the Christmas–New Year's holiday.

Telephones   The phone system for Cancún changed in 1992. The area code, which once was 988, is now 98. All local numbers now have six digits instead of five; all numbers begin with 8. If a number is written 988/4-1234, when in Cancún you must dial 84-1234.

3 Accommodations

Island hotels run almost the gamut, but extravagance is the byword in the more recently built hotels, most of which are awash in a sea of marble, mahogany, brass, and white-gloved bellmen in waistcoats. Others, while sporting a more relaxed attitude, are just as exclusive. The water is placid on the upper end of the island facing Bahía de Mujeres, while beaches lining the long side of the island facing the Caribbean are subject to choppier water on windy days.

During the off-season (from April to November), prices go down. Hotels also often have discounted prices from February up to Easter week. *Important note on prices:* Although rack rates (the hotel's rate to the public) are high and are the ones I list here, a package that includes hotel and airline ticket may save you money. Also ask about special promotional rates and meal credits. Note that the price quoted to you when you call a hotel's reservation number from the United States doesn't include Cancún's 10% tax. Prices can vary widely from hotel to hotel at different times of the year, so it pays to shop around.

Cancún hoteliers, even in budget and moderately priced hotels, are beginning to quote rates in dollars instead of pesos, to buffer themselves against the falling value of the peso. You're usually better off insisting on a quote in pesos. Ciudad Cancún has many good budget and moderately priced hotels. During off-season (from April to November), prices go down, and it doesn't hurt to bargain for further reductions. Ask for the *tarifa promocional* (promotional rate), which hotels often have. The hotels below are categorized by high-season, double-room prices.

If the recommendations below are full, the **Posada Lucy,** Gladiolas 8, ☎ and fax **98/84-4165,** is one of Cancún's budget standbys, good for a long-term stay. And the cheapest beds in town can be found at **Albergue de la Juventud,** Paseo Kukulkán km 3.2, ☎ **98/83-1337.** This youth hostel is located at the beginning of the Zona Hotelera, and a bed costs a mere $5.

The hotel listings in this chapter begin on Cancún Island, the most expensive place to stay, and finish in Cancún City, where bargain lodgings abound.

CANCÚN ISLAND
VERY EXPENSIVE

Caesar Park Beach & Golf Resort
Paseo Kukulcán, Retorno Lacandones km 17, 77500 Cancún, Q. Roo. ☎ **98/81-8000** or 800/228-3000 in the U.S. Fax 98/85-2437. High season standard rooms $275–$350 single or double; Royal Beach Club $295–$485 single or double; suites $375–$500 single or double. Low season standard rooms $200–$300; Royal Beach Club $230–$290; suites $300–$350 single or double.

Downtown Cancún

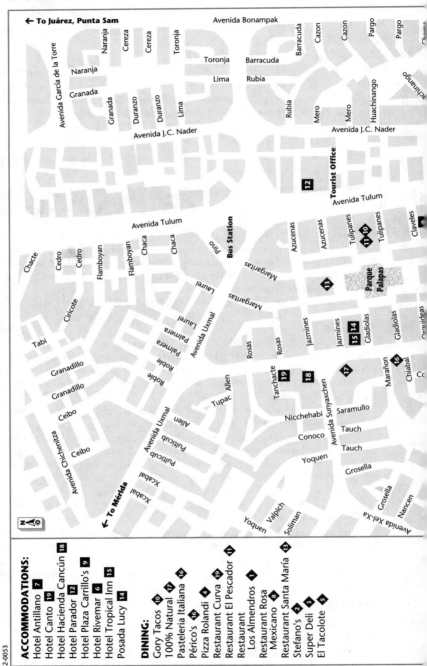

← To Juárez, Punta Sam

Avenida Bonampak

ACCOMMODATIONS:
Hotel Antillano **7**
Hotel Canto **19**
Hotel Hacienda Cancún **18**
Hotel Parador **12**
Hotel Plaza Carrillo's **9**
Hotel Rivemar **6**
Hotel Tropical Inn **15**
Posada Lucy **14**

DINING:
Gory Tacos **10**
100% Natural **11**
Pasteleria Italiana **16**
Périco's **13**
Pizza Rolandi **4**
Restaurant Curva **12**
Restaurant El Pescador **1**
Restaurant
  Los Almendros **1**
Restaurant Rosa
  Mexicano **8**
Restaurant Santa María **13**
Stefano's **2**
Super Deli **3**
El Tacolote **5**

2-0053

74

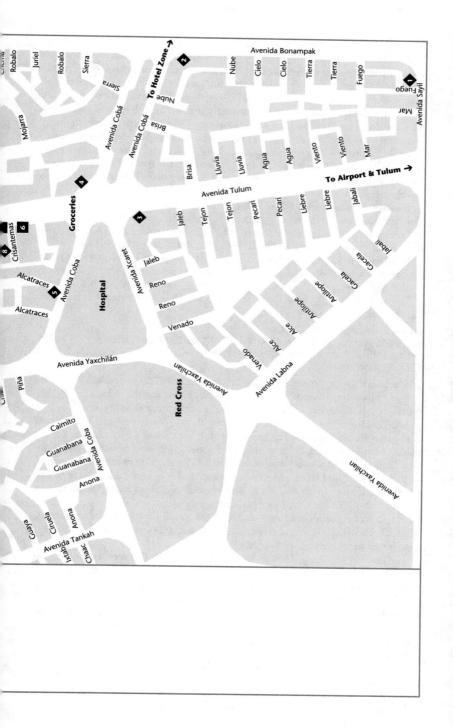

A true resort in every sense of the word, the Caesar Park opened in 1994 on 250 acres of prime Cancún beachfront property with two restaurants, seven interconnected pools, a par-72 golf course across the street, and a location that gives every room a sea view. Like the sprawling resort, rooms are grandly spacious and immaculately decorated in an austere Japanese way (the owners are Japanese). Marble floors and baths throughout are softened with area rugs and pastel furnishings. All rooms have sea views and some have both sea and lagoon views. Other amenities in each luxurious room include robes, house shoes, hair dryers, safety deposit boxes, and remote-control TV. Suites have coffee makers. Royal Beach club guests enjoy nightly cocktails, and each Tuesday a manager's cocktail on the patio. The elegant Royal Beach Club rooms are set off from the main hotel in two-and three-story buildings (no elevators) and with their own check-in and concierge service.

Dining/Entertainment: Spices Restaurant serves the cuisines of Mexico, Argentina, and Italy, while Sirenita offers selections from Japanese cuisine.

Services: Laundry and room service, ice machine on each floor, concierge, tour desk, beauty salon, gift shop and boutiques, golf clinic, car rental.

Facilities: Par-72 golf course, seven interconnected swimming pools with a swim-up bar, two whirlpools, two lighted tennis courts, water sport center, large fully equipped gym with daily aerobics, massage, beauty salon, and sauna. A Kids' Club is part of the gym program. Greens fee is $75 for 18 holes for guests and $95 for nonguests; carts cost $20.

Fiesta Americana Coral Beach

Paseo Kukulkán km 9.5, 77500 Cancún, Q. Roo. ☎ **98/83-2900,** or 800/343-7821 in the U.S. Fax 98/83-3225. 602 suites. A/C MINIBAR TV TEL. High season $325 single or double. Low season $255 single or double.

This sophisticated, spectacular hotel, which opened in 1991, has a lot to recommend it: perfect location; gracious service; grand public areas; and the full gamut of water sports, beach activities, and indoor tennis. It's enormous in a Mexican way and grandly European in its lavish public halls and lobby. It's embellished with elegant dark-green granite from France, deep red granite from South Africa, black and green marble from Guatemala, beige marble from Mexico, a canopy of stained glass from Guadalajara, and hardwood floors from Texas. The elegant choices are, of course, carried into the guest rooms, which are decorated with more marble, area rugs, and tasteful use of Mexican decorative arts. All rooms have balconies facing the ocean, plus remote-control TVs and hair dryers. Master suites have double vanities, dressing room, bathrobes, whirlpool baths, and large terraces. Two concierge floors feature daily continental breakfast and evening cocktails, and a 24-hour receptionist-cashier. Two junior suites are equipped for handicapped guests.

The hotel's great Punta Cancún location (opposite the Convention Center, and within walking distance of shopping centers and restaurants) has the advantage of a north-facing beach, meaning the surf is calm and just perfect for swimming.

Dining/Entertainment: Elegant seafood and Mexican restaurants for dinner; a café-style restaurant with international food and an ocean view serving a breakfast buffet and lunch; a snack bar and stylish outdoor palapa restaurant serve the beach and pool. Five bars.

Services: Laundry and room service, travel agency, car rental, massage.

Facilities: A 660-foot-long free-form swimming pool; swim-up bars; 1,000 feet of beach; three indoor tennis courts with stadium seating; gymnasium with weights, sauna, and massage; water-sport rentals on the beach; business center; tennis pro shop; fashion and spa boutiques; and beauty and barber shops.

Hotel Melia Cancún

Paseo Kukulkán km 14, 77500 Cancún, Q. Roo. ☎ **98/85-1114,** or 800/336-3542 in the U.S., 91-800/2-1779 in Mexico. Fax 98/85-1263. 450 rms and suites. A/C MINIBAR TV TEL. High season $275–$445 single or double. Low season $190–$308 single or double.

You can't miss the palatial exterior of this hotel. The eight-storied circular interior is a jungle of plants set against a fountain. The marble-and-teakwood backdrop is decorated with majolica pottery from Guanajuato and lacquer chests from Olinalá, Guerrero. The spacious rooms, all with sitting areas and balconies, are appropriately stylish and feature in-room security boxes and purified tap water. There are four rooms on the first floor especially equipped with extra-wide bathrooms for guests with disabilities.

Dining/Entertainment: Five restaurants feature foods from France, Mexico, and the United States and include a daily breakfast buffet, seafood, and poolside dining. Five bars serve all guests all day. The lobby bar features Latin rhythms starting at 8pm.

Services: Laundry and room service, travel agency, car rental, and baby cribs and baby-sitters.

Facilities: Two pools; beach; nine-hole golf course on the property; three lighted tennis courts; Ping-Pong; gymnasium with massage, sauna, whirlpool, facials, aerobics, weights, hydromassage showers, and dressing room; and beauty and barber shop. During high season or times of high hotel occupancy there's a full daily list of activities for children posted in the lobby.

Ritz-Carlton Hotel

Retorno del Rey, off Paseo Kukulkán km 13.5, 77500 Cancún, Q. Roo. ☎ **98/85-0808** or 800/ 241-3333. Fax 98/85-1015. 272 rms. 100 suites. A/C MINIBAR TV TEL. High season $365–$985 single or double. Low season $286–$660 single or double. Free guarded parking.

On $7^1/_2$ acres, the nine-story Ritz-Carlton in Cancún is easily the island's most elegant hotel in the finest traditional European sense. People who stay here are accustomed to the finest of everything—impeccable service, crystal chandeliers, stained glass, thick molding, elegant marble, luxurious, upholstered mahogany furniture, large sprays of fresh flowers, silver and crystal in the dining rooms, and lush carpets throughout in muted reds and blues.

The spacious guest rooms are just as sumptuous as public areas. Each room has remote-control TVs, safety-deposit boxes, electronic locks, and maid service twice daily. Suites are large, and some have a large dressing area, two TVs, balconies, and one and a half baths. Marble baths have telephones, separate tubs and showers, lighted makeup mirror, weight scales, and hair dryers. Floors 8 and 9 are for Ritz-Carlton Club members. On these floors there are special amenities including five mini-meals a day. Prices depend on whether your room is oceanfront, or ocean or garden view. Special packages may offer some cost-saving incentives and are worth exploring.

Dining/Entertainment: On the ground level, the Café, a stylishly casual glass-walled restaurant with evening trio entertainment is open for all meals. The dining room, with a large expanse of beveled windows, features northern Italian cuisine in total elegance and is open for all meals. The Club Grill, a stylish English pub, is one of the best restaurants in the city (See "Dining," below), offering grilled specialties, nightly entertainment, and a dance floor. The Caribe Bar and Grill is open for snacks during pool hours. The lobby bar opens at 5pm daily and offers live music between 7:30 and 11pm.

Services: Laundry and dry cleaning, room service, travel agency, concierge.

Facilities: A swimming pool, three tennis courts, fully equipped gym with exercise equipment, massages and lockers, pharmacy/gift shop, boutiques, beauty and barber shops.

EXPENSIVE

Camino Real Cancún

Paseo Kukulkán, 77500 Punta Cancún (Apdo. Postal 14), Cancún, Q. Roo. ☎ **98/83-0100,** or 800/722-6466 in the U.S. Fax 98/83-1730. 381 rms and suites. A/C MINIBAR TV TEL. High season $200–$225 single or double. Low season $120–$215 single or double. Package deals provide the best value. Daily fee for guarded parking adjacent to hotel.

On four acres right at the tip of Punta Cancún, the Camino Real, a member of Leading Hotels of the World, is among the island's most appealing places to stay. The rooms are elegantly outfitted with pink breccia-marble floors, tropical high-backed raffia easy chairs, and drapes and spreads in soft pastel colors. Some rooms in the new 18-story Camino Real Club have elegant Mexican decor, while standard rooms in this section are much like rooms in the rest of the resort. Master suites have expansive views, swivel TVs, large dining tables with four chairs, and hot tubs on the balconies. Camino Real Club guests receive a complimentary continental breakfast daily in the Beach Club lobby, as well as complimentary cocktails and snacks there each evening. Lower-priced rooms have lagoon views.

Dining/Entertainment: Three restaurants serve all meals and include a beach and pool-side snack with seafood specialties; indoor casual dining with flame-broiled meat; and an elegant evening-only restaurant featuring Chinese cuisine. There's a children's menu at the more casual restaurants. A Mexican fiesta takes place on Saturday nights. The lobby bar features Mexican music nightly from 5:30 to 7:30pm, and the oceanview Azucar Disco swings into action Monday through Saturday at 9:30pm.

Services: Laundry and room service, travel agency, car rental, in-room safety boxes, baby-sitting (with advance notice).

Facilities: Freshwater pool; private saltwater lagoon with sea turtles and tropical fish; private beach; sailing pier; water-sports center. There are also three lighted tennis courts, beach volleyball, boutiques, and barber and beauty shops.

Fiesta Americana Cancún

Paseo Kukulkán km 7.5, 77500 Cancún, Q. Roo. ☎ **98/83-1400,** or 800/343-7821 in the U.S. Fax 98/83-2502. 281 rms. A/C MINIBAR TV TEL. High season $200 single or double. Low season $155 single or double. (Ask about summer "Fiesta" packages.) Free parking.

With colorful stucco walls and randomly placed balconies and windows, the Fiesta Americana has Old World charm. Originally built with honeymooners in mind, it's smaller than most island accommodations and is Cancún's most intimate hotel. On the best beach facing the calm Bahia Mujeres, the quiet rooms are beautifully furnished with balconies facing the ocean. Some rooms have in-room safety-deposit boxes. The location is ideal—it's right across the street from shopping malls and restaurants near the Convention Center.

Dining/Entertainment: The hotel's three restaurants cover your dining needs, from formal dining to light meals at poolside (where there's a swim-up bar). The lobby bar, open most of the day, features piano entertainment in the evening between 8 and 11pm. Caliente Sports/TV Betting Bar has big-screen TVs for viewing sporting events.

Services: Laundry and room service, travel agency, wedding arrangements.

Facilities: One swimming pool, water-sports rental on the beach, boutiques, wheelchairs.

Krystal Cancún

Paseo Kukulkán km 7.5, 77500 Cancún, Q. Roo. ☎ **98/83-1133,** or 800/231-9860 in the U.S. Fax 98/83-1790. 364 rms. A/C MINIBAR TV TEL. High season $200–$440 single or double. Low season $135–$165 single or double. Free parking.

The Krystal Cancún lies on Punta Cancún with the Camino Real and Hyatt Regency, near the Convention Center, shops, restaurants, and clubs. The Krystal uses lots of cool marble in its decor. The guest rooms, in two buildings, have bamboo furniture, drapes, and spreads in earthy tones, two double beds, and water views. The hotel's tap water is purified, and there are ice machines on every floor. The presidential suites have private pools. Club Krystal rooms come with in-room safety boxes, complimentary continental breakfast, and evening canapés and drinks; guests in those rooms also have access to the Club Lounge, a rooftop sun lounge with a whirlpool and concierge service.

Dining/Entertainment: Among the hotel's four restaurants are two that have gained countrywide recognition for fine cuisine—Bogart's, a chic dining room with a Moroccan "Casablanca" theme, and the luxurious Hacienda El Mortero, a replica of a colonial hacienda featuring Mexican cuisine. The hotel also hosts theme nights throughout the week. In the evening there's live entertainment in the lobby bar. Christine's, one of the most popular discos in town, is open nightly.

Services: Laundry, room service, travel agency, car and moped rental.

Facilities: Swimming pool complex overlooking the Caribbean and a beach with fairly safe swimming; pharmacy; barber and beauty shop; boutiques and a silver shop; two tennis courts with an on-duty tennis pro; a racquetball court; a dive shop; and a fitness club with whirlpool, sauna, and massage facilities.

Marriott Casamagna

Paseo Kukulkán km 20, 77500 Cancún, Q. Roo. ☎ **98/85-2000,** or 800/228-9290 in the U.S. Fax 98/85-1385. 450 rms and suites. A/C MINIBAR TV TEL. High season $215–$260 single or double. Low season $160–$205 single or double. (Ask about seasonal "supersaver" packages.)

Luxury is this hotel's hallmark. Entering through a half-circle of Roman columns, you pass through a long, domed foyer to a wide, lavishly marbled 44-foot-high lobby. The lobby expands in three directions with wide, Mexican cantera-stone arches branching off outdoors, where columns vanish into shallow pools like Roman baths. All rooms have computer-card entry; most have balconies and contemporary furnishings, tiled floors, and ceiling fans. All suites occupy corners and have enormous terraces, ocean views, and TVs in both the living room and bedroom.

Dining/Entertainment: At this hotel's four restaurants, you'll find the cuisines of Japan, Mexico, and the United States. The lobby bar features nightly mariachi music, while Sixties nightclub features hits from the 1950s through the 1970s, with space for dancing.

Services: Laundry and room service, travel agency, car rental.

Facilities: Beach; swimming pool; two lighted tennis courts; health club with saunas, lockers, whirlpool, aerobics, and juice bar; and beauty and barber shop.

Sheraton Resort

Paseo Kukulkán km 13.5, 77500 Cancún, Q. Roo. ☎ **98/83-1988,** or 800/325-3535 in the U.S. Fax 98/85-0974. 748 rms and suites. A/C MINIBAR TV TEL. High season $225–$240 single or double. Low season $153–$162 single or double. (Ask about summer "Temptation" packages.) Free parking.

These three lavish, pyramid-style buildings are set on their own vast stretch of beach. The impressive lobby has large expanses of green tiles and a dramatic stainless-steel sculpture of birds in flight. Emerald lawns extend in every direction from the main buildings, and a small reconstructed Maya ruin crowns a craggy limestone hillock. Rooms and suites are luxurious, with views of the Caribbean (to the east) or of the lagoon (to the west). In the V-shaped tower section, all units have in-room security boxes, and guests enjoy the services of a personal butler who attends to a variety of tasks from shoe shines to snack service. There's a nonsmoking floor, and rooms are available for guests with disabilities.

Dining/Entertainment: At least four restaurants cover every aspect of eating, from grilled food by the beach to lavish breakfast buffets to Italian feasts to Mexican food. There are five bars, including the lobby bar where there's live music from noon to midnight.

Services: Laundry and room service, travel agency, car rental, massage, baby-sitting.

Facilities: Three swimming pools; six lighted tennis courts with tennis pro on duty; beach; fitness center with sauna, steam bath, and whirlpool; mini-golf; aerobics, swimnastics; arts and crafts; Spanish classes; children's playground; basketball court; table games; pharmacy; beauty and barber shop; business center; flower shop; and boutiques.

MODERATE

Calinda Viva Cancún

Paseo Kukulkán km 8.5, 77500 Cancún, Q. Roo. ☎ **98/83-0800,** or 800/228-5151 in the U.S. Fax 98/83-2087. 210 rms. A/C TV TEL. High season $135–$185 single or double. Low season $115 single or double. Free parking.

From the street, this hotel looks like a blockhouse, but on the ocean side you'll find a small but pretty patio garden and a Cancún's best beach that is safe for swimming. You have a choice of rooms with either lagoon or ocean view. At least 162 rooms have refrigerators and 64 have kitchenettes.

Dining/Entertainment: The main restaurant, La Fuente, serves all three meals. La Palapa and La Parilla, both beside the pool, serve drinks and light meals; Bar La Terraza is in the lobby.

Services: Laundry and room service, travel agency.

Facilities: Swimming pool for adults and one for children, one lighted tennis court, water-sports equipment rental, marina, pharmacy, and gift shop.

Flamingo Cancún

Paseo Kukulkán km 11.5, 77500 Cancún, Q. Roo. ☎ **98/83-1544.** Fax 98/83-1029. 162 rms. A/C MINIBAR TV TEL. High season $125 single or double. Low season $85 single or double. Free unguarded parking across the street in the Plaza Flamingo.

The Flamingo seems to have been inspired by the dramatic, slope-sided architecture of the Camino Real, but the Flamingo is considerably smaller. Guest rooms form a quadrangle or courtyard with the swimming pool. The Flamingo is in the heart of the island hotel district, opposite the Flamingo Shopping Center and close to other hotels, shopping centers, and restaurants.

Dining/Entertainment: La Joy Restaurant and Don Francisco Restaurant are both open daily. El Coral is the lobby bar.

Services: Laundry and room service, travel agency, car rental.

Facilities: Swimming pool and beach.

Hotel Aristos

Paseo Kukulkán km 12 (Apdo. Postal 450), 77500 Cancún, Q. Roo. ☎ **98/83-0011,** or 800/ 527-4786 in the U.S. 244 rms (all with bath). A/C TV TEL. High season $87 single or double. Low season $71 single or double. Free unguarded parking.

One of the island's first hotels, rooms are neat and cool, with red tile floors, small balconies, and yellow Formica furniture. All rooms face either the Caribbean or the paseo and lagoon; rooms with the best views (and no noise from the paseo) are on the Caribbean side. Here you'll find one restaurant and several bars, plus room and laundry service, a travel agency, and baby-sitting service. The central pool overlooks the ocean with a wide stretch of beach one level below the pool and lobby. You'll also find a marina with water-sports equipment and two lighted tennis courts. Beware of spring break here, when the hotel caters to the crowd with loud music poolside all day.

Misión Miramar Park Inn

Paseo Kukulkán km 9.5, 77500 Cancún, Q. Roo. ☎ **98/83-1755.** Fax 98/83-1136. 189 rms. A/C MINIBAR TV TEL. High season $165–$180 single or double. Low season $105–$125 single or double.

Each of the ingeniously designed rooms has views of both the lagoon and ocean. Public spaces throughout the hotel have lots of dark wood, cream-beige stucco, red tile, and pastel accents. The big swimming pool is next to the beach. Rooms are on the small side but comfortable, with bamboo furniture offset by pastel-colored cushions and bedspreads; bathrooms have polished limestone vanities.

Dining/Entertainment: Two restaurants serve cuisine of Mexico and the United States. There's live music nightly in the lobby bar, and the bar by the pool serves guests during pool hours. Batacha also has live music for dancing from 9pm to 4am Tuesday through Sunday.

Services: Laundry and room service, travel agency, car rental.

Facilities: Pool, beach, pharmacy, and gift shop.

Presidente Inter-Continental Cancún

Paseo Kukulkán km 7, 77500 Cancún, Q. Roo. ☎ **98/83-0200,** or 800/327-0200 in the U.S. Fax 98/83-0200. 292 rms. A/C MINIBAR TV TEL. High season $165–$315 single or double. Low season $110–$255 single or double. Free parking.

Elegant and spacious, the Presidente sports a modern design with lavish marble and wicker accents. Rooms have king-size beds, private balconies, tastefully simple unfinished pine furniture, and in-room safes. Sixteen rooms on the first floor have patios with outdoor whirlpool tubs. The club floors offer robes, magnified makeup mirrors, complimentary continental breakfast, evening drinks and canapés, and use of a private key-activated elevator. Two rooms are available for guests with disabilities and two floors are reserved for nonsmokers. Coming from Cancún City, you'll reach the Presidente on the left side of the street before you get to Punta Cancún—/it's behind the golf course and next to million-dollar homes.

Dining/Entertainment: The fine-dining restaurant features foods from France, Greece, Italy, Spain, and Morocco. El Caribeño, a three-level palapa restaurant by the beach and pool, serves all meals (see "Dining," below).

Services: Room and laundry service, travel agency, car rental.

Facilities: Two landscaped swimming pools with a waterfall; whirlpools; fitness center; a great beach fronting the calm Bahía Mujeres; lighted tennis courts; water-sports equipment rental; and marina.

CANCÚN CITY
MODERATE

Hotel Tropical Inn

Yaxchilán 31. SM 22. Cancún, Q. Roo. ☎ **98/84-3078.** Fax 84/34-7881. 81 rms. A/C TV TEL. High season $50–$70 single; $64–$84 double. Low season $46–$52 single; $56–$60 double.

The former Hotel Plaza del Sol has been incorporated into a shopping mall and has new owners. The three stories of rooms (with elevator) front a lovely palm-shaded pool area with comfortable tables and chairs and restaurant. Standard rooms have two double beds framed with wrought-iron headboards, tile floors, large tile baths with separate sink, desks, and overbed reading lights. Single rooms with one double bed are spacious with plenty of room for luggage. It's a nice hotel, but the prices are high for the location. Ask about a discount. The hotel is between Jazmines and Gladiolas, catercorner from Perico's.

INEXPENSIVE

Hotel Antillano

Claveles 37, 77500 Cancún, Q. Roo. ☎ **98/84-1532.** Fax 98/84-1878. 46 rms, 2 suites (all with bath). A/C TV TEL. High season $38 single; $50 double. Low season $31 single; $35 double.

This is an excellent choice and one of the nicer downtown establishments. For the quality, you'd expect to pay a good deal more. Rooms overlook Avenida Tulum, the side streets and the interior pool, with the latter being the most desirable since they are quieter. Each room has nicely coordinated furnishings, one or two double beds, a sink area separate from the bath, red tile floors, and a small TV. There's a small bar to one side of the reception area and a travel agency in the lobby. To find it from Tulum, walk west on Claveles a half block; it's opposite the Restaurant Rosa Mexicana. Parking is on the street.

Hotel Canto

Yaxchilán at Tanchate, 77500 Cancún, Q. Roo. ☎ and fax **98/84-1267.** 23 rms (all with bath). A/C TV TEL. $13 single; $16 double.

Rooms in this three-story hotel (no elevator) are tidy and freshly painted, though maintenance could be better. Each room has a window but no views, plus small TVs broadcasting U.S. channels. The hotel will be on your right by the Hotel Caribe Internacional, at the intersection with Tanchate, as you head south on Yaxchilán. Street parking is scarce.

Hotel Hacienda Cancún

Sunyaxchen 39–40, 77500 Cancún, Q. Roo. ☎ **98/84-3672.** Fax 98/84-1208. 40 rms (all with bath). A/C TV. High season $23 single or double. Low season $17 single or double.

This is an extremely pleasing little hotel with rooms that are clean and plainly furnished but very comfortable. All have two double beds and windows (but no views). There's a nice small pool and café under a shaded palapa in the back. The hotel is also a member of the Imperial Las Perlas beach club in the Zona Hotelera. To find it from Avenida Yaxchilán turn west on Sunyaxchen; it's on your right next to the Hotel Caribe International, opposite 100% Natural. Parking is on the street.

Hotel Parador

Tulum 26, 77500 Cancún, Q. Roo. ☎ **98/84-1922.** Fax 98/84-9712. 66 rms (all with bath). A/C TV TEL. High season $37 single or double. Low season $28 single or double. Ask about promotional rates.

One of the most popular downtown hotels, the three-story Parador is conveniently located. Guest rooms are arranged around two long, narrow garden courtyards leading back to a pool (with separate children's pool) and grassy sunning area. The rooms are modern, each with two double beds, a shower, and cable TV. Help yourself to bottled drinking water in the hall. There's a restaurant/bar, plus it's next to Pop's restaurant almost at the corner of Uxmal. Rates are almost always discounted from those quoted here. Street parking is limited.

Hotel Plaza Carrillo's

Claveles 5, 77500 Cancún, Q. Roo. ☎ **98/84-1227.** Fax 98/84-2371. 43 rms (all with bath). A/C TV TEL. High season $30 single; $33 double. Low season $25 single; $27 double.

Rooms at this three-story hotel (no elevator) are excellently located, comfortable, and well kept, if totally nondescript. You're paying more for location than anything, especially when comparing this hotel to the Hotel Hacienda, for example. Some rooms are small and dark, others large and bright. Some beds are on concrete platforms that occasionally are a little low to the floor. The nice second-story patio facing the street is a good place to relax with a breeze and a book. The scarcely used pool is in the center behind the streetside restaurant. From Avenida Tulum, the hotel is a half block west on Claveles. Parking spaces are available around the Parque Palapas, a half block farther.

Hotel Rivemar

Tulum 49–51, 77500 Cancún, Q. Roo. ☎ **98/84-1199.** 36 rms (all with bath). A/C or FAN TV TEL. $21–$26 single or double.

Right in the heart of downtown Cancún, this hotel is perfectly located. Rooms are clean, each with tile floors, two double beds, and small baths. Most rooms have air-conditioning, with only seven having fan only. All rooms have windows, some with street views and some with hall view. The hotel is at the corner of Crisantemas, $1\frac{1}{2}$ blocks north of the corner of Avenidas Cobá and Uxmal.

4 Dining

Restaurants change names with amazing rapidity in Cancún, so the restaurants I've chosen are a mix of those with dependable quality and staying power and those newly thriving when I checked them for this edition.

One of the first things you'll notice on arrival in Cancún is the invasion of U.S. franchise restaurants. You'll see them almost everywhere you look, including Wendy's, Subway, McDonald's, Pizza Hut, Tony Roma's, Ruth's Chris Steakhouse, KFC, TGI Friday's, and Burger King. Among the most economical chains are Vips and Denny's, which are also in several locations.

CANCÚN ISLAND
VERY EXPENSIVE

Captain's Cove

Paseo Kukulkán km 15, ☎ **98/85-0016.** Breakfast buffet $7–$10; seafood dishes $18–$40; children's menu $4–$5. INTERNATIONAL.

Though it sits almost at the end of Paseo Kukulkán far from everything, the Captain's Cove continues to pack customers in on its several dining levels. Diners face big open windows overlooking the lagoon and Royal Yacht Club Marina. During breakfast there's an all-you-can-eat buffet. Lunch and dinner main courses of steak and seafood are the norm, and there's a menu catering especially to children. For dessert there are flaming coffees, crepes, and Key lime pie. The restaurant is on the lagoon side opposite the Omni Hotel.

China Moon

Hotel Camino Real, Punta Cancún. ☎ **98/83-1730.** Appetizers $5–$15; main courses $15–$30. Nightly 6–11pm. CHINESE.

With its elegantly dressed circular dining room facing the water, you know upon entering that this is a place for leisurely, sophisticated dining. With Chinese cooks in the kitchen you can explore authentically prepared food from several regions in China. As an appetizer, Tsion Ku Pao Pin features artistically placed cool, thin slices of abalone, bamboo shoots, and shiitake mushrooms. Main courses include lobster, in season, prepared any Chinese style, of course Bei Jin duck, and Pa Fa Gai, a delicately flavored meal of chicken in a shrimp and scallop paste, covered with a crabmeat sauce and drizzled with sesame seeds.

Club Grill

Hotel Ritz-Carlton, Km 13.5. ☎ **98/85-0808.** Appetizers $10–$20; main courses $40–$50. Daily 7–11pm. INTERNATIONAL.

Cancún's most elegant and stylish restaurant is also its best. Even rival restaurateurs give it an envious thumbs-up. The gracious service starts as you enter the anteroom with its comfortable couches and chairs and selection of cognacs and Cuban cigars. It continues into the candlelit dining room with padded side chairs and tables shimmering with silver and crystal. Under the trained eye of chef de cuisine John Patrick Gray, elegant plates of peppered scallops, truffles, and potatoes in tequila sauce, or grilled lamb or mixed grill arrive without feeling rushed after the appetizer. Smoking and nonsmoking sections (a rarity in Mexico) add to the pleasure, as does the band playing romantic music for dancing from 8pm on. This is *the* place for that truly special night out.

EXPENSIVE

El Caribeño

In the Presidente Inter-Continental Hotel, Paseo Kukulkán, km 7.5. ☎ **98/83-0200.** Breakfast buffet $10; main courses $9–$17. Daily 7am–11pm. MEDITERRANEAN.

Especially nice for breakfast, lunch, or dinner, El Caribeño sits on the beach with a stunning view of the water and Isla Mujeres in the distance. The breakfast buffet is a sumptuous affair, including made-to-order omelets and a gorgeous array of tropical fruits and fresh sweet rolls. Lunch is a good choice since you'll be able to see the sea and will pay a bit less for your main courses. But dinner is quiet, romantic, and charming; you can order from the lunch menu at dinner, even though there's a less extensive and more expensive dinner menu. Try the fresh fish prepared Yucatecan style in achiote sauce. The restaurant is on the grounds of the Presidente Inter-Continental, on your left as you face toward the Convention Center on Paseo Kukulkán.

✪ La Dolce Vita

Av. Kukulkán, km 14.6, ☎ **98/84-1384.** Reservations required for dinner. Main courses $10–$19. Mon–Fri 1pm–midnight; Sat–Sun 5pm–midnight. ITALIAN.

Prepare to dine on some of the best Italian food in Mexico. Now at its new location on the lagoon, and opposite the Marriot Casamagna, the casually elegant La Dolce Vita is even more pleasant and popular than its old garden location downtown. Appetizers include pâté of quail liver and carpaccio in vinaigrette or watercress salad. You can order such pastas as green tagliolini with lobster medallions, linguine with clams or seafood, or rigatoni Mexican-style (with chorizo, mushrooms, and chives), as an appetizer for half price or as a main course for full price. Other main courses include veal with morels, fresh salmon with cream sauce, scampi, and various fish.

La Fisheria

Plaza Caracol, Second Floor. ☎ **98/83-1395.** Appetizers $3.50–$9; main courses $5.75–$18. Daily 11am–11:30pm. SEAFOOD.

Patrons find a lot to choose from at this restaurant overlooking Boulevard Kukulkán and the lagoon. The expansive menu offers shark fingers with a jalapeño dip, grouper fillet stuffed with seafood in a lobster sauce, Acapulco-style ceviche (in a tomato sauce), New England chowder, steamed mussels, grilled red snapper with pasta—well, I think you can get the idea. The menu changes daily, but there's always tikin xik—that great Yucatecan grilled fish marinated in achiote sauce. And for those not inclined toward seafood, pizza might do, or one of the grilled chicken or beef dishes.

Mango Tango

Km 14, opposite Jack Tar Village. ☎ **98/85-0303.** Main courses $6–$16; dinner show $25–$35. Daily 2pm–2am. INTERNATIONAL.

Mango Tango's made a name for itself with its floor shows (see "Cancún After Dark," below), but its kitchen is no slouch. Try the peel-your-own shrimp, Argentine-style grilled meat with chimichuri sauce, and other grilled specialties. The Mango Tango Salad has shrimp, chicken, avocado, red onion, tomato, and mushrooms on mango slices. Pasta includes Mango Tango rice with seafood and fried bananas. The creole gumbo comes with lobster, shrimp, and squid.

✪ Savios

Plaza Caracol. ☎ **98/83-2085.** Appetizers $4.50–$8.50; main courses $7.75–$20. Daily 10am–11:30pm. ITALIAN.

Savios, in stylish black and white with tile floors and green marble–topped tables, is on two levels, and faces Paseo Kukulkán through two stories of awning shaded windows. Its bar is always crowded with patrons sipping everything from cappuccino to imported beer. Repeat diners look forward to large fresh salads and richly flavored, subtly herbed Italian dishes. I recommend the ravioli stuffed with ricotta and spinach in a delicious tomato sauce.

CANCÚN CITY
EXPENSIVE

✪ La Habichuela

Margaritas 25. ☎ **98/84-3158.** Reservations recommended in high season. Main courses $8–$27. Daily 1pm–midnight. GOURMET SEAFOOD/BEEF/MEXICAN.

In a garden setting with tables covered in pink-and-white linens and soft music in the background, this restaurant is an ideal setting for romance and gourmet dining. For an all-out culinary adventure, try Habichuela (string bean) soup; shrimp in any number of sauces, including Jamaican tamarindo, tequila, and a ginger-and-mushroom combination; and the Mayan coffee with Xtabentun. The grilled seafood and steaks are excellent as well, but this is a good place to try a Mexican specialty such as enchiladas suizas or tampiqueña-style beef. For something totally new try the "Cocobichuela," which is lobster and shrimp in a curry sauce served in a coconut shell and topped with fruit. The restaurant is a few steps from the northwest end of the Parque Palapas on Margaritas.

MODERATE

100% Natural

Av. Sunyaxchen 6. ☎ **98/84-3617.** Breakfast $1.50–$2.50; spaghetti $5; fruit or vegetable shakes $2; sandwiches and Mexican plates $3–$5; coffee $1.50. Daily 7am–11pm. SEMI-VEGETARIAN.

Of all the 100% Naturals around Mexico, this has one of the most appealing settings, with white rattan tables on white tile floor and large dining areas on the street or interior patio. For great mixed-fruit shakes and salads, this is the place. Coffee is expensive but comes with several refills. Full meals include large portions of chicken or fish, spaghetti, or soup and sandwiches. Dine on the pretty patio in back to avoid the roar of Sunyaxchen. The restaurant is near the corner of Avenidas Yaxchilán and Sunyaxchen opposite the Hotel Caribe Internacional. Two other locations with higher prices are in the Zona Hotelera at Plaza Terramar (☎ **83-1180;** open 24 hours) and Plaza Kukulkán (☎ **85-2904;** open 7am to 11pm).

✪ Périco's

Yaxchilán 61. ☎ **98/84-3152.** Appetizers $4–$8; main courses $6–$17. Daily 1pm–1am. MEXICAN/SEAFOOD/STEAKS.

Périco's—with colorful murals that almost dance off the walls, a bar area overhung with baskets and with saddles for bar stools, colorfully bedecked leather tables and chairs, and witty waiters—is always booming and festive. The extensive menu offers well-prepared steak, seafood, and traditional Mexican dishes for moderate rates (except lobster). This is a place not only to eat and drink but to let loose and join in the fun, so don't be surprised if everybody drops their forks and dons huge Mexican sombreros to bob and snake in a conga dance around the dining room. It's fun whether or not you join in. There's marimba music from 7:30 to 10:30pm, and mariachis from 10:30pm to midnight. To find it, go west of Avenida Tulum to the Parque Palapas. Cross the middle of the park, and continue west one block on Gladiolas to Yaxchilán. Périco's is across Yaxchilán at the corner of Chiabal.

✪ Restaurant El Pescador

Tulipanes 28, off Av. Tulum. ☎ **98/84-2673.** Appetizers $5–$10; Seafood $7–$25; Mexican plates $5–$9; beef and chicken $7–$12. Daily 11am–10:30pm. SEAFOOD.

There's often a line at this restaurant, which opened in 1980 serving well-prepared fresh seafood in its streetside patio and upstairs venue overlooking Tulipanes. Feast on cocktails of shrimp, plus conch, fish, octopus, Créole-style shrimp *(camarones a la criolla)*, charcoal-broiled lobster, and stone crabs. Zarzuela is a combination seafood plate cooked in white wine and garlic. There's a Mexican-specialty menu as well. Another branch, La Mesa del Pescador, is in the Plaza Kukulkán and is open the same hours, but is more expensive. The downtown restaurant is a half block east of Avenida Tulum.

✪ Restaurant Los Almendros

Av. Bonampak and Sayil. ☎ **98/87-1332.** Appetizers $1.50–$6; main courses $4–$6. Daily 10:30am–11pm. YUCATECAN.

To steep yourself in Yucatecan cuisine, head directly to this large, colorful, and air-conditioned restaurant. Many readers have written to say they ate nearly every meal here, since the food and service are good and the illustrated menu, with color pictures of dishes, makes ordering easy to do. Some of the regional specialties include lime soup, poc-chuc, chicken or pork pibil, and such appetizers as panuchos yucatecos. The combinado Yucateco is a sampler of four typically Yucatecan main courses—pollo, poc-chuc, sausage, and escabeche. A second location opened in 1994 on Paseo Kukulkán across from the convention center. To find the downtown location, go to the corner of Tulum and Cobá, walk toward Cancún Island (east) two long blocks, and turn right on Avenida Bonampak; it's opposite the bullring seven short blocks ahead.

Restaurant Rosa Mexicano

Claveles 4. ☎ **98/84-6313.** Reservations recommended for parties of six or more. Main courses $6.75–$11; lobster $20. Dinner only daily 5–11pm. MEXICAN HAUTE.

This beautiful little place has candlelit tables and a plant-filled patio in back, and it's almost always packed. Colorful paper banners and piñatas hang from the ceiling, efficient waiters wear bow ties and cummerbunds color-themed to the Mexican flag, and a trio plays romantic Mexican music nightly. The menu features "refined" Mexican specialties. Try the *pollo almendro*, which is chicken covered in a cream sauce sprinkled with ground almonds, plus rice and vegetables, or the pork baked in a banana leaf with a sauce of oranges, lime, chile ancho, and garlic. The steak tampiqueño is a huge platter that comes with guacamole salad, quesadillas, beans, salad, and rice. The restaurant is a half block east of Avenida Tulum.

INEXPENSIVE

⑤ Gory Tacos

Tulipanes 26. No phone. Breakfast $1.50–$2.50; sandwiches $2–$3; tacos $2.25–$3.25; grilled specialties $5–$6; daily special $6.50; soft drinks 65¢; beer 80¢. Daily 9am–11pm. MEXICAN.

The clean decor here, with 10 pine benches and pink-tile tables, welcomes you to sit and sample the excellent food. The hamburgers are close to Stateside fixings, and the french fries are thick. Sandwiches come on big fresh rolls; the quesadillas are packed with cheese and enveloped in fresh flour tortillas. Besides fast food, you can order grilled fish, beef, and chicken—all of which come with french fries, beans, salad, and tortillas. The daily special is a real tanker-upper with two choices of meat or seafood, rice, salad, baked potato, and bread. It's a half block from Tulum on the first Tulipanes and next to the Restaurant El Pescador.

Pizza Rolandi

Cobá 12. ☎ **98/84-4047.** Appetizers $2.50–$7; pasta $5–$7; pizza and main courses $4.50–$9. Mon–Sat 1pm–midnight; Sun 1pm–11pm. ITALIAN.

At this shaded outdoor patio restaurant you can choose from almost two dozen different wood-oven pizzas and a full selection of spaghetti, calzones, and Italian style chicken and beef and desserts. There's a full bar list as well. To find it from the corner of Tulum and Cobá, walk east (toward the island) a few steps; Rolandi's is on the left.

⑤ Restaurant Curva

Av. Yaxchilán at Sunyaxchen. No phone. Breakfast $1.75–$2.50; comida corrida $2.50–$3. Mon-Sat 9am–5pm. MEXICAN.

It's worth a wait for a seat at one of the six tables in this tiny, and spotless, storefront café. You'll join young office workers and students for an inexpensive home-style lunch. The daily comida includes soup, rice, beans, and meat. There's usually a choice of main courses, such as beef tips, pozole, pollo adobado, and pollo frito. Lingering is not appreciated during lunchtime. The restaurant is at the bend where Avenida Yaxchilán meets Avenida Sunyaxchen.

Restaurante Santa María

Azucenas at Parque Palapas. No phone. Appetizers $1.75–$4; tacos 75¢–$5; main courses $3.50–$9. Daily 5pm–10pm. MEXICAN.

The open-air Santa María restaurant is a clean, gaily decked-out place to sample authentic Mexican food. It's cool and breezy with patio dining that's open on two sides and furnished in leather tables and chairs covered in multicolored cloths. A bowl of frijoles de olla and an order of beefsteak tacos will fill you up for a low price. You may want to try tortilla soup or enchiladas, or go for one of the grilled U.S.–cut steaks, order of fajitas, ribs, or grilled seafood, all of which arrive with a baked potato. The restaurant is opposite the north end of the Parque Palapas 2$1/2$ blocks west of Tulum.

Stefano's

Bonampak 177. ☎ **98/84-1715.** Appetizers $3–$5; main courses $4.75–$6.25; pizza $4.75–$6.75. Wed–Mon 2pm–midnight. ITALIAN/PIZZA/PASTA.

Tourists are beginning to find Stefano's, with its Italian decor and food with a few Mexican accents. For example there's a huitlacoche-and-shrimp pizza, rigatoni in tequila sauce, and seafood with chile peppers, nestled proudly with the Stefano special pizza made with fresh tomato, cheese, and pesto, and calzones stuffed with spinach, Mozzarella, and tomato sauce. For dessert the Ricotta strudel is something out of the ordinary, plus tiramisú, and lots of different coffees and mixed drinks. Stefano's is on Bonampak just around the corner from Cobá, on the west side of the street opposite the Pemex station.

⑤ El Tacolote

Av. Coba 19 at Alatraces. ☎ **98/87-3045.** Delivery 87-3045. Appetizers $1.50–$2.50; main courses $5.50–$8; grilled dinner for two $16. Daily noon–2am. MEXICAN/GRILLED MEAT.

The ranch theme of red brick, wagon wheels, glossy dark-wood tables and chairs, and an open grill is fitting for a place specializing in grilled meats. Steaks are the specialty and northern Mexico–style charro beans are a staple. Tacos come many ways and are made with several meats—pork, chicken, beef and al pastor—with a wide variety of garnishes—cheese, onions, bacon, mushrooms, tomatoes, and cilantro. The same meats are featured as dinner specials. There's a nice size drink list. If you'd rather order in, they'll deliver. It's at the corner of Avenidas Cobá and Alcatrases.

COFFEE AND PASTRIES

Pasteleria Italiana

Av. Yaxchilan 67, SM 25, near Sunyaxchen. ☎ **98/84-0796.** Pastries $1.75–$2.25; ice cream $2; coffee $1–$2. Mon–Sat 9am–10pm, Sun 2pm–9pm. COFFEE/PASTRIES/ICE CREAM.

More like a casual neighborhood coffeehouse than a place aimed at tourists, this shady little respite has been doing business here since 1977. You'll spot it by the white awning that covers the small, outdoor, plant-filled table area. Inside are refrigerated cases of tarts, and scrumptious-looking cakes, ready to be carried away in their entirety or by the piece. The coffeehouse is in the same block as Perico's, between Maraño and Chiabal.

A DELICATESSEN

Super Deli

Tulum at Xcaret/Cobá. ☎ **98/84-1412.** Breakfast $2–$7.50; sandwiches $5–$7.50; pizzas $5.75–$8. Daily 24 hours. DELICATESSEN.

You can't miss the trendy awning and outdoor restaurant here. It's very popular for light or substantial meals any time, and inside is a well-stocked, medium-size grocery store with an excellent delicatessen. Dining choices include pizza, pasta, steaks, burgers, baguette sandwiches, and a variety of coffees, wine, and beer. There's another branch on the island in the Plaza Nautilus. This Cancún City location is on the west side of Tulum just past the intersection of Tulum and Xcaret, almost next to the Hotel Handall.

5 Beaches, Water Sports & Other Things to Do

Although most people come to Cancún to kick back and relax on the beach, options for exploring beyond your selected beach chair are numerous. If you need a travel agent, I highly recommend **Mayaland Tours,** Avenida Tulum at Cóba in the Hotel América (☎ **98/87-2450;** fax 98/87-2438). The company pioneered tourism in the Yucatán, and has a better handle on it than most others. I've seen their double-decker buses running the route south to Tulum and Xel-Ha and elsewhere, and now they're a full-service travel agency handling not only tours all over the Yucatán

Peninsula, but plane reservations. They own hotels in Mérida, Uxmal, and Chichén-Itzá and can arrange a free rental car with reservations at their hotels.

The first thing to do is explore the Zona Hotelera on Isla Cancún, just to see the fabulous resort itself and to get your bearings. Frequent **Ruta 1** or **Ruta 2 buses** marked "Hoteles" and those marked "Turismo" run from the mainland city along the full 12 miles to the end of the island and cost around 75¢ per ride. You can get on and off anywhere to visit hotels, shopping centers, and beaches (but you pay to ride again).

THE BEACHES   The best stretches of beach are dominated by the big hotels. All of Mexico's beaches are public property. Be especially careful on beaches fronting the open Caribbean, where the undertow can be deadly. Swim where there's a lifeguard. By contrast, the waters of Mujeres Bay (Bahía Mujeres) at the north end of the island are usually calm. Get to know Cancún's water-safety pennant system, and make sure to check the flag at any beach or hotel before entering the water. Here's how it goes:

- White   Excellent
- Green   Normal conditions (safe)
- Yellow   Changeable, uncertain (use caution)
- Black or Red   Unsafe—use the swimming pool instead!

Here in the Caribbean, storms can arrive and conditions can change from safe to unsafe in a matter of minutes, so be alert: If you see dark clouds heading your way, make your way to shore and wait until the storm passes and the green flag is displayed again.

Playa Tortuga (Turtle Beach) is the public beach. Besides swimming, you can rent a sailboard and take lessons there. There's a small but beautiful portion of public beach on **Playa Caracol,** by the Xcaret Terminal. Both of these face the calm waters of Bahía Mujeres and for that reason are much better than those facing the Caribbean.

WATER SPORTS   Many beachside hotels offer water-sports concessions that include rental of rubber rafts, kayaks, and snorkeling equipment. On the calm Nichupte Lagoon are outlets for renting sailboats, water jets, and waterskis. Prices vary and are often negotiable, so check around.

Besides **snorkeling** at Garrafón National Park (see "Boating Excursions," below), travel agencies offer an all-day excursion to the natural wildlife habitat of Isla Contoy, which usually includes time for snorkeling. It costs more than doing it on your own from Isla Mujeres (see Chapter 4 for details).

You can arrange a day of **deep-sea fishing** at one of the numerous piers or travel agencies for around $150 to $250 for four hours for up to four people.

Scuba trips run around $60 and include two tanks. **Scuba Cancún,** Paseo Kukulkán, km 5, on the lagoon side (☎ **83-1011,** fax 84-2336, open 8:30am to 6pm, phone reservations also available in the evenings from 7:30 to 10:30pm using the fax line), offers a four-hour resort course for $70. Full certification takes four to five days and costs around $350. Scuba Cancún also offers diving trips to 12 nearby reefs, including Cuevones at 30 feet and the open ocean at 50 to 60 feet (offered in good weather only). The average dive is around 35 feet. The farthest reef is about 40 minutes away. Drift diving is the norm here and the big attractions are the coral reefs, where there are hundreds of fish. One-tank dives cost $45, and two-tank dives cost $56. Dives usually start around 10am and return by 2:15. **Snorkeling** trips cost $24 and leave every afternoon after 2pm, going to shallow reefs about a 20-minute boat ride away.

For windsurfing, go to the Playa Tortuga public beach, where there's a **Windsurfing School** (☎ 84-2023) with equipment for rent.

BOATING EXCURSIONS   The island of Isla Mujeres, just 10 miles offshore, is one of the most pleasant day trips from Cancún. At one end is **El Garrafón National Underwater Park,** which is excellent for snorkeling. And at the other end is the delightful village with small shops, restaurants, and hotels, and Playa Norte, the island's best beach. (See Chapter 4 for more on Isla Mujeres.) If you're looking for relaxation and can spare the time, Isla Mujeres is worth several days.

There are four ways to get there: by frequent public ferry from Puerto Juárez, which takes between 20 and 45 minutes; by a shuttle boat from Playa Linda or Playa Tortuga (a one-hour ride but with irregular service); by the Watertaxi (also with limited service), next to the Xcaret Terminal; and by one of the day-long pleasure boats, most of which leave from the Playa Linda pier.

It's easy to go on your own. The Puerto Juárez **public ferries** are just a few miles from downtown Cancún. From Cancún City, take the Ruta 8 bus on Avenida Tulum to Puerto Juárez; the ferry docks in downtown Isla Mujeres by all the shops, restaurants, hotels, and Norte Beach. You'll need a taxi to go to Garrafón Park at the other end of the island. You can stay as long as you like (even overnight) and return by ferry, but be sure to ask about the time of the last returning ferry—don't depend on the posted hours. Taxi fare from downtown Cancún to the pier will cost around $6. The ferry costs $1.50 to $3 one-way. (For more details and a shuttle schedule, see Chapter 4.)

Pleasure boat cruises to Isla Mujeres are a favorite pastime here. Modern motor yachts, catamarans, trimarans, and even old-time sloops take swimmers, sunners, snorkelers, and shoppers out into the limpid waters. Some tours include a snorkeling stop at Garrafón, lunch on the beach, and a short time for shopping in downtown Isla Mujeres. Most leave at 9:30 or 10am; last about five or six hours; and include continental breakfast, lunch, and rental of snorkel gear. Others, particularly the sunset and night cruises, go to beaches away from town for pseudo-pirate shows and include a lobster dinner or Mexican buffet. If you want to actually see Isla Mujeres, go on a morning cruise, or go on your own and return on the public ferry.

Tour companies are also beginning to offer cruises that emphasize Cancún's natural attributes. The **lagoons** along the Zona Hotelera are ideal for spotting herons, egrets, and crabs in the mangroves. Often billed as **jungle cruises,** they don't go to a jungle but they usually include time for lagoon snorkeling. Other excursions go to the **reefs** in glass-bottom boats, so you can have a near-scuba-diving experience and see many colorful fish. However, the reefs are a distance from shore and impossible to reach on windy days with choppy seas. They've also suffered through overuse and their condition is far from pristine. The **Nautibus** (☎ 83-3552 or 83-2119), one of those offering glass-bottom boat trips to the reefs, has been around for years. The trip in a glass bottom boat from the Playa Linda pier to the Chitale coral reef to see colorful fish, takes about one hour and 20 minutes. Around 50 minutes is consumed going to and from the reef. Cokes are included in the price of the trip, which costs $24 per person. Still other boat excursions visit Isla Contoy, a **national bird sanctuary** that's well worth the time. If you are planning to spend time in Isla Mujeres, the Contoy trip is easier and more pleasurable to take from there.

The operators and names of boats offering excursions change often. To find out what's available when you're there, check with a local travel agent or hotel tour desk, for they should have a wide range of options. You can also go to the Playa Linda Pier either a day ahead or the day of your intended outing and buy your own ticket. If you go on the day of your trip, arrive at the pier around 8:45am, since most boats leave around 9 or 9:30am.

RUINAS EL REY   Cancún has its own Maya ruins. It's a small site and not impressive compared to ruins at Tulum, Cobá, or Chichén-Itzá. The Maya fishermen built this small ceremonial center and settlement very early in the history of Maya culture. It was then abandoned, to be resettled later near the end of the Postclassic period, not long before the arrival of the conquistadores. The platforms of numerous small temples are visible amid the banana plants, papayas, and wildflowers. A new golf course has been built around the ruins, but there is a separate entrance for sightseers. You'll find the ruins about 13 miles from town, at the southern reaches of the Zona Hotelera, almost to Punta Nizuc. Look for the Caesar's Palace hotel on the left (east), then the ruins on the right (west). Admission is $4.50 (free on Sundays and holidays); the hours are daily from 8am to 5pm.

A MUSEUM   To the right side of the entrance to the Cancún Convention Center is the **Museo Arqueológico de Cancún,** a small but interesting museum with relics from archaeological sites around the state. Admission is $1.75 (free on Sundays and holidays); the hours are Tuesday to Saturday from 9am to 7pm, Sunday from 10am to 5pm.

BULLFIGHTS   Cancún has a small bullring (☎ **98/84-8372**) near the northern (town) end of Paseo Kukulkán opposite the Restaurant Los Almendros. Bullfights are held every Wednesday at 3:30pm during the winter tourist season. There are usually four bulls. Travel agencies in Cancún sell tickets: $45 for adults and $25 for children.

6 Shopping

Although shops in Cancún are more expensive than their equivalents in any other Mexican city, most visitors spend a portion of their time browsing.

There are several open-air **crafts markets** easily visible on Avenida Tulum in Cancún City and near the convention center in the hotel zone.

Malls on Cancún Island are air-conditioned, sleek, and sophisticated. Most of these are located one after another on Paseo Kukulkán between km 7 and km 12—Plaza Lagunas, Costa Brava, La Mansión, Mayfair, Plaza Terramar, Plaza Caracol, Plaza Flamingo, and Plaza Kukulkán. These malls offer shops selling anything from fine crystal and silver to designer clothing and decorative objects. Numerous restaurants are interspersed among the shops, many with prices higher than their branches on the mainland. Stores are generally open daily from 10am to 8 or 10pm. Stores in malls near the convention center generally stay open all day, but some, and especially in malls farther out, close between 2 and 5pm. Here's a brief rundown on the malls and some of the shops each contain. Inside the **Plaza Kukulkán** you'll find a branch of Banco Serfin, OK Maguey Cantina Grill, a movie theater with U.S. movies, Tikal, a shop with Guatemalan textile clothing, several crafts stores, a liquor store, a bathing suit specialty store, a record and tape outlet, all leather goods including shoes and sandals, and another specializing in silver from Taxco. In the food court are a number of U.S. franchise restaurants, plus one featuring specialty coffee.

Planet Hollywood anchors the **Plaza Flamingo,** but inside you'll also pass a branch of the Bancrecer, Denny's, Subway sandwiches, and La Casa del Habana for Cuban Cigars.

The long meandering **Plaza Caracol** holds outlets for Cartier jewelry, Aca Joe, Guess, Señor Frog clothing, Waterford crystal, Samsonite luggage, Thomas Moore Travel, Gucci, Fuji film, Mr. Papa's, and La Fisheria restaurant.

Mayfair Plaza is the oldest, with an open bricked center that's lively with people sitting in open-air restaurants and bars such as Tequila Sunrise, Fat Tuesday, El Mexicano (a dinner show restaurant), Hard Rock Café, Pizza Hut, and several stores selling silver, leather, and crafts.

7 Cancún After Dark

One of Cancún's draws is its active nightlife. Sometimes there's entertainment enough just strolling along thriving Avenida Tulum, where restaurant employees show off enticing sample plates to lure in passersby. But the **Centro Comercio Mayfair** (shopping center) on the island is just about the liveliest place for spending an evening hanging out, going from restaurant, to drinking establishment, to restaurant. It's one of the first shopping centers on the island, and the only one with a large open-air center that's ideal for sitting outside to eat and drink and meet other vacationers having a good time. Snazzy discos and a variety of lobby entertainment are all part of the island nighttime scene at many of the better hotels.

CONVENTION CENTER   The long-awaited convention center is open with slick (and I mean slick) marble floors, arcades of fashionable shops and restaurants, entertainment, meeting rooms, and an auditorium.

THE PERFORMING ARTS   Nightly performances of the **Ballet Folklórico de Cancún** (☎ 98/83-0199, ext. 193 and 194), are held at the Cancún Convention Center. Tickets are sold between 8am and 9pm at a booth just as you enter the Convention Center. You can go for dinner and the show, or just the show. Dinner/show guests pay around $35, and arrive at 6:30pm for drinks, which is followed by dinner at 7pm, and the show at 8pm. The price includes an open bar, dinner, show, tax, and tip. Guests preferring only the show arrive at 7:30pm and pay $22. Several hotels host **Mexican fiesta nights,** including a buffet dinner and a folkloric dance show; admission, including dinner, ranges from $35 to $50. A Ballet Folklórico appears Monday through Saturday nights in a 1-hour-and-15-minute show at the **Continental Villas Plaza** (☎ 98/85-1444, ext. 5690). The **Hyatt Regency Cancún** (☎ 98/83-1234) has a dinner, folkloric, and mariachi fiesta, Tuesday through Sunday nights during the high season, as does the **Camino Real** (☎ 98/83-1200). **El Mexicano restaurant** (☎ 98/84-4207), in the Costa Blanca shopping center, hosts a tropical dinner show every night as well as live music for dancing. The entertainment alternates each night with mariachis entertaining intermittently from 7:30 to 11pm and a folkloric show from 8 to 9:30pm.

Mango Tango, Paseo Kukulkán km 14. ☎ 98/85-0303. Get in a party mood at this lagoon side restaurant/dinner show establishment. Diners can choose from two levels, one nearer the music and the other overlooking it all. Music is loud and varied. The 1-hour-and-20-minute dinner show begins at 8pm nightly and costs $25 to $35. At 9:30pm live reggae music begins and there's no cover. If you want to enjoy the show without a meal, just order a drink and be seated at an upper-level table. It's opposite the Jack Tar Village.

On Fridays at 7:30pm the downtown **Parque de las Palapas** hosts Noches Caribeños with tropical music and dancing.

THE CLUB & MUSIC SCENE   Clubbing in Cancún, still called discoing here, is a raucous affair. Many of the big hotels have nightclubs, usually a disco or at least live music, and a lobby bar. However, they're expensive: Expect to pay a cover charge of $8 to $20 per person in the discos or show bars and $4 to $7 for a drink. Numerous restaurants, such as **Carlos 'n' Charlie's, Planet Hollywood, Hard Rock Café,**

Señor Frog, TGI Friday's, and **Périco's** (for the last, see "Where to Eat," above), double as late-night party spots; the first four attract hordes of spring-breakers and offer wildish fun at a fraction of the prices of more costly evening entertainment. Certainly the most sophisticated and upscale of all Cancún's nightly gathering spots is the Club Grill restaurant of the **Ritz-Carlton Hotel,** where diners with reservations enjoy soft, low-key music to dance by.

Carlos O'Brien's, Tulum 29, SM 22. ☎ **98/84-1659.** With taped music, this is one of the tamer of the Carlos Anderson restaurants/night spots in town (Señor Frog and Carlos 'n Charlies are two others), but it has its lively moments, depending on the crowd. It's open daily from 11am to 12:30am.

Christine's, at the Hotel Krystal on the island (☎ **98/83-1793**), is one of the most popular discos. The dress code is no shorts or jeans. It's open at 9:30pm nightly.

Dady'O, Paseo Kukulkán, km 9.5., is the current heavyweight champion, with lines long enough to make you think you're in New York or L.A. It opens at 9:30pm nightly.

La Boom, Bulevar Kukulkán, km 3.5 (☎ **98/83-1152**), has two sections: On one side is a video bar, and on the other is a bilevel disco with the required cranium-cracking music. There's blessed air-conditioning in both places. Each night there may be a special client-getting attraction like no cover, free bar, ladies' night, or bikini night. It's open nightly from 8pm to 6am. A sound-and-light show begins at 11:30pm in the disco.

Azucar Bar Caribeño, adjacent to the Hotel Camino Real (☎ **98/83-0441**), offers spicy tropical dancing of the salsa, meringue, and bolero kind, with bands from Cuba, Jamaica, and the Dominican Republic; it's open Monday to Saturday from 9:30pm to 4am.

Tequila Sunrise Grill Bar & Fiesta, in the Mayfair Shopping Center above the Pizza Hut, is a restaurant, but it's also a lively dancing spot with tempting music drifting down to the plaza below; there's no cover, and it's open daily from 7pm to 4am.

Hard Rock Café, also in the Mayfair Shopping Center (☎ **98/83-2024**) entertains with a live band at 10:30pm every night except Wednesday. Other hours you'll get your share of lively recorded music to munch by—the menu combines the most popular foods from American and Mexican cultures. It's open daily from 10am to 2am.

Planet Hollywood, Flamingo Shopping Center, Paseo Kukulkán km 11 (☎ **98/85-3022**), is the trendy brainchild of Sylvester Stallone, Bruce Willis, and Arnold Schwarzenegger. It's both a restaurant and nighttime music/dance spot with megadecible live music. It's open daily from 11am to 2am.

Carlos 'n' Charlie's, Paseo Kukulkán km 4.5 (☎ **98/83-0846**), is a reliable place to find both good food and frat house–level entertainment in the evenings. There's a dance floor to go along with the live music that starts nightly around 9pm. A cover charge is implemented if you're not planning to eat. It's open daily from noon to 2am.

SPORTS WAGERING   This form of entertainment seems to be sweeping Mexico's resorts. TV screens mounted around the room at **LF Caliente** (☎ **98/83-3704**), at the Fiesta Americana Hotel, show all the action in racetrack, football, soccer, and so on in a bar/lounge setting.

8 Road Trips from Cancún

Outside of Cancún are all the many wonders of the Yucatán Peninsula; you'll find the details in Chapters 4 and 5. Cancún can be a perfect base for day- or overnight trips or the starting point for a longer exploration. Any travel agency or hotel tour desk in Cancún can book these tours, or you can elect to do them on your own via local bus or rental car. The Maya ruins to the south at **Tulum** or **Cobá** should be your first goal, then perhaps the *caleta* (cove) of **Xel-Ha** or the new lagoon day trip to **Xcaret.** And if you're going south, consider staying a night or two on the island of **Cozumel** or at one of the budget resorts on the **Tulum coast** or **Punta Allen,** south of the Tulum ruins. **Isla Mujeres** is an easy day trip off mainland Cancún (see Chapter 4).

About 80 miles south of Cancún begins the **Sian Ka'an Biosphere Reserve,** a 1.3 million-acre area set aside in 1986 to preserve a region of tropical forests, savannas, mangroves, canals, lagoons, bays, cenotes, and coral reefs, all of which are home to hundreds of birds and land and marine animals (see Chapter 4 for details). The Friends of Sian Ka'an, a nonprofit group based in Cancún, offers biologist-escorted day trips from Cancún daily (weather permitting) at $115 per person. The price includes lunch, round-trip van transportation to the reserve, a guided boat/birding trip through one of the reserve's lagoons, and use of binoculars. For reservations, contact Amigos de Sian Ka'an, Plaza America (☎ 84-9583; fax 87-3080), or make reservations through a Cancún travel agent.

Although I don't recommend it, by driving fast or catching the right buses, you can go inland to **Chichén-Itzá,** explore the ruins, and return in a day, but it's much better to spend at least two days seeing Chichén-Itzá, Mérida, and Uxmal. See Chapter 5 for transportation details and further information on these destinations.

Isla Mujeres, Cozumel & the Caribbean Coast

Once obscured by Cancún's glitter, Mexico's other Caribbean vacation spots have shouldered their way into the tourist spotlight. **Isla Mujeres,** just a short ferry ride from Cancún, offers low-priced and low-key Caribbean relaxation. The island of **Cozumel,** somewhere on the spectrum between Isla Mujeres's slow pace and Cancún's fast-lane bustle, has scuba and snorkeling possibilities that compare with any in the world. And the Quintana Roo coast, dubbed the **Costa Turquesa** (Turquoise Coast), stretches south from Cancún all the way to Chetumal—230 miles of powdery white-sand beaches, lush jungle, crystal-clear lagoons full of coral and colorful fish, flashy new resorts, and inexpensive hideaways. It also includes some hideaway nuggets on both the **Punta Allen Peninsula** and the **Majahual Peninsula.**

Chapter 5 supplies full information on points west of Cancún, such as Chichén-Itzá and Mérida. Let's look now at the islands off the peninsula, and the mainland coast south of Cancún.

EXPLORING MEXICO'S CARIBBEAN
ISLA MUJERES

Many people enjoy a brief day trip to Isla Mujeres on a party boat from Cancún, which is fine if you don't have much time. However, most of those trips provide little time in the village, and you get no sense of what island life is like. Besides loafing, fishing, and snorkeling, diving is one of its main attractions. I recommend at least two nights in Isla Mujeres, and you could even spend a whole week relaxing here.

Passenger ferries go to Isla Mujeres from Puerto Juárez near Cancún, and car ferries to Isla Mujeres leave from Punta Sam, also near Cancún. More expensive passenger ferries, with less frequent departures than from Puerto Juárez, also go to Isla Mujeres from Playa Linda on Cancún Island.

COZUMEL

This truly laid-back island getaway is a perfect place to relax for a week or more, with opportunities for the best diving in Mexico, good fishing, and excursions to villages and ruins only a ferry ride away on the mainland. If you're considering a package (usually offered for three or four nights) remember that you'll spend a day coming and going. Buy a longer package if you can, but remember that there are many inexpensive places to stay that won't be part of a package deal and you can still do all the diving and sightseeing you want.

A car/passenger ferry runs between Puerto Morelos (south of Cancún) and Cozumel. Passenger ferries also run between Playa del Carmen and Cozumel—the preferred way to go, if you aren't flying.

THE COSTA TURQUESA

Signs pointing to brand-new, expensive resort developments are sprouting up all along Highway 307 from Cancún south to **Tulum,** a stretch known as the "Tulum Corridor." Some are actually under construction and others may never progress further than a big sign and a pipe dream. This frenzy of construction is changing the character of Corridor, but there are still plenty of small, inexpensive beachfront hideaways, as well as luxury places, just a short distance from the highway. And south of Tulum, almost 100 miles of this coast have been saved from developers and set aside as the Sian Ka'an Biosphere Reserve.

A trip down the coast is a great way to spend a day of a vacation centered in Cancún. The most popular agency-led tour out of Cancún is to the ruins of Tulum, followed by a stop at Xel-Ha for a swim and/or snorkeling in the beautiful clear lagoon. Once a placid and little-known spot, Xcaret Lagoon opened in 1991 as a full-blown tourist attraction for people who plan to spend the day.

The Costa Turquesa is best experienced in a car. (See Chapter 3, "Cancún," for information on rentals.) It's not impossible to get about by bus, but doing so requires careful planning, more time, and lots of patience. Besides Cancún, Playa del Carmen has the best selection of bus services. There are frequent buses between Cancún and Chetumal that stop at the more populous towns—Playa del Carmen, Tulum, and Felipe Carrillo Puerto. These buses will also let you off on the highway if you want to go to Xel-Ha, Xcaret, Pamul, or other spots, but you'll have to walk the mile or so from the highway to your destination. However, a few bus lines now take passengers directly into these popular day-trip destinations. (See "By Bus" in Chapter 2, "Planning a Trip to the Yucatán," for details.) To return on buses not offering door-to-door service, you'll have to walk back and wait on a sweltering highway along with hordes of ravenous mosquitoes to flag a passing bus—and be prepared to watch buses pass you by if they're full. Hitching a ride with other travelers is another possibility, though I don't recommend hitchhiking on the highway. You can always hire a taxi for the return to Cancún.

Highway 307 south of Cancún is flanked by jungle on both sides, except where there are beaches and beach settlements. Traffic, which was once scarce, can be dangerously dense. (See "On the Road in the Yucatán," below.)

Here are some drive times from Cancún: Puerto Morelos (port for the car ferry to Cozumel), 45 minutes; Playa del Carmen (a laid-back beachside village) 1 hour; Xcaret Lagoon and Pamul, $1^1/4$ hours; Akumal, $1^3/4$ hours; Xel-Ha and Tulum, around 2 hours; and Chetumal, about 5 hours.

THE PUNTA ALLEN & MAJAHUAL PENINSULAS

These two areas will appeal to people looking for totally off-the-beaten-track travel, and/or for world-class adventure sports. Punta Allen's saltwater fly-fishing is extraordinary, and the Chinchorro Banks, 22 miles off Majahual's little village of Xcalak, is perhaps the last example of a pristine Caribbean reef—the diving is spectacular. Both places are hard to get to, have beautiful beaches, are overrun by exotic birdlife and jungle flora, and have a few laid-back, rustic inns to stay at.

THE RÍO BEC RUIN ROUTE

Between Lago Bacalar and Escarcega is the **Río Bec** ruin route where several "new" sites are open to the public, and others are available with special permission.

CHETUMAL

Though **Chetumal** is the capital of Quintana Roo state, it has little to recommend it. It's best to think of it as a gateway to Guatemala, Belize, the several ruins near the city, and the excellent diving and fishing to be had off the Xcalak Peninsula. This year a fantastic museum opened in Chetumal, and the reexcavation of many of the ruins near Chetumal may be a reason for a detour there, but Lago Bacalar is the preferred place to stay near Chetumal.

1 Isla Mujeres

10 miles N of Cancún

For total, laid-back, inexpensive Caribbean relaxation, it's hard to beat Isla Mujeres. Often called the "poor man's Cancún," Isla Mujeres is a bargain compared to Cancún—and I much prefer it. The sand streets have been bricked, and some of the original Caribbean-style clapboard houses remain to add a colorful and authentic reminder of the island's past. Suntanned visitors hang out in open-air cafés and stroll streets lined with frantic souvenir vendors who beckon them like carnival barkers.

As packed as days can be, with trips to the Isla Contoy bird sanctuary and excellent diving, fishing, and snorkeling, in the evenings most people find the slow, relaxing pace one of the island's biggest draws. Then it's bathed in a cool breeze that's perfect for casual open-air dining and drinking in small streetside eateries. Most people pack it in as early as 9 or 10pm, when most of the businesses close. Restless night owls, however, will find kindred souls at a few bars on Playa Norte that stay open until the wee hours.

There are two versions of how Isla Mujeres ("Island of Women") got its name. The more popular story claims that pirates parked their women here for safekeeping while they were marauding the Spanish Main. The other account attributes the name to conquistador Francisco Hernández de Córdoba, who was reportedly impressed by the large number of female terra-cotta figurines he found in temples on the island.

ESSENTIALS

GETTING THERE & DEPARTING

Puerto Juárez, just north of Cancún, is the dock for the passenger ferries to Isla Mujeres. The *Caribbean Queen* makes the trip many times daily; it takes 45 minutes and the fare is $1.50. The newer *Caribbean Express* makes the trip in 20 minutes; the cost is $3. Ferries run frequently between 6am and 8pm. Pay at the ticket office, or if the ferry is about to leave, you can pay aboard. Taxi fares are now posted at the lot where the taxis park. The fare to the Cancún airport is $10; to downtown Cancún, $4; and to the Hotel Zone, $6 to $8.50.

Isla Mujeres is so small that a vehicle isn't necessary, but if you're taking a vehicle to Isla Mujeres, you'll use the Punta Sam port a little farther past Puerto Juárez. The ferry runs the 40-minute trip five or six times daily all year except in bad weather (check with the tourist office in Cancún for a current schedule). Cars should arrive an hour in advance of the ferry departure to register for a place in line and pay the posted fee.

There are also boats from the Playa Linda pier in Cancún, but they're less frequent and much more expensive—$13 one way—than those from Puerto Juárez. The Playa

Linda ferries simply don't run if there isn't a crowd. When I checked, a new **Watertaxi** (☎ **86-4270** or **86-4847**) to Isla Mujeres was operating from Playa Caracol, between the Fiesta Americana Coral Beach Hotel and the Xcaret terminal on the island, at a cost of $12. Their scheduled departures were 9 and 11am and 1 and 3pm with returns from Isla Mujeres at 10am, noon, 2, and 5pm.

To get to either Puerto Juárez or Punta Sam from Cancún, take any Ruta 8 city bus from Avenida Tulum. If you're coming from Mérida, you can either fly to Cancún and then proceed by bus to Puerto Juárez, or you can take a first- or second-class bus directly from the Mérida bus station to Puerto Juárez; they leave several times a day. From Cozumel, you can either fly to Cancún (there are daily flights) or take a ferry to Playa del Carmen (see the Cozumel section below for details), where you can catch a bus to Puerto Juárez.

ORIENTATION
Arriving

Ferries arrive at the dock in the center of town. Taxis are always lined up in front and ask around $1 to $2 to take you to almost any hotel. The price gets lower if you wait until all passengers have left the area. Negotiate directly with the driver, not a representative who recruits passengers by quoting half the price the driver actually charges. Rates are posted at the taxi co-op to the right of the pier as you leave the ferry. Tricycle taxis are the least expensive and a merry way to arrive at your hotel. Unless you're loaded with luggage, you don't need transportation since most hotels are close by.

Visitor Information

The **City Tourist Office** (☎ and fax **987/7-0316**) has moved again with its latest location on the second floor of the Plaza Isla Mujeres. You'll find it at the northern end of Juárez, between López Mateos and Matamoros, It's open Monday–Friday 9am to 2:30pm and 7 to 9pm. Also look for *Islander,* a free publication with history, local information, advertisements, and list of events (if any).

Island Layout

Isla Mujeres is about 5 miles long and 2$^1/_2$ miles wide. The **ferry docks** are right at the center of town, within walking distance of most hotels. The street running along the waterfront is **Rueda Medina,** commonly called the **malecón.** The **market** (Mercado Municipal) is by the post office on **Calle Guerrero,** an inland street at the north edge of town, which, like most streets in the town, is unmarked.

Getting Around

A popular form of transportation on Isla Mujeres is the electric golf cart, available for rent at many hotels for $10 per hour or $50 per day. They don't go more than 20 miles per hour, so don't expect to speed around the island, but they're fun. Anyway, on Isla Mujeres you aren't there to hurry. Many people enjoy touring the island by moto, the local sobriquet for motorized bikes and scooters. If you don't want to fool with shifting gears, rent a fully automatic one for around $30 per day or $6 per hour. They come with seats for one person, but some are large enough for two. Whatever you rent, take time to get familiar with how the vehicles work, and be careful on the road as you approach blind corners and hills where visibility is poor. There's only one main road with a couple of offshoots, so you won't get lost. Be aware that the rental price does not include insurance, and any injury to yourself or the vehicle will come out of your pocket. Bicycles are also available for rent at some hotels for $5 per day.

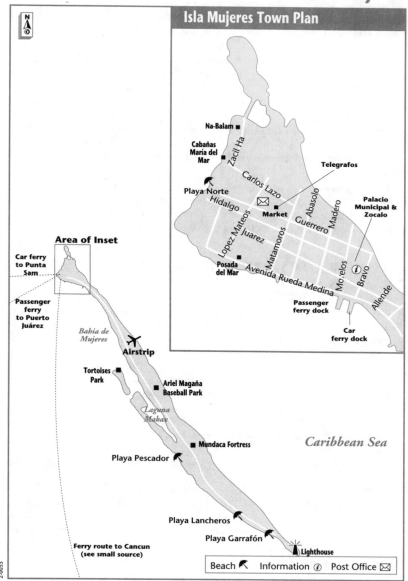

Isla Mujeres

Isla Mujeres Town Plan

N

Area of Inset

Car ferry to Punta Sam

Passenger ferry to Puerto Juárez

Bahia de Mujeres

✈ **Airstrip**

Tortoises Park

Ariel Magaña Baseball Park

Laguna Makaz

Mundaca Fortress

Playa Pescador

Caribbean Sea

Playa Lancheros

Playa Garrafón

Lighthouse

Ferry route to Cancun (see small source)

Na-Balam

Cabañas María del Mar

Zacil Ha

Carlos Lazo

Telegrafos

Playa Norte

Hidalgo

Market

Palacio Municipal & Zocalo

Lopez Mateos

Juarez

Matamoros

Guerrero

Abasolo

Madero

Posada del Mar

Avenida Rueda Medina

Morelos

Bravo

Allende

Passenger ferry dock

Car ferry dock

Beach 🏖   Information ⓘ   Post Office ✉

2-0055

FAST FACTS: Isla Mujeres

Area Code   The area code of Isla Mujeres is 987. The first digit for all telephone numbers on the island has been changed from 2 to 7.

Hospital   The Hospital de la Armada, on Medina at Ojon P. Blanco (☎ 7-0001). It's half a mile south of the town center.

Impressions

It becomes a virtue, almost a necessity, to do some loafing. The art of leisure is therefore one of Mexico's most stubbornly defended practises [sic] and one of her subtle appeals; a lesson in civilization which we of the hectic north need very badly to learn.
—Anita Brenner, *Your Mexican Holiday,* 1932

Post Office/Telegraph Office   The correo is on Calle Guerrero, by the market.

Telephone   There's a long-distance telephone office in the lobby of the Hotel María José, Avenida Madero at Medina, open Monday through Saturday from 9am to 1pm and 4 to 8pm. There are Ladatel phones accepting coins and prepaid phone cards at the plaza.

Tourist Seasons   Isla Mujeres's tourist season (when hotel rates are higher) is a bit different from that of other places in Mexico. High season runs December through May, a month longer than in Cancún; some hotels raise their rates in August and some hotels raise their rates beginning in mid-November. Low season is June through mid-November.

BEACHES, WATER SPORTS & OTHER ATTRACTIONS
THE BEACHES

The most popular beach in town used to be called Playa Cocoteros (Coco for short). Then, in 1988, Hurricane Gilbert destroyed the coconut palms on the beach. Gradually, the name has been changed to **Playa Norte,** referring to the long stretch of beach that extends around the northern tip of the island, to your left as you get off the boat. This is a truly splendid beach—a wide swath of fine white sand and calm, lucidly clear, turquoise-blue water. Topless sunbathing is tolerated here. The beach is easily reached on foot from the ferry and from all downtown hotels. Water-sports equipment, beach umbrellas, and lounge chairs are available for rent. New palms are beginning to sprout all over Playa Norte and it won't be long until it will be deserving of its previous name. The beach is easily reached on foot from the ferry and from all downtown hotels. Water-sports equipment, beach umbrellas, and lounge chairs are available for rent. The latter go for $1.75–$2.25 per day. Those in front of restaurants usually cost nothing if you use the restaurant as your headquarters for drinks and food.

  Garrafón National Park is known best as a snorkeling area, but there is a nice stretch of beach on either side of the park. **Playa Lancheros** is on the Caribbean side of Laguna Makax. Local buses go to Lancheros, then turn inland and return downtown. The beach at Playa Lancheros is nice, but the few restaurants there are high-priced.

WATER SPORTS
Swimming

Wide Playa Norte is the best swimming beach, with Playa Lancheros second. There are no lifeguards on duty on Isla Mujeres, and the system of water-safety flags used in Cancún and Cozumel isn't used here either. Be very careful!

Snorkeling

By far the most popular place to snorkel is **Garrafón National Park,** at the southern end of the island, where you'll see numerous schools of colorful fish. The well-equipped park has beach chairs, changing rooms, lockers, showers, and a snack bar. Taxis from the central village cost around $3.50 one way. Admission is $2; lockers rent for $1.50. Also good for snorkeling is the **Manchones Reef,** which is just off shore and reached by boat, where a bronze cross was installed in 1994.

Another excellent location is around the lighthouse in the **Bahía de Mujeres** (bay) opposite downtown, where the water is about 6 feet deep. Boatmen will take you for around $10 per person if you have your own snorkeling equipment or $15 more if you use theirs.

Diving

Several dive shops have opened on the island, most offering the same trips. The traditional dive center is **Buzos de México,** on Rueda Medina at Morelos (☎ 7-0500), next to the boat cooperative. Dive instructor Carlos Gutiérrez, speaks English, French, and Italian and offers certification (5–6 days for $300), and resort courses ($80 with three dives), and makes sure all dives are led by certified dive masters. **Bahia Dive Shop,** on Rueda Medina 166 across from the car ferry dock (☎ and fax 987/7-0340), is a full-service shop with dive equipment for sale and rent and resort and certification classes. The most popular reefs are Manchones, Banderas, and Cuevones. All 30- to 40-foot dives cost $40 to $70 for a two-tank trip; equipment rental costs $15. Cuevas de los Tiburones (Caves of the Sleeping Sharks) is Isla's most famous dive site and costs $60 to $80 for a two-tank dive at a depth of 70 feet. There are actually two places to see the sleeping sharks—the Cuevas de Tiberones and La Punta. During a storm the arch collapsed that was featured in a Jacques Cousteau film showing the sleeping sharks, but the caves are still there. However, your chance of actually seeing sleeping sharks, by the way, is about one in four; fewer sharks are present than in the past. The best time to see them is January through March. Other dive sites include a wreck 9 kilometers off shore; Banderas, between Isla Mujeres and Cancún, where there's always a strong current; Tabos reef on the eastern shore; and Manchones, 1 kilometer off the southeastern tip of the island where the water is 15 to 35 feet deep. The best season for diving is from June through August, when the water is calm.

Fishing

To arrange a day of fishing, ask at the **Sociedad Cooperativa Turística** (boatmen's cooperative; ☎ 987/7-0274) or the travel agency mentioned below, under Isla Contoy. The cost can be shared with four to six others and includes lunch and drinks. All year you'll find bonito, mackerel, kingfish, and amberjack. Sailfish and sharks (hammerhead, bull, nurse, lemon, and tiger) are in good supply in April and May. In winter, larger grouper and jewfish are prevalent. Four hours of fishing close to shore costs around $100, with 8 hours farther out for $240. The cooperative is open Monday through Saturday from 8am to 1pm and 5 to 8pm and Sunday from 7:30 to 10am and 6 to 8pm.

OTHER ATTRACTIONS

A Turtle Sanctuary

Easily the most interesting outing on the island is to this reserve dedicated to preservation of Caribbean sea turtles, and to educating the public about them.

As few as 20 years ago fishermen converged on the island nightly from May through September waiting for these monster-size turtles to lumber ashore to deposit their flimsy Ping-Pong-ball-sized eggs. Totally vulnerable once the turtles begin laying their eggs, and exhausted when they finished, the turtles were easily captured and slaughtered for their highly prized meat, shell, and eggs. Then a concerned fisherman, Gonzalez Cahle Maldonado, began convincing fishermen to spare at least the eggs, which he protected. It was a start. Following his lead, the Fishing Secretariat founded this **Centro de Investigaciones** 10 years ago; it's funded by both the government and private donations. Since then at least 28,000 turtles have been released and every year local schoolchildren participate in the event, thus planting the notion of protecting the turtles within a new generation of islanders.

Six different species of sea turtles nest on Isla Mujeres. An adult green turtle, the most abundant species, measures 4 to 5 feet in length and can weigh as much as 450 pounds when grown. At the center, visitors walk through the indoor and outdoor turtle pool areas, watching the creatures paddling around. The turtles are separated by age, from newly hatched up to one year. Besides protecting the turtles that nest on Isla Mujeres of their own accord, the program also calls for capturing the turtles at sea and bringing them to enclosed compounds to mate and later to be freed to nest on Isla Mujeres. They are tagged and then released. While in the care of the center these guests receive a high-protein diet and reportedly grow faster than in the wild. People who come here usually end up staying at least an hour, especially if they opt for the guided tour, which enhances a visit. The permanent shelter has large wall paintings of all the sea turtles of the area. Admission is $1; the shelter is open daily from 9am to 5pm.

A Maya Ruin
Just beyond the lighthouse, at the southern end of the island, is a pile of stones that formed a small Maya pyramid before Hurricane Gilbert struck. Believed to have been an observatory built to the moon goddess Ixchel, now it's reduced to a rocky heap. The location, on a lofty bluff overlooking the sea, is still worth seeing. If you're at Garrafón National Park and want to walk, it's not too far. Turn right from Garrafón. When you see the lighthouse, turn toward it down the rocky path.

A Pirate's Fortress
The Fortress of Mundaca is about 2¹/₂ miles in the same direction as Garrafón, about half a mile to the left. The fortress was built by the pirate Mundaca Marecheaga, who in the early 19th century arrived at Isla Mujeres and proceeded to set up a blissful paradise in a pretty, shady spot while making money from selling slaves to Cuba and Belize.

A Visit to Isla Contoy
If at all possible, plan to visit this pristine uninhabited island, 19 miles by boat from Isla Mujeres, that was set aside as a national wildlife reserve in 1981. The oddly shaped 3.8-mile-long island is covered in lush vegetation and harbors 70 species of birds as well as a host of marine and animal life. Bird species that nest on the island include pelicans, brown boobies, frigates, egrets, terns, and cormorants. Flocks of flamingos arrive in April. June, July, and August are good months to spot turtles that bury their eggs in the sand at night. Most excursions troll for fish (which will be your lunch), anchor en route for a snorkeling expedition, and skirt the island at a leisurely pace for close viewing of the birds without disturbing the habitat, then pull ashore. While the captain prepares lunch visitors can swim, sun, follow the nature trails, and visit the fine nature museum. For a while the island was closed to visitors, but it's reopened now. The trip from Isla Mujeres takes a minimum of 1¹/₂ hours one way, more if the waves are choppy. Because of the tight-knit boatmen's cooperative, prices for this excursion are the same everywhere—$50. You can buy a ticket at the **Sociedad Cooperativa Turística** (☎ 7-0274) on Avenida Rueda Medina, next to Mexico Divers and Las Brisas restaurant, or at one of several travel agencies, such as **La Isleña,** on Morelos between Medina and Juárez (☎ 7-0578). La Isleña is open

daily from 7am to 9pm and is a good source for tourist information. Contoy trips leave at 8:30am and return around 4pm.

Three types of boats go to Contoy. Small boats have one motor and seat eight or nine people. Medium-size boats have two motors and hold 10. Large boats have a toilet and hold 16 passengers. Most boats have a sun cover. The first two types are being fazed out in favor of larger, better boats. Boat captains should respect the cooperative's regulations regarding capacity and should have enough life jackets to go around. Snorkling equipment is usually included in the price, but double-check that before heading out. I highly recommend the services of English-speaking boat owner **Ricardo Gaitan** (☎ 7-0434), who has two boats: the *Afroditi,* a 30-foot speedboat holding up to 15 people, and the 37-foot trimaran *Pelicano,* good for day trips and overnight excursions. It sleeps up to six people or carries 15 passengers for day trips. Call him, or write to him directly P.O. Box 42, 77400 Isla Mujeres, Q. Roo.

SHOPPING

Shopping is a casual activity here. There are only a few glittery, sleek shops. Otherwise you are bombarded by shop owners, especially on Hidalgo, selling Saltillo rugs, onyx, silver, Guatemalan clothing, blown glassware, masks, folk art, beach paraphernalia, and T-shirts in abundance. Prices are also lower than in Cancún or Cozumel, but with the overeager sellers, bargaining is necessary to achieve a satisfactory price.

One store stands out from the rest: **La Loma,** Guerrero 6 (☎ 987/7-0223), stocks a great variety of good folk art, including Huichol yarn "paintings," masks, silver chains and coins, a good selection of textiles, Oaxacan wood carvings, Olinalá lacquer objects, and colorful clay candelabras from Izúcar de Matamoros. You'll see it opposite the left side of the church beside La Peña restaurant, and almost next to the Hotel Perla del Caribe II. It's open Monday through Saturday from 10am to 3pm and 5 to 8pm.

ACCOMMODATIONS

There are plenty of hotels in all price ranges on Isla Mujeres. Rates are at their peak during high season, which is the most expensive and most crowded time to go. Elizabeth Wenger of **Four Seasons Travel** in Montello, WI (☎ 800/552-4550) specializes in Mexico travel and especially books a lot of hotels in Isla Mujeres. Her service is invaluable in high season when hotel occupancy is high.

VERY EXPENSIVE

Puerto Isla Mujeres Resort & Yacht Club

Puerto de Abrigo Laguna Macax, Isla Mujeres, Q. Roo. ☎ **987/7-0330,** or 987/83-3208 in Cancún, or 800/960-ISLA in the U.S. Fax 987/83-0485 or 98/83-1228 in Cancún. Reservation address: Paseo Kukulcán km. 4.5 77500 Cancún, Q. Roo. 30 rms. A/C TV TEL MINIBAR. Suites $160–$300 single or double; villas $250–$530 single or double. Rates include transportation from Cancún and daily continental breakfast and dinner.

The concept here—an exclusive glide-up yachting/sailing resort—is new not only to Isla Mujeres, but to all of Mexico. Opened in 1995 and facing an undeveloped portion of the glass-smooth mangrove-edged Macax Lagoon, Puerto Isla Mujeres's modern suites and villas, with sloping white stucco walls and red tile roofs, are spread across spacious palm-filled grounds. Beautifully designed with Scandinavian and Mediterranean elements, guest quarters feature tile, wood-beamed ceilings, natural wood and marble accents, televisions with VCR, stereos with CD changer, and living areas. Villas have two bedrooms upstairs with a full bath and a small bathroom downstairs with a shower. Each villa also features a small stylish kitchen area with dishwasher, microwave, refrigerator, and coffee maker. A whirlpool is on the upper patio off the master bedroom. Since weather is of consideration to the boating crowd, nightly turndown service leaves the next day's weather forecast on the pillow beside the requisite chocolate. The beach club, with refreshments, is a water-taxi ride across the lagoon on a beautiful stretch of beach. A staff biologist can answer questions about birds and water life on Isla Mujeres. Besides two meals, an afternoon snack is delivered to each room. More suites and villas were on the drawing board. The highest rates mentioned above are for high season.

Dining/Entertainment: Two excellent restaurants, one indoor and one outdoors by the pool, gourmet deli, small grocery store.

Services: Transportation from the Cancún airport by Chevy Suburban and private yacht to Isla Mujeres, full-service marina with 60 slips for 30- to 60-foot vessels, short- and long-term dockage, fueling station, charter yachts and sailboats, and sailing school. Mopeds, golf carts, bicycles, and water-sports equipment for rent. Video and CD library.

Facilities: Laundry and room service, nearby beach club, free-form swimming pool with swim-up bar.

EXPENSIVE

Hotel Cabañas María del Mar

Av. Carelos Lazo 1, 77400 Isla Mujeres, Q. Roo. ☎ **987/7-0179.** Fax 987/7-0213. 56 rms. A/C. High season $70–$75 single or double. Low season $45–$50 double. Rates include continental breakfast.

A good choice, the Cabañas María del Mar is located on Playa Norte, a half block from the Hotel Nabalam. There are three completely different sections to this hotel. The older two-story section behind the reception area and beyond the garden offers nicely outfitted rooms facing the beach, all with two single or double beds, refrigerators, and balconies with ocean views. Eleven single-story cabañas closer to the reception and pool are rather dark and these are the lowest priced. The newest addition, El Castillo, is across the street and built over and beside Buho's restaurant. It contains all "deluxe" rooms, but some are larger than others; the five rooms on the ground floor all have large patios and are the most appealing to me. Upstairs rooms have small balconies. Most have one double bed. All have ocean views, blue-and-white tile floors, and tile lavatories and are outfitted in cool cotton bedspreads and natural-toned neocolonial furniture. There's a small, unkempt pool in the garden. The owners also have a bus for tours and a boat for rental, as well as golf cart and moto rental.

To get here from the pier walk left one block, then turn right on Matamoros. After four blocks, turn left on Lazo, the last street. The hotel is at the end of the block.

✪ Hotel Na Balam

Zacil Ha 118, 77400 Isla Mujeres, Q. Roo. ☎ **987/7-0279.** Fax 987/7-0446. 31 suites (all with bath). A/C FAN. High season, $100–$125 suite for one or two. Low season, $80–$115 suite for one or two. Free parking; unguarded.

This two-story hotel near the end of Norte Beach is my favorite of the island's lodgings, with its comfortable rooms on a quiet, ideally located portion of the beach. It seems to get better each year. Rooms are in three sections, with some facing the beach and others across the street in a garden setting where there's a swimming pool. All rooms have either a patio or balcony. Each nicely furnished and spacious suite contains two double beds, a seating area, and folk-art decorations. Though other rooms are newer, my preference is the older section with a bottom-floor patio facing the peaceful palm-filled sandy inner yard and Norte Beach. Tuesday through Thursday yoga lessons are offered; ask about the time and price. The restaurant, Zacil-Ha, is one of the island's most popular (see "Dining," below). To find it from the pier, walk five blocks to López Mateos; turn right and walk four blocks to Lazo (the last street). Turn left and walk to the sandy road parallel to the beach and turn right. The hotel is half a block farther.

MODERATE

✪ Hotel Posada del Mar

Av. Rueda Medina 15, 77400 Isla Mujeres, Q. Roo. ☎ **987/7-0300,** or 800-221-6509 in the U.S. Fax 987/7-0266. 40 rms (all with bath). A/C TEL. $40–$55 single; $45–$65 double. Ask about specials.

Attractively furnished, quiet and comfortable, this long-established hotel faces the water and a wide beach three blocks north of the ferry pier. The very spacious rooms, all with a fresh coat of white paint, are in a large garden palm grove in either a three-story building or in one-story bungalow units. For the spacious quality of the rooms and the location, this is among the best buys on the island. A wide, seldom used but appealing stretch of Playa Norte is across the street. An extremely appealing casual palapa-style bar and a lovely pool are set on the back lawn, and the popular restaurant Pinguino (see "Dining," below) is by the sidewalk at the front of the property. Ask about specials—four nights for the price of three and seven nights for the price of five. From the pier, go left for four blocks; the hotel is on the right.

INEXPENSIVE

Autel Carmelena

Guerrero 4, 77400 Isla Mujeres, Q. Roo. ☎ **987/7-0005.** 18rms. FAN. $7–$10 single; $10–$13.50 double.

With so few cars in Isla, it's odd to see a motel. However, because so few tourists bring a vehicle, it's not odd that no cars are parked here. Nevertheless, there's plenty of room to park in front of the two tiers of coral-and-white-colored rooms, all facing the lot. Rooms, which have windows facing the common walkway and parking lot, are plain but clean, with tile floors, striped cotton bedspreads, desks, and small bathrooms. Only two rooms have air-conditioning and the highest prices are for these. Bike rentals can be arranged at the reception desk, where you can also order roast chicken between 11am and 3:30pm (reflecting another of the owner's interests). It's between Madero and Abasolo.

Hotel Belmar

Av. Hidalgo 110,74000 Isla Mujeres, Q. Roo. ☎ **987/7-0430.** Fax 987/7-0429. 11 rms (all with bath). A/C FAN TV TEL. High season, $30 single; $35 double. Low season, $23 single; $27 double.

Situated above Pizza Rolandi (consider the restaurant noise), this hotel is run by the same people who serve up those wood-oven pizzas. Each of the simple but stylish rooms comes with two twin or double beds and handsome tile accents. Prices are high for no views, but the rooms are very pleasant, and a satellite dish brings in U.S. channels. The hotel is between Madero and Abasolo, 3$^{1}/_{2}$ blocks from the passenger ferry pier.

Hotel Caribe Maya

Av. Madero 9, 77400 Isla Mujeres, Q. Roo. ☎ **987/1-0523.** 26 rms (all with bath). A/C or FAN. $11–$18 single or double.

The rooms in this basic three-story hotel have green-tile floors, nylon ruffled bed-spreads, reading lights over the beds, showers, and furniture that may have seen service in some older and long-gone establishment. Upstairs rooms are brighter and higher prices are for the seven rooms with air-conditioning. To get here from the main pier, turn left 1 block, then go right for 1½ blocks; it's between Guerrero and Hidalgo.

❂ Hotel D'Gomar

Rueda Medina 50, 77400 Isla Mujeres, Q. Roo. ☎ **987/7-0540.** 16 rms. FAN or A/C. High season $23–$27 single or double. Low season $14–$17 single or double.

You can hardly beat this hotel for comfort at reasonable prices. Rooms, in rattan furniture, all have two double beds, pink walls and drapes, and a wall of windows with great breezes and picture views, The higher prices are for air-conditioning, which is hardly needed with fantastic breezes and ceiling fans. Manager Manuel Serano says, "We make friends of all our clients," and indeed I think he does. The only drawback is that there are five stories of rooms and no elevator. But it's conveniently located catercorner (look right) from the ferry pier, and the rooftop views can't be beat anywhere on the island. The name of the hotel is the most visible sign on the "skyline."

❂ Hotel Francis Arlene

Guerrero 7, 77400 Isla Mujeres, Q. Roo. ☎ and fax **987/7-0310,** in Cancún 98/84-3302. 17 rms (all with bath). A/C or FAN. High season $15–$27 single; $20–$27 double. Low season, $12–$15 single; $18–$20 double.

The Magaña family operates this neat little two-story inn behind the family home, which is built around a small shady courtyard. You'll notice the tidy cream-and-white facade of the building from the street. Rooms are clean and comfortable, with tile floors and all-tile baths, and soap and towels laid out on your bed. Each downstairs room has a refrigerator and stove; each upstairs room comes with a refrigerator and toaster. All have either a balcony or a patio. Rates were substantially better if quoted in pesos when I checked, and are reflected above. In dollars they are 15% to 20% higher. It's 5½ blocks inland from the ferry pier, between Abasolo and Matamoros.

Hotel María José

Avs. Madero and Rueda Medina, 77400 Isla Mujeres, Q. Roo. ☎ **987/7-0244** or 987/7-0245. 15 rms (all with bath). FAN. High season, $10 single or double.

Near the ferry dock, this three-story hotel is a good budget deal. Rooms are bright, cheery, clean, and comfortable. Only triple rooms have balconies overlooking the street. Incredibly (considering the already low price), they offer a discount for stays of three or more days. The busy long-distance telephone office is in the lobby. To find it from the main pier, turn left on the Malecón, walk one block to a hot-pink arch, and turn right; the hotel is on your left.

Hotel Vistamar

Av. Rueda Medina, Isla Mujeres, Q. Roo 77400. ☎ **987/7-0209.** 36 rooms (all with bath). A/C or FAN. High season, $9–$15 single; $12–$15 double. Low season, $7–$10 single; $9–$13.50 double.

The name means "sea view," which is indeed what you get if you select a room facing the Malecón. Other rooms have interior windows without views. All units have green-tile floors and ruffled bedspreads and are extremely simple but well kept. Of course, rooms with air-conditioning command the highest prices. The hotel is across from a nice stretch of beach and shoreline, and Playa Norte is almost around the corner. The hotel is on the Malecón, between Abasolo and Matamoros, 1½ blocks to the left of the ferry pier.

Poc-Na

Calle Matamoros 15, 77400 Isla Mujeres, Q. Roo. ☎ **987/7-0090.** Fax 987/7-0059. 4 bunk rms, 3 hammock rms, 3 private rms (none with bath). FAN. $4 bunk; $3 hammock; private room $7–$10; towels 35¢ extra; breakfast $1.50–$2.50; lunch $75¢–$1.75; dinner or pizza $1.75–$4.50.

The Poc-Na claims to be "a basic clean place to stay at the lowest price possible"—and it is. Deposits of your passport or ID are necessary for all rentals. The communal sleeping rooms are arranged around a central palapa-shaded dining area with picnic tables. Meals are served cafeteria-style from a small kitchen. Conveniently located, the hotel is only a short walk from Playa Norte. It's at the end of Calle Matamoros, near the market.

Posada San Jorge

Av. Juárez 29A, 77400 Isla Mujeres, Q. Roo. ☎ **987/7-0155.** 16 rms. FAN. High season $11.50 single, $14.75 double. Low season $11.50 single or double. Rates include continental breakfast.

The two-story (no elevator) San Jorge got a facelift in 1995 that puts it back into the acceptable category again. New paint, mattresses, and bath fixtures have revitalized the hotel, which had deteriorated grimly from lack of care. Most rooms have two double beds, and all have green tile floors, overbed reading lights, and windows opening to the hall. A refrigerator in the lobby is filled with soft drinks for sale to guests, and there's a breezy balcony on the second floor overlooking Juárez. The ambitious plans for the future call for a TV and small refrigerator in each room, a bar in a room off the lobby, and continuation of the small restaurant across the street. Prices will be higher for rooms with TV and air-conditioning. The hotel is located between Matamoros and López Mateos.

DINING

The **Municipal Market,** next door to the telegraph office and post office on Avenida Guerrero, has several little cookshops operated by obliging and hard-working señoras and enjoyed by numbers of tourists. On Sunday, Nacho Beh, El Rey del Taco (The King of the Taco), prepares sublime cochinita pibil tacos. Get there early.

At the **Panadería La Reyna,** at Madero and Juárez, you can pick up inexpensive sweet bread, muffins, cookies, and yogurt. It's open Monday through Saturday from 7am to 9:30pm.

As in the rest of Mexico, a **cocina economica** restaurant literally means "economic kitchen." Usually aimed at the local population, these are almost universally great places to find good food at rock-bottom prices. That's especially so on Isla Mujeres, where you'll find several.

MODERATE

✪ Las Palapas Chimbo's

Norte Beach. No phone. Breakfast $1.85–$3; sandwiches and fruit $2–$3.50; seafood $3.80–$5.50. Daily 8am–6pm. SEAFOOD.

If you're looking for a beachside palapa-covered restaurant where you can wiggle your toes in the sand while scarfing down fresh seafood, this is the best of them. Locals recommend it as their favorite on Norte Beach. Try the delicious fried fish (a whole one), which comes with rice, beans, and tortillas. You'll notice the bandstand and dance floor that's been added to the middle of the restaurant, and especially the sex-hunk posters all over the ceiling—that is, when you aren't gazing at the beach and the Caribbean. Chimbo's becomes a disco at night, and draws a motley crew of drinkers and dancers. (See "Isla Mujeres After Dark" below for details.) To find it from the pier, walk left to the end of the Malecón, then right onto the Playa Norte beach; it's about half a block on the right.

From the pier, walk left to the end of the Malecón, then right onto the Playa Norte Beach; this restaurant is on the right about half a block down.

✪ Pinguino

In the Hotel Posada del Mar, Av. Rueda Medina 15. ☎ **987/7-0300**. Breakfast $1.75–$3; main dishes $3.50–$5.75; daily special $5.75. Daily 7am–9pm; bar open to midnight. MEXICAN/SEAFOOD.

The best seats on the waterfront are on the deck of this restaurant/bar, especially in late evening when islanders and tourists arrive to dance and party. This is the place to splurge on lobster—you'll get a beautifully presented, large, sublimely fresh lobster tail with a choice of butter, garlic, and secret sauces. Breakfasts include fresh fruit, yogurt, and granola or sizable platters of eggs, served with homemade wheat bread. At night it's one of "the" places to be. Pinguino is in front of the hotel, three blocks west of the ferry pier.

Pizza Rolandi

Av. Hidalgo. ☎ **987/7-0429**. Main courses $3.25–$27; pizza $6–$18. Daily 1–11pm. ITALIAN.

Pizza Rolandi, the chain that saves the day with dependably good, reasonably priced food amid other expensive resorts, comes through in Isla Mujeres as well. In the casual dining room, in an open courtyard of the Hotel Belmar, you can munch on plate-size pizzas, pastas, and calzones cooked in a wood oven. There's also a more expensive menu with fish, beef, and chicken dishes. Guitarists often perform in the evenings. It's 3 1/2 blocks inland from the pier, between Madero and Abasolo.

✪ Zacil-Ha

At the Hotel Na Balam, Norte Beach. ☎ **987/7-0279**. Breakfast $3.50–$4.50; main courses $6–$9. Daily 7:30am–10pm; breakfast 7:30–10:30am, lunch 12:30–3:30pm, dinner 7–10pm. INTERNATIONAL.

At this restaurant you can enjoy some of the island's best food while sitting among the palms and gardens at tables on the sand. The serene environment is enhanced by the food—terrific pasta with garlic, shrimp in tequila sauce, fajitas, seafood pasta, and delicious mole enchiladas. Main courses come with vegetable and rice. Between the set hours for meals you can have all sorts of enticing food, such as blender vegetable and fruit drinks, tacos and sandwiches, ceviche, and terrific nachos. It's likely you'll stake this place out for several meals before you leave. It's at the end of Playa Norte and almost at the end of Calle Zacil-Ha.

INEXPENSIVE

✪ Cafecito

Calle Juárez. ☎ **987/7-0438**. Coffee drinks $1–$3; crepes $1.25–$3.25; breakfast $2–$3; main courses $4.25–$6.25. Mon–Wed and Fri–Sat 8am–noon and 6–10pm; Thurs and Sun 8am–noon. CREPES/ICE CREAM/COFFEES/FRUIT DRINKS.

Sabina and Luis Rivera own this cute, Caribbean blue corner restaurant where you can begin the day with flavorful coffee and a croissant and cream cheese, or end it with a hot-fudge sundae. Terrific crepes are served with yogurt, ice cream, fresh fruit, or chocolate sauces, as well as ham and cheese. The two-page ice-cream menu satisfies most any craving—even one for waffles with ice cream and fruit. The three-course fixed-price dinner starts with soup, then a main course such as fish or curried shrimp with rice and salad, followed by dessert. It's four blocks from the pier at the corner of Juárez and Matamoros.

✪ Chen Huaye

Bravo 6. No phone. Breakfast $1.25–$2; appetizers $1–$1.50; main course $1.25–$4.25. Thurs–Tues 9am–11pm. MEXICAN/HOME COOKING.

The Juanito Tago Trego family owns this large lunchroom where tourists and locals find a variety of pleasing dishes at equally pleasing prices. Light meals include empanadas, Yucatecan salubites, panucos, and quesadillas. The *tamal costado,* a tamal stuffed with hunks of chicken and baked in a banana leaf, is a daily special. Main courses might include breaded pork chops, chicken in adobado, or fried chicken. The name, by the way, is Maya for "only here." It's between Guerrero and Juárez; you'll spot it by the wagon wheel in front.

ⓢ Cocina Economica

Juárez 5. ☎ 987/7-0298. Comida Corrida $2.50. Mon–Sat 11am–6pm. HOME COOKING.

Step into another living room just off the street, and enter the homey world of Daniel Canol and his wife Susana Martinez, who is master of the cocina. It's in one of the island's original wood-frame houses with Cuban-style mosaic tile on the floor. It's a very informal place with a few plastic-draped tables and walls with religious memorabilia. The daily menu comes with rice and beans or soup, and a main course that might be pollo adobado, fried fish, milanesa, or a Yucatecan-flavored pork chop seasoned with achiote. There's no sign, but you'll see a handwritten paper menu tacked to the door, and it's next to La Lomita II, between Madero and Morelos.

ⓢ Cocina Economica Carmelita

Calle Juárez 14. ☎ 987/7-0136. Meal of the day $3. Daily 12:30–5pm. MEXICAN/HOME COOKING.

Few tourists find their way to this tiny restaurant, open only for lunch. But locals know they can get a filling, inexpensive, home-cooked meal prepared by Carmelita in the back kitchen and served by her husband at the three cloth-covered tables in the front room of their home. Two or three comida corridas are available each day and are served until they run out. They begin with black bean soup and include a fruit water drink. If offered, try the *Brazo de la Reyna,* which is a large, sliced, very flavorful and filling Maya tamal stuffed with hard-boiled eggs and spices. If it's not on the menu, make a request and see if it can be prepared during your stay. Other selections include paella or *cochinita pibil,* and Sunday is *pozole* day. It's two blocks from the passenger ferry pier, between Bravo and Allende.

La Lomita II

Juárez s/n. No phone. Breakfast $1.50–$1.75; main courses $2.50–$5; comida corrida $2.25. Mon–Sat 9:30am–11pm. MEXICAN.

Narrow and plain, this is a tiny branch of the larger mother restaurant, La Lomita I, on Juárez (the larger restaurant was closed each time I checked, but it's near Cocina Economica Carmelita). This one offers the same menu as the original. The comida corrida starts with soup, then beans or rice, then the main course with a vegetable. Drinks are extra. It's between Madero and Morelos.

ISLA MUJERES AFTER DARK

Those in a party mood by day's end might want to start out at the beach bar of the **Hotel Na Balam** on Playa Norte which hosts a crowd until around midnight. On Saturday and Sunday there's live music here between 4 and 7pm. **Las Palapas Chimbo's** restaurant on the beach becomes a jivin' dance joint with a live band from 9pm until. . . Farther along the same stretch of beach, **Buho's,** the restaurant/beach bar of the Posada María del Mar was a popular, low-key hangout when I was there. **Pinguino's** in the Hotel Posada del Mar has two places to be—the restaurant/bar, where the manager, Miguel, whips up some potent concoctions at the bar, and the band plays nightly during high season from 9pm to midnight—and the more tranquil, but totally delightful poolside bar with its swings at the bar under a giant palapa.

2 Cozumel

44 miles S of Cancún

Cozumel, 12 miles from Playa del Carmen, comes from the Maya word *Cuzamil,* meaning "land of the swallows." It's Mexico's largest Caribbean island, 28 miles long and 11 miles wide, but it's only 3% developed, leaving vast stretches of jungle and uninhabited shoreline. The only town is San Miguel de Cozumel, usually called just San Miguel.

Today Cozumel is one of the Yucatán's top resort destinations as well as the country's scuba-diving capital. It's also home to two species of birds that are found nowhere else—the Cozumel vireo, and the Cozumel thrasher. If Cancún is the jet-set's port of call and Isla Mujeres is the poor man's Cancún, Cozumel is a little bit of both. More remote than the other two, this island (pop. 60,000) is a place where people come to get away from the day-tripping atmosphere of Isla Mujeres or the megadevelopment of Cancún.

All the necessaries for a good vacation are here: excellent snorkeling and scuba places, sailing and water sports, expensive resorts and modest hotels, elegant restaurants and taco shops, and even a Maya ruin or two. If, after a while, you do get restless, the ancient Maya city of Tulum, the lagoons of Xel-Ha and Xcaret, or the nearby village of Playa del Carmen provide convenient and interesting excursions.

During pre-Hispanic times the island was one of three important ceremonial centers (Izamal and Chichén-Itzá were the other two). Salt and honey, trade products produced on the island, further linked Cozumel with the mainland; they were brought ashore at the ruins we know today as Tulum. The site was occupied when Hernán Cortés landed here in 1519. Before his own boat docked, Cortés's men sacked the town and took the chief's wife and children captive. According to Bernal Díaz del Castillo's account, everything was returned. Diego de Landa's account says Cortés converted the Indians and replaced their sacred Maya figures with a cross and a statue of Mary in the main temple at Cozumel. After the Spanish Conquest the island was an important port; however, diseases brought by the foreigners decimated the population, and by 1570 it was almost uninhabited.

The inhabitants returned later, but the War of the Castes in the 1800s severely curtailed Cozumel's trade. Cozumel continued on its economic roller coaster, and after the Caste War it again took its place as a commercial seaport. Merchants exported henequén, coconuts, sugarcane, bananas, chicle, pineapples, honey, and wood products, though in 1955 Hurricane Janet all but demolished the coconut palm plantations. In the mid-1950s Cozumel's fame as a diving destination began to grow, and real development of the island as the site for a vacation resort evolved along with Cancún beginning in the mid-1970s.

ESSENTIALS
GETTING THERE & DEPARTING

By Plane   Aero Cozumel, a Mexicana affiliate, has numerous flights to and from Cancún and Mérida. **Mexicana** flies from Mexico City. **Taesa** flies from Cancún, Chetumal, and Mérida.

Here are some telephone numbers for confirming departures to and from Cozumel: Aero Cozumel (☎ **2-3456** or **988/4-2002** in Cancún; fax 987/2-0877 in Cozumel); Continental (☎ **987/2-0847** in Cozumel); Mexicana (☎ **987/2-0157** or **2-2945** at the airport; fax 987/2-2945); and Taesa (☎ **987/2-4420**).

You can't get a collectivo van from town to the airport, but taxis go to the airport for $5 to $8.

By Ferry   Passenger ferries to Cozumel depart from Playa del Carmen on the mainland; there is also a car ferry from Puerto Morelos. You can catch a bus to Playa del Carmen from Cancún.

The Car Ferry from Puerto Morelos: The first thing to know is that you're better off without a car in Cozumel; parking is difficult. A solution is to drive to Playa del Carmen, find a reliable place to leave your car, and take the passenger ferry. If you do want to take your car over, the terminus in Puerto Morelos (☎ **987/1-0008**), the largest establishment in town, is very easy to find. The car ferry schedule is complicated and may change, so double-check it before arriving in Puerto Morelos. On Monday, the ferry leaves at 7pm; on Tuesday at 11am; on Wednesday through Sunday at 6am. The crossing takes approximately three hours.

Cargo takes precedence over cars. Officials suggest that camper drivers stay overnight in the parking lot to be first in line for tickets. In any case, *always arrive at least three hours in advance of the ferry's departure to purchase a ticket and to get in line.*

Since passenger-boat service between Playa del Carmen and Cozumel is quite frequent now, I don't recommend that foot passengers bother with this boat.

When returning to Puerto Morelos from Cozumel, the ferry departs from the international cruise-ship pier daily. Get in line about three hours before departure, and double-check the schedule by calling ☎ **2-0950.** The fare is $35 for a car and $6 per passenger.

The Passenger Ferry from Playa del Carmen: There are several passenger ferries running between Cozumel and Playa del Carmen. The WJ *México III,* a modern water jet, makes the trip in 45 minutes compared to 60 on the *Cozumeleño.* The WJ *México III* costs $8.25 round-trip and is enclosed, and usually air-conditioned, with cushioned seats and video entertainment. The *Cozumeleño,* an open-top, enclosed-bottom vessel, runs the route for $5 round-trip. In Playa del Carmen, the ferry dock is 1 1/2 blocks from the main square and from where buses let off passengers. Both companies have ticket booths at the main pier in Cozumel. Since schedules change frequently, be sure to double-check them at the docks—especially the time of the last ferry back, if that's the one you intend to use. Be prepared for seasickness on windy days.

From Playa del Carmen to Cozumel, The WJ *Mexico III* runs every hour or every two hours between 5:30am and 8:45pm. The *Cozumeleño* runs five times between 9:30am and 6:30pm.

From Cozumel to Playa del Carmen, the WJ *Mexico III* runs approximately every hour or hour and a half between 4am and 8pm. The *Cozumeleño* runs four times, between 8am and 5:30pm.

ORIENTATION
Arriving

Cozumel's airport is near downtown. Aero Transportes colectivo vans at the airport provide transportation into town for $3 and to either the north or south hotel zone for $5 to $7.50.

Information

The **State Tourism Office** (☎ and fax **987/2-0972**) is on the second floor of the Plaza del Sol commercial building facing the central plaza and is open from Monday through Friday from 8:30am to 3pm.

City Layout

San Miguel's main waterfront street is called **Avenida Rafael Melgar,** running along the western shore of the island. Passenger ferries dock right in the center, opposite the main plaza and Melgar. Car ferries dock south of town near the hotels Sol Caribe, La Ceiba, and Fiesta Inn.

The town is laid out on a grid, with avenidas running north and south, calles running east and west. The exception is **Avenida Juárez,** which runs right from the passenger-ferry dock through the main square and inland. Juárez divides the town into northern and southern halves.

Heading inland from the dock along Juárez, you'll find that the avenidas you cross are numbered by fives: 5a av., 10a av., 15a av. If you turn left and head north, calles are numbered evenly: 2a Norte, 4a Norte, 6a Norte. Turning right from Juárez heads you south, where the streets are numbered: 1a Sur (also called Adolfo Salas), 3a Sur, 5a Sur.

Island Layout

The island is cut in half by one road, which runs past the airport and the ruins of San Gervasio to the almost uninhabited southern coast of the island. The northern part of the island has no paved roads. It's scattered with small, badly ruined Maya sites, from the age when "Cuzamil" was a land sacred to the moon goddess Ixchel. San Gervasio is accessible by motor scooter and car.

Most inexpensive hotels are in the town of San Miguel. Moderate to expensive accommodations are north and south of town. Many cater to divers. Beyond the hotels to the south is **Chankanaab National Park,** centered on the beautiful lagoon of the same name. Beyond Chankanaab are **Playa Palancar** and, offshore, the **Palancar Reef** (*arrecife*). At the southern tip of the island are **Punta Celarain** and the lighthouse.

The eastern, seaward shore of the island is mostly surf beach, beautiful for walking but dangerous for swimming.

Getting Around

You can walk to most destinations in town. The trip from town to the Chankanaab Lagoon by taxi costs around $4. For a day at the beach, finding some like-minded fellow travelers and sharing the cost of a cab is the most economical way to go. Taxis should charge no more than $5 from the town center to the farthest hotels.

Car rentals are as expensive here as in other parts of Mexico. Open-top jeeps are popular for rental, but be aware: They roll over easily and many tourists have been injured or killed using them. See "By Car" under "Getting Around" in Chapter 2 for specifics.

Moped rentals are all over the village and cost about $25 for 24 hours, but terms and prices vary. Carefully inspect the actual moped you'll be renting to see that all the gizmos are in good shape: horn, light, starter, seat, mirror. And be sure to note all damage to the moped on the rental agreement. Most important, read the fine print on the back of the rental agreement, which states that you are not insured, are responsible for paying any damage to the bike (or for all of it if it's stolen or demolished), and must stay on paved roads. It's illegal to ride a moped without a helmet. *Important Note:* North/south streets have the right of way, and these drivers don't slow down.

Cozumel Island

Caribbean Sea

0 — 5 mi / 8 km — N

Punta Molas Lighthouse
Punta Molas

Laguna Xlapak

Punta Norte
Isla de la Pasión

Castillo Real

Downtown Pier

To Playa del Carmen (3/4 hour)

Airport

San Miguel De Cozumel

San Gervasio

Playa Xhanan

Playa Bonita

Cruise Ship Pier & Car Ferry

Cozumel Channel

Chankanaab Reef

Laguna Encantada

CARRETERA TRANSVERSAL (CROSS-ISLAND ROAD)

Santa Rosa

Yucab Reef

Laguna Chankanaab

Punta Ixalbarco

Santa Cecilia

Playa Oriente

Punta Morena

Santa Rosa Reef

Playa San Francisco

El Cedral Ruin

Playa Chen Río
Playa Bonita Beach Club
Punta Chiqueros

Buena Vista

Palancar Reef

Playa Palancar

El Mirador

Tumba de Caracol

Laguna Colombia

Playa Bush

Caribbean Sea

Colombia Reef

Punta Celarain

Celarain Lighthouse

Airport ✈   Ruins ◈

2-0056

FAST FACTS: Cozumel

American Express   The local representative is Fiesta Cozumel, Calle 11 no. 598 (☎ **987/2-0725** or **987/2-0433;** fax 987/2-1044).

Area Code   The telephone area code is 987.

Climate   From October through December there can be strong winds all over the Yucatán, as well as some rain. In Cozumel, wind conditions in November and December can make diving dangerous. May through September is the rainy season.

Diving If you intend to dive, remember to bring proof of your diver's certification. Underwater currents can be very strong here, so be cautious.

Post Office The post office (*correo*) is on Avenida Rafael Melgar at Calle 7 Sur, at the southern edge of town; it's open Monday through Friday from 9am to 6pm and Saturday from 9am to noon.

Recompression Chamber The recompression chamber (*cámara de recompreción*) is on Calle 5 Sur one block off Melgar between Melgar and Avenida 5 Sur (☎ 987/2-2387; fax 987/2-1430). Normal hours are 8am to 1pm and 4 to 8pm.

Seasons High season is Christmas through Easter, and in August.

Telephone The **Calling Station** on Melgar at Calle 3 Sur is a full-services phone center with air-conditioned booths, no surcharges, fax service, and a bulletin board where you can leave messages for friends. It's open Monday through Saturday from 8am to 11pm, and Sunday from 9am to 10pm. You can also make collect calls from the Sports Page restaurant.

Besides these, long-distance telephones are on Salas between Avenidas 5 Sur and 10 Sur on the exterior of the telephone building. Use a credit card to get an American operator; make it collect; or have a pile of coins ready to feed the phone.

DIVING, EXPLORING THE ISLAND & OTHER THINGS TO DO

For **diving** and **snorkeling** it's best to go directly to the recommended shops below. For **island tours, ruins tours** on and off the island, **glass-bottom boat tours, fiesta nights, fishing,** and other activities, I can recommend the travel agency **InterMar Cozumel Viajes,** Calle 4 Norte. 101-B (☎ 987/2-1098; fax 987/2-0895), The office is close to the main plaza between Avenida 5 and 10 Norte. But many of these you can do on your own without purchasing a tour.

A FESTIVAL

Carnaval/Mardi Gras is Cozumel's most colorful fiesta. It begins the Thursday before Ash Wednesday with daytime street dancing and nighttime parades on Thursday, Saturday, and Monday (the best).

FUN ON & UNDER THE WATER
Snorkeling

Anyone who can swim can go snorkeling. Rental of the snorkel (breathing pipe), goggles, and flippers should cost only about $4 for half a day; a two-hour snorkeling trip costs $15. The brilliantly colored tropical fish provide a dazzling show. Chankanaab Park is one of the best places to go on your own for an abundant fish show.

Agency-arranged **snorkeling excursions** cost around $40 for a 10am–3pm trip that includes snorkeling at three different reefs, lunch, beer, and soft drinks. Two-hour snorkeling trips through the dive shops recommended below last two hours, cost $15, and usually leave around 2:30pm.

Scuba Diving

Cozumel is Mexico's dive capital. Various establishments on the island rent scuba gear—tanks, regulator with pressure gauge, buoyancy compensator, weight belts, mask, snorkel, and fins. Many will also arrange a half-day expedition in a boat, complete with lunch, for a set price—usually around $40. Sign up the day before if you're interested. A two-tank morning dive costs around $50; some shops are now offering an additional afternoon one-tank dive for $9 for those who took the morning dives, or $25 for a one-tank dive. However, if you're a dedicated diver, you'll save many

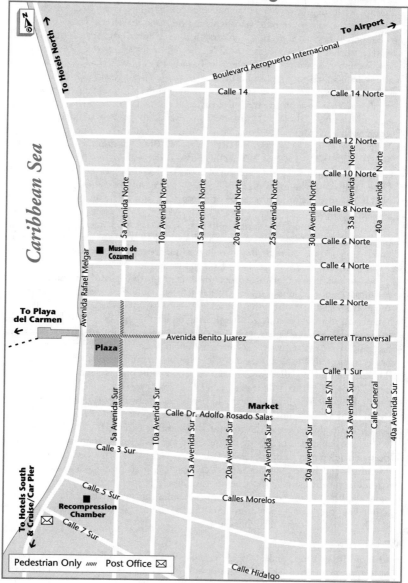

To Airport →

Boulevard Aeropuerto Internacional

Calle 14   Calle 14 Norte

To Hotels North ↗

Calle 12 Norte

Calle 10 Norte

Calle 8 Norte

Calle 6 Norte

Calle 4 Norte

Calle 2 Norte

5a Avenida Norte · 10a Avenida Norte · 15a Avenida Norte · 20a Avenida Norte · 25a Avenida Norte · 30a Avenida Norte · 35a Avenida Norte · 40a Avenida Norte

Caribbean Sea

■ **Museo de Cozumel**

Avenida Rafael Melgar

To Playa del Carmen ←

Avenida Benito Juarez   Carretera Transversal

Plaza

Calle 1 Sur

Calle S/N

Market

Calle Dr. Adolfo Rosado Salas

5a Avenida Sur · 10a Avenida Sur · 15a Avenida Sur · 20a Avenida Sur · 25a Avenida Sur · 30a Avenida Sur · 35a Avenida Sur · Calle General · 40a Avenida Sur

Calle 3 Sur

To Hotels South & Cruise/Car Pier ←

Calle 5 Sur

■ **Recompression Chamber**

Calle 7 Sur

Calles Morelos

Calle Hidalgo

Pedestrian Only /////   Post Office ⊠

2-0057

dollars by buying a diving package that includes air transportation, hotel, and usually two dives a day. There's a recompression chamber on the island (see "Fast Facts," above).

The underwater wonders of the famous **Palancar Reef** are offshore from the beach of the same name. From the car-ferry south to Punta Celarain is more than 20 miles of offshore reefs. In the famous blue depths, divers find caves and canyons, small and large colorful fish, and an enormous variety of sea coral. The **Santa Rosa Reef** is famous for its depth, sea life, coral, and sponges. **San Francisco Reef,** off the beach by the same name south of town, has a drop-off wall, but it's still fairly shallow and the sea life is fascinating. The **Chankanaab Reef,** where divers are joined by schools of tropical fish, is close to the shore by the national park of the same name. It's shallow and good for novice divers, as is **Paradise Reef** by the La Ceiba hotel. Next after Chankanaab going south on the eastern road, **Yucab Reef** has beautiful coral.

Numerous vessels on the island operate daily diving and snorkeling tours, so if you aren't traveling on a prearranged dive package, the best plan is to shop around and sign up for one of those. Of Cozumel's many dive shops, two are among the top: **Aqua Safari,** in front of the Aqua Safari Inn and next to the Vista del Mar Hotel on Melgar at Avenida 5 (☎ **987/2-0101;** fax **987/2-0661**) and in the Hotel Plaza Las Glorias (☎ **987/2-3362** or **2-2422**), is a PADI five-star instructor center, has full equipment and parts, a good selection of books, and its own pier just across the street. **Dive House,** on the main plaza (☎ **987/2-1953** and fax 2-0368), offers PADI, NAUI SSI instruction. Both shops offer morning and night dives, and afternoon snorkeling trips.

You can save money by renting your gear at a beach shop, such as the two mentioned above, and diving from shore. The shops at the Plaza Las Glorias and La Ceiba hotels are good for shore diving—you'll find plenty to see as soon as you enter the water. It costs about $6 to rent one tank and weights.

A new twist in underwater Yucatán is **cenote diving and snorkeling.** The peninsula's underground cenotes (say-*noh*-tehs), or sinkholes—which were sacred to the Maya—lead to a vast system of underground caverns, where the gently flowing water is so clear divers appear to be floating on air through caves that look just like those on dry land, complete with stalagtites and stalagmites, plus tropical fish, eels, and turtles. The caverns were formed millions of years ago during the last two glacial eras, but only in recent years has this other world been opened to certified divers. The experienced cave diver/owners of **Yucatec Expeditions** (☎ and fax **987/2-4618** or **4-7835**), offer this unique experience five times weekly from Playa del Carmen (you take the ferry with your gear and they meet you with vans there). Cenotes are 30 to 45 minutes from Playa and a dive in each cenote lasts around 45 minutes. Snorkelers paddle around the cenotes, while divers explore the depths. Dives are within the daylight zone, about 130 feet into the caverns and no more than 60 feet deep. There's plenty of natural light. Company owners Sheila Gracey, German Yañez Mendoza, and Jorge Gonzalez inspect diving credentials carefully and have a list of requirements divers must meet before cave diving is permitted. They also offer the equivalent of a resort course in cave diving and a full cave diving course. A cenote snorkeling trip to two cenotes runs around $65, while a two-cenote dive costs around $120, and a two-cavern dive runs $150.

Windsurfing

One of Mexico's top windsurfing champions, Raul de Lille, offers windsurfing classes and equipment rentals at the beach in front of Sol Cabañas del Caribe, on the north side. For information call **987/2-0017;** fax 987/2-1942.

Boat Trips

Boat trips are another popular pastime at Cozumel. Some excursions include snorkeling and scuba diving or a stop at a beach with lunch. Various types of tours are offered, including rides in **glass-bottom boats** for around $30. These usually start at 9am and end at 1pm and include beer and soft drinks.

Fishing

The best months for fishing are April through September, when the catch will be blue and white marlin, sailfish, tarpon, swordfish, dorado, wahoo, tuna, and red snapper. Fishing costs $450 for six people all day or $76 per person for a half day for four people.

TOURING THE ISLAND

Travel agencies can book you on a group tour of the island for around $35, depending on whether the tour includes lunch and a stop for snorkeling. A taxi driver charges $60 for a four-hour tour. A four-hour horseback riding tour of the island's interior to the ruins and jungle costs around $40; call Rancho Buenavista (☎ **987/2-1537**) for information, or the InterMar travel agency mentioned above.

You can easily rent a motorbike or car for half a day to take you around the southern part of the island (42 miles). North of town, along Avenida Rafael Melgar (which becomes Carretera Pilar), you'll pass a yacht marina and a string of Cozumel's first hotels as well as some new condominiums. A few of the hotels have nice beaches, which you are welcome to use (on Cozumel this public ownership is more important than ever, since beaches are relatively few—most of the island is surrounded by coral reefs). This road ends just past the hotels; you can backtrack to the transversal road that cuts across the island from west (the town side) to east and link up with the eastern highway that brings you back to town.

The more interesting route begins by going south of town on Melgar (which becomes Costera Sur or Carretera a Chankanaab) past the Hotel Barracuda and **Sol Caribe.** After about 3 miles you'll see a sign pointing left down an unpaved road a short distance to the **Rancho San Manuel,** where you can rent horses. There are only seven horses here, but a guide and soft drink are included in the price. Rides cost $20 per hour. It's open daily from 8am to 4pm.

About 5 miles south of town you'll come to the big **Sol Caribe** (which is closed) and La Ceiba hotels and also the car ferry dock for ferries to Puerto Morelos. Go snorkeling out in the water by the Hotel La Ceiba and you might spot a sunken airplane, put there for an underwater movie. Offshore, from here to the tip of the island at Punta Celarain, 20 miles away, is **Underwater National Park,** so designated to protect the reef from damage by visitors. Dive masters warn not to touch or destroy the underwater growth.

Chankanaab National Park

This lagoon and botanical garden is a mile past the big hotels and 5 1/2 miles south of town. It has long been famous for the color and variety of its sea life. The intrusion of sightseers began to ruin the marine habitat, so now visitors must swim and snorkel in the open sea, not in the lagoon. The beach is wide and beautiful, with plenty of shady thatched umbrellas to sit under, and the snorkeling is good—lots of colorful fish. Arrive early to stake out a chair and palapa before the cruise-ship visitors arrive. There are rest rooms, lockers, a gift shop, several snack huts, a restaurant, and a snorkeling-gear-rental palapa.

Surrounding the lagoon, the botanical garden, with shady paths, has 352 species of tropical and subtropical plants from 22 countries and 451 species from Cozumel. Several Maya structures have been re-created within the gardens to give visitors an idea of Maya life in a jungle setting. There's a small natural history museum as well. Admission to the park costs $3; it's open daily from 8am to 5pm.

BEACHES

After another 10 miles, you'll come to **Playa San Francisco** and, south of it, **Playa Palancar.** Besides the beach at Chankanaab Lagoon, they're the best on Cozumel. Food (usually overpriced) and equipment rentals are available.

The **Playa Bonita Beach Club** near Playa Chiqueros has water sports and windsurfing-equipment rentals. The restaurant is open daily from 10am to 5pm.

Punta Celarain

After Playa San Francisco, you plow through the jungle on a straight road for miles until you're 17½ miles from town. Finally, though, you emerge near the southern reaches of the island on the east coast. The **lighthouse** you see in the distance is at Punta Celarain, the island's southernmost tip. The sand track is unsuitable for motorbikes, but in a car you can drive to the lighthouse in about 25 minutes.

The Eastern Shore

The road along the east coast of the island is wonderful. There are views of the sea, the rocky shore, and the pounding surf. On the land side are little farms and forests. Exotic birds take flight as you approach, and monstrous (but harmless) iguanas skitter off into the undergrowth.

Most of the east coast is unsafe for swimming because the surf can create a deadly undertow that will pull you far out to sea in a matter of minutes. There are always cars pulled off along the road here, with the occupants spending the day on the beach, but not in the churning waters. Three restaurants catering to tourists are along this part of the coast, complete with sombrero-clad iguanas for a picture companion.

Halfway up the east coast, the paved eastern road meets the paved transversal road (which passes the ruins of San Gervasio) back to town, 9½ miles away. The east-coast road ends when it turns into the transversal, petering out to a narrow track of sandy road by a nice restaurant in front of the Chen Río Beach; vehicles, even motorbikes, will get stuck on the sand road. If you're a birdwatcher, leave your vehicle on the highway here and walk straight down the sandy road. Go slowly and quietly and at the least you'll spot many herons and egrets in the lagoon on the left that parallels the path. Much farther on are Maya ruins.

MAYA RUINS

One of the most popular island excursions is to **San Gervasio** (100 B.C. to A.D. 1600). A road leads there from the airport, or you can continue on the eastern part of the island following the paved transversal road. The worn sign to the ruins is easy to miss, but the turnoff (left) is about halfway between town and the eastern coast. Stop at the entry gate and pay the $1 road-use fee. Go straight ahead over the potholed road to the ruins about 2 miles farther and pay the $3.50 to enter; camera permits cost $4 for each still or video camera you want to bring in. A small tourist center at the entrance has cold drinks and snacks for sale.

When it comes to Cozumel's Maya remains, getting there is most of the fun, and you should do it for the trip, not for the ruins. The buildings, though preserved, are crudely made and would not be much of a tourist attraction if they were not the island's only cleared and accessible ruins. More significant than beautiful, the site was once an important ceremonial center where the Maya gathered, coming even from the mainland. The important deity here was Ixchel, known as the goddess of weaving, women, childbirth, pilgrims, the moon, and medicine. Although you won't see any representations of her at San Gervasio today, Bruce Hunter, in his *Guide to Ancient Maya Ruins*, writes that priests hid behind a large pottery statue of her and became the voice of the goddess speaking to pilgrims and answering their petitions. She was the wife of Itzamná, preeminent among Maya gods.

Tour guides charge $10 for a tour for one to six people, but it's not worth it. Find a copy of the green booklet *San Gervasio,* sold at local checkout counters or bookstores, and tour the site on your own. Seeing it takes 30 minutes. Taxi drivers offer a tour to the ruins for about $25; the driver will wait for you outside the ruins.

PARQUE ARQUEOLÓGICA

This park contains reproductions of many of Mexico's important archaeological treasures, including the four-foot-high Olmec head and the Chaac-Mool seen in Chichén-Itzá. A Maya couple demonstrate the lifestyle of the Maya in a *na,* or thatch-roofed oval home. The park is a nice addition to the island's cultural attractions and is well worth visiting—but slather on the bug repellent before you begin exploring. The park is open daily from 8am to 6pm; admission is $1.50. To get there, turn left on the unmarked road across from the International Pier, off Costera Sur just south of the La Ceiba hotel, then left on Avenida 65 Sur and follow the signs.

A HISTORY MUSEUM

The **Museo de la Isla de Cozumel,** on Avenida Melgar between Calles 4 and 6 Norte, is more than just a nice place to spend a rainy hour. On the first floor an excellent exhibit showcases endangered species, the origin of the island, and its present-day topography and plant and animal life, including an explanation of coral formation. Upstairs, showrooms feature the history of the town; artifacts from the island's pre-Hispanic sites; and colonial-era cannons, swords, and ship paraphernalia. It's open daily from 10am to 6pm. Admission is $1.75; guided tours in English are free. There's a rooftop restaurant open long hours.

TRIPS TO THE MAINLAND

Playa del Carmen, Xcaret & Xcalacoco

Going on your own to the nearby seaside village of **Playa del Carmen** and **Xcaret** is as easy as a quick ferry ride from Cozumel (For ferry information, see "Getting There & Departing," above.) All are covered in detail later in this chapter. Cozumel travel agencies offer an Xcaret tour that includes the ferry fee, transportation to the park, and the admission fee for $45 (only about $6 more than it costs to do the trip on your own).

Chichén-Itzá, Tulum & Cobá

Travel agencies can arrange day trips to the fascinating ruins of **Chichén-Itzá** either by air for around $120, or by bus for $85. Departure times vary depending on which transportation you choose. For an excursion to the ruins of **Tulum,** overlooking the Caribbean, and **Cobá,** in a dense jungle setting, you'll shell out $85, but these ruins are closer and are a complete architectural contrast to Chichén-Itzá. Such a trip begins at 9am and returns around 6pm.

SHOPPING

Shopping has improved beyond the ubiquitous T-shirt shops into expensive resortwear, silver, and better decorative and folk art. Most of the stores are on Avenida Melgar; the best shops for high-quality Mexican folk art are **Los Cinco Soles, Talavera,** and **Playa del Angel.** Prices for serapes, T-shirts, and the like are normally less expensive on the side streets off Melgar.

If you want to pick up some Mexican tapes and CDs, head to **Discoteca Holly-wood,** at Juárez 421 (☎ **987/2-4090**); it's open Monday through Saturday from

9am to 10pm. Self-billed as the "Paradise of the Cassette," this store stocks a large selection.

ACCOMMODATIONS

Cozumel's hotels are in three separate locations: The oldest resorts, most of which are expensive, line beaches and coral and limestone outcroppings north and south of town; the more budget-oriented inns are in the central village; and other relatively inexpensive hotels lie both immediately north and south of town. *Note:* There's one **central reservations number** for many (not all) of the island's hotels (☎ **800/ 327-2254** in the U.S. and Canada, or **305/670-9439** in Miami). As an alternative to a hotel, **Casa Cozumel Vacation Villas** and Condos, Av. 10 Sur no. 124, 77600 Cozumel, Q. Roo (☎ **987/2-2259;** fax 987/2-2348 or 800/558-5145 in the U.S.), offers a wide range of accommodations and prices.

NORTH OF TOWN

I'll start with the northernmost hotels going through town, and move onward to the end of the southern hotel zone. Like beaches south of town, those along the northern shore appear sporadically and some hotels have enclosed them with retaining walls. **Carretera Santa Pilar** is the name of Melgar's northern extension, so just take Melgar north and all the hotels are lined up in close proximity to each other on the Santa Pilar Beach a short distance from town and the airport.

Expensive

Hotel Cozumeleño
Km 2 Carretera Santa Pilar (Apdo Postal 53), 77600 Cozumel, Q. Roo. ☎ **987/2-0050** or 2-00149, or 800/221-6509 in the U.S. Fax 987/2-0381. 100 rms. A/C TEL. High season $132–$176 single or double. Low season $110–$150.

After several years as an all-inclusive resort, the Cozumeleño is once again functioning as a regular hotel. But it's kept some of the all-inclusive amenities, such as an 19-hole miniature golf course, a karaoke bar, and water-sports equipment. The five-story hotel (with elevator) has one of the nicest stretches of coral-free beach on the island. The expansive marble-floored lobby scattered with pastel groupings of chairs and couches is a popular gathering place. The glassed-in dining room looks out onto the Caribbean, as do all the spacious and nicely furnished guest rooms. There's a very nice palm-shaded swimming pool as well.

Dining/Entertainment: Two restaurants, one by the beach and pool and the other indoors in a glassed-in area facing the beach, serve all three meals.

Services: Laundry and room service, travel agency, auto and moped rental.

Facilities: A pool, tennis court, water-sports equipment rental.

Moderate

Cabañas del Caribe
Carretera Santa Pilar km 4.5 (Apdo. Postal 9), 77600 Cozumel, Q. Roo. ☎ **987/2-0017** or 987/2-0072 or 800/336-3542 in the U.S. Fax 987/2-1599. 48 rms. A/C. High season $125 single or double. Low season $90 single or double. Free parking.

Built in two sections, the hotel gives you two choices of room styles. Standard rooms in the two-story section adjacent to the lobby are smallish (but very nice) and decorated in southwest shades of apricot and blue. All have small sitting areas and either a porch or balcony facing the beach and pool. The one-story bungalow/cabaña section has a similar decor, but rooms are larger and have patios on the beach.

Dining/Entertainment: The main restaurant is in a glassed-in terrace on the beach, and there's a poolside spot for snacks.

Services: Travel agency.

Facilities: Swimming pool; water-sports equipment for rent including sailboats, jet skis, and diving, snorkeling, and windsurfing equipment; pharmacy; gift shop.

Hotel Fontan

Carretera Santa Pilar km 2.5, 77600 Cozumel, Q. Roo. ☎ **987/2-0300,** or 800/221-6509 in the U.S. Fax 987/2-0105. 48 rms. A/C TV TEL. High season $80–$110 single or double. Low season $70–90 single or double. Free unguarded parking.

Rooms on all four floors of this tan-colored hotel are well maintained and have private balconies; most have ocean views. Baths all have showers. There's a nice pool by the beach (held up by a retaining wall) that's surrounded by lounge chairs. There's a restaurant/bar, plus a dock for water sports. The hotel is an excellent value for your money.

HOTELS IN TOWN

Expensive

Hotel Plaza Las Glorias

Av. Rafael. Melgar km 1.5 77600 Cozumel, Q. Roo. ☎ **987/2-2000** or 800/342-AMIGO. Fax 987/2-1937. 170 rms and suites. A/C MINBAR TV TEL. High season $150–$185 single or double. Low season $135–$170 single or double.

An all-suite hotel, this one offers the top-notch amenities of the expensive hotels farther out, but it's within five blocks of town. Beyond the expansive, comfortable lobby is the pool, with a swim-up bar, a multilevel deck, a shored-up beach, and the ocean. Most of the large nicely furnished rooms all have cool tile floors, separate sunken living rooms and balconies with views. The deluxe suites have whirlpools on the terrace. Standard in-room amenities include hair dryers, purified tap water, and in-room safety deposit boxes.

Dining/Entertainment: During high season there's usually a buffet at breakfast and lunch. The main restaurant features different specialties nightly. There's palapa dining outside for all meals (weather permitting). The popular lobby bar features a large-screen TV which brings in major sports events. In high season there's often live entertainment (soft music) there as well and a happy hour with two-for-one drinks between 5 and 7pm.

Services: Laundry and room service, fully equipped dive shop with PADI and NAUI certification available

Facilities: Swimming pool with swim-up bar by the beach, diving pier, organized pool games, recreational director, travel agency, concierge.

Moderate

Hotel Barracuda

Av. Rafael Melgar 628 (Apdo. Postal 163), 77600 Cozumel, Q. Roo. ☎ **987/2-0002** or 2-1243. Fax 987/2-0884 or 2-3633. 50 rms (all with bath). A/C FAN. High season, $60 single; $65 double. Low season, $42 single; $48 double.

You won't think much of this plain tan-colored building a short walk south of town, but the view from within is outstanding. Rustic carved-wood furnishings decorate the cozy rooms, all with balconies looking out to sea. There's a refrigerator in each room as well. An inner hallway leading to the rooms blocks out the noise from the road. There's no pool, but lounge chairs are lined up on an elevated strip of sand, and stairs lead down to a good snorkeling area. There is a small oceanfront café serving breakfast and snacks, plus a good dive shop. The hotel is on Costera Sur, a 10-minute walk from town; from the pier walk right; the hotel is on your right. Street parking is readily available.

Inexpensive

B & B Caribo

799 Avenida Juárez, 77600 Cozumel, Q. Roo. ☎ and fax **987/2-3195,** or 800/830-5558 in the U.S. 10 rms (8 with bath). FAN. $350 per week single or double; $700 per month single; $850 per month double. Rates include continental breakfast.

The blue-and-white residence behind a short white iron fence looks like one of the finer residences in this neighborhood. The 10 rooms continue the crisp blue-and-white decor and come with cool tile fllors, white furniture, blue bedspreads, and big bottles of purified drinking water. Eight of the rooms have air-conditioning and private baths. Two rooms have a shared bath in the middle and these have fans but no air conditioning. A bakery with breads and pastries is located in the front of the house. To find the Caribo from the plaza, walk 6¹/₂ blocks inland on Juárez, and it's on the left.

Hotel Aguilar

Calle 3 Sur no. 95, 77600 Cozumel, Q. Roo. ☎ **987/2-0307.** Fax 987/2-0769. 32 rms (all with bath). A/C and FAN. High season, $35 single or double. Low season, $29 single or double.

Behind its white stucco walls you'll find a clean, quiet little respite focused on a large pool and a plant-filled courtyard within walking distance of downtown action. The spotless rooms come with fresh paint, lights over the beds, tile floors, two double beds (firm) covered with ruffled spreads, and glass windows with good screens. You can rent a car (expensive), boat, or motor scooter in the lobby. To find the hotel, turn right at the ferry pier on Melgar, then turn left on Calle 3 Sur.

Hotel El Marqués

Av. 5 Sur no. 180, 77600 Cozumel, Q. Roo. ☎ **987/2-0677.** Fax 987/2-0537. 40 rms (all with bath). A/C. High season, $32 single or double. Low season, $22 single or double. Discounts for two or more nights.

Each of the sunny rooms here has gold trim and Formica-marble countertops, French provincial overtones, gray-and-white tile floors, and two double beds. The junior suites have refrigerators; full suites have refrigerators, stoves, and sitting areas. Third-floor rooms have good views. The staff is friendly and attentive. To find it from the plaza, turn right (south) on Av. 5 Sur; the hotel near the corner of Salas, on the right up the stairs next to Coco's restaurant.

⊗ Hotel Flamingo

Calle 6 Norte no. 81, 77600 Cozumel, Q. Roo. ☎ **987/2-1264.** 22 rms (all with bath). FAN. High season, $25 single; $29 double. Low season, $17 single; $21 double.

Built in 1986, the Flamingo offers three floors of quiet rooms, a grassy inner courtyard, and very helpful management. Second- and third-story rooms are spacious. All have white tile floors. Rooms on the front have balconies overlooking the street. Some doubles have one bed; others have two. Soft drinks and bottled water are available from the refrigerator in the lobby. Trade paperbacks are by the reception desk and a TV in the lobby is for guests. You get a lot for your money here. To find it, walk five blocks north on Melgar from the plaza and turn right on Calle 6; the hotel is on the left between Melgar and Avenida 5. Street parking is available.

Hotel Mary-Carmen

Av. 5 Sur no. 4 (Apdo. Postal 14), 77600 Cozumel, Q. Roo. ☎ **987/2-0581.** 30 rms (all with bath). A/C or FAN. High season, $32 single or double. Low season, $27 single or double.

Watched over by eagle-eyed señoras, the two stories of rooms at the Mary-Carmen surround an interior courtyard shaded by a large mamey tree. Rooms are clean and carpeted, with well-screened windows facing the courtyard. Most have two double beds. Upstairs rooms have fan only, while first-floor rooms have both fan and air-conditioning. It's half a block south of the zócalo on the right.

Hotel Maya Cozumel

Calle 5 Sur (Apdo. Postal 23), 77600 Cozumel, Q. Roo. ☎ **987/2-0011.** Fax 987/2-0781. 38 rms (all with bath). A/C TEL. $34 single; $40 double.

Maya touches decorate the lobby and rooms in this pretty, apricot-and-white hotel. A long green lawn and small, clean pool are framed by two three-story buildings and flowering shrubs. Paintings of Maya deities decorate the blue, green, and white walls in the large rooms; some have leather lounge chairs, and TVs with cable connection are available in 15 rooms. The rates stay the same year-round. Street parking is limited. From the ferry pier turn right (south) and walk three blocks on Melgar, then turn left on Calle 5. The hotel is on the left between Melgar and 5 Avenida Sur.

ⓈHotel Pepita

Av. 15 Sur (Apdo. Postal 120), 77600 Cozumel, Q. Roo. ☎ **987/2-0098.** Fax 987/2-0201. 30 rms (all with bath). FAN or A/C. $25 single or double.

Quiet and laid-back, this small two-story inn is an economical hideaway in a peaceful residential neighborhood. The rooms are simple and clean, with good screens on the windows, tiled baths, and mismatched toilet seats. The narrow courtyard is filled with tables and chairs and large bird cages with green parrots. Mornings, between 5 and 10am, complimentary coffee and cookies are available in the lobby. The price seems a bit high, so ask for a discount. To get there from the pier, walk two blocks south on Melgar to Salas, go left three blocks to Avenida 15 Sur, then turn left. The hotel is on your left.

Hotel Safari Inn

Av. Melgar at Calle 5 Sur (Apdo. Postal 41), 77600 Cozumel, Q. Roo. ☎ **987/2-0101.** Fax 987/ 2-0661. 12 rms (all with bath). A/C. High season $42 single; $45 double. Low season $31 single; $35 double.

The nicest budget hotel in town is above and behind the Aqua Dive Shop. Natural colors and stucco pervade the interior of this three-story (no elevator) establishment. The huge rooms come with firm beds, built-in sofas, and tiled floors. The hotel caters to divers and offers some good dive packages through its dive shop on the first floor—one of the most reputable on the island. To find it from the pier, turn right (south) and walk 3¹/₂ blocks on Melgar; the hotel is on your left facing the Caribbean at the corner of Calle 5 Sur.

Hotel Suites Bazar Colonial

Av. 5 Sur no. 9 (Apdo. Postal 286), 77600 Cozumel, Q. Roo. ☎ **987/2-0506.** Fax 987/2-1387. 28 rms (all with bath). A/C TV TEL. High season, $55 single; $60 double. Low season, $40 single; $50 double.

Across the street from the El Marqués is a collection of shops and this nice four-story hotel—with an elevator. It's a good deal for the money. The lobby is far back past the shops. You get a quiet, spacious, furnished studio or a one-bedroom apartment with red tile floors on the first floor; second- and third-floor rooms have kitchenettes. The street is closed to traffic. From the plaza, walk half a block south on Avenida 5 Sur; the hotel is on the left.

Posada Edem

Calle 2 Norte no. 12, Cozumel, 77600 Q. Roo. ☎ **987/2-1166.** 15 rms (all with bath). FAN. $12 single; $14 double.

This small, modest hotel is near the Sports Page restaurant. The rooms are plain but functional, each with tile floors, sheets (but no bedspreads), and a single light hanging from the ceiling. The showers in some bathrooms drip constantly—check it out before you unpack. Four rooms have air conditioning. To get there from the Sports Page turn left and walk 1½ blocks on Calle 2; it's on your right.

HOTELS SOUTH OF TOWN

The best beaches are south of town, but not all the best ones have hotels on them. Each hotel has either a swimming pool, a tiny cove, a dock, or all three. You'll be able to swim, sun, and relax at any of these hotels and most are diver-oriented. **Costera Sur,** also called **Carretera a Chankanaab,** is the southern extension of Melgar, so just follow Melgar south through town to reach these hotels, which are, generally speaking, farther apart than those north of town.

Very Expensive

Presidente Inter-Continental Cozumel

Costera Sur km 6.0, 77600 Cozumel, Q. Roo. ☎ **987/2-0322,** or 800/327-0200 in the U.S. Fax 987/2-1360. 253 rms. A/C MINIBAR TV TEL. High season $165–$365 double. Low season $140–$265 double. Discounts and packages available. Free parking.

The first thing you'll notice here is the palatial scale of the place and the masterful, stylishly grand combination of marble with hot-pink stucco and stone as you enter. Near the Chankanaab Lagoon, the hotel, surrounded by shady palms, spreads out on a beautiful beach with no close neighbors. Rates vary widely, depending on your view and time of year you travel, even within seasons. There are four categories of rooms— some have balconies and garden views, while very spacious rooms come with balconies and ocean views. Deluxe beachfront rooms have comfortable patios and direct access to the beach on the ground floor; on the second floor there are balconies with ocean views. The no-smoking rooms are all on the fourth level, and two rooms are set aside for guests with disabilities. Naturally each category of room has a different price. Absolutely ask about discounts and packages.

Dining/Entertainment: The Arrecife restaurant serves international specialties and is open daily from 6pm to midnight. Caribeño, by the pool and beach, is open from 7am to 7pm.

Services: Room and laundry service; travel agency; car and motorbike rental.

Facilities: Swimming pool; two tennis courts; water-sports equipment rental; dive shop and dive-boat pier; pharmacy; boutiques.

Expensive

La Ceiba Beach Hotel

Costera Sur km 4.5 (Apdo. Postal 284), Cozumel, Q. Roo.☎ **987/2-0815** or 800/437-9609. Fax 800/235-5892. 113 rms. A/C MINIBAR TV TEL. High season $150–$200 single or double. Low season $125 single or double. Diving packages available. Free parking.

Across from the Sol Caribe, on the beach side of the road, La Ceiba is named for the lofty and majestic tree, sacred to the Maya, which grows in the tropics. It's a popular hotel, and the large lobby seems to always be abustle with guests. Rooms all have ocean views and balconies, and bathrooms have combination tubs and showers. The swimming pool is only steps from the beach.

The emphasis here is on water sports, particularly scuba diving, and if this is your passion, be sure to ask about the special dive packages when you call for reservations.

Dining/Entertainment: The Galleon Bar/Restaurant, off the lobby, has walls shaped like an old ship and is open for all meals. Chopaloca, by the beach, is open daily from early morning until almost midnight.

Services: Laundry and room service, travel agency.

Facilities: Large, free-form swimming pool by the beach, tennis court, water sports, dive shop and dive-boat pier, roped-off area for snorkeling.

Moderate

Galápagos Inn

Costera Sur km 1.5 (Apdo. Postal 289), 77600 Cozumel, Q. Roo. ☎ **987/2-0663** or 2-1133, or call Aqua-Sub Tours 800/847-5708 in the U.S. or 713/783-3305 in Texas. 54 rms. A/C. High season three-night package $355 per person. Low season $325 per person. Package rates include all meals and two days diving. Longer diving packages and lower rates for nondivers available.

Homey, shady, and done in colonial style with white stucco and redbrick accents, this older inn is usually peopled by divers who have signed up for one of the several money-saving three-, five-, and seven-night package deals. The inn, located a mile south of the main square, has its own small swimming pool and a bit of walled-in beach. A row of hammocks swings under a long thatched roof by the ocean where there's nothing but the sound of surf and breezes. Some rooms have balconies or terraces on the beach. All have ocean views. One restaurant serves all meals with specific meal times. The bar, with drinks only, is open daily from 7 to 11pm. There's a fully equipped dive shop; dives take off from the hotel's pier.

DINING

Zermatt, a terrific little bakery, is on Avenida 5 at Calle 4 Norte. On Calle 2 Norte, half a block in from the waterfront, is the **Panificadora Cozumel,** excellent for a do-it-yourself breakfast or for picnic supplies. It's open from 6am to 9pm daily.

VERY EXPENSIVE

✪ Café del Puerto

Av. Melgar 3. ☎ **987/2-0316.** Reservations recommended. Main courses $11–$35. Dinner only, daily 5pm–11pm. INTERNATIONAL.

For a romantic dinner with a sunset view, try this restaurant. After being greeted at the door, climb the spiral staircase to the main dining room or continue to a higher loft, overlooking the rest of the dining room. Soft piano music entertains in the background. The service is polished and polite, and the menu is sophisticated, with dishes like mustard steak flambé, shrimp brochette with bacon and pineapple, and prime rib. From the pier cross the street and turn left on Melgar; it's almost immediately on your right.

Pepe's Grill

Av. Rafael Melgar at Salas. ☎ **987/2-0213.** Reservations recommended. Main courses $11–$30; children's menu $7. Daily 5–11:30pm. GRILLED SPECIALTIES.

Pepe's started the grilled-food tradition in Cozumel and continues as a popular trendsetter with low lights, soft music, solicitous waiters, and excellent food; the perpetual crowd is here for a reason. The menu is extensive, with flame-broiled specialties such as beef fillet Singapore and shrimp Bahamas. The children's menu offers breaded shrimp and fried chicken. For dessert try the cajeta crepes.

MODERATE

✪ D'Pub

Calle 4 Norte. ☎ **987/2-4132.** Reservations recommended in high season. Main courses $5–$14. Mon–Sat 11pm–midnight; Sun 5pm–midnight; Pub/Botanera Mon–Sat 11am–5pm. SEAFOOD/INTERNATIONAL.

Nothing here is quite what you expect. It's in a new building that's architecturally like the old island frame houses with cutout wood trim. Then it's a handsome English-style pub with mahogany bar glimmering with shiny glass and brass while coupling the best of Mexican cantina (the equivalent of a Mexican pub) tradition, offering delicious snacks free with inexpensive drinks—but that's only between 11am and 5pm. After 5pm it's transformed from casual to elegant, becoming a stylish restaurant with cloth-covered tables where good service brings terrific crispy fresh salads, curried chicken, large seafood platters, fish and chips, barbecue chicken, dip roast-beef sandwiches, fajitas, stir-fried vegetables, steaks, and an enormous Mexican combo including roasted chicken, rice, beans, guacamole, an enchilada, and a quesadilla. You can dine inside or on the veranda or patio in back overlooking the shaded garden. In the main room as you enter, casual couches and conversational areas are conducive to leisurely drinking, chatting, playing cards or backgammon, or watching ESPN, CNN, WGN Chicago, or sporting events. The latter two are played at low volume. The gracious owners Anibal and Mercedes de Iturbide are almost always on hand. To get there from the plaza turn left (north) on Avenida 5 Norte, walk two blocks and turn right on Calle 4 Norte; it's behind Zermatt bakery, on your right midway up the block.

La Mission

Av. Juárez 23. ☎ **987/2-1641.** Seafood dishes $8–$18; meat dishes $8–$10; Mexican specialties $7–$9. Daily 3pm–midnight. GRILLED MEAT/MEXICAN.

You can tell by the crowds that this is a popular restaurant, where foreign visitors leave saying "We'll see you next year." The first thing you'll notice is the colorfully tiled open kitchen on the right where cooks prepare the dependably good flame-broiled food for which La Mission is known. The tender fajita platter comes with guacamole, beans, rice, and fresh flour tortillas. The seafood platter includes shrimp and lobster, and the garlic bread is great. The owner says, "If you don't like it, don't pay." From the plaza turn right (east) on Juárez and walk one block; it's on your right between Avenidas 10 and 15 Sur.

✪ El Moro

75 bis Norte 124. ☎ **987/2-3029.** Main courses $3–$10; margarita $3.30; beer $1.15. Fri–Wed 1–11pm. Closed Thrusday. REGIONAL.

Crowds flock to El Moro for its wonderfully prepared food and service, but not the decor, which is orange, orange, orange, and Formica. And it's away from everything—a taxi is a must—costing around $1.30 one way. But you won't care as soon as you taste anything, and especially if you sip even a little of their giant, whallop-packing margaritas. The pollo Ticuleño (a specialty from the town of Ticul), is a ribsticking, delicious, layered plate of smooth tomato sauce, mashed potatoes, crispy baked corn tortilla, and batter fried chicken breast, all topped with shredded cheese and green peas. Besides the regional food, other specialties of Mexico march from the kitchen piping hot, such as enchiladas and seafood many ways, plus grilled steaks, sandwiches, and, of course, nachos to go with that humdinger of a margarita. El Moro is $12^{1}/_{2}$ blocks inland from Melgar between Calles 2 and 4 Norte.

✪ La Choza

Salas 198 at Av. 10 Sur. ☎ **987/2-0958.** Breakfast $2.50; appetizers $2.50–$3.50; main courses $7–$12; Daily 7:30am–11pm. YUCATECAN.

The filled tables looking out the big open-air windows on the corner of Salas and 10th Sur announce that this is a favorite of both tourists and locals. It looks like a big Maya house with white stucco walls and thatched roof. Platters of chiles stuffed with shrimp, *pollo en relleno negro* (chicken in a blackened pepper sauce), *puerco entometado* (pork stew), and beefsteak in a poblano pepper sauce, are among the truly authentic specialties.

✪ Prima

Calle Salas 109. ☎ **987/2-4242.** Appetizers $3.30–$9; pizzas $5–$12; pastas $5–$15; calzone $3–$5.25; early bird special $5. Daily 3–11pm. ITALIAN.

One of the few good Italian restaurants in Mexico, Prima gets better every year. Everything is fresh—the pastas, calzones, and sourdough pizza. Owner Albert Domínguez grows most of the vegetables in his hydroponic garden on the island. The menu changes daily and might include shrimp scampi, fettucine with pesto, and lobster and crab ravioli with cream sauce. The fettucine Alfredo is wonderful, as are the puff-pastry garlic "bread" and crispy house salad. Dining is upstairs on the breezy terrace. Next door is **Prima Deli,** serving great sandwiches on fresh-baked bread and aromatic coffee from 9am to 7pm. To get to either place from the pier turn right (south) on Melgar and walk two blocks to Calle 5 Sur and turn left. Prima is visible on your left between Calles 5 and 10 Sur. Hotel delivery is available.

Pizza Rolandi

Av. Melgar, between Calles 6 and 8 Norte. ☎ **987/2-0946.** Appetizers $3.80–$8.25; main courses $8.50–$13; pizza $9–$11; daily specials $4.25–$13. Mon–Sat 11am–11pm; Sun 5–11pm. ITALIAN.

Deck chairs and glossy wood tables make the inviting interior garden a restful place in daytime, and it becomes romantic with candlelight at night. The specialty here (as in their branches in Isla Mujeres and Cancún) is wood-oven–baked pizzas. But for a change, look for pasta prepared five ways and the weekly specials, which may be a special appetizer of sea bass carpaccio, pizza, pasta, or fish with an Italian twist. To get there from the pier turn left (north) on Melgar and walk four block; it's on your right.

INEXPENSIVE

✪ Café Caribe

Av. 10 Sur 215. ☎ **987/2-3621.** Coffee and pastries $1–$3. Mon–Sat 8am–1pm and 6–9:30pm. PASTRIES & COFFEE.

This cute little eatery behind a facade of fuchsia and dark green may become your favorite place to start or finish the day or for something in between. You'll find ice cream, milk shakes, freshly made cheesecake and carrot cake, waffles, bagels, croissants, and biscuits filled with cheese and cream, ham and cheese, or butter and marmalade. Nine different coffees are served, including Cuban, cappuccino, espresso, and Irish. To get there from the plaza turn right (south) on Avenida 5 Sur, walk one block and turn left on Calle Salas, then right on Avenida 10; it's on your left.

✪ Casa de Denis

Calle 1 Sur. ☎ **987/2-0067.** Breakfast $1.25–$3; main courses $4–$12. Mon–Sat 7am–11pm. REGIONAL/INTERNATIONAL.

This yellow wooden house holds a great home-style Mexican restaurant. Small tables are scattered outside on the pedestrians-only street and in two rooms separated by a foyer filled with family photos. More tables are set in the back on the shady patio. You can make a light meal from empanadas filled with potatoes, cheese, or fish, or go for the full comida of fried grouper, rice, and beans, or better yet, try one of the regional specialties such as pollo pibil or pork brochette seasoned with the subtle flavor of achiote. Groups of four or more can request a special meal in advance. To get there from the plaza walk a half block inland up Calle 1 Sur; it's on your right.

ⓢ Cocina Económica Mi Chabelita

Av. 10 Sur. ☎ **987/2-0896**. Breakfast $2.25–$5.75; main courses $3–$7. Mon–Sat 7am–9pm. MEXICAN.

Few tourists have discovered this cheery and informal eatery that caters to locals. It seems to get better every year. Breakfast features omelets and traditional Yucatecan eggs motuleño-style, or more filling fare, such as enchiladas verdes or mole and quesadillas. At lunch and dinner the menu offers tacos, liver and onions, steak and potatoes, fried fish, and soup and homemade mole. To get there from the plaza, walk one block south on Calle 1 Sur and turn right on Avenida 10 Sur; it's on your left near the corner of Salas.

ⓞ Coco's

Av. 5 Sur no. 180, at the corner of Calle Salas. ☎ **987/2-0241**. Breakfast $2.50–$5. Tues–Sun 7am–noon. Closed the last 2 weeks of September and the first week of October. MEXICAN/ AMERICAN.

Once discovered, Coco's becomes a favorite. Tended by owners Terri and Daniel Ocejo, it's clean and welcoming to the tourist, right down to the free coffee refills and the ready purified ice water. Plan to indulge in Stateside favorites like hash browns, cornflakes and bananas, gigantic blueberry muffins, cinnamon rolls, and cream stuffed rolls, plus something unique like a bagelwich or a sandwich on an English muffin. Mexican specialties include huevos rancheros, huevos mexicana, and eggs scrambled with chiles and covered with melted cheese. And you can order them with Egg Beater™ eggs, if you wish. The really famished should inquire about the inexpensive but outrageously filling "Loco" breakfast. A gift section at the front includes gourmet coffee, local honey, bottles of hot pepper, chocolate, *rompope*, and vanilla. Plus there's a paperback book exchange. To get there from the plaza turn right (south) on Avenida 5 Sur. Coco's is on your right beside the entry to the Hotel El Marqués.

Comida Casera Toñita

Calle Salas 265, between Calles 10 and 15 Norte. ☎ **987/2-0401**. Breakfast $1.50–$2; main courses $3.75–$5; daily specials $2.50; fruit drinks $1. Mon–Sat 8am–6pm. HOME-STYLE YUCATECAN.

The owners have taken the living room of their home and made it into a comfortable dining room, complete with filled bookshelves and classical music playing in the background. Whole fried fish, fish fillet, fried chicken, and beefsteak prepared as you wish are on the regular menu. Daily specials give you a chance to taste authentic regional food, including a pollo a la naranja, chicken mole, pollo en escabeche, and pork chops with *achiote* seasoning. To reach Toñita's, walk south from the plaza on Avenida 5 Sur for one block, then turn left on Salas and walk east 1¹/₂ blocks; the restaurant is on your left.

ⓞ Frutas Selectas

Calle Rosado Salas 352. ☎ **987/2-5560**. Breakfast $1.35–$2.75; salads $1.35–$3; sandwiches $1.35–$2; fruit and vegetable juices 75¢–$1.35; coffee 75¢. Mon–Sat 7am–2pm and 5–9pm. FRUIT/PASTRIES.

The sweet smell of fruit will greet you as you enter Frutas Selecta. Downstairs is a grocery store specializing in fresh fruit, and upstairs is the sleek and cheery restaurant with windows on two sides. The yellow and green sign reads only NATURAL. Juices, licuados, "the best coffee in town," yogurt, veggie sandwiches, a salad bar, fruit shakes, baked potatoes with a variety of toppings, and pastries are served. From the plaza, turn right and walk one block south on Avenida 5 Sur, then turn left on Salas and walk three blocks east. It's on your right between 15th and 20th Norte.

✪ The Waffle House

Av. Melgar. ☎ **987/2-0545** or 2-3065. Waffles $2.80–$4.50; breakfast $2.80–$4; main courses $5–$9. Daily 6am–1pm and 6–10pm. BREAKFAST/DESSERTS/MEXICAN.

Tables are often full since the Waffle House has far more business than it has space to handle. The name is a bit misleading since you can order way more than waffles, and you can also have breakfast any time. Jeanie De Lille, the island's premier pastry chef, bakes crisp, light waffles and serves them in many ways, including the waffle ranchero with eggs and salsa, the waffle benedict with eggs and hollandaise sauce, and waffles with whipped cream and chocolate. Hash browns, homemade breads, and great coffee are other reasons to drop in for breakfast mornings and evenings. The menu has been expanded to include fried fish, tamales, *carne asada tampiqueña*, and several pasta dishes, and there is a full bar. To get there from the pier turn right (south) on Melgar and walk four blocks; it's on your left between the Aqua Safari and the Hotel Vista del Mar.

COZUMEL AFTER DARK

Cozumel is a town frequented by sports-minded visitors who play hard all day and wind down early at night. People sit in outdoor cafés around the zócalo enjoying the cool night breezes until the restaurants close. **Carlos 'n' Charlie's** and the **Hard Rock Café,** both on Melgar left of the pier, are two of the liveliest places in town. **Karen's Grill and Pizza,** on Avenida 5 between Juárez and Calle 2 Norte, features live entertainment in the evenings.

Scaramouche, a popular disco, on Melgar at Salas, is open nightly from 10pm to 3am. The cover charge varies.

3 Puerto Morelos

21 miles S of Cancún

Most people come here to take the car-ferry to Cozumel, several hours away. Puerto Morelos has begun to resume the building boom that was beginning when Hurricane Gilbert came through.

ESSENTIALS
GETTING THERE

By Bus   Buses from Cancún's bus station going to Tulum and Playa del Carmen usually stop here, but be sure to ask in Cancún if your bus makes the Puerto Morelos stop.

By Car   Drive south from Cancún along Highway 307 to the km 31 marker. There are a couple of worthwhile stops along Highway 307 on the way to Puerto Morelos. **Croco Cun,** a zoological park where crocodiles are raised, is one of the most interesting attractions in the area—don't be put off by the comical name. Though far from grand, the park has exhibits of crocodiles in all stages of development, as well as animals of nearly all the species that once roamed the Yucatán Peninsula. The snake exhibit is fascinating, though it may make you think twice about roaming in the jungle. The rattlesnakes and boa constrictors are particularly intimidating, and the tarantulas are downright enormous. Children enjoy the guides' enthusiastic tours and are entranced by the spider monkeys and wild pigs. Wear plenty of bug repellent and allow an hour or two for the tour, followed by a cool drink in the restaurant. Croco Cun is open daily from 8:30am to 5:30pm. Admission is $5, and free for children under 6. The park is at km 31 on Highway 307.

About half a mile before Puerto Morelos is a 150-acre **Jardín Botánico,** opened in 1990 and named after Dr. Alfredo Barrera, a biologist who studied the selva (a common geographical term meaning "tropical evergreen broadleaf forest"). A natural, protected showcase for native plants and animals, it's open Tuesday through Sunday from 9am to 4pm. Admission is $3; it's worth the money—and every minute of the hour or more it will take to see it. Slather on the mosquito repellent, though.

The park is divided into six parts: an epiphyte area (plants that grow on others); Maya ruins; an ethnographic area, with a furnished hut and typical garden; a chiclero camp, about the once-thriving chicle (chewing gum) industry; a nature park, where wild vegetation is preserved; and mangroves. Wandering along the marked paths, you'll see that the dense jungle of plants and trees is named and labeled in English and Spanish. Each sign has the plant's scientific and common names, use of the plant, and the geographic areas where it is found in the wild. It's rich in bird and animal life, too, but to catch a glimpse of something you'll have to move quietly and listen carefully.

By the Puerto Morelos–Cozumel Car-Ferry   The dock (☎ 987/1-0008), the largest establishment in town, is very easy to find. Look to the Cozumel section above for details on the car-ferry schedule, but several points bear repeating here: The car-ferry schedule is complicated and may change, so double-check it before arriving. And always arrive at least three hours in advance of the ferry's departure to purchase a ticket and to get in line.

ORIENTATION   There's one public telephone in Puerto Morelos (☎ 987/ 2-0070 and fax 1-0081), at the Caseta de Larga Distancia, next to the Zenaida Restaurant a block south of the main entry street leading to the highway. You can make calls there, and supposedly they'll take messages and pass along hotel-reservation requests. It's open Monday through Saturday from 8am to 1pm and 4 to 7pm. On the highway, near the Puerto Morelos junction, you'll see a gas station with public phones (including Ladatel phones that accept prepaid phone cards) and a supermarket on the right.

EXPLORING AROUND PUERTO MORELOS

Puerto Morelos is attracting more of its own clientele—people seeking seaside relaxation without the crowds and high prices. You make your own fun here. But for **diving and fishing** try **Sub Aqua Explorers** (☎ 987/1-0012; fax 1-0162), on the main square. More than 15 dive sites are nearby and many are close to shore. A two-tank dive costs around $60 and night dives $55. Two hours of fishing costs around $80 and snorkeling excursions run around $5.

ACCOMMODATIONS

Ojo de Agua

Calle Ejer Mexicano, 77500 Puerto Morelos, Q. Roo. ☎ **987/1-0027** (reservations: Calle 12 no. 96, between Calles 21 and 23, Mérida, Yuc. 97050. ☎ 99/25-0292; fax 99/28-3405). 16 rms (all with bath). FAN. High season, $45–$55 single or double. Low season, $40–$50 single or double.

This family-style two-story hotel on the beach is ideal for a long weekend or extended stay, especially in the 12 rooms with kitchens. Each room contains a white tile floor, natural-tone furniture, and a table and chairs. Most rooms have one double and one twin bed, but two come with king-size beds. There's a free-form pool by the ocean. Restaurants are within easy walking distance and dive gear and trips are available

The Yucatan's Upper Caribbean Coast

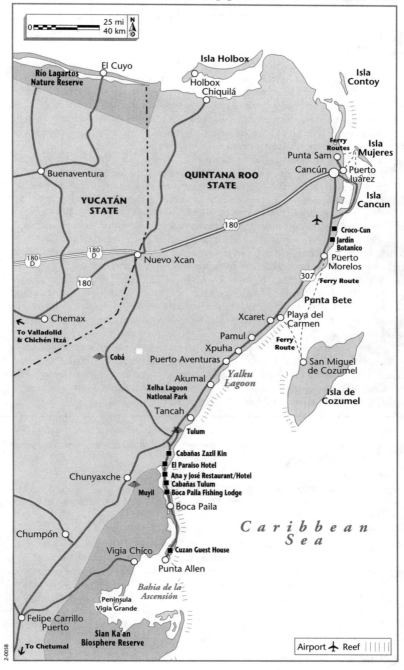

Isla Holbox

Isla Contoy

Río Lagartos
Nature Reserve

El Cuyo

Holbox
Chiquilá

Ferry
Routes

Isla
Mujeres

Punta Sam

Buenaventura

QUINTANA ROO
STATE

Cancún

Puerto
Juárez

YUCATÁN
STATE

Isla
Cancun

180

Croco-Cun

Jardín
Botanico

180
D

180
D

Nuevo Xcan

Puerto
Morelos

307

Ferry Route

180

Punta Bete

Chemax

Xcaret

Playa del
Carmen

To Valladolid
& Chichén Itzá

Pamul

Cobá

Xpuha

Puerto Aventuras

Ferry
Route

San Miguel
de Cozumel

Akumal

Yalku
Lagoon

Xelha Lagoon
National Park

Isla de
Cozumel

Tancah

Tulum

Cabañas Zazil Kin

El Paraíso Hotel

Chunyaxche

Ana y José Restaurant/Hotel

Cabañas Tulum

Muyil

Boca Paila Fishing Lodge

Boca Paila

Caribbean
Sea

Chumpón

Vigia Chico

Cuzan Guest House

Punta Allen

Bahia de la
Ascensión

Peninsula
Vigia Grande

Felipe Carrillo
Puerto

Sian Ka'an
Biosphere Reserve

To Chetumal

0   25 mi
    40 km

N

Airport ✈ Reef |||||

2-0058

On the Road in the Yucatán

Here's a few things to keep in mind if you're planning to hit the road and explore the Yucatán.

Except in Cancún, Isla Mujeres, Playa del Carmen, and Cozumel, exchanging money is difficult along this coast. And though Isla Mujeres and Cozumel are breezy enough to keep them at bay, everywhere else mosquitoes are numerous and fierce on this coast, so bring plenty of mosquito repellent that has DEET as the main ingredient. (Avon's Skin So Soft, a bath oil that's acquired quite a reputation in the States for its unexpected effectiveness as an almost pleasant-smelling mosquito repellent, is practically useless here.)

The most economical way to see the Yucatán is by bus. Although service is still best between the major cities, since 1992 it has improved considerably to other parts of the peninsula as well. There are more deluxe buses. You can sometimes purchase tickets in advance—often selecting your seat on a computer screen. Using buses as the primary means of transportation will add more days to your trip. On highways, you can still flag down buses that are going your way and hop aboard, though you'll spend a lot of time waiting at intersections, particularly near Uxmal and Kabah and along the Caribbean coast. If you're waiting on a busy route—say between Cancún and Tulum—many full buses will pass you by. Distances are deceiving. For example, a bus trip using the new highway from Mérida to Cancún takes four hours; bus travel between Mérida and Palenque takes nine hours. To find the fastest bus, get in the habit of asking if a bus goes *sin escalas* or *directo* (nonstop or direct); either may mean no stops or only a couple of stops as opposed to many stops on a regular bus.

The best way to see the Yucatán is by car. It's one of the most pleasant parts of the country for a driving vacation. The jungle- and beach-lined roads, while narrow and without shoulders, are generally in good condition and have little traffic. And they are straight, except in the southern part of Yucatán state and west to Campeche, where they undulate through the Yucatán "Alps."

through the hotel. To find it from the plaza, turn left on the last street that parallels the ocean. The hotel is at the far end on the left.

Posada Amor

Apdo. Postal 806, 77580 Cancún, Q. Roo. ☎ **987/1-0033.** 20 rms (8 with bath). $16.50 single without bath, $20 double without bath; $22 single with bath, $25 double with bath, $29 for a room with 4 beds and bath.

The simple, cheery little rooms at the Posada Amor, with screens and mosquito netting, are plain but adequate and overpriced. They're clustered around a patio in back of the restaurant. The posada's restaurant is rustic and quaint like an English cottage—with whitewashed walls, small shuttered windows, and open rafters—and decorated with primitive paintings and flowers on each table. The food is tasty, with many regional specialties, sandwiches, a comida corrida for $3.50 and a Sunday buffet for $5. It's open daily from 7:30am to 11pm. To get here, when you enter town, turn right; with the town square on the left, follow the main street leading to the ferry; the hotel is about a block down on the right.

DINING

Besides the above-mentioned Posada Amor, Los Pelicanos is worth trying.

The four-lane toll road between Cancún and Mérida is complete but actually ends short of either city. Costing around $15 one-way, it cuts the trip from five to around four hours. The old two-lane free road is still in fine shape and passes through numerous villages with many speed-control bumps (*topes*)—this route is much more interesting. New directional signs seem to lead motorists to the toll road (*cuota*) and don't mention the free road (*libre*), so if you want to use it, ask locals for directions.

A new four-lane stretch of road is finished going out of Cancún south for several miles. Originally it was to extend to Chetumal, but the local rumor is that a new toll road instead will parallel the existing two-lane Highway 307 and connect Cancún and Chetumal; construction hasn't yet begun. Meanwhile, traffic is quite heavy from Cancún to Tulum, and drivers go too fast. A stalled or stopped car is hard to see, and there are no shoulders for pulling off the roadway. Follow these precautions for a safe journey: Never turn left while on the highway (it's against Mexican law anyway). Always go to the next road on the right and turn around and come back to the turnoff you want. Occasionally, a specially constructed right-hand turnoff, such as at Xcaret, allows motorists to pull off to the right in order to cross the road when traffic has passed. Don't speed and don't follow the next car too closely. There have been many accidents and fatalities on this road lately, and these precautions could save your life. After Tulum, traffic is much lighter, but follow these precautions anyway.

Be aware of the long distances in the Yucatán. Mérida, for instance, is 400 miles from Villahermosa, 125 miles from Campeche, and 200 miles from Cancún. Leaded gas (*Nova*) is readily available in the Yucatán; unleaded gas (*Magna Sin*) is available at most stations. *Note:* Gas stations are found in all major towns, but they're only open from around 8am to around 7pm. If you're planning to rent a car to travel the area, see "Car Rentals" in Chapter 2, "Planning a Trip to the Yucatán."

Los Pelicanos

On the oceanside behind and right of the zócalo. ☎ **1-0014.** Main courses $4–$13; lobster $25. Daily 10am–10pm. SEAFOOD.

Since this village has few restaurants, Los Pelicanos holds almost a captive audience for beachside dining. You'll notice the inviting restaurant down a block to the right of the plaza on the street paralleling the ocean. Select a table inside under the palapa or outside on the terrace (wear mosquito repellent in the evenings). From the terrace you have an easy view of pelicans swooping around the dock. The seafood menu has all the usual offerings, from ceviche to conch made three ways to shrimp, lobster, and fish. There are grilled chicken and steak for those who don't want seafood.

EN ROUTE TO PLAYA DEL CARMEN

Heading south on Highway 307 from Puerto Morelos, you'll find the village of Muchi to be the next landmark. It's only 20 miles from Puerto Morelos to Playa del Carmen, so you'll be there in half an hour or less. However, you'll pass several small beach resorts en route. The two more upscale places below are run by the very reputable Turquoise Reef Group. And less than three miles before Playa del Carmen, you'll pass several roads that head out to the very relaxed, isolated small hotels at

Sea Turtles of the Yucatán

At least four of Mexico's nine species of marine turtles nest on the beaches of Quintana Roo—the loggerhead, green, hawksbill, and leatherback varieties. Of these, the leatherback is almost nonexistent, and the loggerhead is the most abundant—but all are endangered.

Most turtles lay eggs on the same beach year after year, and as often as three times in a season. Strolling along the beach late at night in search of giant turtles (prime egg-laying hours are between 10pm and 3am) is a special experience that will make you feel closer to the Yucatán's environment. It may take you a while to get used to the darkness, but don't use your flashlight—lights of any kind repel the turtles. Laying the eggs is tough work—a female will dig nonstop with back flippers for more than an hour; the exercise leaves its head and legs flushed. Depositing the 100 or more eggs takes only minutes, then she makes the nest invisible by laboriously covering it with sand and disappears into the sea. Each soft-shelled egg looks like a Ping-Pong ball.

Hatchlings scurry to the sea 60 days later, but successful incubation depends on the temperature and depth of the nest. When conditions are right, the hatch rates of fertile eggs are high; however, only 5% of those that do make it to the sea escape predators long enough to return.

Despite recent efforts to protect Mexico's turtles, the eggs are still considered an aphrodisiac and there's a market for them; turtles are killed for their shells and meat as well. Since turtle life expectancy is more than 50 years, killing one turtle kills thousands more. Costly protection programs include tagging the female and catching the eggs as they are deposited and removing them to a protected area and nest of identical size and temperature.

Punta Bete, which is the name of a fine beach—not a town. If you turn left and follow a small unpaved trail at the 52 km marker and PUNTA BETE sign you'll find three small groups of inexpensive bungalows at the end of the trail and on a fine stretch of beach which you'll have almost to yourself.

If you come here between July and October, you can walk the beach at night to watch for **turtles** lumbering ashore to lay their eggs, or watch the eggs hatch and the tiny vulnerable turtles scurry to the ocean in the last two months. However, turtles will not lay eggs where there is too much light, so as development continues (and more lights are installed) we'll see fewer turtles nesting.

ACCOMMODATIONS & DINING
Expensive

La Posada del Capitán Lafitte
Carretera Cancún-Tulum km 62, 77710 Playa del Carmen, Q. Roo. ☎ **987/3-0214** or 303/674-9615, or 800/538-6802 in the U.S. Fax 987/3-0213. 40 bungalows. A/C FAN. Low season $80–$90 single; $90–$340 double. Christmas, New Year's, Thanksgiving, and part of Feb are higher. Minimum 3-night stay. No credit cards. Rates include breakfast and dinner. Free parking.

After the Punta Bete sign, you'll see the sign on the highway pointing left toward Capitán Lafitte, and then you'll drive a mile down a rough dirt road that heads from the highway towards the ocean. The numerous units of Capitán Lafitte stretch out along a huge portion of powdery white beach with space enough between them to feel luxuriously separate from other guests. The one- and two-story white stucco bungalows are smallish but very comfortable, stylishly furnished, and equipped with tile floors, small tiled bathrooms, and either two double or one king-size bed and an oceanfront porch. There's 24-hour electicity (a plus you learn to value on isolated stretches of this coast). If you wish, coffee can be served in the room as early as 6:30am. There's a turtle patrol in which guests can participate during summer on nearby beaches where green and loggerhead turtles nest. Divers from North America make up a sizable portion of the clientele here, as well as repeat visitors who come annually just for the peace, quiet, beach, and relaxation.

Dining/Entertainment: One restaurant takes care of all meals.

Services: Room and laundry service, travel agency, and dive shop.

Facilities: You'll find a large raised swimming pool and sunning deck, clubhouse, and excellent dive shop.

Shangri-La Caribe

Carretera Cancún-Tulum km 69.5 (Apdo. Postal 253), Playa del Carmen, Q. Roo 77710. ☎ **987/3-0611** or 303/674-9615, or 800/538-6802 in the U.S. Fax 987/3-0500. FAN. 50 oceanview bungalows, 5 beachfront cabañas. High season $165 oceanview single or double, $209 beachfront single or double, $352 family unit; low season $114 oceanview single or double, $150 beachfront single or double, $245 family unit (book well in advance during high season). Free parking.

After the Punta Bete sign—and only a mile or so before you reach Playa del Carmen on Highway 307—you'll see the Volkswagen Plant and a huge sign for the Shangri-La Caribe and another resort called Las Palapas. Turn left at the VW building and you'll find the Shangri-La a mile down a semipaved road. The two-story, high-domed, palapa-topped bungalows meander to the ocean linked by sidewalks and edged by tropical vegetation. All come with two double beds, nice tile baths, and a hammock strung on the patio or balcony. Prices get higher the closer you get to the beach and are higher for two-bedroom casas. Though you're very close to Playa del Carmen, hotel guests are the only ones using the beach and the feeling is one of being many relaxing miles from civilization. You'll share this beachside retreat with lots of European vacationers to whom wearing a whole bathing suit is not important.

Dining/Entertainment: One restaurant serves all three meals, and the bar is open long hours.

Services: Car rental and bus or taxi tours to nearby lagoons and to Tulum, Cobá, and Chichén-Itzá.

Facilities: The large inviting pool is surrounded by a sundeck, and there are horses for rent at $25 an hour. The Cyan-Ha Diving Center on the premises offers diving, snorkeling, and fishing trips, and equipment rental for these sports. May and June are best for fishing with abundant marlin, sailfish, and dorado.

INEXPENSIVE

Cabañas Bahia Xcalacoco

Apdo. Postal 176, 77710 Playa del Carmen, Q. Roo. No phone. 2 rms (all with bath).

Ricardo and Rosa Novelo opened their own small inn in 1996, with two small white-washed rooms in a shady thicket by the beach. Rosa, the powerhouse cook and general manager, keeps things running smoothly, while Ricardo takes guests fishing and snorkeling. The rooms are small and plain, but comfortable—however, there's no electricity, so you learn to work the kerosene lamp. Rosa serves guests in the small restaurant—expect sizable portions at very reasonable prices. The fish dinner is large and excellent. Ask about jungle trails to Maya ruins near the cabañas.

Cabañas Xcalacoco

Carretera Cancún-Tulum km 52 (Apdo. Postal 176), 77710 Playa del Carmen, Q. Roo. No phone. 7 cabañas (all with bath). $25 with one bed, $35 with two beds; RVs and campers $4 per person. Discounts available in low season. Free parking.

Next door to the Cabañas Bahia is this long-established set of cabañas, which are tidy whitewashed buildings with small porches, all right on the beach. All have baths; five have king-size beds, and the others have two double beds each. Since there's no electricity, kerosene lamps light rooms in the evenings. Camping facilities are available for those in recreational vehicles and others wishing to hang a hammock under a thatched-roof covering. For these folks there's a shower and bathroom but no electricity. A small restaurant serves guests, but it's always a good idea to bring along packaged and canned snacks, water, and soft drinks.

4 Playa del Carmen

20 miles SW of Puerto Morelos, 44 miles SW of Cancún

This rapidly expanding Caribbean village grew up around the mainland terminus of the passenger-boat service to Cozumel. Travelers soon discovered that Playa del Carmen's long stretches of white beach were far better than those on Cozumel and it has developed quite a tourist trade of its own. The tide of progress is rolling on with the appearance of the all-inclusive Diamond Resort and the Hotel Continental Plaza Playacar, both new resorts south of the center of town, as well as new sewage and water lines, telephone service, and more brick-paved streets. Playa del Carmen severed its political apron strings from Cozumel and now has its own mayor, and is contained in its own separate *municipio* (like a county). The town doubled in size in 1993 and is preparing for 50,000 inhabitants by the year 2000.

Time-share hawkers ply their same fake friendly ways in Playa, but not in the numbers present in Puerto Vallarta or Cancún. Topless sunbathing, though against the law in Mexico, seems condoned here—including leisurely topless strolling anywhere there's a beach. It's so casually topless, in fact, that there was a sign in the post office to the effect of NO TOPLESS IN HERE.

Avenida Juárez (also known as Avenida Principal) leads into town and has always been considered "main street," but the four-lane Avenida 30, five blocks from the beach, has been paved and is positioned as another "main street."

Playa del Carmen is something of a fork in the road for southbound travelers—you can go by ferry east to Cozumel or continue south to Akumal, Tulum, Cobá, Punta Allen, and Chetumal on Highway 307.

Though Playa has lost its innocence, it's still a peaceful place where you can hang out on the beach for hours without feeling the need to explore. However, get there quickly—it's changing fast.

ESSENTIALS
GETTING THERE & DEPARTING

By Bus   There are three bus stations in Playa del Carmen, all on Avenida Principal (the main street): **Transportes de Oriente, Playa Express,** and **ATS** are a half block north of the main square and Avenida 5 on Avenida Principal; **Expreso Oriente** is on the corner of Avenida 5 and Avenida Principal; and the **ADO** station is four blocks north of the ferry dock and two blocks north of the plaza.

ATS offers service to and from Cancún every 15 minutes. ATS buses also go to Xcaret (five times) and to Tulum (11 times), as well as to Cobá, Chetumal, and Palenque. Second-class Oriente buses travel the route to and from Tulum, Cobá, and

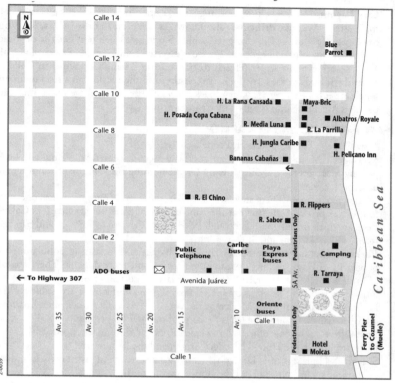

Bacalar. Several de paso ADO buses pass through Playa del Carmen on the way to Cancún. And several ADO buses go to Valladolid, Chichén-Itzá, and Mérida.

Expreso Oriente goes to Villahermosa, Mérida, Tulum, Cancún, Felipe Carrillo Puerto, and Chetumal.

By Car   The turnoff to Playa del Carmen from Highway 307 is plainly marked, and you'll arrive on the town's widest street, Avenida Principal, also known as Avenida Benito Juárez (not that there's a street sign to that effect).

By the Playa del Carmen–Cozumel Passenger Ferry   See the Cozumel section above for the details on the passenger ferry service between Playa del Carmen and Cozumel.

By Taxi   Taxi fares to the Cancún airport are prohibitively high, but there is a service offering shared taxi rides for $10 per person. Check at your hotel or at the Caribe Maya restaurant on Avenida 5 at Calle 8 for information and reservations.

ORIENTATION

Arriving   The ferry dock in Playa del Carmen is 1½ blocks from the main square and within walking distance of hotels. Buses are along Avenida Principal, a short distance from hotels, restaurants, and the ferry pier. Tricycle taxis are the only vehicular traffic allowed between the bus stations and the ferry. A number of these efficient taxis meet each bus and ferry and can transport you and your luggage between the two or to any hotel in town.

City Layout   Villagers know and use street names, but few street signs exist. The main street, **Avenida Principal,** also known as **Avenida Benito Juárez,** leads into town from Highway 307, crossing Avenida 5 one block before it ends at the beach next to the main plaza or zócalo. Traffic is diverted from Avenida Principal at Calle 10. The other main artery (closed to traffic from Avenida Principal to Calle 8), **Avenida 5,** leads to the ferry dock, two blocks from the zócalo; most restaurants and hotels are either on Avenida 5, or a block or two off of it. The village's beautiful beach parallels Avenida 5 and is only a block from it.

FAST FACTS: PLAYA DEL CARMEN

Area Code   The telephone area code is 987.

Messages   Mom's Hotel acts as an unofficial message center, with a bulletin board posting messages for traveling friends, people needing rides, house or room rentals, or items for sale.

Money Exchange   There are two branches of the Cicsa Money exchange, one at the foot of the pier and the other at the Rincón del Sol plaza on Avenida 5 at Calle 8. Both are open from Monday through Friday from 7:30am to 7:30pm and Saturday from 7:30am to 1pm and 3:30–6:30pm.

Parking   Because of the pedestrians-only blocks and increasing population and popularity of Playa, parking close to hotels has become more difficult. There was talk of prohibiting vehicular traffic inside the village by corralling all vehicles into a pay lot, which would be serviced by special taxis. For now, the most accessible parking lot is the Estacionamiento Mexico at the corner of Avenida Principal and Avenida 10, open daily 24 hours; the fee is $1.25 per hour and $8 per day.

Post Office   The post office is on Avenida Principal three blocks north of the plaza, on the right past the Hotel Playa del Carmen and the launderette.

Seasons   High season is December through Easter and August. Low season is all other months, but November is becoming very popular.

Spanish Lessons   The Centro Bilingue de Playa del Carmen (☎ and fax **987/ 3-0558**), offers informal classes in conversational Spanish as well as Spanish geared toward government and business. For a reasonable fee they'll arrange transport to the Cancún airport and confirm airline tickets. The school is on Avenida 5 between Calles 4 and 6 above the Panadería Caribe.

Telephones   Most hotels have phones and faxes now; often both are on the same phone line. So, to send a fax call and ask for the fax tone: "Por favor, dar me el tono por el fax." The **Calling Station** on the street leading up from the ferry pier is a full-services phone center with air-conditioned booths, no surcharges, fax service, and a bulletin board where you can leave messages for friends. It's open Monday through Saturday from 8am to 11pm, and Sunday from 9am to 10pm.

WHAT TO DO

Playa is for relaxing. But beyond that, the island of Cozumel is an quick ferry ride away; Tulum, Xel-Ha, Xcaret, and Xcalacoco are easy excursions. Avenida 5a is lined with two dozen nice-looking, small shops selling imported batik clothing, Guatemalan fabric clothing, masks, pottery, hammocks, and a few T-shirts. Reef diving can be arranged through **Tank-Ha Dive Shop** (☎ **987/3-0302**), at the Hotel Maya Bric. Snorkeling trips cost $25 and include soft drinks and equipment. Two-tank dive trips are $60; resort courses are available. For **cavern diving,** see "Scuba Diving" in "Cozumel," above, where small groups are met in Playa del Carmen for this new one-of-a-kind experience. An 18-hole championship **golf course**

(☎ 3-0624), designed by Robert Von Hagge, is open adjacent to the Continental Plaza Playacar. Greens fee is $72 and the price includes a cart and tax. Two **tennis** courts are also available at the club there.

ACCOMMODATIONS
VERY EXPENSIVE

Continental Plaza Playacar

Frac. Playacar km 62.5, Playa del Carmen, Q. Roo 77710. ☎ **987/3-0100,** or 800/88-CONTI in the U.S. Fax 987/3-0105. 185 rms. A/C TV TEL. High season $150–$450 double. Low season $90–$330 double. (Ask about special packages.)

Rates vary depending on your view—garden, ocean, parking lot, or brick wall—and on whether you have one or two bedrooms. To find it from the ferry pier, turn left when you get off the ferry and follow the road a short distance until you see the Playacar sign.If you're driving in, turn right at the last street before the main street dead-ends and you'll see signs to the hotel about two blocks ahead.

Dining/Entertainment: La Pergola, with pool, beach, and ocean view, serves international food daily from 7 to 11am and 6 to 11pm. La Sirena, the poolside restaurant, is open from 11am to 5pm daily. The stylish and welcoming lobby bar is open between 7am and 1am daily with live music in the evenings.

Services: Room and laundry service, baby-sitting, gift shop and boutiques, travel agency, and tours to nearby archaeological zones and lagoons.

Facilities: Oceanside pool with swim-up bar, water-sports equipment, one lighted tennis court.

MODERATE

✪ Albatros Royale

Calle 8 (Apdo. Postal 31), 77710 Playa del Carmen, Q. Roo. ☎ **987/3-0001,** or 800/538-6802 in the U.S. and Canada. 31 rms (all with bath). FAN. High season, $60–$80 single or double. Low season, $50–$60 single or double. Rates include breakfast.

This "deluxe" sister hotel to the neighboring Pelicano Inn (see below) rises up on a narrow bit of land facing the beach. The two stories of rooms all have tile floors, tile baths with marble vanities and showers, balconies or porches and most have ocean views. Most have two double beds, but seven have queen-size beds. Breakfast is taken almost next door at the Pelicano Inn. To get here from the corner of Avenida 5 and Calle 8 (where you'll see the Rincón del Sol center) turn toward the water on Calle 8; it's midway down the block on your left. Street parking is scarce.

Hotel Alejari

Calle 6 (Apdo. Postal 166), 77710 Playa del Carmen, Q. Roo. ☎ **987/3-0374.** Fax 987/3-0005. 23 rms (all with bath). A/C FAN. High season, $50 single or double; $60 single or double with kitchenette; $55 single or double two-story unit with kitchen. Low season, $45 single or double; $55 single or double two-story unit with kitchen. Rates include breakfast. Free guarded parking.

Built around a fastidiously kept flower-filled inner yard, this small hotel is just off Avenida 5 and half a block from the beach. Though somewhat overpriced, rooms are clean, each with white walls, ruffled nylon bedspreads, and a small vanity with mirror in the bedroom. Ground-level rooms have two double beds. Rooms with kitchens have a kitchen and living room downstairs, and the bedroom, with a king-size bed, is up a narrow stairway. The restaurant is open daily from 8am to 4pm and breakfast is served between 8 and 11am.

La Jungla Caribe

Av. 5 Norte at Calle 8 (Apdo Postal 180), 77710 Playa del Carmen, Q. Roo. ☎ **987/3-0650.**
25 rms. A/C TV. High season standard rooms $55–$65 single or double; suites $85–$120. Low
season standard rooms $46–$55 single or double; suites $65–$100 single or double.

La Jungla was almost finished when I traveled for this edition and appeared to offer
a lot of quality for the bucks. Rolf Albrecht, the mastermind behind the hotel, en-
visioned a lot of space and comfort for guests, so even the standard rooms have plenty
of room, with grey-and-black marble floors and large bathrooms. There's a catwalk
to the "tower" section of suites. A pool is on the first level and a restaurant overlooking Calle 8 was in the planning stages.

✪ Pelicano Inn

On the beach between Calles 6 and 8 (Apdo. Postal 31), 77710 Playa del Carmen, Q. Roo.
☎ **987/3-0997,** or 800/538-6802 in the U.S. Fax 987/3-0998. 38 rms. FAN or A/C. High season $75 single or double garden view; $85 single or double sea view. Low season, $55 single;
$60 double. Rates include breakfast.

Larry Beard demolished his old seaside hotel Albatros and in its place created a
handsome white-stucco pueblo-style hotel bearing no resemblance to its funky pre-
decessor. The spacious rooms, in one-, two-, and three-level tiers, have tile floors and
baths, overbed reading lights, and balconies or patios outfitted with hammocks. Most
rooms have two double beds, but several have only one—but none have bedspreads.
Once you see it, you'd expect to pay a good deal more. The restaurant, open 7:30am–
6pm is one of the best (see "Dining," below), and guests partake of the all-you-can-
eat breakfast buffet. From the Avenida Principal, walk four blocks north on Avenida
5, then turn right half a block on Calle 8, where a path on the right between two lots
leads into the hotel. (You don't have to trudge across the beach as in the past.)

INEXPENSIVE

Cabañas Tuxatah

Calle 5 Sur, 77710 Playa del Carmen, Q. Roo. ☎ **987/3-0025.** Fax 987/3-0148. 9 rms (all with
bath). FAN. High season, $18 single; $25 double. Low season, $15 single; $20 double.

In a Robinson Crusoe–like setting, with stone pathways meandering through a ra-
vine of overgrown jungle foliage, this place will appeal to many for its casual, offbeat
rusticity. Caged birds are scattered about and house cats skitter from sight, while family dogs join in lockstep as you head toward the rooms hidden behind the greenery.
The German owner, María Weltin, speaks English, French, German, and Spanish.
The tidy quarters in a two-story building all have one double bed on a concrete
platform, speckled tile floors, screened and louvered windows, and nice baths. To find
Tuxatah, walk inland from the pier on Avenida Principal two blocks. Turn left on
Calle 5 at the Continental Plaza Playacar sign and walk 1 1/2 blocks. The hotel is on
your right; the entrance is down a pathway behind the sign for Villas y Condominios
Playacar. There is ample parking in front of the entrance.

✪ Hotel Maya-Bric

Av. 5 Norte, 77710 Playa del Carmen, Q. Roo. ☎ and fax **987/3-0011.** 29 rms (all with bath).
A/C or FAN. High season, $35 single or double. Low season, $25 single or double. Free guarded
parking.

The colorful exterior and flowers will draw your eye to this two-story beachfront inn.
Each of the well-kept rooms has two double beds with fairly firm mattresses; some
have ocean views. The buildings frame a small pool where guests gather for card
games and conversation. The Maya-Bric is one of the quietest hotels in town; it's well-
supervised by the Briseño family owners and is frequented by loyal guests who return

annually. The gates are locked at night, and only guests are allowed to enter. A small restaurant by the office sometimes serves breakfast and snacks during the high season. Air-conditioning is being added to all rooms. The on-site dive shop, Tank-Ha (See "What to Do" above), rents diving and snorkeling gear and arranges trips to the reefs.

⑨ Mom's Hotel

Av. 30 at Calle 4. 77710 Playa del Carmen, Q. Roo. ☎ and fax **987/3-0315.** 12 rms (all with bath). FAN. High season, $25 single; $35 double. Low season (May, June, Sept–Nov), $20 single; $25 double. Discounts for lengthy stays.

Though away from the beach, this is a good choice if all the beachside inns are full or if your stay is long. Rooms, all facing the interior courtyard, are fairly large and sunny; each comes with tile floors, one or two double beds, and bedside reading lights. Three rooms have air-conditioning. There's a small pool in the sunny courtyard, and a bulletin board for messages to other travelers. A bar and restaurant were in the planning stage when I checked. To find it from the corner of Avenida 5 and Calle 4, walk five blocks inland and it's at the corner of Calle 4 and Avenida 30.

Posada Copa Cabana

Av. 5 (Apdo. Postal 103), 77710 Playa del Carmen, Q. Roo. ☎ **987/3-0218.** 8 rms, 2 cabañas (all with bath). FAN. High season, $30 single; $35 double. Low season, $20 single; $30 double.

Hammocks are stretched in front of each room and on the porch of each cabaña at this pleasant palm-shaded inn, and the patio Restarant Soluna fills up the courtyard to the right. Each of the clean, simply furnished rooms has one or two double beds on concrete platforms and pink-and-gray tile floors. Vanities and sinks are conveniently placed outside the baths. There's good cross-ventilation through well-screened windows. To get here from the plaza, turn right on Avenida 5 and walk 3 blocks; it's on your right between Calles 6 and 8. There is no parking on Avenida 5, but there's limited parking nearby.

La Rana Cansada

Calle 10, 77710 Playa del Carmen, Q. Roo. ☎ and fax **987/3-0389.** 12 rms (all with bath). High season, $50 single or double. Low season, $20 single or double.

The "Tired Frog" is one of the most simply pleasant inns in the village, though it's a bit overpriced in high season. Behind an elegant hacienda-style wall and handsome iron gate, the plainly furnished, but neat and clean rooms face an inner courtyard with a small snack bar under a large thatched palapa. Hammocks are strung on the covered porch outside the row of rooms. Some have concrete ceilings and others a thatched roof, and all have well-screened doors and windows. New rooms were on the drawing board as well as a small pool and breakfast service. Trade paperbacks are available at the front desk, and manager John Swartz is very accommodating with tips on seeing the area. It's a block and a half inland from the beach. To find it from the main plaza, walk five blocks north on Avenida 5 and turn left on Calle 10; the hotel is on the left.

Treetops

Calle 8 s/n, 77710 Playa del Carmen, Q. Roo. ☎ and fax **987/3-0351.** 15 rms (all with bath). FAN. High season, $30–$50 single or double. Low season, $25–$45 single or double.

Owners Sandy and Bill Dillon changed the name from Cuevo Pargo and added more rooms during their stem-to-stern cleaning and revamp. Set in a small patch of undisturbed jungle, with bungalows linked by stone pathways, this place is cooler than any in town and comes complete with its own cenote. The older bungalows (each a separate unit) are rustic but comfortable and come with small charms like thatched roofs and rock walls and unusual architecture—no two are alike. Two bungalows have kitchens. One room has a loft bed overlooking a living area. The new rooms, in a two-story fourplex, have a choice of air conditioning or fan (you pay extra to turn on the A/C), refrigerators, and nice balconies or patios. The hotel's restaurant serves free coffee to guests each morning, a limited menu of charcoal-broiled hot dogs and hamburgers (with U.S. beef), homemade potato salad, and Tex-Mex chili, tacos, and pizza. The Safari bar, to the left after you enter, is a good place to come for an evening drink and meet fellow travelers. The bar is open daily from 3pm to midnight. Happy hour is from 5 to 7pm. There's a TV broadcasting U.S. channels in the "lobby." A new restaurant, to be built over a new swimming pool, was in the planning stages. From the Avenida Principal, walk four blocks north on Avenida 5, then turn right for half a block on Calle 8; the hotel is on the left, half a block from the beach.

A YOUTH HOSTEL

From the bus station, walk toward the highway and follow the signs. A bed in an 18-bunk room with cold and hot water costs $5, including sheets, pillowcase, and a locker. You can also rent a cabaña with shared bath for $15. The hostel is a 10- to 15-minute walk from the bus station.

CAMPING

Playa del Carmen has many little camping areas down along the water. Turn to the left at the beach and head for **Campamiento, Cabañas Las Ruinas** (☎ 987/ 3-0405), right on the beach and across the street from a tiny Maya ruin. Everyone pays a refundable entry deposit of $8, and cabin renters deposit $20. Hammocks rent for $2, and sheets, towels, and blankets (no pillows) rent for 75¢. Lockers cost $1.50; safety boxes cost $5 for money, passports, and so forth. Hammock space in a covered palapa comes with a locker and costs $5. Small cabins cost $10 to $35 (with bath in high season); tent, trailer, and camper spaces run $4 to $8; and auto space is $4. The property is very rundown and casually operated; I strongly recommend you get a locker or safety deposit box for your valuables. A shady palapa serves as a restaurant and general gathering area.

Coming in from the highway, turn left (north) on Avenida Principal, left on Avenida 10, and right on Calle 6; go straight for one block and cross Avenida 5 and it's a half block down on the left near the beach.

DINING

Make your own delicious doughnut breakfast and savor aromatic Chiapan coffee at **Daily Doughnuts,** on Avenida 5, between Calles 8 and 10 (☎ 987/3-0396). It's open Monday through Saturday from 7am to 9pm.

EXPENSIVE

○ **Flippers**
Av. 5 at Calle 4. No phone. Grilled specialties $5–$15; seafood platter $20. Daily 3–10:30pm.
MEXICAN/GRILLED MEAT.

There's almost always a crowd at Flippers, which is noticeable from the street for its nautical theme, created by fishnets and ropes under a thatched palapa. There's an extensive bar list as well as a varied menu that includes grilled specialties from sea and land plus hamburgers, poc-chuc, and beef tampiqueña. Happy hour, when drinks are two for the price of one, runs from 5 to 11pm and live music springs forth between 7 and 10pm most evenings.

La Parrilla

Av. 5 at Av. 8. ☎ **987/3-0687.** Breakfast specials $2–$3; main courses $4.50–$14. Daily 7am–1am. MEXICAN/GRILLED MEATS.

The Rincón del Sol plaza is one of the prettiest buildings in Playa, and now it houses one of the most popular restaurants in town. The dining room is set in two levels above the street with the open kitchen in back, and the aroma of grilling meat permeates the air. The huge chicken fajitas come with plenty of homemade tortillas and beans, and if you want to splurge on lobster, this is the place to do it. The tables fill quickly in the evening, but there are smaller bar tables set out in the plaza's courtyards, where you can wait.

MODERATE

✪ El Chino

Calle 4 at Av. 15. ☎ **987/3-0015.** Breakfast $1.50–$2.50; main courses $3–$7.50. Daily 8am–11pm YUCATÁN/MEXICAN.

Despite its name, there's nary a Chinese dish on the menu. But locals highly recommend this place, as do I. Though slightly off the popular Avenida 5 row of restaurants, it has its own clean, cool ambience, with tile floors and plastic-covered polished wood tables set below a huge palapa roof with whirring ceiling fans. A side patio is open-air with uncovered tables that are good for evening meals. The standard breakfast menu applies, plus you can order fresh blended fruit drinks. Main courses include such regional favorites as poc-chuc, chicken pibil, and Ticul-style fish, plus shrimp-stuffed fish and beef and chicken and shrimp borcettes. Other selections are lobster and shrimp crepes, fajitas, and ceviche.

✪ Media Luna

Av 5, corner of Calle 8. No phone. Breakfast $2.50–$4; main courses $3–$7. Tues–Sun 7:30am–3pm and 6:30–11:30pm. INTERNATIONAL.

Open only a short while when I passed by, I couldn't resist adding it to my list. Few restaurants have such mouthwatering aromas coming from the kitchen. When you read the menu you'll know why. The spinach-and-mushroom breakfast crepes arrive with fabulous herb-, onion-, and garlic-flavored potatoes. Other crepes are filled with fresh fruit. For dinner there are savory Greek salads, black bean quesadillas, grilled shrimp salads, fresh grilled fish, and pastas with fresh herbs and sauces, plus other entrées featuring Indian, Italian, Mexican, and Chinese specialties. It's a casual, inviting place, with soft taped guitar music in the background, and decorated in textiles from Guatemala, with a few unfinished pine tables for dining outside on the street or a larger area inside.

Pelicano Inn

On the beach, at Calle 6. ☎ **987/3-0997.** Buffet breakfast $6; main courses $2–$30. Buffet breakfast daily 7–11am; lunch daily 11:30–6pm (happy hour noon–1pm and 4–6pm). MEXICAN/AMERICAN.

Located on the beach, this is a good place to meet Americans who live here and while away some hours munching and people-watching. The food is dependably good. The breakfast buffet is an "all you can eat" affair, so arrive hungry. Apart from breakfast you have a choice of peel-your-own cajun-flavored shrimp with U.S.-style tarter and shrimp sauce, hamburgers, hot dogs, quesadillas, pastries, ice cream, beer, wine, and coffee. From Avenida Principal, walk four blocks north on Avenida 5, turn right ¹/₂ block on Calle 8 to a marked Pelican Inn pathway, and turn right, or go to the beach and turn right; the hotel/restaurant is on the beach.

INEXPENSIVE

Daily Doughnuts

Av. 5, between Calles 8 and 10. ☎ **987/3-0396.** Doughnuts 75¢; doughnut centers 30¢; sandwiches $2–$3; molletes $1; coffee 75¢. Mon–Sat 7am–9pm. DOUGHNUTS/CROISSANTS/SANDWICHES.

Paulino and Federico Suárez, a pair of enterprising Mexico City youths, opened this delicious doughnut shop in 1993. The variety is mouthwatering—50 kinds in all, with terrific toppings of glaze or chocolate or nuts or combined flavorings of coffee, almonds, cream, blueberries, strawberries, peanut butter, and more. The Chiapan blend they use makes the best cup of coffee in town.

✪ Sabor

Av. 5 between Calles 2 and 4. No phone. Yogurt and granola $1–$1.75; sandwiches $1.50–$2; vegetarian plates $1.50–$2.50; pastries 50¢–$1. Daily 8am–11pm. BAKERY/HEALTH FOOD.

The patio full of patrons—it's always full—attests to the popularity of this modest restaurant. The list of hot and cold drinks has expanded to include espresso and cappuccino, café frappe, hot chocolate, tea, and fruit and vegetable drinks, and Sabor now has Blue Bell ice cream (a favorite of Texans), and light vegetarian meals. Try a cup of something with a slice of pie and watch village life stroll by.

El Tacolote

Av. Juárez. ☎ **987/3-0066.** Main courses $2–$11. Daily 11am–3am. (Shortened hours in low season.) GRILLED MEATS/SEAFOOD.

There's a good selection of tacos, hamburgers, and mixed brochettes offered here. The "vegetarian plate" is grilled shrimp with peppers; the "gringas plate" comes with flour tortillas, grilled pork, and cheese. The restaurant faces the main plaza and has expanded to fill up half the block. Marimbas and mariachis play on weekend nights in high season. There's another branch of this restaurant in Cancún; if you've tried and enjoyed that one, you'll likely enjoy this one, too, especially with its cool patio in back.

✪ Tarraya Restaurant/Bar

Calle 2 Norte at the beach. No phone. Appetizers $1.50–$3.50; main courses $3–$6; whole fish $5. Daily noon–9pm. SEAFOOD.

"THE RESTAURANT THAT WAS BORN WITH THE TOWN," proclaims the sign. This is also the restaurant locals recommend as the best for seafood. Since it's right on the beach, with the water practically lapping at the foundations, and since the owners are fishermen, the fish is so fresh it's practically still wiggling. The wood hut doesn't look like much, but you can have fish fixed almost any way imaginable. If you haven't tried the Yucatecan specialty Tikinxic fish—this would be a good place. It's on the beach opposite the basketball court.

PLAYA DEL CARMEN AFTER DARK

It seems like everyone in town is out on Avenida 5 or Juárez across from the square until 10 or 11pm; there's pleasant strolling, meals and drinks at streetside cafés, buskers to watch and listen to, and shops to duck into. Later in the evening your choices diminish: a **Señor Frog's** down by the ferry dock, dishing out its patented mix of thumping dance music, Jell-O shots, and frat-house antics; **Karen's Pizza** on Avenida 5, with live entertainment nightly; the **Safari Bar,** at the Treetops hotel always has a congenial crowd gathered around the bar and television until midnight; and then there's the beachside bar at the **Blue Parrot,** which seems to draw most of the European and American expatriate community, has swings for barstools, and stays open late (somewhere around 2 to 3am). This last is the coolest.

Caution: Ladies—stay clear of Playa's unusual number of would-be gigolos—they're slick. And lately there have been a few reports of drug involvement in tourist robberies—don't do drugs in Mexico, and don't flash money.

5 Highway 307 from Xcaret to Xel-Ha

This section of the mainland coast—between Playa del Carmen and Tulum—is right on the front lines of the Caribbean coast's transformation from idyllic backwater to developing tourist destination. South of Playa del Carmen along Highway 307 are a succession of brand-new planned resorts and nature parks, commercially developed beaches, and—for now, anyway—a few rustic beach hideaways and unspoiled coves. From north to south, this section will cover Xcaret, Pamul, Xpuha, Puerto Aventuras, Akumal, and Xel-Ha.

Of the fledgling resorts south of Playa del Carmen, **Akumal** is one of the most developed, with moderately priced hotels and bungalows scattered among the graceful palms that line the beautiful, soft beach and gorgeous bay. **Puerto Aventuras** is a privately developed, growing resort city aimed at the well-heeled traveler and private-condo owner. **Paamul** and **Xpuha** offer inexpensive inns on gorgeous beaches $2^1/2$ miles apart. If the offbeat beach life is what you're after, grab it now before it disappears. (Other little-known and inexpensive getaways can be found on the Punta Allen Peninsula south of Tulum; see the next section for details.) You'll also enjoy a swim in the nearby lagoon of **Xel-Ha,** one of the coast's prettiest spots. And the new parklike development of **Xcaret** will appeal to some for an all-day excursion.

EN ROUTE SOUTH FROM PLAYA DEL CARMEN   Bus transportation from Playa del Carmen south is no longer as chancy as it used to be, but it's still not great. There are four bus companies in Playa; buses depart fairly frequently for Chetumal, stopping at every point of interest along the way. There's even bus service to and from Cobá three times a day. Though buses originate here, you may be told you can't buy tickets ahead of time. If you choose to hire a car and driver, be sure to find a driver you like; remember, you'll be with him all day.

XCARET: A DEVELOPED NATURE PARK

Three miles south of Playa del Carmen is the turnoff to Xcaret ("*ish*-car-et"), a heavily commercialized, specially-built tourist destination that promotes itself as a 150-acre ecological park. Meant as a place to spend the day, it's open daily from 9am to 5:30pm. Without exaggeration, everywhere you look in Cancún are signs advertising Xcaret, or someone handing you a leaflet about it. They even have their own bus terminal to take tourists from Cancún at regular intervals, and they've added an evening extravaganza.

Xcaret may celebrate mother nature, but its builders rearranged quite a bit of her handiwork in completing it. If you're looking for a place to escape the commercialism of Cancún, this may not be it; it's expensive and contrived and may even be very crowded, thus diminishing the advertised "natural" experience. Children, however, seem to love it, and the palm-lined beaches are beautiful. Once past the entry booths (built to resemble small Maya temples) you'll find pathways that meander around bathing coves, the snorkeling lagoon, and the remains of a group of Maya temples. You'll have access to swimming beaches with canoes and pedal boats; limestone tunnels to snorkel through; marked palm-lined pathways; and a visitor's center with lockers, first aid, and gifts. There's also a museum, a "farm," and a botanical garden. Visitors aren't allowed to bring in food or drinks, so you're at the mercy of the high-priced restaurants. Personal radios are a no-no, as is use of suntan lotion if you swim in the lagoon; chemicals in lotion will poison the lagoon habitat.

The price of $30 per person entitles you to all the facilities—boats, life jackets, and snorkeling equipment for the underwater tunnel and lagoon, and lounge chairs and other facilities. However, there are often more visitors than equipment (such as beach chairs), so bring a beach towel and your own snorkeling gear. Travel agencies in Cancún offer Xcaret as a day trip that includes transportation and admission. You can also buy a ticket to the park at the Xcaret Terminal (☎ 8-30654 or 8-30743) next to the Hotel Fiesta Americana Coral Beach on Cancún island. Xcaret's colorfully painted buses haul people to and from Cancún. From Cancún the price including transportation and admission is $45 for adults and $33 for children. "Xcaret Night" costs $80 for adults and $70 for children and includes round-trip transportation from Cancún, a *charreada* festival, lighted pathways to Maya ruins, dinner, and folkloric show.

PAAMUL: A BEACH HIDEAWAY

About 10 miles south of Xcaret, 60 miles southwest of Cancún, and half a mile east of the highway is Paamul (also written Pamul), which in Maya means "a destroyed ruin." Turn when you see the Minisuper (a place to pick up reasonably priced snacks and drinks), which is also owned by the Cabañas Paamul (see below). Here you can enjoy a beautiful beach and a safe cove for swimming; it's a delightful place to leave the world behind. Thirty years ago the Martin family gave up coconut harvesting on this wide stretch of land which includes a large shallow bay, gained title to the land, and established this comfortable out-of-the-way respite. They plan to soon build more rooms on the unoccupied portion of the bay.

Mark and Lester Willis established their PADI- and SSI-certified fully-equipped dive shop here a few years ago and opened **Scuba Max** (☎ **987/3-0667** and fax **987/ 4-1729**), next to the cabañas. Using three 38-foot boats, they take guests on dives 5 miles in either direction. If it's too choppy, the reefs in front of the hotel are also excellent. The cost per dive is $25–$45 if you have your own equipment or $35–$65 if you rent. The snorkeling is excellent in this protected bay and the one next to it. They were establishing an office at the Hotel La Jungla in Playa del Carmen when I checked.

ACCOMMODATIONS & DINING

✪ Cabañas Paamul

Carretera Cancún-Tulum, km 85 (Apdo. Postal 83), Playa del Carmen, Q. Roo 77710. ☎ **99/ 25-9422** and fax 99/25-6913 in Mérida. 12 bungalows (all with bath); 80 trailer spaces (all with full hookups). FAN. Dec–Feb $40 single or double. March–June $30 single or double. July–Aug $40 single or double. Sept–Nov $30 single or double. RV space with hookups $13 per day, $300 per month.

When you reach this isolated, relaxing hotel you'll see an extremely tidy lineup of mobile homes and beyond them a row of coral-and-white beachfront bungalows with covered porches, steps away from the Caribbean. Despite the number of mobile homes (which are occupied more in winter than any other time) there's seldom a soul on the beautiful little beach. I eagerly anticipate reaching Paamul, for the bit of peace it provides during hectic days of updating. Each bungalow contains two double beds, tile floors, rattan furniture, ceiling fans, hot water, and 24-hour electricity. A new large breezy palapa restaurant serves delicious food at more than reasonable prices. Try the pescado Paamul or shrimp Paamul; both are wonderful baked medleys devised by the gracious owner Eloiza Zapata. For stays longer than a week, ask for a discount, which can sometimes be as much as 10% to 20%. The trailer park isn't what you might expect—some trailers have decks or patios and thatched palapa shade covers. Trailer guests have six showers and separate baths for men and women. Laundry service is available. Turtles nest here June through September. The Paamul turnoff is clearly marked on the highway; then it's almost a mile on a straight, narrow, paved-but-rutted road to the bungalows. Visitors not staying here are welcome to use the beach, though the owners request that they not bring in drinks and food and use the restaurant instead.

PUERTO AVENTURAS: A RESORT COMMUNITY

About 2½ miles south of Paamul (65 miles southwest of Cancún), you'll come to the new city-size development of Puerto Aventuras on Chakalal Bay. Though it's on 900 oceanfront acres, you don't see the ocean unless you walk through one of the three hotels. A complete resort, it includes a state-of-the-art marina, hotels, several restaurants, and multitudes of fashionable condominiums winding about the grounds and around the marina. The golf course has nine holes open for play. I don't recommend this resort for a vacation at this time because it's so far from anything. If you're touring this part of the world you won't see much of it by staying here. Architecturally sophisticated, it's like being on the island of Cancún without the crowds or nightlife. It's aimed more at well heeled Mexicans who've purchased condominiums here, than at foreign tourists who've come to experience the culture.

Even if you don't stay here, the **Museo CEDAM** on the grounds is worth a stop. CEDAM means Center for the Study of Aquatic Sports in Mexico, and the museum houses displays on the history of diving on this coast from pre-Hispanic times to the present. Besides dive-related memorabilia, there are displays of pre-Hispanic pottery, figures, and copper bells found in the cenotes of Chichén-Itzá, shell fossils, and sunken ship contents. It's supposed to be open daily from 10am to 1pm and 2 to 6pm. Donations are requested.

If you're hungry, there's a restaurant opposite the museum.

XPUHA: ANOTHER BEACH HIDEAWAY

Almost 3 miles beyond Pamul, east of the highway, is an area known as Xpuha (*ish-poo-hah*) consisting of an incredibly beautiful wide bay and fine stretch of sand. Before October 1995's Hurricane Roxanne, tall palms leaned over the beach, but unfortunately the storm destroyed the trees and toppled the encroaching jungle, revealing the seamier side of Xpuha. Some of this heavenly beach is junked with trashy-looking abodes and tacky restaurants, with the all-inclusive Robinson Club at the far southern end (though it was closed when I was there). If you're looking for something totally offbeat, clean, but not at all posh, then consider two of the humble inns on this beach. These are on a nicely kept part of beach (comparatively speaking), where you can still enjoy its uninhabited appeal. Finding them can be confusing since from Highway 307 several crude signs mark entry down even cruder, narrow rutted roads cutting through the jungle. To get to these hotels and the best portion of beach take the one marked Villas Xpuha.

The **restaurant** of the Villas Xpuha offers home-style cooking with a simple-but-varied menu and several fish entrées to choose from. It's open daily from 7am to 8pm. It's ideal for day-trippers who want to spend the day on the beach and have restaurant facilities, too; they request that visitors not bring food. As long as you use the restaurant of the Villas Xpuha, there's no charge for the two public baths and showers. Besides the beach, a huge lagoon is within walking distance, and the reef is not far offshore.

WHERE TO STAY & EAT

Villas del Caribe Xpuha
Carretera Cancún-Tulum, km 88, Playa del Carmen, Q. Roo 77710. No phone. 9 rms (all with bath). High season, $30 single or double. Low season, $22 single or double.

Not quite as nice as its neighbor (see "Villas Xpuha," below), this inn is still a good choice. The two stories of rooms face the beach, with communal porches for lounging. Rooms have blue tile floors and matching blue walls, and each comes with one or two double beds, an all-tile bath, and windows facing the beach; one room has a kitchen. There's 24-hour electricity and hot water here, too. The management has radio communication with the Hotel Flores in Cozumel (☎ 987/2-1429), so if you're there, you can reserve a room ahead (or vice versa).

Villas Xpuha and Restaurant
Carretera Cancún-Tulum, km 88 (Apdo. Postal 115), Playa del Carmen, Q. Roo 77710. No phone. 5 rms (all with bath). FAN. High season, $40 single or double. Low season, $32 single or double.

The five rooms here line up in a row of blue buildings; four have a porch area on the beach and ocean, and one is an island-style wooden structure. The rooms are plain but clean, each with nice tile floors, two windows, two single beds, two plastic chairs, hammock hooks, and a place for a suitcase—but no closet. A single bare bulb in the center of each ceiling provides light. Count on 24-hour electricity and hot water. The hotel has a dive shop offering diving and snorkeling trips and kayak rentals.

AKUMAL: RESORT ON A LAGOON

Continuing south on Highway 307 a short distance, you'll come to Akumal, a resort development built around and named after a beautiful lagoon. Signs point the way in from the highway, and the white arched Akumal gateway is less than half a mile toward the sea. The resort complex here consists of five distinct establishments sharing the same wonderful, smooth palm-lined beach and the adjacent Half Moon Bay and Yalku Lagoon. The hotel's signs and white entry arches are clearly visible from Highway 307.

You don't have to be a guest to enjoy the **beach,** swim in the beautiful clear bay, and eat at the restaurants. It's an excellent place to spend the day while on a trip down the coast. Besides the excellent snorkeling, ask at the reception desk about **horseback rides** on the beach and or join a tour of the Sian Ka'an Biosphere Reserve that meets at the Cabañas Ana y José on the Punta Allen Peninsula. Equipment rental for snorkeling and windsurfing are readily available. For **scuba diving,** two completely equipped dive shops with PADI-certified instructors serve the hotels and bungalows in this area. Both are located between the two hotels. There are almost 30 dive sites in the region (from 30 to 80 feet), and two-tank dives cost around $55. Both shops offer resort courses as well as complete certification. **Fishing trips** can also be arranged through the dive shops. You're only 15 minutes from good fishing. Two hours (the minimum period) costs $80, and each additional hour is $25 for up to four people with two fishing lines.

Hotel-Club Akumal Caribe Villas Maya
Carretera Cancún-Tulum (Hwy. 307) km 63. ☎ 987/3-0596. For reservations, P.O. Box 13326, El Paso, TX 79913; ☎ 915/584-3552 or 800/351-1622 in the U.S. outside Texas, 800/343-1440 in Canada. 73 rms. A/C TEL. High season $90 bungalow, $110 hotel room, $155–$375 villa; low season $75 bungalow, $90 hotel room, $145–$210 villa.

The white arches you drive under and the entry are not impressive, but the lodging varieties here are. The 41 spacious **Villas Maya Bungalows** have beautiful tile floors and comfortable, nice furniture, all with fully-equipped kitchens. The 21 rooms in the new three-story **beachfront hotel** are similarly furnished but with small kitchens (no stove), a king-size or two queen-size beds, pale tile floors, and stylish Mexican accents. The **Villas Flamingo** are four exquisitely designed and luxuriously (but comfortably) furnished two-story homes facing Half Moon Bay. Each has one, two, or three bedrooms; large living, dining, and kitchen areas; and a lovely furnished patio just steps from the beach. The hotel has its own pool separate from other facilities on the grounds. Akumal's setting is truly relaxing and there's a restaurant facing the beach and lagoon, plus a grocery store with all the common necessities. If you're traveling with children, ask about the **children's program** that functions during specific times of year.

A CAVERN TOUR/SCUBA DIVING OPERATOR

On the right side of the road (if coming from Cancún) about 11½ miles south of Xcacel (and about 9 miles north of Tulum), is **Divers of the Hidden Worlds** (☎ **98/74-4081;** it's a cellular phone in Cancún). Experienced divers lead certified divers, snorkelers, and hikers on a variety of unusual trips. Some require hiking in the jungle to dry caves, others to caves where divers penetrate the underground world of watery caves with glass-clear water. Snorkelers investigate the *cenotes* (sinkholes leading to underground caves). Some dives are for more advanced divers, and some trips last all day, while others consume half a day. They also offer reef dives and resort courses and cave diving certification. They'll provide transporation from Cancún.

XEL-HA: SNORKELING & SWIMMING

The Caribbean coast of the Yucatán is carved by the sea into hundreds of small *caletas* (coves) that form the perfect habitat for tropical marine life, both flora and fauna. Many caletas remain undiscovered and pristine along the coast, but Xel-Ha, 8 miles south of Akumal, is enjoyed daily by throngs of snorkelers and scuba divers who come to luxuriate in its warm waters, and swim among its brilliant fish. Xel-Ha (pronounced "Shell-hah") is a swimmers' paradise, with no threat of undertow or pollution. It's a beautiful, completely calm cove that's a perfect place to bring kids for their first snorkeling experience (experienced snorkelers may be disappointed—the crowds here seem to have driven out the living coral and a lot of the fish, and you can find more abundant marine life and avoid an admission charge by going to Akumal, among other spots).

The entrance to Xel-Ha is half a mile in from the highway. You'll be asked to pay a "contribution" to the upkeep and preservation of the site of $10 per adult and $7 for children ages 5 to 12. It's open daily from 8am to 4:30pm.

Once in the park, you can rent snorkeling equipment and an underwater camera—but it's much cheaper to bring your own. You can also buy an outrageously priced drink or a meal, change clothes, take showers, and count lizards—the place is teeming with iguanas and other species. When you swim, be careful to observe the SWIM HERE and NO SWIMMING signs. (The greatest variety of fish can be seen right near the ropes marking off the no swimming areas and near any groups of rocks.)

Just south of the Xel-Ha turnoff on the west side of the highway, don't miss the **Maya ruins** of ancient Xel-Ha. You'll likely be the only one there as you walk over limestone rocks and through the tangle of trees, vines, and palms. There is a huge, deep, dark cenote to one side and a temple palace with tumbled-down columns, a jaguar group, and a conserved temple group. A covered palapa on one pyramid guards a partially preserved mural. Admission is $2.50.

Xel-Ha is close to the ruins at Tulum—it's a good place for a dip when you've finished clambering around the Maya castles. You can make the short 8-mile hop north from Tulum to Xel-Ha by bus. When you get off at the junction for Tulum, ask the restaurant owner when the next buses come by—otherwise you may have to wait as much as two hours on the highway. Most tour companies in Cancún and Cozumel include a trip to Tulum and a swim at Xel-Ha in the same journey.

6 Tulum, Punta Allen & Sian Ka'an

Tulum (80 miles southwest of Cancún) and the Punta Allen Peninsula (110 miles southwest of Cancún at its tip) are the southernmost points many travelers reach in their wanderings down the Caribbean coast (although there is more to discover farther on). The walled Maya city of Tulum—a large Postclassic Maya site that dramatically overlooks the Caribbean—is a natural beacon to visitors to Quintana Roo, and from Cancún it's within a two-hour drive. Tour companies and public buses make the trip regularly from Cancún and Playa del Carmen. And for those who want to leave the modern world a long, long way behind, Punta Allen (which can take between $1^{1}/_{2}$ to 3 hours to reach from Tulum, depending on how miserable the road's condition is) may be the ultimate. It's a place without the crowds, frenetic pace, or the creature comforts of the resorts to the north—down here, the generator shuts down at 10pm (if there is one). What you will find is great fishing and snorkeling, the natural and archaeological riches of the Sian Ka'an Biosphere Reserve, and a chance to rest up at what truly feels like the end of the road. A few beach cabañas now offer reliable power, telephones, and hot showers.

ESSENTIALS
ORIENTATION

When traveling south of Highway 307, get your bearings on Tulum by thinking of it as several distinct areas: First, on your left will be the junction of Highway 307 and the old access road to the Tulum ruins (it no longer provides access); here you'll find two small hotels, two restaurants, and a Pemex gas station. Next, a few feet south of the old road on Highway 307, also on the left, is the new Tulum ruins access road, leading to a large parking lot. And a few feet farther along 307 is the left turn onto the road leading to the hotels and campgrounds south of the ruins.

This is the road south along the narrow **Punta Allen Peninsula** to **Boca Paila,** a portion of the **Sian Ka'an Biosphere Reserve,** and **Punta Allen,** a lobstering/fishing village at the tip's end. Though most of this 30-mile-long peninsular stretch of sandy, potholed road is uninhabited, there are several rustic inns along a fabulous beach south of the ruins.

(Across the highway from the turnoff to the Punta Allen Peninsula on Highway 307 is the road to Cobá, another fascinating Maya city 40 miles inland. See "Cobá," below, for details.)

Finally, south of the Punta Allen road on Highway 307 is the **village of Tulum.** The highway here is lined with businesses, including the bus stations, auto repair shops, markets, and pharmacies. The village of Tulum, by the way, has the look of an up-and-coming place, with sidewalks and restaurants it's never sported before.

EXPLORING THE TULUM ARCHAEOLOGICAL SITE

Located 8 miles south of Xel-Ha, Tulum is a Maya fortress overlooking the Caribbean. At the end of the Classic period, in A.D. 900, Maya civilization began to decline and most of the large ceremonial centers were deserted. During the Postclassic period (A.D. 900 to the Spanish Conquest), small rival states developed with a few imported traditions from north central Mexico. Tulum is one such walled city-state; built in the 10th century, it functioned as a seaport. Aside from the spectacular setting, Tulum is not an impressive city when compared to Chichén-Itzá or Uxmal. There are no magnificent pyramidal structures as are found in the Classic Maya ruins. The stone carving is crude, and the site looks as though it was put together in a hurry or by novice apprentices rather than skilled masters. The primary god here was the diving god, depicted on several buildings as an upside-down figure above doorways. Seen at the Palace at Sayil and Cobá, this curious, almost comical figure is also known as the bee god.

The most imposing building in Tulum is the large stone structure on the cliff called the **Castillo** (castle), actually a temple as well as a fortress, once covered with stucco and painted. In front of the Castillo are several unrestored palacelike buildings partially covered with stucco. And on the beach below, where the Maya once came ashore, tourists frolic, combining a visit to the ruins with a dip in the Caribbean.

The **Temple of the Frescoes,** directly in front of the Castillo, contains interesting 13th-century wall paintings inside the temple, but entrance is no longer permitted. Distinctly Maya, they represent the rain god Chaac and Ixchel, the goddess of weaving, women, the moon, and medicine. On the cornice of this temple is a relief of the head of the rain god. If you get a slight distance from the building you'll see the eyes, nose, mouth, and chin. Notice the remains of the red-painted stucco on this building—at one time all the buildings at Tulum were painted a bright red.

Much of what we know of Tulum at the time of the Spanish Conquest comes from the writings of Diego de Landa, third bishop of the Yucatán. He wrote that Tulum was a small city inhabited by about 600 people, who lived in dwellings situated on platforms along a street and who supervised the trade traffic from Honduras to the Yucatán. Though it was a walled city, most of the inhabitants probably lived outside the walls, leaving the interior for priestly hierarchy and religious ceremonies. Tulum survived about 70 years after the Conquest, when it was finally abandoned.

Because of the excessive amount of visitors this site receives, it is no longer possible to climb the ruins. Visitors are asked to remain behind roped-off areas to view them.

In late 1994 a new entrance to the ruins was constructed about a 10-minute walk from the archaeological site. Cars and buses enter a large parking lot; some of the public buses from Playa del Carmen go directly to the visitors' center, where there's are artisans' stands, bookstore, and a museum, restaurant, several large rest rooms, and a ticket booth for Inter-Playa buses, which depart for Playa del Carmen and Cancún frequently between 7:40am and 4:40pm. After walking through the center, visitors pay the admission fee to the ruins, and another fee ($1.50 round-trip) to ride an open-air shuttle to the ruins. You can easily walk, however. Admission is $5; free on Sunday. There's an additional charge of $4 for a permit to use a video camera at the site. Parking costs $1.50. Licensed guides have a stand by the path to the ruins and charge $20 for a 45-minute tour in English, French, or Spanish for up to four persons. They will point out many architectural details you might otherwise miss, but their history information may not be up-to-date.

WHERE TO STAY & EAT AT TULUM

Motel El Crucero

Carretera Cancún-Tulum (Hwy. 307), Tulum Junction (Apdo. Postal 4), Tulum, Q. Roo. ☎ **987/ 3-0230** or 3-0232. 16 rms (all with bath). FAN. $121 single; $15 double. Free unguarded parking.

The Sian Ka'an Biosphere Reserve

Down the peninsula a few miles south of the Tulum ruins, you'll pass the guard-house of the Sian Ka'an Biosphere Reserve, 1.3 million acres set aside in 1986 to preserve tropical forests, savannas, mangroves, coastal and marine habitats, and 70 miles of coastal reefs. The area is home to jaguars, pumas, ocelots, margays, jagua-rundis, spider and howler monkeys, tapirs, white-lipped and collared peccaries, manatees, brocket and white-tailed deer, crocodiles, and green, loggerhead, hawks-bill, and leatherback sea turtles. It also protects 366 species of birds—you might catch a glimpse of an ocellated turkey; a great curassow; a brilliantly colored par-rot; a toucan or trogon; a white ibis; a roseate spoonbill; a jabiru, or wood stork; a flamingo; or one of 15 species of herons, egrets, and bitterns.

The park is separated into three parts: a "core zone," restricted to research; a "buffer zone," where visitors and families already living there have restricted use; and a "cooperation zone," outside the reserve but vital to its preservation. If you drive on Highway 307 from Tulum to an imaginary line just below the Bahía (bay) of Espíritu Santo, all you see on the Caribbean side is the reserve; but except at the ruins of Muyil/Chunyaxche, there's no access. At least 22 archaeological sites have been charted within Sian Ka'an. The best place to sample the reserve is the Punta Allen Peninsula, part of the "buffer zone." The inns were already in place when the reserve was created. Of these, only the Cuzan Guest House (see "Where to Stay and Eat at Tulum," below) offers trips for birding. But bring your own binoculars and birding books and have at it—the birdlife anywhere here is rich. At the Boca Paila bridge you can often find fishermen who'll take you into the lagoon on the landward side, where you can fish and see plenty of birdlife; but it's unlikely the boatman will know bird names in English or Spanish. Birding is best just after dawn, especially during the April through July nesting season.

Day trips to the Sian Ka'an are led from Cozumel (see "Cozumel," earlier in this chapter) and by a biologist from the **Friends of Sian Ka'an** in Cancún. For more information about the reserve or trip reservations, contact them at Plaza América, Av. Cobá 5, 3a Piso, Suite 48–50, Cancún, Q. Roo 77500 (☎ **988/4-9583;** fax 988/7-3080). From Cozumel, **Viajes Internacionales Palancar,** Av. 10 Sur no. 124, Cozumel, Q. Roo 77600 (☎ **987/2-2259;** fax 987/2-2348), offers day-long excursions to the reserve.

This motel, opposite the more expensive Hotel Acuario, has a very good and festive restaurant with the best food in the area; main courses cost $4 to $6. The pollo pibil is excellent. The guest rooms, however, are quite basic and may or may not have hot water. There's also a tiny "convenience store."

EN ROUTE TO FELIPE CARRILLO PUERTO

If you continue along the main Highway 307 past the Cobá turnoff, it heads south-west through Tulum village. About 14 miles south of Tulum village are the ruins of **Muyil** (ca. A.D. 1–1540) at the settlement of **Chunyaxche,** on the left side. Although archaeologists have done extensive mapping and studies of the ruins, only a few of the more than 100 or so buildings, caves, and subterranean temples have been exca-vated; new excavations take place off and on, so keep checking the progress. One of the objects of this research is to find evidence of an inland port, since canals link the site to the Caribbean 9 miles east of the Boca Paila cut.

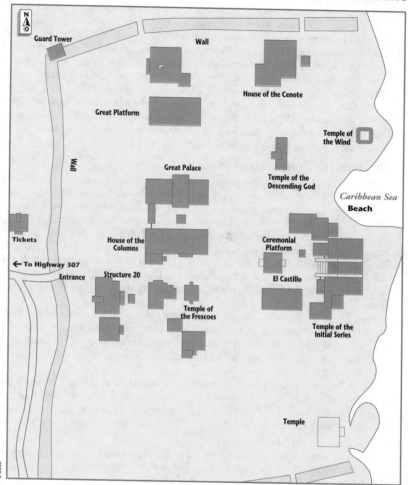

The Friends of Sian Ka'an in Cancún (see "Sian Ka'an Biosphere Reserve," above) organizes trips through the canals from Boca Paila. The Cuzan Guest House in Punta Allen and the Restaurant y Cabañas Ana y José south of the Tulum ruins (see listings below) also guide visitors here through the lagoons and canals. *Note:* The mosquito and dive-bombing fly population is fierce, but this is one of the best places along the coast for birding—go early in the morning.

Admission is $1.75; free for children under 12 and free for everyone on Sunday and festival days. It's open daily from 8am to 5pm.

After Muyil and Chunyaxche, Highway 307 cuts through 45 miles of jungle to Felipe Carrillo Puerto (see below).

THE PUNTA ALLEN PENINSULA

About 3 miles south of the Tulum ruins on the Punta Allen Road, the pavement ends and the road becomes narrow and sandy, with many potholes during the rainy season. Beyond this point is a 30-mile-long peninsula called Punta Allen, split in two at a cut called Boca Paila, where a bridge connects the two parts of the peninsula and the Caribbean enters a large lagoon on the right. It's part of the far eastern edge of the 1.3-million-acre **Sian Ka'an Biosphere Reserve** (see above). Along this road you'll find several cabaña-type inns, all on beautiful beaches facing the Caribbean. Taxis from the ruins can take you to most of these; then you can find a ride back to the junction at the end of your stay. *A Note About Huricane Roxanne:* Tulum and the Punta Allen Peninsula were among the hardest hit when Hurricane Roxanne raged through in October 1995. However, within a month hotels sported new paint, windows, roofs, and furnishings. The path of the storm was evident by the acres of broken trees, but the businesses seemed to have survived.

EXPLORING THE PUNTA ALLEN PENINSULA

The natural environment is the peninsula's marquee attraction, whether your tastes run to relaxing on the beaches or going on bird-watching expeditions (these are available between June and August, with July being best). Sea turtles nest on the beaches along here from May to October. The turtles lumber ashore at night, usually between 10pm and 3am. *A Note About Provisions:* Since the Punta Allen Peninsula is rather remote and there are no stores, handy provisions to bring along include a flashlight, mosquito repellent, mosquito coils, and water. Most hotels along here charge for bottled water in your room and for meals. From October through December winds may be accompanied by nippy nights, so come prepared—the hotels don't have blankets.

Lodgings here vary in quality—some are simple but quite comfortable, while others are a lot like camping out. One or two have electricity for a few hours in the evening—but shut it off around 10pm—and there are no electrical outlets; most don't have hot water. The first one is half a mile south of the ruins, and the farthest is 30 miles down the peninsula.

The following hotels are listed in the order you'll find them as you drive south on the Punta Allen road (from Tulum). To reach the first one you'll need to take the Punta Allen exit from Highway 307, then turn left when it intersects the coastal road. The rest of the hotels are to the right.

Cabañas Zazil Kin Don Armando

Apdo. Postal 44, 77780 Tulum, Q. Roo. ☎ **987/4-3856.** 30 bungalows (none with bath). $10 bed with hammock; $13 double with two beds. $10 deposit for bedding, key, and flashlight. Free unguarded parking.

Casual accommodations on a big beautiful beach, these stick-walled bungalows are spread over the large stretch of sand, mingled with clotheslines flapping with guests' laundry and a restaurant that's notably good. Each of these basic bungalows has a bed on a concrete slab, sheets, a blanket, and occasional mosquito netting, but there's electricity only in the restaurant. (Bring your own soap and towel and mosquito netting.) Some of the bungalows have no windows or ventilation, except through the cracks, unless the door is open. There are separate shared-bath facilities for men and women. The friendly English-speaking owners also run the restaurant. An average meal of chicken, beans, and rice costs $3 to $5. At night Don Armando's restaurant is *the* place to be while you're in the area, offering the best food and service and conviviality among guests.

From here you can arrange taxi service to and from the Tulum ruins and to the Cancún airport. It's half a mile south of the Tulum ruins; the sign on the right as you drive toward the ruins says zazil kin.

Restaurant y Cabañas Ana y José

Punta Allen Peninsula, Carretera Tulum, km 7 (Apdo. Postal 15), 77780 Tulum, Q. Roo. ☎ **988/ 0-6022** in Cancún. Fax 98/80-6021 in Cancún. 16 rms (all with bath). High season, $50–$60 single or double. Low season, $40–$50 single or double. Free unguarded parking.

This place started as a restaurant and blossomed into a comfortable inn on the beach, although it's somewhat overpriced. All rooms have tiled floors, one or two double beds, baths with cold-water shower, patios or balconies, and electricity between 6 and 10pm. However, 24-hour electricity is said to be on its way, so expect prices to skyrocket. The rock-walled cabañas in front are a little larger, and some face the beautiful wide beach just a few yards off, but these are also the most expensive rooms. New rooms have been added on a second level in back. The only drawback is the lack of cross-ventilation in some of the lower rooms in the back section, which can be uncomfortable at night without electricity to power fans. The inn also offers bicycle and kayak rentals, snorkeling, and dive trips. Biologist-led boat excursions to the Sian Ka'an Biosphere Reserve begin here at 9:30am Monday and Tuesday and Friday and Saturday (weather permitting) for $50 per person. The price includes chips and soft drinks and round-trip van transportation to the reserve from the cabañas.

The excellent, screened-in restaurant, with sand floors under the palapa, offers modest prices and is open daily from 8am to 9pm. It's 4 miles south of the Tulum ruins. Reservations are a must in high season, or arrive very early in the day before it fills up.

Cabañas Tulum

Punta Allen Peninsula, Carretera Tulum, km 7 (Apdo. Postal 63), 77780 Tulum, Q. Roo. No phone. 18 rms (all with bath). FAN. High season, $34 single or double. Low season, $23 single or double.

Next door to Ana y José's (above) is a row of bungalows facing a heavenly stretch of ocean and beach. Each bungalow includes a cold-water shower, two double beds, screens on the windows, a table, one electric light, nice-size tiled baths, and a verandah where you can hang a hammock. Mattresses, which rest on a cement platform, are too thin to cushion against the hard surface. Flat topsheets, which are also used as bottom sheets, immediately work off the mattress, leaving guests either wrestling with them all night or giving up to settle in on the bare mattress. The electricity is on from 5:30 to 10pm only, so bring candles or a flashlight. A small restaurant serves beer, soft drinks, and all three meals for reasonable prices—just don't expect a gourmet meal. The cabañas are often full between December 15 and Easter and July and August, so arrive early or make reservations. It's 4 miles south of the ruins.

Boca Paila Fishing Lodge

Apdo. Postal 59, Cozumel, Q. Roo 77600. ☎ and fax **987/872-0053** or 987/872-1176. For reservations contact Frontiers, P.O. Box 959, 100 Logan Rd., Wexford, PA 15090; ☎ 412/ 935-1577 or 800/245-1950 in the U.S.; fax 412/935-5388. 8 cabañas. FAN. High season (Dec 3–June 2) $2,000 per person double. Low season $1,600 per person double. Rates for 6 days and 7 nights, including all meals and a private boat and bonefishing guide for each cabaña. Ask about prices for a nonangler sharing a double with an angler. Nonfishing drop-in prices July–Sept, $200 per person double with three meals; $275 one or two people for day of fishing with lunch but no overnight.

Easily a top contender for the nicest spot along this road, the white stucco cabañas offer a friendly beachside comfort that makes it an ideal choice. Spread out on the beach and linked by a nice walkway, each individual unit has a mosquito-proof palapa roof, large tiled rooms comfortably furnished with two double beds, rattan furniture, hot water in the bathrooms, wall fans, 24-hour electricity, and comfortable screened porch. The Boca Paila attracts a clientele that comes for saltwater fly-fishing in the flats, mostly for bonefish. Prime fishing months are March through June. But when occupancy is low, nonfishing guests can be accommodated with advance notice. Overnight nonfishing rates are priced high as a discouragement to drop-ins. The lodge is about midway down the Punta Allen Peninsula, just before the Boca Paila bridge.

✪ Cuzan Guest House

Punta Allen (reservations: Contact Apdo. Postal 24, 77720 Felipe Carrillo Puerto, Q. Roo; ☎ **983/4-0358** and fax 983/4-0383 in Felipe Carrillo Puerto). 8 rms (6 with bath). $40–$60 single or double. All inclusive 7-day fly-fishing package $1,499.

About 30 miles south of the Tulum ruins is the end of the peninsula and Punta Allen, the Yucatán's best-known lobstering and fishing village planted on a palm-studded beach. Isolated and rustic, it's part Indiana Jones, part Robinson Crusoe, and certainly the most laid-back end of the line you'll find for a while. The small town has a lobster cooperative, a few streets with modest homes, and a lighthouse at the end of a narrow sand road dense with coconut palms and jungle on both sides. So it's a welcome sight to see the beachside Cuzan Guest House and its sign in English that reads STOP HERE FOR TOURIST INFORMATION. A stay here could well be the highlight of your trip, provided you're a flexible traveler.

Two rooms are plainly furnished Maya-style oval stucco buildings with concrete floors, shared bath, and a double bed with mosquito netting. Three comfortable, spacious huts with thatched roofs and private bathrooms are at the water's edge, with three more similar accommodations set back from the water, but with an ocean view. A room in the owner's house with a front verandah is sometimes available. A house in the village is often rented as well, but readers have reported that it's extremely noisy at night. Unfortunately, Cuzan's delightful thatched teepees disappeared during hurricane Roxanne. Everything is solar-powered. The real charmer here is the sand-floored restaurant run by coowner Sonja Lilvik, a Californian who makes you feel right at home. If it's lobster season, you may have lobster at every meal, always prepared with a deliciously different recipe. But you might also be treated to a pile of heavenly stone crabs or some other gift from the sea.

Sonja arranges fly-fishing trips for bone, permit, snook, and tarpon to the nearby saltwater flats and lagoons of Ascension Bay. The $25 per-person boat tour of the coastline that she offers is a fascinating three hours of snorkeling, slipping in and out of mangrove-filled canals for birdwatching, and skirting the edge of an island rookery loaded with frigate birds. November through March is frigate-mating season and the male frigate shows off his big billowy red breast pouch to impress potential mates. The all-day Robinson Crusoe Tour costs $100 per person and includes a boat excursion to remote islands, beaches, reefs, ruins (Muyil/Chunyaxche), jungles, lagoons, and birdwatching areas. Or you can simply relax in a hammock on the beach or in your room or go kayaking along the coast.

7 Cobá

105 miles SW of Cancún

From the turnoff at the Tulum junction, you travel inland an hour or so to arrive at these mystical ruins jutting up from the forest floor.

The impressive Maya ruins at Cobá, deep in the jungle, are a worthy detour from your route south. You don't need to stay overnight to see the ruins, but there are a few hotels. The village is small and poor, gaining little from the visitors who pass through to see the ruins. **Used clothing** (especially for children) would be a welcome gift.

ESSENTIALS
GETTING THERE & DEPARTING
By Bus

From Playa del Carmen there are three buses to Cobá. Two buses leave Valladolid for Cobá, but they may fill early, so buy tickets as soon as possible.

Several buses a day leave Cobá: At 6:30am and 3pm a bus goes to Tulum and Playa del Carmen, and at noon and 7pm there's a bus to Valladolid.

By Car

The road to Cobá begins in Tulum, across Highway 307 from the turnoff to the Punta Allen Peninsula. Turn right when you see the signs to Cobá and continue on that road for 40 miles. When you reach the village, proceed straight until you see the lake; when the road curves right, turn left. The entrance to the ruins is at the end of that road past some small restaurants. Cobá is also about a three-hour drive south from Cancún.

ORIENTATION

The highway into Cobá becomes one main paved street through town, which passes El Bocadito restaurant and hotel on the right (see "Accommodations & Dining," below) and goes a block to the lake. If you turn right at the lake you reach the Villas Arqueológicas a block farther. Turning left will lead past a couple of informal/primitive restaurants on the left facing the lake, and to the ruins, straight ahead, the equivalent of a block.

EXPLORING THE COBÁ RUINS

The Maya built many breathtaking cities in the Yucatán, but few were grander in scope than Cobá. However, much of the 42-square-mile site, on the shores of two lakes, is unexcavated. A 60-mile-long *sacbe* (a pre-Hispanic raised road or causeway) through the jungle linked Cobá to Yaxuná, once a large and important Maya center 30 miles south of Chichén-Itzá. It's the Maya's longest-known sacbe, and there are at least 50 or more shorter ones from here. An important city-state, Cobá, which means "water stirred by the wind," flourished between A.D. 632 (the oldest carved date found here) until after the founding of Chichén-Itzá, around 800. Then Cobá slowly faded in importance and population until it was finally abandoned. Scholars believe Cobá was an important trade link between the Yucatán Caribbean coast and inland cities.

Once in the site, keep your bearings—it's very easy to get lost on the maze of dirt roads in the jungle. Bring your bird and butterfly books; this is one of the best places to see both. Branching off from every labeled path you'll notice unofficial narrow paths into the jungle, used by locals as shortcuts through the ruins. These are good for scouting for birds, but be careful to remember the way back.

The **Grupo Cobá** boasts a large, impressive pyramid, the **Temple of the Church** (La Iglesia), which you'll find if you take the path bearing right after the entry gate. Walking to it, notice the unexcavated mounds on the left. Though the urge to climb the temple is great, the view is better from El Castillo in the Nohoc Mul group farther back at the site.

From here, return back to the main path and turn right. You'll pass a sign pointing right to the ruined *juego de pelota* (ball court), but the path is obscure.

Continuing straight ahead on this path for 5 to 10 minutes, you'll come to a fork in the road. To the left and right you'll notice jungle-covered, unexcavated pyramids, and at one point you'll cross a raised portion crossing the pathway—this is the visible remains of the sacbe to Yaxuná. Throughout the area, intricately carved stelae stand by pathways, or lie forlornly in the jungle underbrush. Though protected by crude thatched roofs, most are so weatherworn as to be indiscernible.

The left fork leads to the **Nohoc Mul Group,** which contains El Castillo, the tallest pyramid in the Yucatán (rising even higher than the great El Castillo at Chichén-Itzá and the Pyramid of the Magician at Uxmal). So far, visitors are still permitted to climb to the top. From the magnificent lofty position you can see unexcavated jungle-covered pyramidal structures poking up through the forest all around. The right fork (more or less straight on) goes to the **Conjunto Las Pinturas.** Here, the main attraction is the **Pyramid of the Painted Lintel,** a small structure with traces of the original bright colors above the door. You can climb up to get a close look. Though maps of Cobá show ruins around two lakes, there are really only two excavated buildings to see after you enter the site.

Note: Because of the heat, visit Cobá in the morning or after the heat of the day has passed. Mosquito repellent, drinking water, and comfortable shoes are imperative.

Admission is $5; children under 12 enter free daily, and Sunday and holidays it's free to everyone. Camera permits are $8.50 for each video. The site is open daily from 8am to 5pm.

ACCOMMODATIONS & DINING

⑤ El Bocadito

Calle Principal, Cobá, Q. Roo. No phone. For reservations contact Apdo. Postal 56, Valladolid, Yuc. 97780. 8 rms (all with bath). FAN. $12–$15 double. Free unguarded parking.

El Bocadito, on the right as you enter town, could take advantage of being the only game in town besides the much more expensive Villas Arqueológicas—but it doesn't. Next to the hotel's restaurant of the same name, the rooms are arranged in two rows facing an open patio. They're simple, each with tile floors, two double beds, no bedspreads, a ceiling fan, and a washbasin separate from the toilet and cold-water shower cubicle. It's agreeable enough and always full by nightfall, so to secure a room, arrive no later than 3pm.

The clean open-air restaurant offers good meals at reasonable prices, served by a friendly, efficient staff. Busloads of tour groups stop here at lunch (always a sign of approval). I enjoy the casual atmosphere of El Bocadito, and there's a bookstore and gift shop adjacent to the restaurant.

✪ Villas Arqueológicas Cobá

Cobá, Q. Roo. ☎ **5/203-3086** in Mexico City, or **800/258-2633** in the U.S. 44 rms (all with bath). A/C. $70 single; $80 double. Rates include all charges and taxes. Free guarded parking.

Operated by Club Med but nothing like a Club Med Village, this lovely lakeside hotel is a five-minute walk from the ruins. The hotel has a French polish, and the restaurant is top-notch, though expensive. Breakfast costs $10; lunch and dinner cost $20. A room rate including meals is available. The rooms, built around a plant-filled courtyard and beautiful pool, are stylish and soothingly comfortable. The hotel also has a library on Mesoamerican archeology (with books in French, English, and Spanish). Make reservations—this hotel fills with touring groups.

To find it, drive through town and turn right at the lake; the hotel is straight ahead on the right.

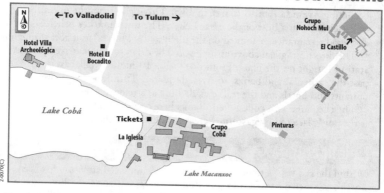

←To Valladolid   **To Tulum →**

Hotel Villa
Archeológica

Hotel El
Bocadito

Grupo
Nohoch Mul

El Castillo

Lake Cobá

Tickets ■

La Iglesia

Grupo
Cobá

Pinturas

Lake Macanxoc

2-0070(C)

8 Muyil & Chunyaxche

From Tulum you continue along the main Highway 307 past the Cobá turnoff; it heads southwest through Tulum village. About 14 miles south of Tulum village are the ruins of **Muyil** (ca. A.D. 1–1540) at the settlement of **Chunyaxche,** on the left side. Although archaeologists have done extensive mapping and studies of the ruins, only a few of the more than 100 or so buildings, caves, and subterranean temples have been excavated; it's actually more historically significant than it is interesting, and for most people it may not be worth the time or admission price. Birding in the early morning, however, is quite worthwhile. New excavations take place off and on, so keep checking the progress. One of the objects of this research is to find evidence of an inland port, since canals link the site to the Caribbean 9 miles east of the Boca Paila cut.

Note: The mosquito and dive-bombing fly population is fierce, but this is one of the best places along the coast for birding—go early in the morning.

Admission is $3; free for children under 12 and free for everyone on Sunday and festival days. It's open daily from 8am to 5pm.

After Muyil and Chunyaxche, Highway 307 cuts through 45 miles of jungle to Felipe Carrillo Puerto.

9 Felipe Carrillo Puerto

134 miles SW of Cancún

Felipe Carrillo Puerto (pop. 47,000) is a busy crossroads in the jungle along the road to Ciudad Chetumal. It has gas stations, a market, a small ice plant, a bus terminal, and a few modest hotels and restaurants.

Since the main road intersects the road back to Mérida, Carrillo Puerto is the turning point for those making a "short circuit" of the Yucatán Peninsula. Highway 184 heads west from here to Ticul, Uxmal, Campeche, and Mérida.

As you pass through, consider its strange history: This was where the rebels in the War of the Castes took their stand, guided by the "Talking Crosses." Some remnants of that town (named Chan Santa Cruz) are still extant. Look for signs in town pointing the way. For the full story, see the features on Yucatecan history in Chapter 5.

ESSENTIALS

Coastal Highway 307 from Cancún leads directly here. There's frequent bus service south from Cancún and Playa del Carmen. The highway goes right through the town, becoming **Avenida Benito Juárez** in town. Driving in from the north, you'll pass a traffic circle with a bust of the great Juárez. The town **market** is here. Small hotels and good restaurants are located on the highway (Av. Juárez) as it goes through town.

The directions given above assume you'll be driving. If you arrive by bus, the **bus station** is right on the plaza. From there it's a 10-minute walk east down Calle 67, past the cathedral and banks, to Avenida Juárez. Turn left onto Juárez to find restaurants and hotels and the traffic circle I use as a reference point.

The telephone **area code** is 983. **Banks** here don't exchange foreign currency. This is the only place to buy **gasoline** between Tulum and Chetumal.

10 Majahual, Xcalak & the Chinchorro Reef

Within the last year, a tremendous amount of commercial attention has been focused on this remote part of Quintana Roo, with resorts rumored both north of the Majahual turnoff and in the tiny village of Xcalak itself. Several small inns have also opened between Majahual and Xcalak since the last edition. But the peninsula is still a little-known area—at least for the moment. A roll-with-the-punches kind of traveler will savor its rustic and remote appeal—especially those preferring this coast's offbeat offerings, divers looking for new underwater conquests, bird lovers seeking an abundance of colorful tropical birdlife, and anyone looking for quiet, beachfront relaxation. Your destination is the Cabañas Costa de Cocos diving resort and the nearby fishing village of Xcalak near the end of the peninsula. Offshore reefs and the little-known Chinchorro reef offer great diving possibilities. The village of Xcalak once had a population as large as 1,200 before the 1958 hurricane; now it has only 200 inhabitants. You'll pass many down-and-out places on the way, so the clean Costa de Cocos will stand out when you see it.

ESSENTIALS

Driving south from Felipe Carrillo Puerto, you'll come to the turnoff (left) onto Highway 10, $1^1/_2$ miles after Limones, then it's a 30-mile drive to the coastal settlement of Majahual (mah-*hah*-wahl), and another 35 miles to the end of the peninsula at the tiny fishing village of Xcalak (eesh-*kah*-lahk). To orient you further, the turnoff from Highway 307 is 163 miles southwest of Cancún, 88 miles southwest of Tulum and just south of the small village of Limones.

Driving from the turnoff at Highway 307 to Xcalak takes around two hours. At Mahajual, where you turn right (south), there's a military guard station. Tell the guard your destination and continue on the sandy, sometimes potholed road for 35 more miles—about an hour. *Slow down at settlements. Residents aren't expecting much traffic, and dogs and children play on the road.*

Public Transportation Note: From Chetumal, two full-size **buses** daily go to Xcalak from Chetumal's bus station. There's combi transportation too, from behind the Holiday Inn, but they cram in twice as many passengers as will fit comfortably and may carry a pig or goat on top as well.

By Ferry   When I checked, ferry docks, and two 20-car ferries (with passenger space) were being prepared to ply Chetumal Bay running between the capital of Chetumal and village of Xcalak, eliminating the tedious road trip through Limones and Majahual. Check with the State Tourism Office in Chetumal about the status of this service.

Important Note About Provisions: Since this is a remote part of the world, travelers should expect inconveniences. When things break down or food items run out, replacements are a long way off. You might arrive to find that the dive boat's broken, or that there's no beer, or that the generator powering the water pumps, toilets, and electricty is off for hours or days. Needless to say, a flashlight might come in handy. Bring a large quantity of strong mosquito repellent with DEET as a main ingredient—the mosquitoes are undaunted by anything else. You might want to stow a package or two of mosquito coils to burn at night. Your last chance for gas is at Felipe Carrillo Puerto, although if you're desperate, the tire repairman's family in Limones might sell you a liter or two. Look for the big tire leaning against the fence.

DIVING THE CHINCHORRO REEF

The **Chinchorro Reef Underwater National Park** is a 24-mile-long, eight-mile-wide oval-shaped reef with a depth of three feet on the reef's interior to 3,000 feet on the exterior. Locals claim it's the last virgin reef system in the Caribbean. It's invisible from the ocean side; one of its diving attractions is the number of shipwrecks—at least 30 of them—along the reef's eastern side. One is on top of the reef. Divers have counted 40 cannon at one wreck site. On the west side are walls and coral gardens, but it's too rough to dive there.

Aventuras Chinchorro is the fully-equipped dive shop for Sandwood Villas and Villa Caracol (see below) as well as other establishments in the area. Local diving just off shore costs $30 per diver for a two-tank dive. Chinchorro Banks diving costs between $15 and $50 per person, depending on how long you stay, how far you go, and how many divers are in the group. Fishing and snorkeling excursions and trips into Belize can also be arranged, as well as rental of kayaks and horses. For reservations for diving, or for rooms at the abovementioned inns, contact Aventuras Chinchorro, 812 Garland Ave. Nokomis, FL 34275 (☎ **941/488-4505** or **800/ 480-4505**).

ACCOMMODATIONS & DINING

Besides the Costa de Cocos Dive Resort described below, two other small, cozy inns have opened about a half a mile from each other and near the village of Xcalak. **Sandwood Villas** are four two-bedroom apartments renting for $45 per person double; the **Villa Caracol,** where rooms rent for $60 per person double, is a four-room inn with air-conditioning, balconies, 24-hour electricity, hot water, free snorkeling and fishing equipment, and a beachside bar and grill. Rates at both places include breakfast and dinner, and lunch is available. Discounts are offered for stays of a week or more. Thirteen RV hookups are also available, at $13.50 per night for one or two people, but no camping is permitted. Contact **Aventuras Chinchorro,** listed above, for reservations.

Aside from those connected to the establishments mentioned here, a couple of restaurants in Xcalak offer good seafood meals—ask at your hotel which one is the current favorite.

Costa de Cocos Dive Resort

Carretera Majahual-Xcalak km 52. Q. Roo. For reservations ☎ **708/529-4473** or 800/443-1123; fax 813/488-4505. 8 cabañas. FANS. $35 double with 1bed, $40 double with 2 beds; $30 triple. Dive package (daily rate including dives, breakfast, and dinner) $105 double with 1 bed, $95 triple. Three-night minimum stay with dive package. Rates include breakfast and dinner.

Far and away the most sophisticated hostelry along this route, this place will seem a welcome respite in a palm grove just before the fishing village of Xcalak, which is a half mile farther at the end of the peninsula. The beautifully constructed thatch-roofed cabañas are fashioned after Maya huts but with sophisticated details like limestone walls halfway up, followed by handsomely crafted mahogany-louvered and screened windows, beautiful wood plank floors in the bedroom, large tile bathrooms, comfortable furnishings, shelves of paperback books, hot water, and mosquito netting. Nice as it is, it still won't hurt to inspect your shoes daily for hidden critters— this is the jungle, after all. All dive equipment is available and included in dive packages or rented separately for day guests. The resort operates a 40-foot dive boat for diving Chinchorro. Water-sports equipment for rent includes an ocean kayak and windsurf board. PADI open-water certification can be arranged also at an additional cost. Beer and soft drinks are sold at the resort, but bring your own liquor and snacks. Besides the rates quoted above, there are separate diving rates for individuals without package arrangements.

Anytime the sea gets choppy, your planned dive at Chinchorro Reef (22 miles offshore) may be grounded. However, the diving five minutes offshore from the Costa de Cocos Resort is highly rewarding when weather prohibits Chinchorro diving.

11 Lago Bacalar

65 miles SW of Felipe Carrillo Puerto, 23 miles NW of Chetumal

If you can arrange it, staying in Bacalar sure beats staying in Chetumal or Felipe Carrillo Puerto. The crystal-clear spring-fed waters of Lake Bacalar, which is Mexico's second largest lake at slightly over 65 miles long, empty into the Caribbean. Known as the Lake of Seven Colors, mismanagement of the natural mixture of spring and seawater in recent years changed the characteristic varied deep blue colors. It's still beautiful to gaze upon, and the colors range from crystal clear and pale blue to deep blue-green and Caribbean turquoise. Spaniards fleeing coastal pirates used Maya pyramid stones to build a fort in Bacalar, which is now a modest museum. The area is very quiet—the perfect place to swim and relax. At least 130 species of birds have been counted in the area. If you're in a car, take a detour through the village of Bacalar and down along the lakeshore drive. To find the lakeshore drive, go all the way past town on Highway 307, where you'll see a sign pointing left to the lake. When you turn left, that road is the lakeshore drive. You can double back along the drive from there to return to the highway. The Hotel Laguna is on the lakeshore drive. From here it's a 30-minute drive to Chetumal and to the Corozol Airport in Belize. Besides its location on Lago Bacalar, this area is also perfect for launching excursions into the Río Bec ruin route, described below.

ESSENTIALS

Buses going south from Cancún and Playa del Carmen stop here and there are frequent buses from Chetumal. Signs into Bacalar are plainly visible from Highway 307.

ACCOMMODATIONS

Hotel Laguna

Costera de Bacalar 143, 77010 Lago Bacalar, Q. Roo. ☎ **983/2-3517** in Chetumal. 30 rms, 4 bungalows (all with bath). FAN. $23 single or double. $50 bungalow for 5 persons.

The Laguna is off the beaten path, so there are almost always rooms available— except in winter, when it's full of Canadians. Rooms overlook the pool and have a lovely view of the lake. The water along the shore is very shallow, but you can dive from the hotel's dock into 30-foot water. The hotel's restaurant offers main courses costing about $4 to $8. It's open daily from 8am to 8pm. To find it, go through town toward Chetumal. Just at the edge of town you'll see a sign pointing left to the hotel and lakeshore drive.

✪ Rancho Encantado

Carretera Felipe Carrillo Puerto-Chetumal (Apdo. Postal 233), 77000 Chetumal, Q. Roo. ☎ and fax **983/8-0427.** For reservations contact P.O. Box 1256, Taos, NM 87571. ☎ 800/505 MAYA in the U.S.; fax 505/776-5878. 12 casitas. FAN. Including continental breakfast and dinner, Nov–April, $120 single or double; May–Oct, $96 single or double ($17.50 per person less without food).

What an Edenic, serene place to unwind. Rancho Encantado's immaculate white stucco individual casitas are spread out on a shady manicured lawn beside the smooth Lago Bacalar. Each spacious, sublimely comfortable, and beautifully kept room has mahogany-louvered windows, a shiny red tile floor, mahogany dining table and chairs, a living room or sitting area, a porch with chairs, and hammocks strung between trees. Some have a handsome blue-tile kitchenette and others have a coffee area; coffee makers and coffee are provided in each room. Some rooms have cedar ceilings and red tiled roofs and others have handsome thatched roofs. All are decorated with folk art, foot-loomed pastel-colored bedspreads, and Zapotec rugs from Oaxaca. The newest rooms are the four waterfront casitas (rooms 9 through 12) with white stucco walls, thatched roofs, and fabulous hand-painted murals inspired by those at Bonampak. Two of these have murals plus a striking large rust-colored plaster face resembling those Olmeclike faces at nearby Kohunlich. These rooms prime you for a trip to nearby archaeological sites. Casita 8 sleeps five, and casita 1 sleeps four.

The large palapa-topped restaurant overlooks the lake and serves all three meals. There's no beef on the menu, but plenty of chicken, fish, vegetables, and fresh fruit. The honey here is from Rancho hives. You can swim from the hotel's dock, and kayaks and canoes are available for guest use. Orange, lime, mango, sapote, ceiba, banana, palm, and oak trees, wild orchids, and bromiliads on the expansive grounds make great bird shelter, attracting flocks of chattering parrots, turquoise-browed motmots, toucans, and at least a hundred more species, many of which are easy to spot outside your room. Ask the manager, Luis Tellez, for a copy of the extensive birding list.

Tellez also keeps abreast of developments at the nearby archaeological sites and is the only source of current information before you reach the ruins. He's developed a lot of knowledge about the sites and leads several trips himself. Almost a dozen excursions are available through the hotel. Among them are day trips to the Río Bec ruin route, an extended visit to Calakmul, a ruins visit and lunch with a local family (a guest favorite), outings to the Majahual Peninsula, and a riverboat trip to the Maya ruins of Lamanai deep in a Belizian forest. This is the only hotel offering guided trips to the Rio Bec ruins, many of which are available only by special permit, which Tellez can obtain. Several ruins are easily reachable from the road, and others are so deep in the jungle that a guide is necessary to find them and a four-wheel-drive vehicle is a must. With advance notice, the hotel can arrange guides and transportation. They also work with Río Bec specialist Serge Rìou (see "Exploring Chetumal," below). Excursions range in price from $55 to $115 per person, depending on the length and difficulty of the trip, and several have a three-person minimum. Groups interested in birding, yoga, archaeology, and the like are invited to bring a leader and use Rancho Encantado as a base. Special packages and excursions can be arranged in advance from the hotel's U.S. office. To find it, look for the hotel's sign on the left about 1 mile before Bacalar.

WHERE TO EAT

Besides the lakeside restaurant of Rancho Encantado (see "Accommodations," above), you may enjoy the **Restaurant Cenote Azul,** a comfortable open-air thatched-roof restaurant on the edge of the beautiful Cenote Azul. In both places, main courses cost from $5 to $10. To get there, follow the highway to the south edge of town and turn left at the restaurant's sign; follow that road around to the restaurant. At Rancho Encantado you can swim in Lago Bacalar, and at the Restaurant Cenote you can take a dip in placid Cenote Azul—but without skin lotion of any kind, because it poisons the cenote.

12 West from Bacalar: The Río Bec Ruin Route

A few miles west of Bacalar begins the Yucatán's southern ruin route, generally called the Río Bec region, although other architectural styles are present. Until recently the region enjoyed little attention. However, all that is rapidly changing. Within the last several years, the Mexican government has spent millions of pesos to build a new highway, conserve previously excavated sites and uncover heretofore unexcavated ruins. This is an especially ruin-rich but little-explored part of the peninsula. With the opening in late 1994 of **Dzibanché,** an extensive "new" site, paved-road access to **Calakmul** in 1994, and the **Museo de la Cultura Maya** also in 1995 in Chetumal, together with other "new sites" and discoveries at existing ruins, the region is poised to become the peninsula's "newest" tourist destination. With responsible guides, other jungle-surrounded but difficult-to-reach sites may also be available soon. A new four-lane highway leads from close to Bacalar for several miles before it becomes two-lane again; construction crews are continuing to work widening the road even further. Touristic services (restaurants, hotels) are slowly being added along the route, informed guides must be arranged before you arrive, and there are no visitor's centers. Rancho Encantado trucks in water to the bathrooms at the ruins of Kohunlich, making them the only public rest rooms on the route. Part of what makes this area so special is the feeling of pioneering into unmarked land—and with that comes a bit of inconvenience. However, this area is definitely worth watching and visiting now. And finally I must mention the richness of the bird and animal life in the whole route. Toucans flying across the highway and orioles are extremely common. Grey fox, wild turkey, and tesquintle (a bushy-tailed plant-eating rodent), the raccoon relative coatimundi, with its long tapered snout and tail, and armadillos will surely cross your path. At Calakmul a family of howler monkeys resides in the trees overlooking the parking area. To make the most of your visit, preparatory reading would include *A Forest of Kings: The Untold Story of the Ancient Maya* by Linda Schele and David Friedel (William Morrow, 1990), *The Blood of Kings: Dynasty and Ritual in Maya Art* by Linda Schele and Mary Ellen Miller (George Braziller, Inc., 1968), and *The Maya Cosmos* by David Freidel and Linda Schele (William Morrow, 1993). *Arqueológica Mexicana* magazine, which is written in Spanish, devoted its July-August 1995 issue to the Quintana Roo portion of the Río Bec ruin route. And finally, though it lacks historic and cultural information, and many sites have ex-panded since it was written, Joyce Kelly's *An Archeological Guide to Mexico's Yucatán Peninsula* (University of Oklahoma, 1993), is the best companion book to have. For a crash course, focus your learning on the meaning of the jaguar, Xibalba (the underworld), and the earth monster.

The route starts just 9 miles from the edge of Bacalar where there's the turnoff from Highway 307 to Highway 186, which leads to the Río Bec ruin route as well as to Escarcega, Villahermosa, and Palenque. You can divide your sightseeing into several day trips. If you get an early start, many of the ruins mentioned below can be easily visited in a day from Bacalar. These sites will be changing, though, since swarms of laborers are still busy with further exploration. Evidence shows that these ruins, especially Becán, were part of the trade route linking the Caribbean coast at Cobá to Edzná and the Gulf coast and with Lamanai in Belize and beyond. Once this region was dense with Maya cities, cultivated fields, lakes, and an elaborate system of rivers that connected the region with Belize and Central America. Today many of these ancient cities hide under a dense cover of jungle, which has overtaken the land from horizon to horizon. There are no visitor facilities or refreshments at these sites, so bring your own water and food. However, in the village of Xpujil (just before the ruins of Xpujil), the **Restaurant Posada Calakmul** (☎ 983/2-3304), under the watchful eye of Doña María Cabrera, serves excellent home-style food and caters to ruins enthusiasts—hung about the room are photos and descriptions of little-known sites by Serge Rìou. The new **hotel rooms** behind the restaurant cost $16 single or double and are clean and comfortable, with tile floors, private bathrooms with hot water, good beds, and a small porch. Near the entrance to the Chicanná ruins, on the north side of the road, is the new **Ramada Inn Eco Village,** km. 144 Carretera Excarcega (☎ 983/2-8863). Though the name suggests an ecological bent, approximately 20 acres of jungle were completely leveled to build an as yet unpaved parking lot for all the buses and cars that will one day come, a swimming pool, restaurant, and 28 nicely furnished rooms in sets of two stories. One room is single-level and built like a Maya house. Manicured lawns with flower beds and pathways link the rooms, which have a Polynesian architecture. There are no ecologically oriented tours. For the moment, the hotel attracts primarily bus tours and individual travelers. Electricity is generated between 6pm and 10am. Restaurant prices are high, and don't include the 15% tax. A 15% service charge might also be added. Single rooms go for $90 single and $100 double, including breakfast.

Luis Tellez at Rancho Encantado, at Bacalar (see "Accommodations," above), is the best source of information about the status of these sites and any new ones. Entry to each site is $1.75 to $3, and all are free on Sunday. Informational signs at each building within the sites are in Maya, Spanish, and English. Wear loads of mosquito repellent. The following list of sites is in order if you're driving from Bacalar or Chetumal.

DZIBANCHÉ

Dzibanché (or Tzibanché) means "place where they write on wood." Exploration began here in 1993, and it opened to the public in late 1994. Scattered over 26 square miles (though only a small portion is excavated), it's both a Preclassic and a Postclassic site (A.D. 300–900) that was occupied for around 700 years. Two enormous and adjoining plazas have been cleared. The site shows influence from Río Bec, Petén, and Teotihuacán. The Temple of the Owl, on the Plaza de Xibalbá, has a miniature version of Teotihuacán-style *talud tablero* (slant and straight facade) architecture flanking the sides of the main stairway leading to the top with its lintel and entrance to an underground tomb. (Teotihuacán ruins are near Mexico City, but their influence was strong as far as Guatemala.) Despite centuries of an unforgiving wet climate, a wood lintel, in good condition and with a date carving, still supports a partially preserved corbeled arch on top of this building. Inside the temple, a tomb was discovered, making this the second known temple in Mexico built specifically as a tomb (the first discovered is the Temple of Inscriptions at Palenque). However, the tomb at Dzibanché predates Pacal's at Palenque by about 350 years. A diagram of this temple shows interior steps leading from the top, then down inside the pyramid to ground level, just as at Palenque. The stairway is first reached by a deep, well-like drop that held remains of a sacrificial victim and which was sacked during pre-Hispanic times. Uncovered at different levels of the stairwell were a number of beautiful polychromed lidded vessels, one of which has an owl painted on the top handle, with its wings spreading onto the lid. White owls were messengers of the gods of the underworld in the Maya religion. This interior stairway isn't open to the public, but you can clearly see the lintel just behind the entrance to the tomb. Further exploration of the tomb awaits stabilization of interior walls. Opposite the Temple of the Owl is the Temple of the Cormorant, so named after a polychromed drinking vessal found there picturing a cormorant. Here too archaeologists have found evidence of an interior tomb similar to the one in the Temple of the Owl, but excavations of it have not begun. Other magnificently preserved pottery pieces found during excavations include an incense burner with an almost three-dimensional figure of the diving god attached to the outside, and another incense burner with an elaborately dressed figure of the god Itzamná attached. The site also incorporates another section of ruins called Kinichná (keen-*eech*-nah), about 1¹/₂ miles north, and which is reachable only by a rutted road that's impassable in the rainy season. There, an Olmec-style jade figure was found. A formal road to these ruins had not yet been built, but there's a sign pointing to the right turn to Morocoy approximately 18 miles from the Highway 307 turnoff. You follow that paved road, which turns into an unpaved road, and pass the small settlement (not really a town) of Morocoy to another rough dirt road to the right (there's a sign to the ruins there), and follow it for about a mile to the ruin entrance. Ask at Rancho Encantado, near Bacalar (see "Accommodations," above), about the condition of the unpaved portion of road.

KOHUNLICH

Kohunlich (koh-*hoon*-leek), 26 miles from the intersection of Highways 186 and 307, dates from around A.D. 100 to 900. Turn left off the road, and the entrance is 5¹/₂ miles ahead. From the parking area you enter the grand parklike site, crossing a large and shady ceremonial area flanked by four large conserved pyramidal edifices. Continue walking, and just beyond this grouping you'll come to Kohunlich's famous **Pyramid of the Masks** under a thatched covering. The masks, actually enormous plaster faces, date from around A.D. 500, and are on the facade of the building. Besides characteristic Olmec undulating lips, the masks show vestiges of blue and red paint. Note the carving on the pupils, which show a cosmic connection possibly with the night sun that illuminated the underworld. It's speculated that masks covered much of the facade of this building, which is built in the Río Bec style with rounded corners, false stairway, and false temple on the top. At least one theory is that the masks are a composite of several rulers at Kohunlich. During recent excavations of buildings immediately to the left after you enter, two intact pre-Hispanic skeletons and five decapitated heads were uncovered that were once probably used in a ceremonial rite. To the right after you enter (follow a shady path through the jungle) is another recently excavated plaza. It's thought to have housed elite citizens, due to the high quality of pottery found there and the fine architecture of the rooms. Scholars believe that Kohunlich became overpopulated, leading to its decline. The bathrooms here are the only ones at any site on the route.

CHACAN BACAN

Chacan Bacan (chah-*kahn* bah-kahn), which dates from around 200 B.C., was first discovered in 1980 with excavation begining in 1995. It's scheduled to open some time in 1997, with 30 to 40 buildings uncovered. Only one imposing 107-foot-high pyramid was being excavated when I was there. However, the discovery of huge Olmec-style heads on the facade of it can only lend excitement to future digs. The heads, showing from the middle of the skull forward, have helmetlike caps similar in style to the full multiton Olmec heads unearthed in Veracruz and Tabasco on Mexico's Gulf coast, where the Olmecs originated. These heads are thought to be older than the figures at both Kohunlich and Balamkú. The exact size of the site hasn't been determined, but it's huge. In a densely forested setting, with thousands of tropical hardwood trees, plants, birds, and wild animals, it's been earmarked as an ecological/touristic center. Though not open to the public when I was there, it's about 50 miles and a 1½-hour drive from Bacalar. The turnoff (left) to it is at Caoba, where you follow a paved road for about 1½ miles, then turn left on an unmarked path. From the paved portion you can look left and see the uncovered pyramid protruding over the surrounding jungle. Ask at Rancho Bacalar about the accessibility of this site.

XPUJIL

Xpujil (also spelled Xpuhil) means either "cattail" or "forest of kapok trees" and flourished between A.D. 400 and 900. Ahead on the left after you enter, you'll see a rectangular ceremonial platform 6½ feet high and 173 feet long holding three once-ornate buildings. These almost-conical edifices resemble the towering ruins of Tikal in Guatemala and rest on a lower building with 12 rooms. Unfortunately, they are so ruined you can only ponder how it might have been. To the right after you enter are two newly uncovered structures, one of which is a large acropolis. From the highway, a small sign on the right points to the site that is just a few yards off the highway and 49 miles from Kohunlich.

BECÁN

Becán, about 4½ miles beyond Xpujil and once surrounded by a moat, means "canyon filled by water" and dates from Early Classic to Late Classic—600 B.C. to A.D. 1200. The moat, which isn't visible today, once had seven bridges leading to the seven cities that were pledged to Becán. Extensive excavations will continue through 1997. Following jungle paths beyond the first visible group of ruins, you'll find at least two recently excavated acropoli. Though the site was abandoned by 850, ceramic remains indicate there may have been a population resurgence between A.D. 900 and 1000, and it was still used as a ceremonial site as late as A.D. 1200. Becán was a governmental and ceremonial center with political sway over at least seven other cities in the area, including Chicanná, Hormiguerro, and Payan. To really understand this site, you need a good guide. But for starters, the first plaza group you see after you enter was the center of grand ceremonies. From the highway you see the backside of a pyramid (Temple 1) with two temples on top. From the highway you can see between the two pyramid-top temples to Temple 4, which is opposite Temple 1. When the high priest appeared through the mouth of the earth monster in the center of Temple 4 (which he reached via a hidden side stairway that's now partly exposed), he was visible from what is now the highway. It's thought that commoners had to watch ceremonies from outside the ceremonial plaza; thus the site was positioned for good viewing purposes. The backside of Temple 4 is believed to have been a civic plaza where rulers sat on stone benches while pronouncing judgments. The recently uncovered second plaza group dates from around A.D. 850 and has perfect twin towers on top, where there's a big platform. Under the platform are 10 rooms that are thought to be related to Xibalba (shee-*bahl*-bah), the underworld. Earth monster faces probably covered this building (and they appeared on other buildings as well). Remains of at least one ball court have been unearthed. Becán is about 4½ miles beyond Xpujil and is visible on the right side of the highway, about half a mile down a rutted road.

CHICANNÁ

Slightly over a mile beyond Becán, on the left side of the highway, is Chicanná, which means "house of the mouth of snakes." Trees loaded with bromeliads shade the central square surrounded by five buildings. The most outstanding edifice features a monster-mouth doorway and an ornate stone facade with more superimposed masks. As you enter the mouth of the earth monster, note that you are walking on a platform which functions as the open jaw of the monster with stone teeth on both sides.

CALAKMUL

This area is both a massive Maya archaeological zone with at least 60 sites and a 178,699-acre rain forest designated in 1989 as the Calakmul Biosphere Reserve, which includes territory in both Mexico and Guatemala.

THE ARCHAEOLOGICAL ZONE

Since 1982, archaeologists have been excavating the ruins of Calakmul, which dates from 100 B.C. to A.D. 900. It's the largest of the area's 60 known sites. Nearly 7,000 buildings have been discovered and mapped. At its zenith at least 60,000 people may have lived around the site, but by the time of the Spanish Conquest of Mexico in 1519, there were fewer than 1,000 inhabitants. Discoveries include more stelae than any other site. One of them by building 13 is a stelae of a woman dating from A.D. 652. Of the buildings, Temple 3 is the best preserved. In it were found offerings of shells, beads, and polychromed tripod pottery. The tallest, at 178 feet, is Temple II. From the top of it you can see the outline of the ruins of El Mirador, 30 miles across the forest in Guatemala. Temple 4 charts the line of the sun from June 21 when it falls on the left (north) corner, to September 21 and March 21, when it lines up in the east behind the middle temple on the top of the building, to December 21 when it falls on the right (south) corner. Numerous jade pieces, including spectacular jade masks, were uncovered here, most of which are on display in the Museo Regional in Campeche. Temple 7 is largely unexcavated except for the top, where in 1984 the most outstanding jade mask yet to be found at Calakmul was uncovered. In *A Forest of Kings,* Linda Schele and David Freidel tell of wars between Calakmul, Tikal, and Naranjo (the latter two in Guatemala) and how Ah-Cacaw, king of Tikal (75 miles south of Calakmul) captured King Jaguar-Paw in A.D. 695 and later Lord Ox-Ha-Te Ixil Ahau, both of Calakmul. From January to May the site is open Tuesday through Sunday from 7am to 7pm. The site will be so wet during the rainy season from June through October that it's best not to go.

CALAKMUL BIOSPHERE RESERVE

Set aside in 1989, this is the peninsula's only high forest selva, a rain forest that annually records as much as 16 feet of rain. Among the plants are cactus, epiphytes, and orchids. Endangered animals include the white-lipped peccary, jaguar, and puma. So far more than 250 species of birds have been recorded. At the moment there are no guided tours in the reserve, and no overnight stays or camping are permitted. But a hint of the region can be seen around the ruins. Howler monkeys are often peering down on visitors as they park their cars near the entrance to the ruins.

The turnoff on the left for Calakmul is located approximately 145 miles from the intersection of Highways 186 and 307, just before the village of Conhuas. There's a guard station there where you pay to enter the road/site. From the turnoff it's a 1¹/₂ hour drive on a newly-paved, but very narrow and somewhat rutted road that may be difficult during the rainy season from May through October. *A driving caution:* Numerous curves in the road make seeing oncoming traffic (what little there is) difficult, and there have been head-on collisions. (I nearly had one).

BALAMKÚ

Balamkú (bah-*lahm*-koo) was literally snatched from the incredibly destructive hands of looters by INAH archaeologist Florentino García Cruz in October 1990. Amateur archaeologist and guide Serge Rìou was close behind him to photograph the site before looters hit one last time, destroying the head of one of the figures. An uncharted site at the time, it was saved by García, who had been alerted by locals that looters were working there. Today it's open to the public, and though small, it's worth the time to see it since the facade of one building is among the most unusual on this route. When you reach the clearing, about 2 miles from the highway via a narrow dirt path through the jungle are two buildings, one on the right and one on the left. The right building is really three continuous, tall, but narrow, pyramids dating from around A.D. 700. The left building, which dates from around A.D. 400, holds the most interest because of the cross-legged figures resembling those found at Copan, in Honduras. Originally there were four of these regal figures (probably representing kings), seated on crocodiles or frogs above the entrance to the underworld, but looters destroyed two on each end and further disfigured the others. Still, enough remains to see the beauty; the whole concept of this building, with its molded stucco facade, is of life and death. On the head of each almost-three-dimensional figure are the eyes, nose, and mouth of a jaguar figure, followed by the full face of the human figure, then a neck formed by the eyes and nose of another jaguar, and an Olmeclike face on the stomach, its neck decorated by a necklace, then the crossed legs of the figure seated upon a frog or crocodile. The earth monster is represented by a half-snake, half-crocodile animal, all symbols of death, water, and life. The May 1992 issue of *Mexico Desconocido* features the discovery of Balamkú written by Florentino García Cruz.

13 Chetumal

85 miles S of Felipe Carrillo Puerto, 23 miles S of Lago Bacalar

Quintana Roo became a state in 1974, and Chetumal (pop. 170,000) is its capital. While Quintana Roo was still a territory, it was a free-trade zone to encourage trade and immigration between neighboring Guatemala and Belize. The old part of town, down by the river (Río Hondo), has a Caribbean atmosphere and wooden buildings, but the newer parts are modern Mexican. There is lots of noise and heat, so your best plan would be not to stay—it's not a particularly interesting or friendly town. It is, however, worth a detour to see the wonderful **Museo de la Cultural Maya,** especially if your trip involves seeing the Río Bec ruin route described above.

ESSENTIALS

GETTING THERE & DEPARTING

By Plane

Aerocaribe (Mexicana) has daily flights to and from Cancún and flights several times weekly between Chetumal and the ruins of Tikal in Guatemala. **Avio Quintana** (☎ 983/2-9692) flies Monday through Friday to Cancún in a 19-passenger plane for around $45 one way. **Taesa** flies from Cancún and Cozumel.

By Bus

The bus station of **Autotransportes del Caribe** (☎ 2-0740) is 20 blocks from the town center on Insurgentes at Niños Héroes. Buses go to Cancún, Tulum, Playa del

Carmen, Puerto Morelos, Mérida, Campeche, Villahermosa, and Mexico City. **Caribe Express** (☎ 2-7889 or **2-8001**) has deluxe buses to Mérida and Cancún. This service features a 28-seat bus with video movies, steward service, and refreshments. Sixteen second-class buses run to and from Bacalar daily.

To Belize: Two companies make the run from Chetumal (through Corozal and Orange Walk) to Belize City. **Batty's Bus Service** runs 10 buses per day, and **Venus Bus Lines** (☎ **04/2-2132** in Corozal) has seven daily buses, the first at 11am; the 2pm bus is express, with fewer stops. Seven buses go to Belize City (☎ **02/7-3354** in Belize); the first leaves at 4am and the last at 10am. Though it's a short distance from Chetumal to Corozal, it may take as much as $1^1/_2$ hours, depending on how long it takes the bus to pass through Customs and Immigration.

To Limones, Majahual, and Xcalak: Two buses a day run between these destinations.

By Car

It's a $2^1/_2$-hour ride from Felipe Carrillo Puerto. If you're heading to Belize you'll need a passport and special auto insurance, which you can buy at the border. You can't take a rental car over the border, however.

To get to the ruins of Tikal in Guatemala you must first go through Belize to the border crossing at Ciudad Melchor de Mencos. For more details on crossing into Guatemala and Belize, see *Frommer's Costa Rica, Guatemala & Belize.*

By Ferry

When I checked, ferry docks and two 20-car ferries (with passenger space) were being prepared to ply the water route between Chetumal and the Xcalak/Majahual Peninsula, making that once-tedious road trip much shorter. Check with the State Tourism Office for the latest word on this new service.

INFORMATION

The State Tourism Office (☎ **983/2-0266** or **2-0855.** Fax 983/2-5073 or 2-6097) is at Avenida Hidalgo 22, corner of Carmen Ochoa.

ORIENTATION

The **telephone area code** is 983. Chetumal has many "no left turn" streets, with hawk-eyed traffic policemen at each one. Be alert—they love to nail visitors and may even motion you into making a traffic or pedestrian violation, then issue a ticket, or take a bribe instead.

You'll arrive following Obregón into town. Niños Héroes is the other main cross street. When you reach it, turn left to find the hotels mentioned below.

ACCOMMODATIONS & DINING

Hotel Nachacan

Calz. Veracruz 379, 77000 Chetumal, Q. Roo. ☎ **983/2-3232.** 20 rms. A/C TV. $15 single; $19 double.

Opposite the new market, this nice hotel offers rooms that are plain, but clean and comfortable. A restaurant is off the lobby. It's relatively convenient to the bus station, but not close enough to walk if you arrive by bus, and it's within walking distance of the Museo de la Cultura Maya. To find it from Avenida Obregón, turn left on Calzada Veracruz and follow it for at least 10 blocks; the hotel will be on the right.

Hotel Holiday Inn Caribe

Niños Héroes 171, Chetumal, Q. Roo 77000. ☎ **983/2-1100** or 800/465-4329 in the U.S. Fax 983/2-1676. 75 rms (all with bath). A/C TV TEL. $50–$75 single or double. Free parking.

This modern hotel (formerly the Hotel Continental) across from the central market was remodeled in 1995 and became a Holiday Inn. The hotel has a good-size pool (a blessing in muggy Chetumal) and a good restaurant. If you stay here it's only two blocks farther to the Museo de la Cultura Maya. You can contact Río Bec specialist Serge Rìou (see below) through the travel agency here. To find it as you enter the town on Obregón, turn left on Niños Heroes, go six blocks and look for the hotel on the right, opposite the market.

EXPLORING CHETUMAL

Chetumal is really the gateway to Belize or to the Río Bec ruins, and not a touristically interesting city. But it's worth a detour to Chetumal to see the Museo de la Cultura Maya. If you can arrange it, see the museum before you tour the Río Bec ruins, since it will all make more sense after getting it in perspective here.

If you're coming to this part of the Yucatán specifically to see the Río Bec ruins, the services of Serge Rìou, "Maya Lowland Specialist," will probably be indispensable to you. Several years ago young Mr. Rìou visited the Río Bec ruin route on a vacation from France. He fell so in love with the culture, romance, and history of the ruins that he returned to live and learn all that was possible about these little-known ruins. Living in Xpujil, he hiked the forests daily in search of ruins, worked with archaeologists on the trail of new sites, photographed the ruins, attended conferences of Maya specialists, and read everything he could find on Mexican archaeology. Today his encyclopedic knowledge of the nearby ruins makes him the most informed guide. He speaks excellent English and Spanish and charges around $60 to $100 per person a day to guide up to three people to a variety of sites. The higher price is for Calakmul, the farthest site from Chetumal. He can arrange necessary permits to unopened sites. You can contact him directly (Apartado Postal 238, 77000 Chetumal, Q. Roo; ☎ **983/2-9819** or **2-1251**) or arrange for his services through Rancho Encantado at Lago Bacalar (see "Bacalar," above), which has all the necessary types of vehicles, or contact him through the Holiday Inn in Chetumal.

Museo de la Cultura Maya

Av. Heroes s/n. ☎ **2-6838.** Admission $1; children 50¢. It's open Tuesday through Thursday from 9am to 7pm, Friday and Saturday from 9am to 8pm and Sunday from 9am to 2pm. It's on the left between Colón and Primo de Verdad, 8 blocks from Avenida Obregón, on the left past the Holiday Inn.

Sophisticated, impressive, and informative, this new museum unlocks the complex world of the Maya. Push a button and an illustrated description appears explaining the medicinal and domestic uses of plants with their Maya and scientific names, another describes the five social classes of the Maya by the way they dress, and yet another shows how the beauty signs of cranial deformation, crossed eyes, and facial scarification were achieved. An enormous screen flashes moving pictures taken from an airplane flying over more than a dozen Maya sites from Mexico to Honduras. Another large television shows the architectural variety of Maya pyramids and how they were probably built. Then a walk on a glass floor takes you over representative ruins in the Maya world, clearly showing the variety of pyramidal shapes and particular sites. And finally one of the most impressive sections is the three-story sacred ceiba tree, which the Maya believed represented the underworld (Xibalba) on the bottom (the bottom floor of the museum), earth (the middle floor of the museum), and the 13 heavens (the third floor of the museum). From this you'll have a better idea of the significance of symbolism on the pyramids in the Maya world. Plan no less than two hours here. Even then, especially if your interest is high, you may want to take a break and return with renewed vigor—there's a lot to see and learn. What a museum!

ONWARD FROM CHETUMAL

From Chetumal you have several choices: You can take the ferry to the Xcalak/Majahual Peninsula for excellent diving, fishing, and hanging out in a laid-back portion of the state; you go south to Belize and Guatemala (though not in a rental car)—the Maya ruins of Lamanai are an easy day trip into Belize if you have transportation; you can explore the Río Bec ruin route north of the city; and after Bacalar you can cut diagonally across the peninsula to Mérida or retrace your steps to Cancún. You can take Highway 186 west to Escarcega, Villahermosa, and Palenque, but I don't recommend it. It's a long, hot, and lonely trip on a highway that is often riddled with potholes after you cross into Campeche state. Permanent ZONA DE DESLAVE signs warn motorists that parts of the roadbed are missing entirely or so badly dipped they might cause an accident. It improves from time to time, but annual rains cause constant problems. At the Campeche state line there's a military guard post with drug-sniffing dogs; every vehicle is searched. A military guard post at the Reforma intersection just before Bacalar requires motorists to present the identification you used to enter Mexico (birth certificate or passport), plus your Tourist Permit. Other photo identification may be required, as well as information on where you are staying or where you are headed. The whole procedure should take only minutes.

Mérida & the Maya Cities 5

Mérida and its environs in Campeche and Yucatán states in the western Yucatán are abundantly endowed with the qualities that can make a Mexican vacation something to remember. The area is rich in living pre-Hispanic traditions—you'll find clothing, crafts, and village life that hearken back to Maya ways of 10 centuries ago. And there are plenty of the more traditional reminders of the past—the ruins of spectacular Maya cities such as Chichén-Itzá, Uxmal, and others, along with walled Spanish colonial cities like Campeche. The western half of the Yucatán also offers the budget-minded traveler a wide choice of economical lodgings, and you'll enjoy the relaxed pace of Yucatecan life and warm, friendly people.

Maya village women wear cool, embroidered cotton shifts and go about village life oblivious to the peninsula's fame as a premier resort destination. Their day-to-day cultural and belief system holds many elements that can be traced to pre-Hispanic times.

Though shy, the Maya are immensely courteous and helpful, and they eagerly chat with strangers even when there's a language barrier. More than 350,000 Maya living in the Yucatán Peninsula's three states speak a Maya dialect, and many, particularly men, speak Spanish, too. Many, especially those serving tourists, slip easily between Maya, Spanish, and English. You'll get along even if English is your only language.

EXPLORING THE YUCATÁN'S MAYA HEARTLAND

The cultural center of the Yucatán, beautiful Mérida is a natural launching pad for trips to the Yucatán's major archaeological sites, to the Gulf coast, and to the Yucatán's northern coast. This part of the Yucatán Peninsula is among the best places in Mexico to take a driving tour—there are no mountains; roads, though only two-lane, are fairly well-maintained; traffic is light; and stops in the many rock-walled villages are delightful.

CELESTÚN NATIONAL WILDLIFE REFUGE: A WETLANDS RESERVE

This flamingo sanctuary and offbeat sand-street fishing village on the Gulf coast is a 1¹/₂-hour drive from Mérida. Plan a long day—with a very early start—for the 7am flamingo trip. However, people looking for solitude might find this a welcome respite for a week.

DZIBILCHALTÚN: MAYA RUINS

This Maya site, now a national park, is located 9 miles north of Mérida along the Progreso Road. Here you'll find a number of pre-Hispanic structures, nature trails, and the new Museum of the Maya. Make this one a half-day trip in the cool of the morning.

PROGRESO: GULF COAST CITY

A modern city and Gulf coast beach escape 21 miles north of Mérida, Progreso has a beautiful oceanfront drive and a vast beach lined with coconut palms that's popular on the weekends. Plan a full day trip if you like beaches, but there's not a lot else to do.

UXMAL: SPECTACULAR MAYA RUINS

The best way to visit the splendid archaeological zone of Uxmal ("oosh-mahl"; it's about 50 miles to the south of Mérida) is to rent a car, stay two nights in a hotel at Uxmal or a less expensive hotel in Ticul, and allow for two to three full days of sightseeing. It's also possible—though a bit rushed—to see Uxmal and the quartet of ruins south of there on a day trip by special excursion bus from Mérida. Sunday is a good day to go, since admission is free to the archaeological sites.

CAMPECHE: WALLED COLONIAL CITY

A pretty colonial city with a relaxed pace, Campeche is also somewhat off the main tourist path. It's about three hours southwest of Mérida. Two nights and a full day should give you enough time to see Campeche's architectural highlights and museums.

Don't miss the **Museo Regional de Campeche,** especially the clay and jade objects taken from the freshly excavated southern Campeche ruins of Calakmul. You can stay at either the handsome, oceanfront **Ramada Inn** (Av. Ruíz Cortínez 51; ☎ **981/6-2233**) or the much cheaper **Posada del Angel** (Calle 10 no. 307; **981/6-7718**). For meals try either the classic **Parroquia** (Calle 55 no. 9) or **La Pigua** (Av. Miguel Alemán no. 197A), which is a good place to spend a leisurely afternoon.

CHICHÉN-ITZÁ & VALLADOLID

From Mérida, it's 75 miles to the famed ruins of **Chichén-Itzá,** and 100 miles to the somnolent town of **Valladolid.** The ruins at Chichén-Itzá are so vast that you'll want to spend the better part of two days, taking your time in the heat, to see this site. The colonial city of Valladolid offers an inexpensive alternative to staying at Chichén-Itzá, where lodgings are considerably more expensive.

1　Mérida: Gateway to the Maya Heartland

900 miles NE of Mexico City, 200 miles W of Cancún

Mérida, capital of the state of Yucatán, has been the major city in the area since the mid-1500s, when the Spanish founded it on the site of the defeated Maya city of Tihó. Although it's a major touristic crossroads—within range of both the peninsula's archaeological ruins and its glitzy coasts, this modern city is easygoing, and the friendliness of its people remains its trademark.

Downtown Mérida is full of fine examples of colonial-style architecture. Vestiges of the opulent 19th-century era of the Yucatán's henequen boom remain in the ornate mansions sprinkled throughout the city.

ESSENTIALS
GETTING THERE & DEPARTING
By Plane

For carriers serving Mérida from the United States, see Chapter 2, "Planning a Trip to the Yucatán." **Mexicana** (☎ **24-6633, 24-7421,** or **23-0508; 46-1332** at the airport) flies in from Mexico City. **Aeroméxico** (☎ **27-9000; 46-1305** at the airport) flies to and from Cancún and Mexico City. **AeroCaribe,** a Mexicana affiliate (☎ **28-6786; 28-6790** at the airport), provides service to and from Cozumel, Cancún, Oaxaca, Tuxtla Gutierrez, Veracruz, Villahermosa, and points in Central America. **Taesa** (☎ **46-1826** at the airport) flies in from Monterrey and Mexico City. **Aviateca** (☎ **24-4354**) flies in from Guatemala City. **Aviacsa** (at the airport ☎ **46-1344**) provides service from Cancún, Monterrey, Villahermosa, Tuxtla Gutiérrez, Tapachula, Oaxaca, and Mexico City. Taxis to and from the city to the airport cost nearly $10.

By Bus

The second-class **Central Camionera** is seven blocks southwest of Plaza Mayor at Calle 68, between Calles 69 and 71. The new first-class station, **CAME,** is directly behind it on Calle 70, between Calles 69 and 71. A separate station for travelers to **Progresso** is at Calle 62 no. 524, between Calles 65 and 67.

To/From Uxmal: Autotransportes del Sur (☎ **24-9374**) buses depart at 6 and 9am, noon, and 2:30pm; return trips are at 2:30, 3:30, and 7:30pm. The same company also offers one bus daily on the Mérida–Uxmal–Kabah–Sayil–Labná–Xlapak route. The trip costs $11; it departs Mérida at 8am and returns at 4pm. The driver allows passengers to spend around two hours at Uxmal and 30 minutes at each of the other archaeological sites before returning. There is no evening departure for the sound-and-light show at Uxmal.

To/From Chichén-Itzá: There are first-class **ADO** (☎ **24-8391**) buses at 7:30am and 3:30pm, leaving from the CAME. If you're planning a day trip (something I don't recommend because you'll want more time to see the impressive ruins), take the 7:30am bus and reserve a seat on the 3:30pm return bus.

To/From Pisté: Autotransportes de Oriente (☎ **22-2387**) runs second-class buses every hour from 5am till midnight, and a luxury bus at 11am.

To/From Valladolid and Cancún: Expresso de Oriente (☎ **22-2387**) offers deluxe service—video, rest room, and refreshments—to Cancún (a four- to five-hour trip) 19 times daily between 6am and 11:15pm. The line also has eight deluxe buses daily to Valladolid between 6am and 11:45pm. **Caribe Express** (☎ **24-4275**) runs nine deluxe buses daily to Cancún between 7:15am and 10pm. **Autotransportes del Caribe** goes to Cancún at 6:30am and 5:30 and 11:45pm, and **ADO** runs three buses to Valladolid.

To/From Playa del Carmen, Tulum, and Chetumal: Three deluxe **ADO** buses go to Valladolid and on to Playa del Carmen between 7:30am and midnight. ADO also has deluxe buses to Chetumal at 10:10am and 5:30pm. **Caribe Express** buses to Playa del Carmen and Tulum depart at 6:15am and 11pm; Caribe Express buses to Chetumal depart at 7:30 and 10:30am and 1, 10, and 11pm. **Autotransportes Peninsulares** (☎ **24-1844**) offers Servicio Plus deluxe service to Chetumal at 8:30am and 6pm.

To/From Campeche: Autotransportes Peninsulares offers deluxe service to Campeche at 8am and 3pm. **ADO** has first-class service to Campeche every half hour between 6am and 10pm; **Autotransportes del Sur** (☎ **24-9374**) buses leave every 45 minutes from 6am to 11:30pm.

To/From Palenque and San Cristóbal de las Casas: ADO has first-class service to Palenque at 8am and 10pm. **Autotransportes del Sureste** offers second-class service to Palenque and San Cristóbal de las Casas at 6pm.

To/From Progreso, Dzibilchaltún, and Celestún: Buses depart from the Progreso Station at Calle 62 no. 524, between Calles 65 and 67.

By Car

Highway 180 from Cancún, Chichén-Itzá, or Valladolid leads into Calle 65 past the market and within one block of the Plaza Mayor. Highway 281 from Uxmal (via Muna and Uman) becomes Avenida Itzáes (if you arrive by that route, turn right on Calle 63 to reach the Plaza Mayor). From Uxmal (via Ticul and the ruins of Mayapán) the road passes through Kanasín before joining Highway 180 from Valladolid into Mérida.

A traffic loop encircles Mérida, making it possible to skirt the city and head for a nearby city or site. Directional signs are generally good into the city, but going around the city on the loop requires constant vigilance.

The eight-lane toll highway (autopista) between Mérida and Cancún was completed in 1993 and cuts the driving between the two cities by about one hour. The highway begins about 35 miles east of Mérida at Kantuníl, intersecting with Highway 180. It ends at Nuevo Xcan, which is about 50 miles before Cancún. One-way tolls cost about $15.

See "En Route to Uxmal," below, at the end of the Mérida section for suggested routes from Mérida.

ORIENTATION

Arriving By Plane

Mérida's airport is 8 miles from the city center on the southwestern outskirts of town where Highway 180 enters the city. The airport has desks for renting a car, reserving a hotel room, and getting tourist information. *A Note of Caution:* Customs inspectors at the Mérida airport have been known to hassle tourists by confiscating and refusing to return the legal, legitimate, and allowable contents of their luggage. Upon arrival at all airports in Mexico passengers receive a customs statement with all allowable items listed. If you are within your rights according to that list, tell the officials that you are reporting them to SEDOCAM ("say-doh-kahm"), which is the Comptroller and Administrative Development Secretariat (☎ **91-800/ 0-0148** in Mexico). Of course their idea is to relieve you of your possessions, but threatening to go over their heads to their superiors *may* save you further discussion. The allowable items per person include a portable computer, a video camera, two still cameras, personal clothing, used fishing equipment for one person, etc.

Taxi tickets to town are sold outside the airport doors under the covered walkway. A collectivo ticket costs $6 per person, but you have to wait for a group of five to assemble. Private taxis cost $10.

City bus no. 79 ("Aviación") operates between the town center and the airport (40¢), but the buses do not have frequent service. Other city buses run along Avenida Itzáes, just out of the airport precincts, heading for downtown.

Arriving By Bus

From Mérida's main bus station you're only six blocks from the Plaza Mayor and within walking distance of several hotels. Buses to town stop on the corner to the left of the bus station's front door.

Information

The most convenient source of information is the downtown branch of the **State of Yucatán Tourist Information Office,** in the hulking edifice known as the Teatro Peón Contreras, on Calle 60 between Calles 57 and 59 (☎ **99/24-9290** or **24-9389**). It's open Monday through Sunday from 8am to 8pm, as are the information booths at the **airport** (☎ **99/24-6764**), the bus station, and on Calle 62 next to the Palacio Municipal. **Yucatán Information Office,** P.O. Box 140681, Coral Gables, FL 33114-0681, is a nonprofit service of the Mesoamerica Foundation. They offer helpful information about the Yucatán, such as the current cost of admission to archaeological sites, reports on new museums, and updates on customs scams.

City Layout

As in many colonial Mexican cities, Mérida's streets were originally laid out in a grid: **Even-numbered streets** run north—south; **odd-numbered streets** run east—west. In the last few decades the city has expanded well beyond the grid, and several grand boulevards have been added on the outskirts to ease traffic flow.

When looking for an address, you'll notice that street numbers progress very slowly because of the many unnumbered dwellings and the addition of letters (A, B, C, etc.) to numbered dwellings. For example, the distance between 504 to 615D on Calle 59 is 12 blocks.

The center of town is the very pretty **Plaza Mayor** (sometimes called the Plaza Principal), with its shady trees, benches, vendors, and a social life all its own. Around the Plaza Mayor are the massive cathedral, the Palacio de Gobierno (state government headquarters), the Palacio Municipal, and the Casa de Montejo. Within a few blocks are several smaller plazas, the University of Yucatán, and the sprawling market district.

Mérida's most fashionable address is the broad tree-lined boulevard called **Paseo de Montejo** and the surrounding neighborhood. The Paseo de Montejo begins seven blocks northwest of the Plaza Mayor and is home to Yucatán's anthropological museum, several upscale hotels, and the U.S. Consulate. New high-rise deluxe hotels are opening just off the Paseo on **Avenida Colón,** another shaded boulevard containing some of the city's finest old mansions. Within the next few years, this neighborhood will become Mérida's more exclusive tourism zone, with fine restaurants and boutiques catering to the travelers drawn to the new hotels.

GETTING AROUND

By Bus

A ride on a city bus costs only 40¢. You can take a bus to the large, shady Parque Centenario on the western outskirts of town. Look for a bus of the same name ("Centenario") on Calle 64. Most buses on Calle 59 go to the zoo or to the Museum of Natural History. "Central" buses stop at the bus station, and any bus marked "Mercado" or "Correo" (post office) will take you to the market district.

By Taxi

Taxi drivers are beginning to overcharge tourists in Mérida the way they do in Mexico City. Taxi meters start at $2.50.

By Car

A car is handy for your explorations of Mayapán, Uxmal, and Kabah, but you don't need one to get around Mérida or to reach Chichén-Itzá or Cancún. Rental cars are expensive, averaging $45 to $75 per day for a VW Beetle. As you scour the city for a rental-car deal, be sure the price quoted includes tax, insurance, and unlimited mileage, and get deductible information before settling the deal. For tips on saving money on car rentals by renting in advance from your home country see "Getting Around" in Chapter 2. Also you may want to look into the free car rental (you pay for insurance) offered by Mayaland Tours if you stay at their hotels at Chichén-Itzá and Uxmal. Ask about pick-up or drop-off in Cancún if your trip starts or ends there. For information contact Mayaland Resorts, Av. Colón 502, Mérida, Yuc. 97000; ☎ **99/25-2122**, or **800/235-4079** in the U.S.; fax 99/25-7022.

On Foot
Most tourist attractions are within walking distance of the Plaza Mayor.

FAST FACTS: Mérida

Area Code   The telephone area code is 99.

Bookstore   The Librería Dante, Calle 60 at Calle 57 (☎ **99/24-9522**), has a selection of English-language cultural-history books on Mexico. It's open Monday through Friday from 8am to 9:30pm, Saturday from 8am to 2pm and 5 to 9pm, and Sunday from 10am to 2pm and 4 to 8pm.

Climate   From November through February the weather can be chilly, windy, and rainy. You'll need a light jacket or sweater for occasional cool winter weather and thin, light clothes for summer days. Light rain gear is suggested for the brief showers in late May, June, and July, but there's a chance of rain year-round in the Yucatán.

Complaints   Tourists experiencing difficulties with public officials such as police officers can call ☎ **91-800/0-0148** in Mexico to report incidents.

Consulates   The U.S. Consulate is at Paseo de Montejo 453, at the corner of Avenida Colón (☎ **99/25-5011**), near the Holiday Inn. It's open Monday through Friday from 7:30am to 4pm. Visa matters are dealt with only on Monday, Tuesday, Wednesday, and Friday from 7:30 to 11am; other kinds of problems are considered on the same days from noon to 3:30pm and Thursday until 4pm. The telephone number of a duty officer is posted at the entrance. The British Vice-Consulate is at Calle 58 no. 498 (☎ **99/28-6152**). Though in theory it's open Monday through Friday from 9:30am to 1pm, you may find no one there. The vice-consul fields questions about travel to Belize as well as British matters.

Currency Exchange   Banamex, in the Palacio Montejo on the Plaza Mayor, usually provides a better rate of exchange than other banks, but the lines are often maddeningly long. Exchange hours are Monday through Friday from 9:30am to 1:30pm. Another option is the money-exchange office just as you enter the bank gates, and more banks are located on and off Calle 65 between Calles 62 and 60.

Hospitals   Hospital O'Horan is on Avenida Itzáes at Calle 59A (☎ **99/24-8711**), north of the Parque Centenario.

Post Office   Mérida's main post office ("correo") is located in the midst of the market at the corner of Calles 65 and 56. A branch office is located at the airport. Both are open Monday through Friday from 8am to 5pm and Saturday from 8am to 2pm.

Seasons   There are two high seasons—one in July and August when the weather is very hot and humid and when Mexicans most commonly take their vacations, and one between November 15 and Easter Sunday when the northerners flock to the Yucatán to escape winter weather and when weather in the Yucatán is cooler.

Spanish Classes   Maya scholars, Spanish teachers, and archaeologists from the United States are among the students at the **Centro Idiomas del Sureste,** Calle 14 no. 106 at Calle 25, Colonia México, Mérida, Yucatán 97000 (☎ **99/26-1155;** fax 99/26-9020). The school has two locations: in the Colonia México, a northern residential district, and on Calle 66 at Calle 57 in the downtown area. Students live with local families or in hotels; sessions running two weeks or longer are available for all levels of proficiency and areas of interest. For brochures and applications, contact Chloe Conaway de Pacheco, directora.

Telephones   There are long-distance *casetas* at the airport and the bus station. Look also for the blue-and-silver Ladatel phones appearing in public places all over Mexico. Also see "Telephones/Fax" in "Fast Facts: Mexico" in Chapter 2. *Important Note:* Telephone numbers are being changed throughout the city, so if you have difficulty reaching a number, ask the telephone operator for assistance.

EXPLORING MÉRIDA

Most of the city's attractions are within walking distance of each other in the downtown area.

FESTIVALS & EVENTS

On the evening of the **first Friday** of each month, Dennis LaFoy of the Yucatán Trails Travel Agency (☎ **99/28-2582**) invites the English-speaking community to a casual get-together. They usually gather at the Hotel Mérida Misión Park Plaza on Calle 60, across from the Hotel Casa del Balam, but call Dennis to confirm the location.

Many Mexican cities offer weekend concerts in the park, but Mérida surpasses them with almost-daily high-quality public events, most of which are free.

Sunday   Each Sunday from 9am to 9pm there's a fair called **Domingo en Mérida** (Sunday in Mérida). The downtown area, blocked off from traffic for the day, bustles with activity; there are children's art classes, antiques vendors, and food stands, as well as concerts of all kinds. At 11am in front of the Palacio del Gobierno, musicians play everything from jazz to classical and folk music. Also at 11am the police orchestra performs Yucatecan tunes at the Santa Lucía park. At 11:30am, marimba music brightens the Parque Cepeda Peraza (Parque Hidalgo) on Calle 60 at Calle 59. At 1pm in front of the Palacio Municipal on the Plaza Mayor, folk ballet dancers re-enact a typical Yucatecan wedding. All events are free.

Monday   The **City Hall Folklore Ballet** and the **Police Jaranera Band** perform at 8pm in front of the Palacio Municipal. The music and dancing celebrate the Vaquerías feast, which occurs after the branding of cattle on Yucatecan haciendas. Among the featured performers are dancers with trays of bottles or filled glasses on their heads—a sight to see. Admission is free.

Tuesday   The theme for the Tuesday entertainment, held at 9pm in Parque Santiago, on Calle 59 at Calle 72, is **Musical Memories.** Tunes range from South American and Mexican to North American. Admission is free. Also at 9pm in the Teatro Peón Contreras on Calle 60 at Calle 57 the **University of Yucatán Folklore Ballet** presents "Yucatán and Its Roots." Admission is $5.

Wednesday   The **University of Yucatán Folklore Ballet,** along with guitarists and poets, performs at 8pm at the Mayab Culture House on Calle 63, between Calles 64 and 66. Admission is free.

Thursday   Typical Yucatecan music and dance are presented at the **Serenata** in Parque Santa Lucía at 9pm. Admission is free.

Friday   At 9pm in the patio of the University of Yucatán, Calle 60 at Calle 57, the **University of Yucatán Folklore Ballet** often performs typical regional dances from the Yucatán. Admission is free.

WALKING TOUR
Mérida

Start: Plaza Mayor.
Finish: Palacio Cantón.
Time: Allow approximately two hours, not counting time for browsing or refreshment.
Best Times: Tuesday through Sunday before noon.
Worst Time: Monday, when the Anthropology Museum is closed.

Downtown Mérida is a visitor's visual delight, with several tree-shaded parks and most of the finest examples of both colonial and late 19th-century architecture the city has to offer. The downtown is within an easy stroll of the:

1. **Plaza Mayor.** Flanked east and west by Calles 61 and 63 and north and south by Calles 60 and 62, the plaza began its history as the Plaza de Armas—a training field for Montejo's troops. It was renamed Plaza de la Constitución in 1812 and then Plaza de la Independencia in 1821 before assuming its current name. Other common names for it include Plaza Grande, Plaza Principal, and the zócalo. Today this beautiful town square, shaded by topiary laurel trees, is decked out in manicured shrubs and lawns with iron benches. Numerous entertainment events open to the public take place here throughout the year. On the east side of the plaza stands the:

2. **Cathedral.** Built between 1561 and 1598, it looks like a fortress, as do many other early churches in the Yucatán. (For several centuries, defense was actually one of the functions of such churches, as the Maya did not take kindly to European domination.) Much of the stone in the cathedral's walls came from the ruined buildings of Tihó, the former Maya city. Inside, decoration is sparse, with altars draped in fabric colorfully embroidered like a Maya woman's shift. The most notable feature is a picture over the right side door of Ah Kukum Tutul Xiú visiting the Montejo camp. (For more information on the Montejos and the Spanish Conquest of the Yucatán, see the box below, "Centuries of Conflict: Spanish & Maya in the Yucatán.")

   To the left of the main altar is a smaller shrine with a curious charred cross recovered from the church in the town of Ichmul, which burned down. The figure was carved by a local artist in the 1500s from a miraculous tree that burned but did not char. The figure, along with the church, broke out in blisters as the flames enveloped it. The local people named it Cristo de las Ampollas (Christ of the Blisters). Also take a look in the side chapel (open from 8 to 11am and 4:30 to 7pm), which contains a lifesize diorama of the Last Supper. The Mexican Jesus is covered with prayer crosses brought by supplicants asking for intercession.

   To the right (south) of the cathedral is a:

3. **Seminary** and the former site of the archbishop's palace. The palace was torn down during the Mexican Revolution in 1915; part of the seminary remains but now contains shops. On the south side of the Plaza Mayor is the:

4. **Palacio Montejo,** also called the Casa de Montejo. Started in 1542 by Francisco Montejo *el mozo* (the Younger, i.e., the first Montejo's natural son) it was occupied by Montejo descendants until the 1970s. It now houses a Banamex bank

Walking Tour—Mérida

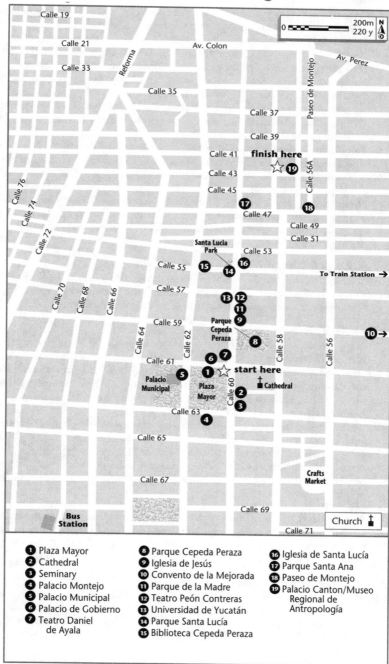

1. Plaza Mayor
2. Cathedral
3. Seminary
4. Palacio Montejo
5. Palacio Municipal
6. Palacio de Gobierno
7. Teatro Daniel de Ayala
8. Parque Cepeda Peraza
9. Iglesia de Jesús
10. Convento de la Mejorada
11. Parque de la Madre
12. Teatro Peón Contreras
13. Universidad de Yucatán
14. Parque Santa Lucía
15. Biblioteca Cepeda Peraza
16. Iglesia de Santa Lucía
17. Parque Santa Ana
18. Paseo de Montejo
19. Palacio Canton/Museo Regional de Antropología

branch, which means you can get a look at parts of the palace just by wandering in during banking hours: Monday through Friday from 9am to 1:30pm. Note the arms of the Spanish kings and of the Montejo family on the plateresque facade, along with figures of the conquistadores standing on the heads of "barbarians." Look closely and you'll find the bust of Francisco Montejo the Elder, his wife, and his daughter. Facing the cathedral across the Plaza Mayor (on the west side) is the:

5. **Palacio Municipal** (City Hall) with its familiar clock tower. It started out as the *cabildo*—the colonial town hall and lockup—in 1542. It had to be rebuilt in the 1730s and again in the 1850s, when it took on its present romantic aspect. On the north side of the Plaza Mayor is the:

6. **Palacio de Gobierno,** dating from 1892. Large murals painted by the Meridiano artist Fernando Pacheco Castro between 1971 and 1973 decorate the interior walls. Scenes from Maya and Mexican history abound, and the painting over the stairway depicts the Maya spirit with ears of sacred corn, the "sunbeams of the gods." Nearby is a painting of the mustachioed benevolent dictator Lázaro Cárdenas, who in 1938 expropriated 17 foreign oil companies and was hailed as a Mexican liberator. The palace is open Monday through Saturday from 8am to 8pm and Sunday from 9am to 5pm.

☕ **TAKE A BREAK**   Revive your motor with a cup of coffee and some pan dulce or a bolillo from the Pan Montejo on the southwest side of the plaza on the corner of Calles 63 and 62. Add a glass of fresh orange or papaya juice from Jugos California next door, take a seat at the plaza, and enjoy the morning sun.

Exploring Calle 60

Continuing north from the Plaza Mayor up Calle 60, you'll see many of Mérida's old churches and little parks. Several stores catering to tourists along Calle 60 sell gold-filigree jewelry, pottery, and folk art. A stroll along this street leads to the Parque Santa Ana and continues to the fashionable boulevard Paseo de Montejo and its Museo Regional de Antropología. On your left as you leave the northeast corner of the Plaza Mayor, the:

7. **Teatro Daniel de Ayala** offers a continuous schedule of performing artists from around the world. A few steps beyond and across the street is the:

8. **Parque Cepeda Peraza** (also called the Parque Hidalgo), named for the 19th-century general Manuel Cepeda Peraza, was part of Montejo's original city plan. Small outdoor restaurants front hotels on the *parque*, making it a popular stopping-off place at any time of day.

☕ **TAKE A BREAK**   Any of the several outdoor restaurants on the Parque Cepeda Peraza makes an inviting respite. My favorite is **Giorgio,** where you can claim a table and write postcards while bartering for hammocks, amber jewelry, and baskets displayed by wandering artisans. It's in front of the Gran Hotel.

Bordering Parque Cepeda Peraza across Calle 59 is the:

9. **Iglesia de Jesús,** or El Tercer Ordén (the Third Order), built by the Jesuit order in 1618. The entire city block on which the church stands was part of the Jesuit establishment, and the early schools developed into the Universidad de Yucatán. Walk east on Calle 59, five blocks past the Parque Cepeda Peraza and the church, and you'll see the former:

10. **Convento de la Mejorada,** a late-1600s work by the Franciscans. While here, go half a block farther on Calle 59 to the **Museo Regional de Artes Populares**

(see "More Attractions," below). Backtrack to Calle 60 and turn north. Just beyond the church (Iglesia de Jesús) is the:

11. **Parque de la Madre** (also called the Parque Morelos), which contains a modern statue of the Madonna and Child. The statue is a copy of the work by Renoir that stands in the Luxembourg Gardens in Paris. Beyond the Parque de la Madre and across the pedestrian way is:

12. **Teatro Peón Contreras,** an enormous beige edifice designed by Italian architect Enrico Deserti in the early years of this century. In one corner you'll see a branch of the State Tourist Information Office facing the Parque de la Madre. The main theater entrance, with its Carrara marble staircase and frescoed dome, is a few steps farther. Domestic and international performers appear here frequently. On the west side of Calle 60, at the corner of Calle 57, is the:

13. **Universidad de Yucatán,** founded in the 19th century by Felipe Carrillo Puerto with the help of General Cepeda Peraza. The founding is illustrated by a fresco (1961) by Manuel Lizama.

A block farther on your left, past the Hotel Mérida Misión Park Inn, is the:

14. **Parque Santa Lucía.** Surrounded by an arcade on the north and west sides, the *parque* once was where visitors first alighted in Mérida after arriving in their stagecoaches. On Sunday, Parque Santa Lucía holds a used-book sale and small swap meet, and several evenings a week it hosts popular entertainment. On Thursday nights performers present Yucatecan songs and poems. A block west from the *parque* on Calle 55 at the corner of Calle 62 is:

15. **Biblioteca Cepeda Peraza,** a library founded by the general in 1867. Back to the Parque Santa Lucía and facing it is the ancient:

16. **Iglesia de Santa Lucía** (1575). To reach Paseo de Montejo, continue walking north on Calle 60 to the:

17. **Parque Santa Ana,** four blocks up Calle 60 from the Parque Santa Lucía. Turn right here on Calle 47 for 1¹/₂ blocks; then turn left onto the broad, busy boulevard known as the:

18. **Paseo de Montejo,** a broad tree-lined thoroughfare with imposing banks, hotels, and several 19th-century mansions erected by henequen barons, generals, and other Yucatecan potentates. It's Mexico's humble version of the Champs-Elysées.

☕ **WINDING DOWN**   Before or after tackling the Palacio Cantón (see below), stop for a break at the **Dulcería y Sorbetería Colón,** on Paseo de Montejo one block north of the Palacio between Calles 39 and 41. Far grander than its sister café at the Plaza Mayor, this bakery/ice-cream shop/candy shop has a long glass counter displaying sweet treats. Unfortunately, coffee and tea are not available.

At the corner of Calle 43 is the:

19. **Palacio Cantón** (entrance on Calle 43), which houses the **Museo Regional de Antropología** (Anthropology Museum; ☎ **99/23-0557**). Designed and built by Enrico Deserti, the architect who designed the Teatro Peón Contreras, this is the most impressive mansion on Paseo de Montejo and the only one open to the public. It was constructed between 1909 and 1911 during the last years of the Porfiriato as the home of General Francisco Cantón Rosado. The general enjoyed his palace for only six years before he died in 1917. The house was converted into a school and later became the official residence of the governor of the Yucatán.

This is an interregional museum covering not only the state but also the rest of the peninsula and Mexico. Its exhibits include cosmology, pre-Hispanic time computation and comparative timeline, musical instruments, weaving examples and designs, and stone carving from all over the country.

On the right as you enter is a room used for changing exhibits, usually featuring "the piece of the month." After that are the permanent exhibits with captions mostly in Spanish. Starting with fossil mastodon teeth, the exhibits take you through the Yucatán's history, paying special attention to the daily life of its inhabitants. You'll see how the Maya tied boards to babies' skulls in order to reshape their heads, giving them the slanting forehead that was then a mark of great beauty, and how they filed teeth to sharpen them or drilled teeth to implant jewels. Enlarged photos show the archaeological sites, and drawings illustrate the various styles of Maya houses and how they were constructed. The one of Mayapán, for instance, clearly shows the city's ancient walls. Even if you know only a little Spanish, the museum provides a good background for explorations of Maya sites. The museum is open Tuesday through Saturday from 8am to 8pm and Sunday from 8am to 2pm. Admission is $2.50; free on Sunday. There's a museum bookstore on the left as you enter.

MORE ATTRACTIONS

The **Museo de la Ciudad** is on Calle 61 at Calle 58, in recently renovated quarters. The museum collection relates the city's past in the form of photographs, drawings, and dioramas. It's open Tuesday through Saturday from 9am to 8pm, Sunday 9am to 1pm. Admission is $2.

The **Museo de Arte Contemporáneo Ateneo de Yucatán** (MACAY) opened in April 1994 in a rambling 15-room building from colonial days. Now refurbished, it has on permanent exhibit the works of Fernando García Ponce, Gabriel Ramirez Asnar, and others, and it hosts traveling exhibits every three months or so. It is located on Paseo de la Revolución (Calle 61-A), just south across the street from the cathedral; it's open Wednesday through Monday from 9am to 5pm. Admission is $3.50.

For a tour by **horse-drawn carriage,** look for a line of *coches de caleta* near the cathedral and in front of the Hotel Casa del Balam. Haggle for a good price; a 1-hour tour of the city costs around $6.

ECO-TOURS & ADVENTURE TRIPS

Companies that organize nature and adventure tours of the Yucatán Peninsula are just beginning to establish themselves. **Ecoturismo Yucatán,** Calle 3 no. 235, Col. Pensiones, Mérida, Yuc. 97219 (☎ **99/25-2187;** fax 99/25-9047), is run by Alfonso and Roberta Escobedo. Alfonso has been guiding adventure tours for more than a dozen years, and Roberta runs the office with professional efficiency. The various tours emphasize remote ruin sites and culture in the Yucatán, Campeche, Chiapas, Tabasco, Oaxaca, Belize, and Guatemala. Customized tours are available.

Another specialty tour agency is **Yucatán Trails,** Calle 62 #482 (☎ **99/28-2582**). Canadian Dennis LaFoy, well-known and active in the English-speaking community, is a font of information and can arrange a variety of individualized tours.

Roger Lynn at **Casa Mexilio Guest House** (☎ **99/28-2505**), mentioned in "Accommodations," below, arranges a variety of specialized trips. Concentrating on nature, Yucatán train trips, and haciendas, these are among the most unique trips in the area. Roger is operations manager for the Turquoise Reef Group, so you can request information through them at P.O. Box 2664, Evergreen, CO 80439 (☎ 800-538-6802).

SHOPPING

Mérida is known for hammocks, guayaberas (short-sleeve, lightweight men's shirts that are worn untucked), and Panama hats. And there are good buys in baskets made in the Yucatán and pottery, as well as crafts from all over Mexico, especially at the central market. Mérida is also the place to pick up prepared achiote—a pastelike mixture of ground achiote, oregano, garlic, masa, and other spices used in Yucatecan cuisine. It makes a great marinade, especially on grilled meat and fish, when mixed with vinegar to a soupy consistency. It's also the sauce that makes baked chicken and cochinta pibil. On occasion, achiote is also found bottled and already mixed with juice of the sour orange. I don't leave the Yucatán without some achiote, but buy the prepared achiote only if you're heading directly home from Mérida—it needs refrigeration.

Mérida's bustling **market district,** bounded by Calles 63 to 69 and Calles 62 to 54, is a few blocks southeast of the Plaza Mayor. The streets surrounding the market can be as interesting and crowded as the market itself. Heaps of prepared achiote are sold in the food section.

Crafts

Casa del Las Artesanías
Calle 63 no. 513, between Calles 64 and 66. ☎ **99/23-5392.**

This beautiful restored monastery houses an impressive selection of crafts from throughout Mexico. Stop by here before going to the various crafts markets to see what high-quality work looks like. The monastery's back courtyard is used as a gallery, with rotating exhibits on folk and fine arts. It's open Monday through Saturday from 8am to 8pm.

Crafts Market
In a separate building of the main market, Calle 67 at Calle 56.

Look for a large pale-green building behind the post office. Climb the steps and wade into the clamor and activity while browsing for leather goods, hammocks, Panama hats, Maya embroidered dresses, men's formal guayabera shirts, and craft items of all kinds.

Museo Regional de Artes Populares
Calle 59 no. 441, between Calles 50 and 48. No phone.

A branch of the Museo Nacional de Artes y Industrías Populares in Mexico City, this museum displays regional costumes and crafts in the front rooms. Upstairs is a large room full of crafts from all over Mexico, including filigree jewelry from Mérida, folk pottery, baskets, and wood carving from the Yucatán. Open Tuesday through Saturday from 8am to 8pm and Sunday from 9am to 2pm. Admission is free.

Guayaberas

T-shirts, polo shirts, dress shirts, and the like can be horrendously hot and uncomfortable in Mérida's soaking humidity. For this reason, businessmen, politicians, bankers, and bus drivers alike don the guayabera—a loose-fitting button-down shirt worn outside pants. Mérida could well be called the hotbed of guayaberas, which can be purchased for under $10 at the market or for over $50 custom-made by a tailor. A guayabera made of Japanese linen can set you back about $65. The most comfortable shirts are made of light, breathable cotton, though polyester is surprisingly common, despite its tendency to seal in perspiration against the skin. Several guayabera shops are located along Calle 59; most display ready-to-wear shirts in several price ranges.

Jack Guayaberas
Calle 59 no. 507A. ☎ **99/28-6002.**

The tailors at Jack's, known for their craftsmanship since the mid-1950s, can make you the guayabera of your dreams in three hours. Connoisseurs have very definite opinions on color, the type of tucks that will run down the front, and the embroidery that will swirl around the buttons. Check out the shirts on the racks for your first guayabera or perhaps a blouse or dress. The shop is open daily from 9am to 1pm and 4 to 8pm.

Hammocks

The comfortable Yucatecan fine-mesh hammocks *(hamacas)* are made of string woven from silk, nylon, or cotton. Silk is extremely expensive and only for truly serious hammock sleepers. Nylon is long-lasting. Cotton is attractive, fairly strong, and inexpensive, but it wears out sooner than nylon. Here's how to select a hammock: Hold the hammock loosely and make sure the space between the weave is no larger than the size of your little finger. Grasp the hammock at the point where the wide part and the end strings meet and hold your hand level with the top of your head. The body should touch the floor; if not, the hammock is too short for you.

Hammocks are sold as *sencillo* (single, about $15); *doble* (double, $20); and *matrimonial* (larger than double, about $25). The biggest hammock of all is called *matrimonial especial.* Buy the biggest hammock you can afford—the bigger ones take up no more room than smaller ones and are more comfortable, even for just one person.

Street vendors selling hammocks will approach you at every turn, *"¿Hamacas, señor, señorita?"* Their prices will be low, but so is the quality of their merchandise. If you buy from these vendors, be sure to examine the hammock carefully. Booths in the market have a larger selection and offer hammocks at only slightly higher prices.

La Poblana
S.A., Calle 65 no. 492, between Calles 60 and 58. No phone.

La Poblana has been well recommended for years. Prices are marked, so don't try to bargain. Upstairs there's a room hung wall-to-wall with hammocks where you can give your prospective purchase a test-drive. La Poblana sells ropes and mosquito nets for hammocks, as well as Maya women's dresses and men's guayaberas. The store is open Monday through Saturday from 8am to 7pm.

Panama Hats

Another very popular item are these soft, pliable hats made from the palm fibers of the jipijapa in several towns along Highway 180, especially Becal, in the neighboring state of Campeche. There's no need to journey all the way to Campeche, however, as Mérida sells the hats in abundance. Just the thing to shade you from the fierce Yucatecan sun, the hats can be rolled up and carried in a suitcase for the trip home. They retain their shape quite well.

Jipi hats come in three grades determined by the quality (pliability and fineness) of the fibers and closeness of the weave. Hats with the coarser, more open weave of fairly large fibers cost a few dollars (street vendors in Cancún and Cozumel charge up to $10). The middle grade—a fairly fine, close weave of good fibers—should cost about $15 in a respectable shop. The finest weave, truly a beautiful hat, can cost more than $50.

Maquech—The Legendary Maya Beetle

One of the most unusual items for sale in the Yucatán is the live maquech beetle. Storekeepers display bowls of the large dusty-brown insects with long black legs and backs sprinkled with multicolored glass "jewels" attached to small gold chains. The chain hooks to a small safety pin and behold—you have a living brooch to wear.

One version of the maquech legend goes that a Maya princess became the forbidden love object of a Maya prince. Without her knowledge, he crept into her garden one night, and just as they met, he was captured by the princess's guards. To save the prince, a sorceress turned him into a beetle and put him on a decaying tree near where he was captured. When the princess recovered from her faint, she looked for the prince where she had last seen him and found the bejeweled beetle instead; in an instant she knew it was the prince. Using a few strands of her long hair, she harnessed the beetle and kept it over her heart forever. Another version has it that the prince asked a sorceress to put him close to the heart of his beloved princess, and because he was very rich, she turned him into a bejeweled beetle pin.

No matter which legend you believe, putting a beetle close to your heart costs $5 to $8 and comes with a piece of its favorite wood, a nice little box with air holes to carry it in, and a chain and safety pin. U.S. Customs, however, doesn't permit the beetle to cross the border, so plan to find it a home before you leave Mexico.

ACCOMMODATIONS

Mérida is easier on the budget than other Yucatán cities. Most hotels offer at least a few air-conditioned rooms, and a few of the places also have pools. You may find every room taken in July and August, when Mexicans vacation in Mérida.

VERY EXPENSIVE

Hyatt Regency Mérida

Calle 60 no. 344, 97000 Mérida, Yuc. ☎ **99/25-6722,** or 800/228-9000 in the U.S. Fax 99/25-7002. 300 rms and suites. A/C MINIBAR TV TEL. High season $110–$125 single or double. Ask about "supersaver rates."

The most luxurious place in town, this 17-story hotel far surpasses the services and style to which Mérida is accustomed. The large, modern rooms have channels on satellite TV, 24-hour room service, direct-dial long-distance phone service, and personal safes. Regency Club rooms take up two floors of the hotel; guests here receive complimentary continental breakfast, evening cocktails, and hors d'oeuvres; special concierge service; and private lounges and boardrooms. The hotel is at the intersection of Calle 60 and Avenida Colón.

Dining/Entertainment: Several restaurants and bars.

Services: Complete business center, travel agency, and shops.

Facilities: Pool with swim-up bar.

EXPENSIVE

✪ Casa del Balam

Calle 60 no. 48, 97000 Mérida, Yuc. ☎ **99/24-8844,** or 800/624-8451 in the U.S. Fax 99/24-5011. 54 rms, 2 suites. A/C MINIBAR TV TEL. $80 double; $110 suite. Free parking.

One of Mérida's most popular and centrally located hotels, the Casa del Balam is built around a lush interior courtyard. In two sections of three and six stories respectively, the colonial-style rooms are accented with Mexican textiles, folk art, dark furniture, iron headboards, and tile floors with area rugs. It's hard to top this place for location and comfort. There's a travel agency and a rental-car agency in the lobby, as well as a popular restaurant and bar with trio entertainment in the evenings. The tables scattered around the courtyard have become a favorite romantic spot for evening cocktails and appetizers.

The owners also run the Hacienda Chichén-Itzá hotel, at the entrance of the ruins of Chichén-Itzá, so you can make arrangements here to stay there. To find the hotel, walk three blocks north of the Plaza Mayor.

✪ Hotel Misión Park Inn

Calle 60 no. 491, 97000 Mérida, Yuc. ☎ **99/23-9500** or 800/448-8355. Fax 99/23-7665. 73 rms. A/C TV TEL. $70 double; $80–$95 suite.

The Misión Park Inn is actually a large modern addition grafted onto a gracious older hotel. The location is excellent—right across the street from the university and the Teatro Peón Contreras, at the corner of Calle 57 and only two short blocks from the Plaza Mayor. Enter the hotel's cool lobby from the noisy street, and you'll find yourself in an oasis complete with bubbling fountain, high ceilings, and a nice little swimming pool. Though the public rooms are colonial in style, the guest units are Spartan in a modern way with blond furniture, tile floors, drapes and shutters, and two double beds in most rooms. Some of the suites have small kitchens and separate living-room areas.

Dining/Entertainment: One restaurant serves all meals. La Trova Bar has live piano entertainment Monday through Saturday evenings.

Services: Laundry and room service, and a travel agency.

MODERATE

✪ Casa Mexilio Guest House

Calle 68 no. 495, 97000 Mérida, Yuc. ☎ and fax **99/28-2505,** or 800/538-6802 in the U.S. 7 rms, 1 suite (all with bath). High season $55–$75 single or double. Low season $35–$55 single or double (including breakfast). Parking on street.

Roger Lynn, part owner and host, has created the atmosphere of a private home rather than that of a hotel in this 19th-century town house. Guests have the run of this three-story home built around indoor and outdoor patios. Each room is unique, and throughout the house pleasant decorative use is made of Mexican crafts. On the back patio are a small pool and whirlpool. The hotel is connected with the Turquoise Reef Group, which runs inns on Mexico's Caribbean coast between Cancún and Chetumal. You can make reservations here for those inns and sign up for a variety of trips in the Yucatán (see "Eco-Tours & Adventure Trips," above).

To find the hotel from the Plaza Mayor, walk one block north on Calle 62. Turn left on Calle 59 and walk for three blocks. Turn right on Calle 68; the hotel is half a block down on the left.

✪ Hotel Caribe

Calle 59 no. 500, 97000 Mérida, Yuc. ☎ **99/24-9022,** or 800/826-6842 in the U.S. Fax 99/24-8733. 18 rms, 38 suites (all with bath). A/C (2) or FAN (16) TV TEL. $28–$32 single; $30–$37 double; $45 suite for two with A/C. Free guarded parking.

Step inside the entry of this small two-story central hotel and discover a well-located, comfortable jewel. Well-coordinated colonial-style furnishings accent new pastel tile floors. Comfortable sitting areas along the three stories of covered open-air walkways are like extended living rooms offering a cozy respite at any time of day. From the top floor, where there's a small pool and sundeck, are great views of the cathedral and town. Rooms with air-conditioning are the most expensive. The interior restaurant is arranged around a quiet central courtyard, while the hotel's sidewalk café, El Mesón, is set out in front in the shady Parque Cepada Peraza. *A Reservation Note:* If you reserve a room through the 800 number, all the nights of your reservation will be charged on your credit card, which may arrive before you leave home; the rate will be higher than if you paid and reserved directly with the hotel. To get to the hotel from the Plaza Mayor, walk a half block to the Parque Cepeda Peraza. The hotel is in the back right corner of the park.

INEXPENSIVE

⊛ Hotel Dolores Alba

Calle 63 no. 464, 97000 Mérida, Yuc. ☎ **99/28-5650.** Fax 99/28-3163. 40 rms (all with bath). A/C or FAN. $19 single; $21 double. Limited free, unguarded parking.

The Sánchez family converted the family home into this comfortable hotel, which boasts a large open court and a smaller courtyard with a nice clean pool. The rooms, half of which have air-conditioning, are decorated with local crafts and all have showers. The highest prices are for rooms with air-conditioning. A small dining room opens for breakfast between 7 and 9am. The Sánchez family also operates the Hotel Dolores Alba outside Chichén-Itzá, so you can make reservations at one hotel for another. To find this hotel from the Plaza Mayor, walk east on Calle 63 for 3 1/2 blocks; it's between Calles 52 and 54.

⊛ Hotel Mucuy

Calle 57 no. 481, 97000 Mérida, Yuc. ☎ **99/28-5193.** Fax 99/23-7801. 22 rms (all with bath). FAN. $10 single; $12 double.

One of the most hospitable budget hotels in the country, the Mucuy is named for a small dove said to bring good luck to places where it alights. You'll see doves fluttering about the flower-filled interior courtyard. Owners Alfredo and Ofelia Comin strive to make guests feel welcome with conveniences such as a communal refrigerator in the lobby and laundry and clothesline facilities for guest use. Outside there are comfortable tables and chairs. Inside, two floors of freshly painted rooms with window screens, showers, and ceiling fans face the courtyard. Señora Comin speaks English. To find the hotel from the Plaza Mayor walk two blocks north on Calle 60, then turn right on Calle 57 and go a block and a half; it's between Calles 56 and 58.

Hotel Santa Lucía

Calle 55 no. 508, 97000 Mérida, Yuc. ☎ **99/24-6233.** Fax 99/28-2662. 51 rms (all with bath). A/C or FAN TV TEL. $17–$23 single; $19–$21 double. Free guarded parking nearby.

This small hotel opened in 1990. The rooms are in a three-story building with windows facing the inner hallways or the courtyard, which contains a long, inviting pool. The highest rates are for rooms with air-conditioning. The management is very helpful, providing information on tours, restaurants, and sights. They also run the Hotel San Clemente in Valladolid. To find the hotel from the Santa Lucía Park, walk west on Calle 55; the hotel is on the left less than half a block down, between Calles 60 and 62.

Hotel Trinidad Galería

Calle 60 no. 456, 97000 Mérida, Yuc. ☎ **99/23-2463.** Fax 99/24-2319. 31 rms, 1 suite (all with bath). A/C or FAN. $14 single; $15 double; $18–$20 suite with A/C and TV. Limited free parking.

Once an enormous home, this rambling hotel offers its guests a small shaded pool, a communal refrigerator, a shared dining room, oodles of original art and antiques, and lots of relaxing nooks with comfortable furniture. Upstairs, a covered porch decorated with antiques and plants runs the length of the hotel, providing yet another place to read or converse. Rooms are rather dark and simply furnished, and most don't have windows, but the overall ambience of the hotel is comparable to that of more expensive inns. To find the hotel from the Plaza Mayor, walk five blocks north on Calle 60; it's at the corner of Calle 51, two blocks north of the Santa Lucía Park.

Posada Toledo

Calle 58 no. 487, 97000 Mérida, Yuc. ☎ **99/23-1690.** Fax 99/23-2256. 21 rms, 2 suites (all with bath). A/C (16) or FAN (5) TEL. $19–$21 single; $21–$23 double. Free parking next door.

This colonial inn was once a private mansion. It's now a cross between a garden dripping with vines and a fading museum with beautifully kept antique furnishings. Two of the grandest rooms have been remodeled into a suite with ornate cornices and woodwork. Most rooms have no windows, but high ceilings and appropriately creaky hardwood floors are standard. The highest rates are for air-conditioned rooms. The rooftop lounge area is excellent for viewing the city. Five rooms have TVs. To find the inn from the Plaza Mayor, walk two blocks north on Calle 60, then right one block on Calle 57 to Calle 58; it's on the left.

DINING

Calle 62 between the Plaza Mayor and Calle 57 contains a short string of small budget food shops. To make your own breakfast, try the **Panificadora Montejo,** at the corner of Calles 62 and 63 on the southwest corner of the Plaza Mayor, and choose from a number of delectable treats. For those who can't start a day without fresh orange juice, **juice bars** have sprouted up all over Mérida, and several are on or near the Plaza Mayor.

EXPENSIVE

✪ Alberto's Continental

Calle 64 no. 482. ☎ **99/28-5367.** Reservations recommended. Main courses $7–$16. Daily 11am–11pm. LEBANESE/YUCATECAN/ITALIAN.

Created from a fine old town house, the large elegantly furnished rooms are built around a plant- and tree-filled patio that's framed in Moorish arches. Cuban floor tiles from a bygone era and antique furniture and sideboards create an Old World mood. The eclectic menu features Lebanese, Yucatecan, and Italian specialties. There's a sampler plate of four Lebanese favorites, plus traditional Yucatecan specialties such as pollo pibil and fish Celéstun (bass stuffed with shrimp). Polish off your selections with Turkish coffee. Alberto's is at the corner of Calle 57.

MODERATE

✪ Los Almendros

Calle 50A no. 493. ☎ **99/28-5459.** Main courses $3–$7; daily special $4–$8. Daily 9am–11pm. YUCATECAN.

The original Los Almendros is located in Ticul, deep in the Maya hinterland, but the branch in Mérida has become a favorite spot to sample local delicacies. The colorful chairs and tables will put you in a festive mood. Ask to see the menu with color photographs of the offerings accompanied by descriptions in English. Their famous poc chuc—a marinated and grilled pork dish created at the original restaurant in Ticul some years ago—is a must. To arrive at the restaurant from the Parque Cepeda Peraza, walk east on Calle 59 for five blocks, then left on Calle 50A; it's half a block on the left facing the Parque de Mejorada.

✪ La Casona

Calle 60 no. 434. ☎ **99/23-8348.** Reservations recommended. Pasta courses $4–$7; meat courses $5–$8. Daily 1pm–midnight. CONTINENTAL/ITALIAN.

A gracious old Mérida house and its lush interior garden makes a charming and romantic restaurant. The cuisine is Yucatecan and continental, especially Italian, so you can choose among such dishes as *pollo pibil,* filet mignon with brandy and cream, linguine with mushrooms, and lasagne. It's also a fine place to wind up the day sipping espresso or cappuccino. To find it from the Plaza Mayor, walk north on Calle 60 six blocks and it's at the corner of Calle 47.

El Patio de Las Fajitas

Calle 60 no. 467. ☎ **99/28-3782.** Main courses $5–$8; comida corrida $4–$6. Mon–Sat 1–11pm. MEXICAN.

Fajitas are the specialty at this mansion-turned-restaurant where you dine around a central courtyard decorated with plants and colorful tablecloths. The fajitas, grilled before you on the patio, come with guacamole, tortillas, and fresh Mexican salsa cruda. The portions are not large, so you may want to order a baked potato on the side. The menu also offers an economical fixed-price afternoon meal, which can include soup, poc-chuc or *pollo mole,* rice, beans, and tortillas. To find the restaurant, walk north on Calle 60 for four blocks; it's at the corner of Calle 53.

✪ Restaurante Portico del Peregrino

Calle 57 no. 501. ☎ **99/28-6163.** Reservations recommended. Main courses $5–$8. Daily noon–11pm. MEXICAN/INTERNATIONAL.

This romantic restaurant captures the spirit of 19th-century Mexico with its patio dining on the side of the street and outdoor patio dining in back. Inside is an air-conditioned dining room decorated with antique mirrors and elegant sideboards. The extensive menu offers soup, fish fillet, grilled gulf shrimp, spaghetti, *pollo pibil,* baked eggplant with chicken and cheese, and coconut ice cream topped with Kahlúa. To find it from the Plaza Mayor, walk 2¹/₂ blocks north on Calle 60, turn left on Calle 57, and it's half a block down on the right before Calle 62.

INEXPENSIVE

Café Alameda

Calle 58 no. 474. ☎ **99/28-3635.** Breakfast $2.25–$2.50; main courses $3–$6. Mon–Sat 8am–10pm. YUCATECAN/MIDDLE EASTERN.

At about 10am on weekdays, the Alameda is filled with businesspeople all eating the same late breakfast—a shish kebab of marinated beef, a basket of warm pita bread, and coffee. If eggs are more your style, order them with beans; otherwise, you'll get a small plate with a little pile of eggs. Vegetarians can choose from tabbouleh, hummus, cauliflower, eggplant or spinach casseroles, and veggie tamales. The umbrella-shaded tables on the back patio are pleasant places to eat. To find the café from the Plaza Mayor, walk east on Calle 61 for one block, then turn left on Calle 58 and walk three blocks north, near the corner of Calle 55.

Café Amaro

Calle 59 no. 507. ☎ **99/28-2451.** Breakfast $2–$2.50; main courses $3–$3.75. Mon–Sat 8am–11pm. REGIONAL/VEGETARIAN.

This pleasant, small restaurant serves guests in an open courtyard to the accompaniment of soft background music. Their *crema de calabacitas* soup is delicious, as is the apple salad. The avocado pizza is terrific. There is also a limited menu of meat and chicken dishes. To find it from the Plaza Mayor, walk one block north on Calle 60 and turn left on Calle 59.

El Louvre

Calle 62 no. 499. ☎ **99/24-5073.** Main courses $2–$4; comida corrida $3. Daily 24 hours (comida corrida served 1–5pm). MEXICAN.

This big, open restaurant feeds everybody from farm workers to townspeople. There's also an English menu. The comida corrida might include beans with pork on Monday, pork stew on Tuesday, and so on, plus there are sandwiches, soups, and other full meals. From the Palacio Municipal, cross Calle 61 and walk north on Calle 62 a few steps; it's near the corner of Calle 61.

Ⓢ Restaurante Los Amigos

Calle 62 no. 497. ☎ **99/23-1957.** Comida corrida $2.50. Tues–Sun noon–midnight. MEXICAN.

This place serves a comida corrida of Yucatecan specialties that includes soup, main course, and dessert. It's not classy, but the price is right. To find it from the Palacio Municipal (which faces the Plaza Mayor), walk north on Calle 62 half a block; it's on the left between Calles 61 and 59.

Ⓞ Vito Corleone

Calle 59 at Calle 60. ☎ **99/28-5777.** Pizza $2–$6; spaghetti $2; beer $1. Daily 9:30am–11:30pm. PIZZA/SPAGHETTI.

Aside from the food, the most impressive aspect of this tiny pizza parlor is the interesting use of ollas (clay pots) embedded in the wall above the hand-painted tile oven. The oven's golden yellow tiles are as handsome as those that decorate church domes. The tables by the sidewalk are the only bearable places to sit when it's warm, since the oven casts incredible heat. Another section upstairs in the back is also tolerable. The thin-crusted pizzas taste smoky and savory, and on Thursdays there's a pizza special of two pizzas for the price of one. To find it from the Plaza Mayor, walk north on Calle 60 one block and turn left on Calle 59; it's half a block ahead.

MÉRIDA AFTER DARK

For a full range of free or low-cost evening entertainment, as well as daily public events in Mérida, see "Festivals & Events," above.

Teatro Peón Contreras, at Calles 60 and 57, and the **Teatro Ayala,** on Calle 60 at Calle 61, both feature a wide range of performing artists from around the world. Stop in and see what's showing.

The scenes at the hotel bars, lounges, and discos depend on the crowd of customers presently staying at each hotel. Most of Mérida's downtown hotels, however, are filled with tour groups whose members prefer to rest after an exhausting day of sightseeing.

ROAD TRIPS FROM MÉRIDA
CELESTÚN NATIONAL WILDLIFE REFUGE: FLAMINGOS & OTHER WATERFOWL

This flamingo sanctuary and offbeat sand-street fishing village on the Gulf coast is a 1¹/₂-hour drive from Mérida. To get here, take Highway 281 (a two-lane road) past numerous old henequen haciendas. Around 10 **Autobuses de Occidente** buses leave Mérida for Celestún from the terminal at Calles 50 and 67 daily between 6am and 6:30pm.

One **telephone** at the Hotel Gutiérrez (☎ **99/28-0419**) serves as the public phone for the entire village. You'll find a bank, two gas stations (but no unleaded gas), and a grocery store. Bus tickets are purchased at the end of the row of market stalls on the left side of the church. Celestún hotels don't furnish drinking water, so bring your own or buy it in town.

December 8 is the Feast Day of the Virgen de Concepción, the patron saint of the village. On the Sunday that falls nearest to **July 15,** a colorful procession carries Celestún's venerated figure of the Virgen de Concepción to meet the sacred figure of the Virgen de Asunción on the highway leading to Celestún. Returning to Celestún, they float away on decorated boats and later return to be ensconced at the church during a mass and celebration.

Seeing the Waterfowl

The town is on a narrow strip of land separated from the mainland by a lagoon. Crossing over the lagoon bridge, you'll find the 14,611-acre **wildlife refuge** spreading out on both sides without visible boundaries. You'll notice small boats moored on both sides waiting to take visitors to see the flamingos. In addition to flamingos, you may see frigate birds, pelicans, cranes, egrets, sandpipers, and other waterfowl feeding on shallow sandbars at any time of year. Of the 175 bird species that come here, some 99 are permanent residents. At least 15 duck species have also been counted. Flamingos are found here all year; some nonbreeding flamingos remain year-round, even though the larger group takes off around April to nest on the upper Yucatán Peninsula east of Río Lagartos.

A 1¹/₂- to 2-hour **flamingo-sighting trip** costs around $25 for four persons or twice that much if you stay half a day. The best time to go is around 7am, and the worst is midafternoon, when sudden storms come up. Be sure not to allow the boatmen to get close enough to frighten the birds; they've been known to do it for photographers, but it will eventually cause the birds to permanently abandon the habitat. Your tour will take you a short distance into the massive mangroves that line the lagoon to a sulfur pool, where the boatman kills the motor and poles in so you can experience the stillness and density of the jungle, feel the sultry air, and see other birds.

Accommodations

To find restaurants and hotels, follow the bridge road a few blocks to the end. On the last street, Calle 12, paralleling the oceanfront, you'll find restaurants and hotels, all of which have decent rooms but marginal housekeeping standards. Always try to bargain for lower rates, which can go down by as much as 30% in the off-season.

Hotel María del Carmen

Calle 12 no. 111, Celestún, Yuc. 97367. ☎ **99/28-0152.** 9 rms (all with bath). FAN. $10 single; $12 double.

New in 1992, this three-story hotel on the beach is a welcome addition to Celestún's modest accommodations lineup. Spare but clean and large, each room has terrazzo floors, two double beds with sheets but no bedspread, screened windows (check screens for holes), and a small balcony or patio facing the ocean. Best of all, there's hot water in the baths (not necessarily a hallmark of other Celestún hotels), but not always toilet seats. Lorenzo Saul Rodríguez and María del Carmen Gutiérrez own the hotel and are actively involved in local conservation efforts, particularly in protecting the sea turtles that nest on the beach in early summer. Look for the sign for Villa del Mar, the hotel's restaurant; the rooms are behind it across the parking area.

Dining

Calle 12 is home to several rustic seafood restaurants aside from the place listed below. All have irregular hours of operation.

✪ Restaurant Celestún

Calle 12, on the waterfront. No phone. Main courses $3–$7. Daily 10am–6pm (sometimes). SEAFOOD/MEXICAN.

I highly recommend this ocean-view restaurant, owned by Elda Cauich and Wenseslao Ojeda; the service is friendly and swift. Tables and chairs fill a long room that stretches from Calle 12 to the beach. The house specialty is a super-delicious shrimp, crab, and squid omelet (called a *torta*). But if you're a fan of stone crabs (*manitas de cangrejo* on the menu), this is definitely the place to chow down. Trapped in the gulf by Celestún fishermen, they come freshly cooked and seasoned with lime juice. Also popular during the fall season is *pulpo* (octopus). Other local specialties include *liza* (mullet) and caviar de Celestún (mullet eggs). To find the restaurant, follow the bridge road to the waterfront (Calle 12); turn left and the restaurant is immediately on the right.

DZIBILCHALTÚN: MAYA RUINS

This Maya site, now a national park located 9 miles north of Mérida along the Progreso road and 4¹/₂ miles east off the highway, is worth a stop. Though it was founded about 500 B.C. and flourished around A.D. 750, Dzibilchaltún was in decline long before the coming of the conquistadores but may have been occupied until A.D. 1600—almost a hundred years after the arrival of the Spaniards. Since its discovery in 1941, more than 8,000 buildings have been mapped. The site, which was probably a center of commerce and religion, covers an area of almost 10 square miles with a central core of almost 65 acres. At least 12 *sacbeob* (causeways), the longest of which is 4,200 feet, have been unearthed. Dzibilchaltún means "place of the stone writing," and at least 25 stelae have been found, many of them reused in buildings constructed after the original ones were covered or destroyed.

Today, the most interesting buildings are grouped around the **Cenote Xlacah,** the sacred well, and include a complex of buildings around Structure 38; the **Central Group** of temples; the raised **causeways**; and the **Seven Dolls Group,** centered on the **Temple of the Seven Dolls.** It was beneath the floor of the temple that seven weird little dolls (now in the museum) showing a variety of diseases and birth defects were discovered. The Yucatán State Department of Ecology has added nature trails and published a booklet (in Spanish) of birds and plants seen at various points along the mapped trail. The booklet tells where in the park you are likely to see specific plants and birds.

The federal government has spent over a million pesos for the **Museum of the Maya** on the grounds of Dzibilchaltún; the museum opened in 1995. The museum is a replica of a Maya village of houses, called *nas,* staffed by Maya demonstrating traditional cooking, gardening, and folk-art techniques.

To get to Dzibilchaltún by bus from Mérida, go to the Progreso bus station at Calle 62 no. 524, between Calles 65 and 67. There are five buses per day on Monday through Saturday at 7:10 and 9am and 1, 2, and 3:20pm to the pueblo of Chanculob; it's a 1-kilometer walk to the ruins from there. On Sunday there are only three buses to Chanculob—at 5:40 and 9am and 2pm. The return bus schedule is posted at the ticket window by the ruins. The last bus is at 4:15pm.

The site and nature trails are open daily from 8am to 5pm. Admission is $2.75, free on Sunday; video camera use costs $4. Parking costs $1, and a guided tour costs about $15 for a small group.

PROGRESO: GULF COAST CITY

For another beach escape, go to Progreso, a modern city facing the gulf less than an hour from Mérida. Here, the Malecón, a beautiful oceanfront drive, borders a vast beach lined with coconut palms that's popular on the weekends. A long pier, or *muelle* (pronounced "mu-wey-yeh"), extends 5 miles out into the bay to reach water deep enough for oceangoing ships. Progreso is part-time home to many Americans and Canadians who come to escape northern winters and also to many Meridianos who want to escape Mérida.

Along or near the Malecón are several of the more desirable restaurants and hotels.

From Mérida, buses to Progreso leave the special bus station at Calle 62 no. 524, between Calles 65 and 67, every 15 minutes during the day, starting at 5am. The trip takes 45 minutes.

In Progreso, the bus station is about four blocks south of Calle 19, or Malecón, which runs along the beach.

EN ROUTE TO UXMAL

There are three routes to Uxmal, about 50 miles south of Mérida. The most direct is Highway 261 via Uman and Muna. A second possibility is to follow Highway 180 through Uman and the ruins of Oxkintok near Maxcanú and Calcehtok, turn east onto Highway 184, then at Muna rejoin Highway 261 South to Uxmal. And your third choice is a scenic but meandering trip down State Highway 18. Additional details on this last route are provided in "The Ruins of Mayapán & Village of Ticul," below.

HIGHWAY 261: YAXCOPOIL & MUNA   Ten miles beyond Uman along Highway 261 is Yaxcopoil (yash-koh-poe-*eel*), the tongue-twisting Maya name of a fascinating 19th-century hacienda on the right side of the road between Mérida and Uxmal. It's difficult to reach by bus.

This hacienda, dating from 1864, was originally a cattle ranch comprising over 23,000 acres. Around 1900, it was converted to growing henequen (for the manufacture of rope). Take half an hour to tour the house (which boasts 18-foot ceilings and original furniture), factory, outbuildings, and museum. You'll see that such haciendas were the administrative, commercial, and social centers of vast private domains; they were almost little principalities carved out of the Yucatecan jungle. It's open Monday through Saturday from 8am to 6pm and Sunday from 9am to 1pm.

From Mérida via Uman, it's 20 miles to the Hacienda Yaxcopoil and 40 miles to Muna on Highway 261. Uxmal is 10 miles from Muna.

HIGHWAY 180: OXKINTOK & GRUTAS CALCEHTOK   Only 35 miles south of Mérida and 28 miles northwest of Uxmal is a Maya site that dates from Preclassic times, perhaps as early as 300 B.C., and covers three square miles. Before recent excavations it suffered extensive looting, but new discoveries still thrill archaeologists. Although the architecture is predominantly Puuc, as in other nearby sites, scholars believe it was an important crossroads because there is great evidence of influence from as far away as Guatemala. Building and habitation continued until at least the Late Classic period, around A.D. 1000.

Archaeologists have mapped more than 200 buildings, including at least 12 pyramids. Deep inside several pyramids, numerous tombs containing jade masks have been uncovered. Today several restored structures are visible, including the Tzat Tun Tzat, the Ch'ich Palace, and the Devil's Palace. The most interesting of these is probably the Tzat Tun Tzat. Its depths revealed a labyrinth of tunnels, passageways, stairs, and rooms, one of which was a tomb. Based on the placement of its windows, it was probably an observatory. The 10-room Ch'ich Palace still has two of the four anthropomorphic columns that once decorated the portico. The Devil's Palace contains an anthropomorphic column with holes in its head supporting the northern portico.

The Mysteries of the Maya's Beginnings

Ever since New York lawyer and amateur anthropologist John L. Stephens recorded his adventures traveling in the Yucatán, Chiapas, and Central America in a fascinating series of travel book adventures, foreigners have been touring the Yucatán to view its vast crumbling cities and ponder the fall of the great Maya civilization, which developed mathematical theories far in advance of European thought and perfected an extremely accurate calendar. For a detailed list of suggested background reading, see "Recommended Books" in Chapter 1.

The Olmec civilization took shape between 1500 B.C. and A.D. 300 (the **Preclassic period**) on the Gulf coast of Mexico. Historians speculate that the Maya were descended from the mysterious Olmecs, but a definitive link in the cultures is missing, except for a few archaeological finds like Izapa, a huge site found almost intact on the Pacific coast of Chiapas. Izapa is considered a transitional culture between the Olmec and the Maya that arose between 400 B.C. and A.D. 400.

Other than conclusions drawn from the stone carvings and historic significance of Izapa, the development of the Maya culture remains a mystery. Somewhere along the way the Maya perfected the Olmec calendar and refined and developed their ornate system of hieroglyphic writing and their early architecture. The Maya religion, with its 166 deities, was also being shaped in these early centuries, which were contemporaneous with the Roman empire. The Maya guided their lives by using a number of interwoven and complex calendars (see the section on Chichén-Itzá).

The great years of Maya culture (the so-called **Classic period**), lasted from A.D. 320 to 925, when Rome was falling to the barbarians and the Dark Ages were spreading over Europe. The finest examples of Maya architecture date from these years, well before the Gothic style made its appearance in Europe. These supreme achievements of Maya art can be seen at Palenque (near Villahermosa), at Copán in Honduras, and at Quirigua in Guatemala. All these sites flourished during the last part of the 700s.

The Classic period ended with a century of degradation and collapse, roughly equivalent to the A.D. 800s. By the early 900s the great ceremonial centers were abandoned and the jungle took them over, but why classic Maya culture collapsed so quickly is still something of a mystery.

After the Classic period, the Maya migrated from their original home in Guatemala and Chiapas into the northern lowlands of the Yucatán (roughly the modern states of Yucatán and Campeche), where they spent six centuries (A.D. 900–1500) trying to recover their former greatness.

During this **Postclassic period**, the cities near the Yucatán's low western Puuc hills were built. The architecture of the region, called Puuc style, is generally characterized by elaborate exterior stonework appearing above door frames and extending to the roofline. Examples of this can be seen in Kabah, Sayil, Labná, and Xlapak. Even though Maya architecture never gained the heights achieved at Palenque or Tikal, the Puuc buildings, such as the Codz Poop at Kabah and the palaces at Sayil and Labná, it is quite beautiful and impressive.

The Putún Maya   The Yucatán was also profoundly affected by a strong influence from central Mexico. Some theories claim that a distantly related branch of the Maya people, the Putún Maya, came from the borders of the peninsula and crowded into the Yucatán during the Postclassic period. The Putún Maya were traders and navigators who had controlled the trade routes along the coast and rivers between mainland Mexico and the classic Maya lands in Petén and Chiapas. They spoke the Maya language poorly and used many Náhuatl (Aztec) words.

The Itzáes   When the Putún Maya left their ships and moved inland, they became known as the Itzáes because, after unsuccessfully trying to conquer Yaxuná, they settled 12 miles north in what eventually became known as **Chichén-Itzá** (Well of the Itzá), a perfect place because of its access to water and its proximity to population centers ripe for conquering. They brought with them years of experience in trading far and wide (thus perhaps explaining the influence of the Toltecs that shows up so strongly at Chichén-Itzá). Eventually they were successful in conquering other peninsular kingdoms and creating the vast city of Chichén-Itzá.

The Toltec Invasion Theory   Research revealed in Linda Schele and David Freidel's *A Forest of Kings* shows that the bas-relief history found at Chichén-Itzá does not support a Toltec invasion theory. They believe Chichén-Itzá's adoption of Toltec architecture demonstrates it was a cosmopolitan city that absorbed elements brought from the central Mexican region occupied by Toltecs, and that the continuity of buildings and bas-relief figures show it was a continuous Maya site.

The Legend of Kukulkán   Legend has it that when the great man-god Quetzalcoatl fled Tula in central Mexico in shame after succumbing to a series of temptations, he took refuge first on the east coast of Mexico and later in the Yucatán, where he became known as Kukulkán. Scholars once placed him leading the invasion of Chichén-Itzá or establishing Mayapán, which came after Chichén-Itzá. Now the jury is out again. That Kukulkán existed is not in doubt, but precisely how he fit in is being reexamined.

The Xiú   According to some authorities, Uxmal was inhabited during this same period (around A.D. 1000) by a tribe known as the Tutul Xiú, who came from the region of Oaxaca and Tabasco. Some scholars think the Xiú took the city from earlier builders because evidence shows the region around Uxmal was inhabited as early as 800 B.C.

The three great centers—Chichén-Itzá, Mayapán, and Uxmal—lived in peace under a confederation: The Itzá ruled in Chichén-Itzá, the Cocom tribe in Mayapán, and the Xiú in Uxmal. Authorities don't agree on the exact year, but sometime during the 12th century the people of Mayapán overthrew the confederation, sacked Chichén-Itzá, conquered Uxmal, and captured the leaders of the Itzá and the Xiú. Held in Mayapán, the Itzá and the Xiú princes reigned over, but did not rule, their former cities. Mayapán remained the seat of the confederation for over 200 years.

The Xiú took their revenge in 1441 when they marched from Uxmal on Mayapán, capturing and destroying the city and killing the Cocom rulers. They founded a new city at Maní. Battles and skirmishes continued to plague the Maya territory until it was conquered by the Spanish conquistadores.

Visually, the site doesn't rival Uxmal or Chichén-Itzá, but it's interesting if you're following a ruins itinerary. The site is open more or less daily from 8am to 5pm. Admission is $2.50, free on Sunday; use of a personal video camera costs $8.

The undeveloped **Grutas (caves) Calcehtok,** with almost 3 miles of underground passageways in which to get lost, are about 2 miles from Oxkintok. To explore them, contact Roger Cuy, a guide in Calcehtok.

To get to Oxkintok, follow Highway 180 south through Uman to an intersection 2 miles short of Maxcanú. Turn east here (an overhead sign points to Manu) for about 5 miles. This takes you to the village of Calcehtok. A sign points south (right) to the Grutas Calcehtok and Oxkintok. After about a mile, another sign points to the Grutas (straight ahead) or to Oxkintok (right). Follow this road (which gives new meaning to the word *narrow*) for a mile and a half (the last half mile is dirt) to a locked gate. A caretaker *may* show up to let you in and accept admission.

HIGHWAY 18: KANASIN, ACANCEH, MAYAPÁN & TICUL   Taking Calle 67 east, head out of Mérida toward Kanasin ("Kahn-ah-seen") and Acanceh ("Ah-kahn-keh"), for about 12 miles. When Calle 67 ends, bear right, then go left at the next big intersection. Follow the wide divided highway with speed bumps. At Mérida's periférico (the road that circles the city), you'll see signs to Cancún. You can either cross the periférico and go straight into Kanasin or turn and follow the Cancún signs for a short distance and then follow the signs into Kanasin. In **Kanasin,** watch for signs that say "circulación" or "desviación." As in many Yucatán towns, you're being redirected to follow a one-way street through the urban area. Go past the market, church, and the main square on your left and continue straight out of town. The next village you come to, at km 10, is **San António Tehuit,** an old henequen hacienda. At km 13 is **Tepich,** another hacienda-centered village, with those funny little henequen-cart tracks crisscrossing the main road. After Tepich comes **Petectunich** and finally Acanceh.

Across the street from and overlooking **Acanceh's** church is a partially restored pyramid. From Acanceh's main square, turn right (around the statue of a smiling deer) and head for **Tecoh** with its huge crumbling church (5¹/₂ miles farther along Highway 18) and **Telchaquillo** (7 miles farther). This route takes you past several old Yucatecan haciendas, each with a big house, chapel, factory with smokestack, and workers' houses.

Shortly after the village of Telchaquillo, a sign on the right side of the road will point to the entrance of the ruins of Mayapán.

2   The Ruins of Mayapán & Village of Ticul

THE RUINS OF MAYAPÁN
30 miles S of Mérida; 25 miles NE of Ticul; 37 miles NE of Uxmal

Founded, according to Maya lore, by the man-god Quetzalcoatl (Kukulkán in Maya) in about A.D. 1007, Mayapán ranked in importance with Chichén-Itzá and Uxmal and covered at least 2¹/₂ square miles. For more than two centuries, it was the capital of a Maya confederation of city-states that included Chichén and Uxmal. But before the year 1200 the rulers of Mayapán ended the confederation by attacking and conquering Chichén and by forcing the rulers of Uxmal to live as vassals in Mayapán. Eventually a successful revolt by the captive Maya rulers brought down Mayapán, which was abandoned during the mid-1400s.

Though ruined, the main pyramid is still impressive. Next to it is a large cenote (a natural limestone cavern used as a well), now full of trees, bushes, and banana

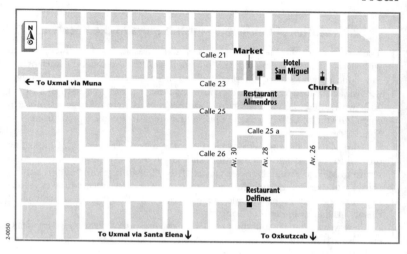

plants. Beside it is a small temple with columns and a fine high-relief mask of Chaac, the hook-nosed rain god. Jungle paths lead to other small temples, including El Caracol, with its circular tower. These piles of stones do not reflect the grandeur of the walled city of Mayapán in its heyday. Supplied with water from 20 cenotes, it had over 3,000 buildings in its enclosed boundaries of several square miles. Today, all is covered in dense jungle.

The site is open daily from 8am to 5pm. Admission is $1.25; free on Sunday; use of a personal video camera is $4.

FROM MAYAPÁN TO TICUL   The road is a good one, but directional signs through the villages are almost nonexistent. Stop and ask directions frequently. From Mayapán, continue along Highway 18 to **Tekit** (5 miles), turn right and go to **Mama** on a road as thrilling as a roller-coaster ride (4¹/₃ miles), then turn right again for **Chapab** (8 miles).

If you're ready for a break, take time out to visit the **tortilla factory** in Chapab. Turn left when you see a building named Centro Educativo Comunitario Chapab, and the factory will be a couple of blocks farther on the left. As you came into town, you probably noticed young Maya girls, masa dough up to their elbows, carrying large pans and buckets of it atop their heads. They're returning from the daily ritual of corn grinding, and they'll use the masa to make their own tortillas at home. Other young-sters are carrying large stacks of finished tortillas hot off the press. The Matos Sabino family owns the factory, and they don't mind if you stop in and watch the action, which goes on daily from 8am to around 3pm. Better yet, buy some tortillas; fill them with avocados, tomatoes, and cheese; and have a picnic on the lawn across the street. After Chapab you reach **Ticul** (6¹/4 miles), the largest town in the region.

TICUL

12 miles E of Uxmal, 53 miles SE of Mérida

Many of the 27,000 inhabitants of this sprawling town make their living embroider-ing huipiles (the Maya women's shiftlike dress), weaving straw hats, making shoes and gold-filigree jewelry, and shaping pottery. Workshops and stores featuring most of these items are easy to find, especially in the market area.

Centuries of Conflict: Spanish & Maya in the Yucatán

The Conquest of the Yucatán took 20 years and was achieved by three men, all with the same name: Francisco de Montejo, the Elder (also called El Adelantado, the pioneer), who started the process; his son Francisco Montejo, the Younger (known as El Mozo, the lad); and a cousin. Montejo the Elder sailed from Spain in 1527 with 400 soldiers and landed at Cozumel but was forced to relaunch his campaign from the western coast, where he could more easily receive supplies from New Spain (Mexico).

From Mexico, he conquered what is now the state of Tabasco (1530), pushing onward to the Yucatán. But after four difficult years (1531–35) he was forced to return to Mexico penniless and exhausted. In 1540, Montejo the Younger and his cousin (another Francisco de Montejo) took over the cause, successfully establishing a town at Campeche and another at Mérida (1542); by 1546, virtually all of the peninsula was under their control.

A few weeks after the founding of Mérida, the greatest of the several Maya leaders, Ah Kukum Xiú, head of the Xiú people, offered himself as Montejo's vassal and was baptized, giving himself the name Francisco de Montejo Xiú. With the help of Montejo's troops, Montejo the Younger and his cousin then accomplished their objective, the defeat of the Cocoms. By allying his people with the Spaniards, Xiú triumphed over the Cocoms but surrendered the freedom of the Yucatecan Maya. In later centuries warfare, disease, slavery, and emigration all led to the decline of the peninsula's population. Fray Diego de Landa, second bishop of Yucatán, destroyed much of the history of the Maya culture when he ordered the mass destruction of the priceless Maya codices, or "painted books," at Maní in 1562; only three survived.

The Yucatán struggled along under the heavy yoke of Spanish colonial administration until the War of Independence (begun in 1810) liberated Mexico and the Yucatán in 1821. In that same year, the Spanish governor of the Yucatán resigned, and the Yucatán, too, became an independent country. Though the Yucatán decided to join in a union with Mexico two years later, this period of sovereignty is testimony to the Yucatecan spirit of independence. That same spirit arose again in 1846 when the Yucatán seceded from Mexico.

ESSENTIALS

GETTING THERE & DEPARTING   There are frequent buses from Mérida. The Ticul bus station is near the town center on Calle 24 between Calles 25 and 25A. Buses return to Mérida daily at 7 and 10am and 5:30 and 7pm. Also check with the drivers of the minivans that line up across from the bus station. Buses run twice hourly to Muna, where you can change for a bus to Uxmal. For car information, see "En Route to Uxmal," above.

ORIENTATION   The market, most hotels, and Los Almendros, Ticul's best-known restaurant, are on the main street, **Calle 23,** also called Calle Principal. The **telephone area code** is 997. Since cars, buses, trucks, bicycles, and tricycles all compete for space on the narrow potholed streets, **parking and driving** have become difficult. Consider parking several streets away from the center of town and walking around from there. Directional signs that allow drivers to bypass the most congested part of town are beginning to appear.

After the war, sugarcane and henequen cultivation were introduced on a large scale, organized around vast landed estates called haciendas, each employing hundreds of Maya virtually as slaves. During the war for secession, weapons were issued to the Maya to defend independent Yucatán against attack from Mexico or the United States. The Maya turned these same weapons on their local oppressors, setting off the **War of the Castes** in 1847.

The Maya ruthlessly attacked and sacked Valladolid and strengthened their forces with guns and ammunition bought from British merchants in Belize (British Honduras). By June 1848, they held virtually all the Yucatán except Mérida and Campeche—and Mérida's governor had already decided to abandon the city.

Then followed one of the strangest occurrences in Yucatecan history. It was time to plant the corn, and the Maya fighters dropped their weapons and went off to tend the fields. Meanwhile, Mexico sent reinforcements in exchange for the Yucatán's resubmission to Mexican authority. Government troops took the offensive, driving many of the Maya to the wilds of Quintana Roo, in the southeastern reaches of the peninsula.

Massed in southern Quintana Roo, the Maya, seeking inspiration in their war effort, followed the cult of the Talking Crosses, which was started in 1850 by a Maya ventriloquist and a mestizo "priest," who carried on a tradition of "talking idols" that had flourished for centuries in several places, including Cozumel. The "talking cross" first appeared at Chan Santa Cruz (today's Felipe Carrillo Puerto), and soon several crosses were talking and inspiring the Maya.

The Yucatecan authorities seemed content to let the rebels and their talking crosses rule the southern Caribbean coast, which they did with only minor skirmishes until the late 1800s. The rebel government received arms from the British in Belize, and in return allowed the British to cut lumber in rebel territory.

At the turn of the century, Mexican troops with modern weapons penetrated the rebel territory, soon putting an end to this bizarre, if romantic, episode of Yucatecan history. The town of Chan Santa Cruz was renamed in honor of a Yucatecan governor, Felipe Carrillo Puerto, and the Yucatán was finally a full and integral part of Mexico.

EXPLORING TICUL

Ticul's **annual festival,** complete with bullfights, dancing, and carnival games, is held during the first few days of April.

Shopping

Ticul is best known for the cottage industry of *huipil* embroidery and for the manufacture of ladies' dress shoes. It's also a center for large-size commercially produced pottery. Most of the widely sold sienna-colored pottery painted with Maya designs comes from Ticul. If it's a cloudy, humid day, the potters may not be working since part of the process requires sun drying, but they still welcome visitors to purchase finished pieces.

Arte Maya

Calle 23 no. 301, Carretera Ticul Muna. ☎ **997/2-1095.** Fax 997/2-0334.

Owned and operated by Luis Echeverria and Lourdes Castillo, this shop and gallery produces museum-quality art in alabaster, stone, jade, and ceramics. Much of the work is done as it was in Maya times; soft stone or ceramic is smoothed with the leaf of the siricote tree, and colors are derived from plant sources. If you buy from them, hang onto the written description of your purchase—their work looks so authentic that U.S. customs have delayed entry of people carrying their wares, thinking that they're smuggling real Maya artifacts into the States.

ACCOMMODATIONS

Only 12 miles northeast of Uxmal, Ticul is an ideal spot from which to launch regional sightseeing trips and to avoid the high cost of hotels in Uxmal.

Hotel Bougambillias Familiar

Calle 23 no. 291A, 97860 Ticul, Yuc. ☎ **997/2-0761.** 20 rms (all with bath). FAN. $9 single or double, one bed; $12 double, two beds. Free parking; secure.

Ticul's nicest inn is more like a motel, with parking outside the rooms. The half-circle drive into the arched entrance is lined with plants and pottery from the owner's local factory. Ceiling-height windows don't let in much light, the rooms have saggy beds, and bathrooms come without shower curtains and toilet seats. But the cool tile floors and ready hot water are attractions. In back is the hotel's pretty restaurant, Xux-Cab. To find the hotel, follow Calle 23 through Ticul on the road to Muna. It's on the right before you leave town, past the Santa Elena turnoff.

DINING

Decent restaurants in Ticul are few. The busy market on Calle 23 is a good place to mingle with chatty Maya women while you select fresh fruit or grab a bite at one of the little eateries.

✪ Los Almendros

Calle 23 no. 207. ☎ **997/2-0021.** Main courses $4–$7. Daily 9am–7pm. YUCATECAN.

Set in a big old Andalusian-style house with interior-courtyard parking, this is the first of a chain that now has branches in Mérida and Cancún. The Maya specialties include papadzules (sauce-covered, egg-filled tortillas) poc-chuc (which originated here), and the spicy pollo ticuleño; as in Mérida, the quality of the food can vary. Ask for the illustrated menu in English (also Spanish and French) that explains the dishes in detail. To find it, walk one and a half blocks west of the plaza/church on Calle 23; it's on the left.

Restaurant Los Delfines

Calle 27, no. 216. No phone. Main courses $4–$5. Daily 8am–6pm. MEXICAN.

A favorite, although I've often found it closed, the Restaurant Los Delfines is in a beautiful garden setting near the center of town. The menu offers chiles rellenos stuffed with shrimp, *carne raja asada* with achiote, pork, garlic-flavored fish, and other seafood. The filling complimentary *botanas* (appetizers) are a refreshing treat. You can park off the street in the courtyard. If the restaurant appears to be closed, just bang on the large metal doors and someone will open. To find the restaurant from the corner of Calles 23 and 26 (by the church), go two blocks west on Calle 23 to Calle 28; turn left (south) for three blocks to Calle 27, then right half a block. It's on the left.

A SIDE TRIP: SPELUNKING IN THE YAXNIC CAVES

Just outside the village of Yotolín (also spelled Yohtolín), between Ticul and Oxkutzcab (along Highway 184), are some impressive caves called **Yaxnic** (yash-*neek*), on the grounds of the old, private Hacienda Yotolín. Virtually undeveloped and full of colored stalactites and stalagmites, the caves are visited by means of a perilous descent in a basket let down on a rope.

Arranging this spelunking challenge takes time, but the thrill may be worth it. Here's the procedure: Several days (or even weeks or months) before your intended cave descent, go to Yotolín and ask for the house of the *comisario,* a village elder. He will make the proper introductions to the hacienda owners, who in turn will tell you how to prepare for the experience.

FROM TICUL TO UXMAL

From Ticul to Uxmal, follow the main street (Calle 23) west through town. Turn left at the sign to **Santa Elena.** It's 10 miles to Santa Elena; then, at Highway 261, cut back right for about 2 miles to Uxmal. The easiest route to follow is via Muna, but it's also longer and less picturesque. To go this way drive straight through Ticul 14 miles to Muna. At Muna, turn left and head south on Highway 261 to Uxmal, 10 miles away.

3 The Ruins of Uxmal

50 miles SW of Mérida, 12 miles W of Ticul, 12 miles S of Muna

One of the highlights of a vacation in the Yucatán, the ruins of Uxmal, noted for their rich geometric stone facades, are the most beautiful on the peninsula. Remains of an agricultural society indicate that the area was occupied possibly as early as 800 B.C. However, the great building period took place a thousand years later, between A.D. 700 and 1000, during which time the population probably reached 25,000. Then Uxmal fell under the sway of the Xiú princes (who may have come from the Valley of Mexico) after the year 1000. In the 1440s, the Xiú conquered Mayapán, and not long afterward the glories of the Maya ended when the Spanish conquistadores arrived.

Close to Uxmal, four other sites—Sayil, Kabah, Xlapak, and Labná—are worth visiting. With Uxmal, these ruins are collectively known as the Puuc route, for the Puuc hills of this part of the Yucatán. See the "Puuc Maya Sites" section below if you want to explore these sites.

ESSENTIALS
GETTING THERE & DEPARTING

By Bus   See "Getting There & Departing" in Mérida, above, for information about bus service between Mérida and Uxmal. To return, wait for the bus on the highway at the entrance to the ruins. There is no evening departure from Mérida for the sound-and-light show at Uxmal.

By Car   Three routes to Uxmal from Mérida—via Highway 261, via Highways 180 and 184, or via State Highway 18—are described in "En Route to Uxmal," at the end of the Mérida section, above. *Note:* There's no gasoline at Uxmal, so top off the tank in Mérida, Muna, or Ticul before continuing.

ORIENTATION

Uxmal consists of the archaeological site and its visitor center, four hotels, and a highway restaurant. The visitor center—open daily from 8am to 9pm—has a restaurant (with good coffee); toilets; a first-aid station; and shops selling soft drinks, ice cream, film, batteries, and books. There are no phones except at the hotels. Restaurants at hotels near Uxmal and at the visitor center are expensive, so if you're coming for the day, bring a lunch. Most public buses pick up and let off passengers on the highway at the entrance to the ruins. The site itself is open daily from 8am to 5pm. Admission to the archaeological site of Uxmal is $3.75, but a Sunday visit will save money since admission is free to Uxmal and other recommended sites nearby. *There's a*

$4 charge for each video camera you bring in (save your receipt; it's good for other area sites on the same day). Parking costs $1.

Guides at the entrance of Uxmal give tours in a variety of languages and charge $20 for one person or a group. The guides frown on an unrelated individual joining a group (presumably a group is people traveling together). They'd rather you pay as a single entity, but you can hang around the entrance and ask other English speakers if they would like to join you in a tour and split the cost. As at other sites, the guides' information is not up-to-date, but you'll see areas and architectural details you might otherwise miss.

A 45-minute **sound-and-light show** is staged each evening in Spanish for $2 at 7pm and in English for $3 at 9pm. The bus from Mérida is scheduled to leave near the end of the Spanish show; confirm the exact time with the driver. If you stay for the English show, the only return to Mérida is via an expensive taxi. After the impressive show, the chant *"Chaaac, Chaaac"* will echo in your mind for weeks.

A TOUR OF THE RUINS

The Pyramid of the Magician As you enter the ruins, note the *chultún* (cistern) inside the entrance to the right. Besides the natural underground cisterns (such as cenotes) formed in the porous limestone, chultúns were the principal source of water for the Maya.

Just beyond the chultún, Uxmal's dominant building, the Pyramid of the Magician (also called the Soothsayer's Temple) with its unique rounded sides, looms majestically on the right as you enter. The name comes from a legend about a mystical dwarf who reached adulthood rapidly after being hatched from an egg and who built this pyramid in one night. Beneath it are five temples, since it was common practice for the Maya to build new structures atop old ones as part of a prescribed ritual.

The pyramid is unique because of its oval shape, height, steepness, and odd doorway on the opposite (west) side near the top. The doorway's heavy ornamentation, a characteristic of the Chenes style, features 12 stylized masks of the rain god Chaac, and the doorway itself is a huge open-mouthed Chaac mask.

The tiring and even dangerous climb to the top is worth it for the view. From on top you can see Uxmal's entire layout. Next to the Pyramid of the Magician, to the west, is the Nunnery Quadrangle, and left of it is a conserved ball court, south of which are several large complexes. The biggest building among them is the Governor's Palace, and behind it lies the partially restored Great Pyramid. In the distance is the Dovecote, a palace with a lacy roofcomb (false front) that looks like the perfect apartment complex for pigeons. From this vantage point, note how Uxmal is special among Maya sites for its use of broad terraces or platforms constructed to support the buildings; look closely and you'll see that the Governor's Palace is not on a natural hill or rise but on a huge square terrace, as is the Nunnery Quadrangle.

The Nunnery The 16th-century Spanish historian Fray Diego López de Cogullado gave the building its name because it resembled a Spanish monastery. Possibly it was a military academy or a training school for princes, who may have lived in the 70-odd rooms. The buildings were constructed at different times: the northern one was first, then the southern, then the eastern, then the western. The western building has the most richly decorated facade, composed of intertwined stone snakes and numerous masks of the hook-nosed rain god Chaac.

The corbeled archway on the south was once the main entrance to the Nunnery complex; as you head toward it out of the quadrangle to the south, look above each doorway in that section for the motif of a Maya cottage, or *na,* looking just like any

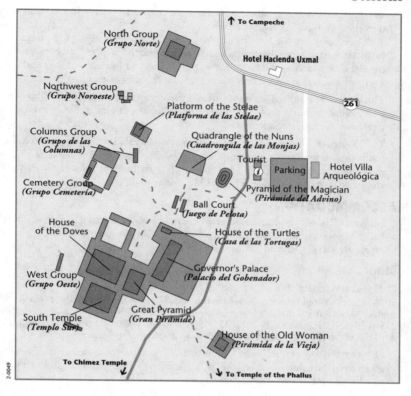

number of cottages you'd see throughout the Yucatán today. All this wonderful decoration has been restored, of course—it didn't look this good when the archaeologists discovered it.

The Ball Court   The unimpressive ball court is conserved to prevent further decay, but keep it in mind to compare with the magnificent restored court at Chichén-Itzá.

The Turtle House   Up on the terrace south of the ball court is a little temple decorated with colonnade motif on the facade and a border of turtles. Though it's small and simple, its harmony is one of the gems of Uxmal.

The Governor's Palace   In size and intricate stonework, this is Uxmal's masterwork—an imposing three-level edifice with a 320-foot-long mosaic facade done in the Puuc style. Puuc means "hilly country," the name given to the hills nearby and thus to the predominant style of pre-Hispanic architecture found here. Uxmal has many examples of Puuc decoration, characterized by elaborate stonework from door tops to the roofline. Fray Cogullado, who named the Nunnery, also gave this building its name. The Governor's Palace may have been just that—the administrative center of the Xiú principality, which included the region around Uxmal. It probably had astrological significance as well. For years, scholars pondered why this building was constructed slightly turned from adjacent buildings. Originally they thought the strange alignment was because of the *sacbe* (ceremonial road) that starts at this building and ends 11 miles distant at the ancient city of Kabah. But recently scholars of archaeoastronomy (a relatively new science that studies the placement of archeological sites in relation to the stars), discovered that the central doorway, which is larger than the others, is in perfect alignment with Venus.

Before you leave the Governor's Palace, note the elaborately stylized headdress patterned in stone over the central doorway. As you stand back from the building on the east side, note how the 103 stone masks of Chaac undulate across the facade like a serpent and end at the corners where there are columns of masks.

The Great Pyramid A massive, partially restored nine-level structure, it has interesting motifs of birds, probably macaws, on its facade, as well as a huge mask. The view from the top is wonderful.

The Dovecote It wasn't built to house doves, but it could well do the job in its lacy roofcomb—a kind of false front on a rooftop. The building is remarkable in that roofcombs weren't a common feature of temples in the Puuc hills, although you'll see one (of a very different style) on El Mirador at Sayil.

ACCOMMODATIONS

Unlike Chichén-Itzá, which has several classes of hotels from which to choose, Uxmal has (with one exception) only one type: comfortable but expensive. Less expensive rooms are also available in nearby Ticul.

MODERATE

✪ Hotel Hacienda Uxmal
Km 80 Carretera Mérida-Uxmal, 97840 Uxmal, Yuc. ☎ & fax **99/49-4754.** For reservations contact Mayaland Resorts, Av. Colón 502, Mérida, Yuc. 97000; ☎ 99/25-2122, or 800/ 235-4079 in the U.S.; fax 99/25-7022. 75 rms (all with bath). A/C (21) or FAN (54). High season $130 single or double. Low season $110 single or double. Free guarded parking.

One of my favorites, this is also the oldest hotel in Uxmal. Located on the highway across from the ruins, it was built as the headquarters for the archaeological staff years ago. Rooms are large and airy, exuding an impression of a well-kept yesteryear, with patterned tile floors, heavy furniture, and well-screened windows. All rooms have ceiling fans, and TVs are being added. Guest rooms surround a handsome central garden courtyard with towering royal palms, a bar, and a pool. Other facilities include a dining room and gift shop. At the restaurant breakfast costs $4 to $6; lunch $7 to $11; dinner, $9 to $15. A guitar trio usually plays on the open patio in the evenings. Checkout time is 1pm, so you can spend the morning at the ruins and take a swim before you hit the road again. It's on the highway opposite the road entrance to the ruins.

Mayaland Resorts, owners of the hotel, offers tour packages that include free car rental for the nights you spend in its hotels. Car rental is free, but there's a daily insurance charge, which for a manual-shift Volkswagen Beetle is $18 per day. They also have Ford Escorts at a higher price. Mayaland also has a transfer service between the hotel and Mérida for about $30 one-way.

✪ Villa Arqueológica
Ruinas Uxmal, Uxmal. Yuc. 97844. ☎ **99/49-6284,** or 800/258-2633 in the U.S. Fax 99/ 49-5961. 40 rms and 3 suites. A/C. High season $72 single; $85 double. Low season $56 single; $70 double. Free guarded parking.

Operated by Club Med, the Villa Arqueológica offers a beautiful two-story layout around a plant-filled patio and a pool. At guests' disposal are a tennis court, a library, and an audiovisual show on the ruins in English, French, and Spanish. Each of the serene rooms has two oversize single beds. French-inspired meals are a la carte only and cost $6–$8 for breakfast and $5.75–$10 for lunch or dinner. It's easy to find—

follow the signs to the Uxmal ruins, then turn left to the hotel just before the parking lot at the Uxmal ruins.

INEXPENSIVE

Rancho Uxmal

Km 70 Carretera Mérida-Uxmal, 97840 Uxmal, Yuc. No local phone. For reservations contact Sr. Macario Cach Cabrera, Calle 26 #156, Ticul, Yuc, 97860; ☎ **997/2-0277** or 99/23-1576. 20 rms (all with bath.) A/C or FAN. $18–$24 single or double; $4 per person campsite. Free guarded parking.

This modest little hotel is an exception to the high-priced places near Uxmal, and it gets better every year. Air-conditioning has been added to 10 of the rooms, all of which have good screens, hot-water showers, and 24-hour electricity. The restaurant is good; a full meal of poc chuc, rice, beans, and tortillas costs about $5, and breakfast is $2.25 to $3. It's a long hike to the ruins from here, but the manager may help you flag down a passing bus or combi or even drive you himself if he has time. A primitive campground out back offers electrical hookups and use of a shower. The hotel is 2¼ miles north of the ruins on Highway 261.

DINING

Besides the hotel restaurants mentioned above and the restaurant at the visitor's center, there are few other dining choices.

Café-Bar Nicte-Ha

In the Hotel Hacienda Uxmal, across the highway from the turnoff to the ruins. ☎ **24-7142.** Soups and salads $2–$4; pizzas and enchiladas $5; main courses $5–$8; fixed-price lunch $9. Daily 1–8pm. MEXICAN.

This small restaurant attached to the Hotel Hacienda Uxmal is visible from the crossroads entrance to the ruins. The food is decent, though the prices tend to be high. If you eat here, take full advantage of the experience and spend a few hours by the pool near the café—use is free to customers. This is a favorite spot for bus tours, so come early.

Las Palapas

Hwy. 261. No phone. Breakfast $3; comida corrida $3.75; soft drinks $1. Daily 9am–6pm (comida corrida served 1–4pm). MEXICAN/YUCATECAN.

Three miles north of the ruins on the road to Mérida you'll find this pleasant restaurant with open-air walls and large thatched palapa roof. The amiable owner, María Cristina Choy, has the most reasonable dining prices around. Individual diners can sometimes become lost in the crowd if a busload of tourists arrives, but otherwise the service is fine and the food quite good. There's also a small gift shop with regional crafts and a few books.

THE PUUC MAYA ROUTE & VILLAGE OF OXKUTZCAB

South and east of Uxmal are several other Maya cities worth exploring. Though smaller in scale than either Uxmal or Chichén-Itzá, each has gems of Maya architecture. The facade of masks on the Palace of Masks at **Kabah,** the enormous palace at **Sayil,** and the fantastic caverns of **Loltún** may be among the high points of your trip. Also along the way are the **Xlapak** and **Labná** ruins, and the pretty village of **Oxkutzcab.**

Note: All these sites are currently undergoing excavation and reconstruction, and some buildings may be roped off when you visit. And for photographers: You'll find afternoon light the best. The sites are open daily from 8am to 5pm. Admission is

$1.75 each for Sayil, Kabah, and Labná, and for Xlapak $1.25, and Loltún $2.75. All except the caves of Loltún are free on Sunday. Use of a video camera at any time costs $4, but if you're visiting Uxmal in the same day, you pay only once for video permission and present your receipt as proof at each ruin. The sites are open daily from 8am to 5pm.

Kabah is 17 miles southeast of Uxmal. From there it's only a few miles to Sayil. Xlapak is almost walking distance (through the jungle) from Sayil, and Labná is just a bit farther east. A short drive beyond Labná brings you to the caves of Loltún. And Oxkutzcab is at the road's intersection with Highway 184, which can be followed west to Ticul or east all the way to Felipe Carillo Puerto.

If you are driving, between Labná and Loltún you'll find a road and a sign pointing north to Tabi. A few feet west of this road is a narrow dry-weather track leading into the seemingly impenetrable jungle. A bit over a mile up this track, the jungle opens to remains of the fabulous old henequen-producing **Hacienda Tabí.** The hewed-rock, two-story main house extends almost the length of a city block, with the living quarters above and storage and space for carriages below. In places it looks ready to collapse. Besides the house, you'll see the ruined chapel, remnants of tall chimneys, and broken machinery. Though not a formal public site, the caretaker will ask you to sign a guestbook and allow you to wander around the hulking ruins—without climbing to the second story.

If you aren't driving, a daily bus from Mérida goes to all these sites, with the exception of Loltún and Tabí. (See "By Bus" under "Getting There & Departing," in Mérida, above, for more details.)

PUUC MAYA SITES

KABAH If you're off to Kabah, head southwest on Highway 261 to Santa Elena ($8^1/2$ miles), then south to Kabah (8 miles). The ancient city of Kabah is on both sides along the highway. Make a right turn into the parking lot.

The most outstanding building at Kabah is the huge **Palace of Masks,** or Codz Poop ("rolled-up mat"), named for a motif in its decoration. You'll notice it first on the right up on a terrace. Its outstanding feature is the Chenes-style facade, completely covered in a repeated pattern of 250 masks of the rain god Chaac, each one with curling remnants of Chaac's elephant trunklike nose. There's nothing like this facade in all of Maya architecture. For years stone-carved parts of this building lay lined up in the weeds like pieces of a puzzle awaiting the master puzzlemaker to put them into place. Now workers are positioning the parts, including the broken roofcomb, in place. Sculptures from this building are in the museums of anthropology in Mérida and Mexico City.

Once you've seen the Palace of Masks, you've seen the best of Kabah. But you should take a look at the other buildings. Just behind and to the left of the Codz Poop is the **Palace Group** (also called the East Group), with a fine Puuc-style colonnaded facade. Originally it had 32 rooms. On the front you see seven doors, two divided by columns, a common feature of Puuc architecture. Recent restoration has added a beautiful L-shaped colonnaded extension to the left front. Further restoration is under way at Kabah, so there may be more to see when you arrive.

Across the highway, a large, conical dirt-and-rubble mound (on your right) was once the **Great Temple,** or Teocalli. Past it is a **great arch,** which was much wider at one time and may have been a monumental gate into the city. A sacbe linked this arch to a point at Uxmal. Compare this corbeled arch to the one at Labná (below), which is in much better shape.

SAYIL   Just about 3 miles south of Kabah is the turnoff (left, which is east) to Sayil, Xlapak, Labná, Loltún, and Oxkutzcab. And 2¹/₂ miles along this road are the ruins of Sayil (which means "place of the ants").

Sayil is famous for **El Palacio,** the tremendous 100-plus-room palace that's a masterpiece of Maya architecture. Impressive for its simplistic grandeur, the building's facade, stretching three terraced levels, is breathtaking. Its rows of columns give it a Minoan appearance. On the second level, notice the upside-down stone figure of the diving god of bees and honey over the doorway; the same motif was used at Tulum several centuries later. From the top of El Palacio there is a great view of the Puuc hills. Sometimes it's difficult to tell which are hills and which are unrestored pyramids, since little temples peep out at unlikely places from the jungle. The large circular basin on the ground below the palace is an artificial catch basin for a chultún (cistern) because this region has no natural cenotes (wells) to catch rainwater.

In the jungle past El Palacio is **El Mirador,** a small temple with an oddly slotted roofcomb. Beyond El Mirador, a crude **stele** has a phallic idol carved on it in greatly exaggerated proportions.

XLAPAK   Xlapak (pronounced "shla-pahk") is a small site with one building; it's 3¹/₂ miles down the road from Sayil. The **Palace at Xlapak** bears the masks of the rain god Chaac. It's open daily from 8am to 5pm, and the admission is $2.25 (free on Sunday); use of your video camera costs an additional $8.

LABNÁ   Labná, which dates to between A.D. 600 and 900, is 18 miles from Uxmal and only 1³/₄ miles past Xlapak. Like other archaeological sites in the Yucatán, it's also undergoing significant restoration and conservation. Descriptive placards fronting the main buildings are in Spanish, English, and German.

The first thing you see on the left as you enter is **El Palacio,** a magnificent Puucstyle building much like the one at Sayil but in poorer condition. There is an enormous mask of Chaac over a doorway with big banded eyes, a huge snout nose, and jagged teeth around a small mouth that seems on the verge of speaking. Jutting out on one corner is a highly stylized serpent's mouth out of which pops a human head with a completely calm expression. From the front you can gaze out to the enormous grassy interior grounds flanked by vestiges of unrestored buildings and jungle.

From El Palacio you can walk across the interior grounds on a newly reconstructed sacbe leading to Labná's **corbeled arch,** famed for its ornamental beauty and for its representation of what many such arches must have looked like at other sites. This one has been extensively restored, although only remnants of the roofcomb can be seen, and it was part of a more elaborate structure which is completely gone. Chaac's face is on the corners of one facade, and stylized Maya huts are fashioned in stone above the doorways.

You pass through the arch to **El Mirador,** or **El Castillo,** as the rubble-formed, pyramid-shaped structure is called. Towering on the top is a singular room crowned with a roofcomb etched against the sky.

There's a refreshment/gift stand with restrooms at the entrance.

LOLTÚN   The caverns of Loltún are 18¹/₂ miles past Labná on the way to Oxkutzcab, on the left side of the road. The fascinating caves, home of ancient Maya, were also used as a refuge and fortress during the War of the Castes (1847–1901). Inside, examine statuary, wall carvings and paintings, chultúns (cisterns), and other signs of Maya habitation, but the grandeur and beauty of the caverns alone are impressive. In front of the entrance is an enormous stone phallus. The cult of the phallic symbol originated south of Veracruz and appeared in the Yucatán between A.D. 200 and 500.

The entrance fee is $2 on Sunday; 1¹/₂-hour tours in Spanish are given daily at 9:30 and 11am and 12:30, 2, and 3pm and are included in the price. Before going on a tour, confirm these times at the information desk at Uxmal.

To return to Mérida from Loltún, drive the 4¹/₂ miles to Oxkutzcab and from there go northwest on Highway 184. It's 12 miles to Ticul, and (turning north onto Highway 261 at Muna) 65 miles to Mérida.

OXKUTZCAB

Oxkutzcab (pronounced "ohsh-kootz-*kahb*"), seven miles from Loltún, is the heartland of the Yucatán's fruit-growing region, particularly oranges. The tidy village of 21,000, centered around a beautiful 16th-century church and the market, is worth a stop if for no other reason than to eat at Su Cabaña Suiza (see below) before heading back to Mérida, Uxmal, or Ticul.

During the last week in October and first week in November is the **Orange Festival,** when the village goes nuts with a carnival and orange displays in and around the central plaza.

Dining

Su Cabaña Suiza
Calle 54 no. 101. ☎ **997/5-0457.** Main dishes $3; soft drinks or orange juice 75¢. Daily 7:30am–6:30pm. CHARCOAL-GRILLED MEAT/MEXICAN.

It's worth a trip from Loltún, Ticul, or Uxmal just to taste the delicious charcoal-grilled meat at this unpretentious eatery dripping with colorful plants. Park in the gravel courtyard, then take a seat at one of the metal tables either under the palapa roof or outdoors where caged birds sing. Señora María Antónia Puerto de Pacho runs the spotless place with an iron hand, and family members provide swift, friendly service. The primary menu items include filling portions of charcoal-grilled beef, pork, or chicken served with salad, rice, tortillas, and a bowl of delicious bean soup. But you can also find a few Yucatecan specialties, such as costillos entomatados, escabeche, queso relleno, and pollo pibil. The restaurant is between Calles 49 and 51 in a quiet neighborhood three blocks south of the main square.

EN ROUTE TO CAMPECHE
From Oxkutzcab, head back 27 miles to Sayil, then drive south on Highway 261 to Campeche (78 miles). Along the way are several ruins and caves worth visiting.

XTACUMBILXUNA CAVES   Highway 261 heads south for several miles, passing through a lofty arch marking the boundary between the states of Yucatán and Campeche. Continue on through Bolonchén de Rejón (Bolonchén means "nine wells").

About 1³/₄ miles south of Bolonchén a sign points west to the Grutas de Xtacumbilxuna, though the sign spells it XTACUMBINXUNAN. Another sign reads: IT'S WORTH IT TO MAKE A TRIP FROM NEW YORK TO BOLONCHÉN JUST TO SEE XTACUMBILXUNA CAVES (John Stephens—explorer). The caves are open whenever the guide is around, which is most of the time. Follow him down for the 30- or 45-minute tour in Spanish, after which a $1 to $3 tip is customary.

Legend has it that a Maya girl escaped an unhappy love affair by hiding in these vast limestone caverns, which wouldn't be hard to do, as you'll see. Unlike the fascinating caves at Loltún, which are filled with traces of Maya occupation, these have only the standard bestiary of limestone shapes: a dog, an eagle, a penguin, a Madonna and child, a snake, and so on—figments of the guide's imagination.

CHENES RUINS On your route south, you can also take a detour to see several unexcavated, unspoiled ruined cities in the Chenes style. You have to be adventurous for these; pack some food and water. When you get to Hopelchén, take the turn-off for Dzibalchén. When you get back to Dzibalchén (25 1/2 miles from Hopelchén), ask for directions to Hochob, San Pedro, Dzehkabtún, El Tabasqueño, and Dzibilnocac.

EDZNÁ From Hopelchén, Highway 261 heads west, and after 26 miles you'll find yourself at the turnoff for the ruined city of Edzná, 12 miles farther along to the south.

Founded probably between 600 and 300 B.C. as a small agricultural settlement, it developed into a major ceremonial center during the next 1,500 years. Archaeologists estimate that to build and maintain such a complex center must have required a population in the tens of thousands. Once a network of Maya canals crisscrossed this entire area, making intensive cultivation possible.

The **Great Acropolis** is a unique five-level pyramid with a temple complete with roofcomb on top. Edzná means "House of Wry Faces," which undoubtedly there were at one time. Though the buildings at Edzná were mostly in the heavily baroque Chenes, or "well country" style, no vestige of these distinctive decorative facades remains at Edzná. Several other buildings surround an open central yard. Farther back, new excavations have revealed the **Temple of the Stone Mask,** a structure with several fine stucco masks similar to those of Kohunlich in the Río Bec region near Chetumal. The site takes only 30 minutes or less to see and is perhaps not worth the price of entry, especially if you've seen many other sites in the Yucatán. (*Note:* The afternoon light is better for photographing the temple.)

It's open daily from 8am to 5pm. Admission costs $2.50, plus $4 to use your video camera.

Back on Highway 261, it's 12 miles to the intersection with Highway 180, then another 26 miles to the very center of Campeche.

4 Campeche

157 miles SW of Mérida, 235 miles NE of Villahermosa

Campeche, capital of the state bearing the same name, is a pleasant, beautifully kept coastal city (pop. 172,000) with a leisurely pace. You'll be able to enjoy this charming city without the crowds because many tourists bypass Campeche on their way to Mérida in favor of the road via Kabah and Uxmal.

Founded by Francisco de Córdoba in 1517 and claimed for the Spanish Crown by the soldier Francisco de Montejo the Elder in 1531, Campeche was later abandoned and refounded by Montejo the Younger in 1540. To protect it against pirates who pillaged the gulf coastal towns, the townspeople built a wall around the city in the late 1600s. Remnants of this wall, called *baluartes* (bulwarks), are among the city's proudest links with the past.

ESSENTIALS
GETTING THERE & DEPARTING

By Plane **Aeroméxico** (at the airport ☎ 6-6656) flies once daily to and from Mexico City.

By Bus The **Camioneros de Campeche** line (☎ 6-2332) runs second-class buses to Mérida every half hour for the two- to three-hour trip. There are direct buses to Mérida at 7am and 1:30 and 5:30pm, daily buses to Uxmal at 7 and 11am and 5pm, and buses to Edzná at 8am and 2:30pm (this bus drops you off and picks you up 1 km from the ruins). These tickets are sold on the Calle Chile side of the bus station at the Camioneros de Campeche ticket booth. **ADO** (☎ **6-0002**), in the front of the station, offers a first-class de paso bus to Palenque at 11pm and buses to Mérida every hour or less from 5:30am to midnight. **Caribe Express** (☎ **1-3972**) has direct deluxe service to and from Mérida and Cancún. Their office and bus yard is on the north side of the Centro Comercial Ah Kin Pech, Local 304.

By Car Highway 180 goes south from Mérida, passing near the basket-making village of Halacho and near Becal, known for Panama-hat weavers. At Tenabo, take the shortcut (right) to Campeche rather than going farther to the crossroads near Chencoyí. The longer way from Mérida is along Highway 261 past Uxmal. From Uxmal, Highway 261 passes near some interesting ruins and the Xtacumbilxuna caves (see "En Route to Campeche" in previous section).

When driving the other direction, toward Celestún and Mérida, use the Vía Corta (short route) by going north on Avenida Ruíz Cortínez, bearing left to follow the water (this becomes Avenida Pedro Sainz de Baranda, but there's no sign). Follow the road as it turns inland to Highway 180, where you turn left (there's a gas station at the intersection). The route takes you through Becal and Halacho. Stores in both villages close between 2 and 4pm.

If you're leaving Campeche for Edzná and Uxmal, go north on either Cortínez or Gobernadores and turn right on Madero, which becomes Highway 281. To Villahermosa, take Cortínez south; it becomes Highway 180.

ORIENTATION

Arriving The **airport** is several miles northeast of the town center, and you'll have to take a taxi ($5) into town. The **ADO bus station,** on Avenida Gobernadores, is nine long blocks from the Plaza Principal. Turn left out the front door and walk one block. Turn right (Calle 49) and go straight for five blocks to Calle 8. Turn left here, and the Plaza Principal is three blocks ahead. Taxis cost around $5 to the plaza.

Information The **State of Campeche Office of Tourism** (☎ **981/6-6767** or fax **6-6068**) is in the Baluarte Santa Rosa on the south side of town on Circuito Baluartes, between Calles 12 and 14. It's open Monday through Friday from 9am to 9pm, Saturday and Sunday from 9am to 1pm.

City Layout Most of your time in Campeche will be spent within the confines of the old city walls. The administrative center of town is the modernistic **Plaza Moch-Couoh** on Avenida 16 de Septiembre near the waterfront. Next door to the plaza rises the modern office tower called the Edificio Poderes or Palacio de Gobierno, headquarters for the state of Campeche. Beside it is the futuristic Cámara de Diputados or Casa de Congreso (state legislature chamber), which looks like an enormous square clam. Just behind it, the **Parque Principal** (central park) on Calle 8 will most likely be your reference point for touring.

Campeche's systematic street-numbering plan can be both clear-cut and confusing. Streets in the primary grid of downtown Campeche are all called "Calle" regardless of which way they run—that's the confusing part. The easy part is that those running roughly north to south have even numbers, and those running east to west have odd numbers. In addition, the streets are numbered so that numbers ascend toward the south and west. After walking around for 5 minutes you'll have the system down pat.

Getting Around Most of the recommended sights, restaurants, and hotels are within walking distance of the Parque Principal. Campeche isn't easy to negotiate by bus, so I recommend taxis for the more distant areas.

Campeche

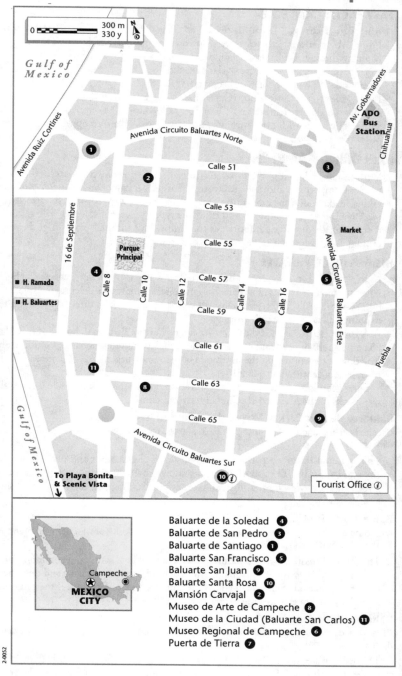

Gulf of Mexico

Avenida Ruiz Cortines

Avenida Circuito Baluartes Norte

Calle 51

Calle 53

Calle 55

16 de Septiembre

Parque Principal

Calle 8

Calle 10

Calle 12

Calle 57

Calle 14

Calle 16

Calle 59

Calle 61

Calle 63

Calle 65

Avenida Circuito Baluartes Sur

To Playa Bonita & Scenic Vista

Av. Gobernadores

ADO Bus Station

Chihuahua

Market

Avenida Circuito Baluartes Este

Puebla

H. Ramada

H. Baluartes

Gulf of Mexico

Tourist Office ⓘ

Campeche

MEXICO CITY

Baluarte de la Soledad ④
Baluarte de San Pedro ③
Baluarte de Santiago ①
Baluarte San Francisco ⑤
Baluarte San Juan ⑨
Baluarte Santa Rosa ⑩
Mansión Carvajal ②
Museo de Arte de Campeche ⑧
Museo de la Ciudad (Baluarte San Carlos) ⑪
Museo Regional de Campeche ⑥
Puerta de Tierra ⑦

2-0052

213

FAST FACTS: CAMPECHE

American Express Local offices are at Calle 59 no. 4–5 (☎ **1-1010**), in the Edificio Belmar, a half block toward town from the Ramada Hotel. They're open Monday through Friday from 9am to 2pm and 5 to 7pm and Saturday from 9am to 1:30pm. They do not cash traveler's checks.

Area Code The telephone area code is 981.

Post Office The post office (Correo) is in the Edificio Federal at the corner of Avenida 16 de Septiembre and Calle 53 (☎ **981/6-2134**), near the Baluarte de Santiago; it's open Monday through Saturday from 7:30am to 8pm. The telegraph office is here as well.

EXPLORING CAMPECHE

With its city walls, clean brick-paved streets, friendly people, easy pace, and orderly traffic, Campeche is a lovely city worthy of at least a day in your itinerary. Besides taking in the museums built into the city walls, you'll want to stroll the streets (especially Calles 55, 57, and 59) and enjoy the typical Mexican colonial-style architecture. Look through large doorways to glimpse the colonial past—high-beamed ceilings, Moorish stone arches, and interior courtyards.

INSIDE THE CITY WALLS

As the busiest port in the region during the 1600s and 1700s, Campeche was a choice target for pirates. The Campechanos began building impressive defenses in 1668, and by 1704, the walls, gates, and bulwarks were in place. Today three of the seven remaining baluartes are worth visiting.

A good place to begin is the pretty zócalo, or **Parque Principal,** bounded by Calles 55 and 57 running east and west and Calles 8 and 10 running north and south. Construction of the church on the north side of the square began in 1650 and was finally completed a century and a half later.

For a good introduction to the city, turn south from the park on Calle 8 and walk five blocks to the Museo de la Ciudad (city museum).

Baluarte de San Carlos/Museo de la Ciudad

Circuito Baluartes and Avenida Justo Sierra. No phone. Free admission. Tues–Sat 8am–8pm; Sun 8am–2pm.

This museum features a permanent exhibition of photographs and plans about the city and its history. The model of the city shows how it looked in its glory days and gives a good overview for touring within the city walls. There are several excellent ship models as well.

Baluarte de Santiago

Av. 16 de Septiembre and Calle 49. No phone. Free admission. Tues–Fri 8am–3pm and 6–8:30pm, Sat–Sun 9am–1pm.

The **Jardín Botánico Xmuch'haltun** grows in a jumble of exotic and common plants within the stone walls of this baluarte. More than 250 species of plants and trees share what seems like a terribly small courtyard. Some are identified and, if the projector is working, a film explains the garden.

Baluarte de la Soledad

Calle 57 and Calle 8, opposite the Plaza Principal. No phone. Free admission. Tues–Sat 8am–8pm, Sun 8am–1pm.

This bastion houses the Sala de Estelas, or **Chamber of Stelae,** a display of Maya votive stones brought from various sites in this ruin-rich state. Many are badly worn, but the excellent line drawings beside the stones allow you to admire their former beauty. Three additional rooms also have interesting artifacts; each room is dedicated to a different Maya scholar.

Museo de Arte de Campeche

Calles 10 and 63. ☎ 6-1424. Admission 50¢. Tues–Fri 9am–1pm and 4–8pm.

To glimpse colonial glitter and a touch of modern art, visit this museum, which is actually the restored Templo de San José (1640). The museum displays traveling exhibits of Mexican art. The temple also holds the library for the university next door, and students' paintings and photographs are displayed in the gallery space. Peer around corners and behind shelves at the walls. Don't miss the large mural of the Virgin of Guadalupe. The temple is one block inland from the Museo de la Ciudad (see above).

Museo Regional de Campeche

Calle 59 no. 36, between Calles 14 and 16. ☎ **6-9111.** Admission $3. Tues–Sat 8am–8pm, Sun 8am–1pm.

Just 2¹/₂ blocks farther inland from the Museo de Arte de Campeche (see above) is the city's best museum. Housed in the former mansion of the Teniente de Rey (royal governor), it features original Maya artifacts, pictures, drawings, and models of Campeche's history. The exhibit on the skull-flattening of babies practiced by the Maya includes actual deformed skulls. Another highlight is the Late Classic (A.D. 600–900) Maya stele carved in a metamorphic rock that does not exist in the Yucatán but was brought from a quarry hundreds of miles away. Many clay figures show scarified faces and tools, such as manta ray bones, obsidian, and jade, used for cutting the face.

Other unusual pre-Hispanic artifacts include clay figures with movable arms and legs, as well as jade masks and jewelry from the tomb of Calakmul—a site in southern Campeche that is undergoing study and excavation. Among the other Calakmul artifacts found in Structure VII are the remains of a human between 30 and 40 years old; the remains show the burial custom of partially burning the body, then wrapping it in a woven straw mat and cloth. Beans, copal, and feathers—all items deemed necessary to take the person through the underworld after death—were discovered in pottery vessels.

A model of the archaeological site at Becán shows Maya society in daily life. Other displays demonstrate Maya architecture; techniques of water conservation; and aspects of their religion, commerce, art, and considerable scientific knowledge. There's a bookstore on the left as you enter.

Puerta de Tierra (Land Gate)

Calle 59 at Circuito Baluartes/Av. Gobernadores. No phone. Museum, free; show, $3. Tues–Sun 8am–2pm and 4–8pm.

At the Land Gate there's a small museum displaying portraits of pirates and the city founders. The 1732 French 5-ton cannon in the entryway was found in 1990. On Tuesday and Friday at 8pm there's a light-and-sound show.

Mansión Carvajal

Calle 10 no. 584. No phone. Free admission. Mon–Sat 9am–2pm and 4–8pm.

Restoration was completed in 1992 on this early 20th-century mansion, originally the home of the Carvajal family, owners of a henequen plantation. In its latest transformation, the blue-and-white Moorish home contains government agencies. Join the crowd purposefully striding along the gleaming black-and-white tile and up the curving marble staircase. No signs mark the entrance to the building—look for fresh blue-and-white paint inside the entrance on the west side of Calle 10 between Calles 53 and 51.

MORE ATTRACTIONS

If you're looking for a **beach,** the Playa Bonita is 4 miles south of town; it's often dirty.

A Scenic Vista

For a dramatic view of the city and gulf, go south from the tourism office on Avenida Ruíz Cortínez and turn left on Ruta Escénica, winding up to the **Fuerte San Miguel.** Built in 1771, this fort was the most important of the city's defenses. Santa Anna later used it when he attacked the city in 1842. It is currently being used as a museum with a recent exhibit of pirate-related items.

Shopping

Artesanías DIF
Calle 55 #25 (between Calles 12 and 14). ☎ **6-9088.**

This newly opened store in a restored mansion features quality textiles, clothing, and locally made furniture. DIF is the family-assistance arm of the government, and proceeds support government programs. It's open Monday through Friday from 9am to 1:30pm and 5 to 8pm, Saturday from 9am to 1:30pm.

WHERE TO STAY

Campeche's tourist trade is small and there are relatively few good places to stay. If you're driving, there are a few motels on the waterfront road, but you don't get a lot for the money.

DOUBLES FOR LESS THAN $35

Hotel América
Calle 10 no. 252, 24000 Campeche, Camp. ☎ **981/6-4588.** 52 rms (all with bath). FAN TV. $14 single; $19 double. Free guarded parking three blocks away.

This centrally located hotel is a choice only if La Posada del Angel is full. It is old and worn, semi-clean, and gets no high marks for maintenance. The three stories of rooms (no elevator) have one, two, or three double beds and come with tile floors. Corner rooms are quieter than those with windows on the street. To find the hotel from the Parque Principal, walk south on Calle 10 for 2½ blocks; it's on the right between Calles 61 and 63.

La Posada del Angel
Calle 10 no. 307, 24000 Campeche, Camp. ☎ **981/6-7718.** 14 rms (all with bath). FAN A/C. $12–$14 single; $14–$16 double.

Rooms, with windows opening onto the dim narrow hall, are a little dark in this three-story hotel, but they are clean and freshly painted, and each comes with either two double beds or a single and a double. Carpeted halls in the upper two stories cut down on noise. To find the hotel from the Parque Principal, walk north on Calle 10 (with the cathedral on your left); the hotel is opposite the cathedral's right wall, a half block north of the Plaza Principal.

WHERE TO EAT

For regional food, try *colados,* which are delicious regional tamales, *tacos de salchicha* (an unusual pastry), *cazón de Campeche* (a tasty shark stew), and *pan de cazón* (another shark dish for those with more adventurous palates).

MEALS FOR LESS THAN $5

Panificadora Nueva España

Calle 10 no. 256. ☎ **6-2887.** All items 50¢–$2. Mon–Sat 6:30am–9:30pm. BAKERY.

A block and a half south of the Parque Principal is Campeche's best downtown bakery. Besides the usual assorted breads and pastries, you can stock up on food for the road—mayonnaise, catsup, cheese, butter, yogurt, and fruit drinks. This is the place to try the unusual *tacos de salchicha*, also called *feite*. Fresh breads come out of the oven at 5pm. A second location is on Calle 12 between Calles 57 and 59.

La Parroquia

Calle 55 no. 9. ☎ **6-8086.** Breakfast $1–$3; main courses $2–$5; comida corrida $3. Daily 24 hours (comida corrida served 1–4pm). MEXICAN.

La Parroquia, a popular local hangout, has friendly waiters and offers excellent inexpensive fare. Here, you can enjoy great breakfasts and colados, the delicious regional tamal. Selections on the comida corrida might include pot roast, meatballs, pork or fish, rice or squash, beans, tortillas, and fresh-fruit-flavored water.

La Perla

Calle 10 no. 345. ☎ **6-4092.** Breakfast $1:75; main courses $2–$4; sodas 75¢. Mon–Sat 7am–10pm. MEXICAN.

A popular student lounge (the Instituto Campechano is down the street near the Templo San José), La Perla has a youthful clientele with prices to match student budgets. The *arroz con camarones*, a filling meal of rice and shrimp, is a great bargain, and the *licuados* made with purified water and fresh pineapple or cantaloupe are refreshing. The coffee is instant, not brewed! At times, La Perla is noisy, but sometimes just a few customers are scattered about, seriously reading textbooks. To find the lounge from the Art Museum (at Calle 63 and Calle 10), walk one block north.

MEALS FOR LESS THAN $10

Restaurant Miramar

Calle 8 no. 293 (corner of Calle 61). ☎ **6-2883.** Main courses $3.25–$6; sandwiches $2–$3. Mon–Fri 8am–midnight, Sat 8am–1am, Sun 11am–7pm. SEAFOOD/MEXICAN.

One of the best choices in Campeche, this restaurant has airy and pleasant decor with light-colored stone arches, dark wood, and ironwork. The menu offers typical Campeche seafood dishes, including lightly fried breaded shrimp (ask for *camarones empanizados*); *arroz con mariscos* (shellfish and rice); and *pargo poc-chuc*. For dessert there's *queso napolitana*, a very rich, thick flan. Ask about the changing daily specials. To find the restaurant from the Plaza Principal, walk two blocks south on Calle 8; it's near the corner of Calle 61.

✪ La Pigua

Av. Miguel Alemán no. 197A. ☎ **1-3365.** Main courses $4–$6. Daily noon–6pm. SEAFOOD/MEXICAN.

You can easily pass the entire afternoon in this junglelike dining room with glass walls between the diners and the trees. The most filling meal on the menu (in a sharkskin folder) is the plateful of rice with octopus and shrimp; the most unusual is chiles rellenos stuffed with shark. The *cangrejo* (stone crab) is a house specialty. To reach La Pigua from the Plaza Principal, walk north on Calle 8 for three blocks. Cross the Avenida Circuito by the botanical garden, where Calle 8 becomes Miguel Alemán. The restaurant is 1¹/₂ blocks north, on the east side of the street.

5 The Ruins of Chichén-Itzá & Village of Pisté

112 miles SW of Cancún, 75 miles SE of Mérida

The fabled pyramids and temples of Chichén-Itzá are the Yucatán's best-known ancient monuments. You must go, since you can't say you've *really* seen the Yucatán until you've gazed at the towering El Castillo, seen the sun from the Maya observatory called El Caracol, or shivered on the brink of the gaping cenote that may have served as the sacrificial well.

This Maya city was established by Itzáes perhaps sometime during the 9th century A.D. Linda Schele and David Friedel, in *A Forest of Kings* (Morrow, 1990), have cast doubt on the legend that Kukulkán (called Quetzalcoatl by the Toltecs—a name also associated with a legendary god) came here from the Toltec capital of Tula, and, along with Putún Maya coastal traders, built a magnificent metropolis that combined the Maya Puuc style with Toltec motifs (the feathered serpent, warriors, eagles, and jaguars). Not so, say Schele and Friedel. Readings of Chichén's bas-reliefs and hieroglyphs fail to support that legend and instead shows that Chichén-Itzá was a continuous Maya site which was influenced by association with the Toltecs but not by an invasion. Kukulkán's role in the Yucatán is once again in question.

Though it's possible to make a round trip from Mérida to Chichén-Itzá in one day, it will be a long, tiring, and very rushed day. Try to spend at least one night at Chichén-Itzá (you'll actually stay in the nearby village of Pisté) or two if you can, and take your time seeing the ruins in the cool of the morning or the afternoon after 3pm; take a siesta during the midday heat. The next morning, get to the ruins early; when the heat of the day approaches, catch a bus to your next destination. This may involve paying the admission fee more than once (unless you're there on a Sunday, when it's free), but the experience is worth it. Day-trip groups generally arrive when it's beginning to get hot, rushing through this marvelous ancient city in order to catch another bus or have lunch.

ESSENTIALS

GETTING THERE & DEPARTING

By Plane   Day-trips on charter flights from Cancún and Cozumel can be arranged by travel agents in the United States or in Cancún.

By Bus   From Mérida, first-class **ADO buses** leave at 7:30am and 3:30pm. If you go round-trip in a day (a 2^1/$_2$-hour trip one way), take the 8:45am bus and reserve a seat on the return bus. There are direct buses to Cancún at 11:15am and 6pm and to Mérida at 3pm. De paso buses to Mérida leave hourly day and night, as do those to Valladolid and Cancún.

By Car   Chichén-Itzá is on the main Highway 180 between Mérida and Cancún.

ORIENTATION

Arriving   You'll arrive in the village of Pisté, at the bus station next to the Pirámide Inn. From Pisté there's a sidewalk to the archaeological zone, which is a mile or so east of the bus station.

City Layout   The small town of **Pisté,** where most hotels and restaurants are located, is about a mile and a half from the ruins of Chichén-Itzá. Public buses from Mérida, Cancún, Valladolid, and elsewhere discharge passengers here. A few hotels are at the edge of the ruins, and one, the **Hotel Dolores Alba** (see

"Accommodations," below), is out of town about 1½ miles from the ruins on the road to Valladolid.

Area Code   The telephone area code is 985.

EXPLORING THE RUINS

The site occupies four square miles, and it takes a strenuous full day (from 8am to noon and 2 to 5pm) to see all the ruins, which are open daily from 8am to 5pm. Service areas are open from 8am to 10pm. Admission is $3.50, free for children under 12 and free for all on Sunday and holidays. A permit to use your own video camera costs an additional $4. Parking costs $1. *You can use your ticket to reenter on the same day, but you'll have to pay again for another day.*

The huge visitor center, at the main entrance where you pay the admission charge, is beside the parking lot and consists of a museum, an auditorium, a restaurant, a bookstore, and rest rooms. You can see the site on your own or with a licensed guide who speaks either English or Spanish. These guides are usually waiting at the entrance and charge around $30 for one to six people. Although the guides frown on it, there's nothing wrong with your approaching a group of people who speak the same language and asking if they would like to share a guide with you. The guide, of course, would like to get $30 from you alone and $30 each from other individuals who don't know one another and still form a group. Don't believe all the history they spout— some of it is just plain out-of-date, but the architectural details they point out are enlightening.

Chichén-Itzá's light-and-sound show was completely revamped in 1993, and is well worth seeing. The Spanish version is shown nightly at 7pm and costs $2.50; the English version is at 9pm and costs $3. The show may be offered in French and German as well. Ask at your hotel.

There are actually two parts of Chichén-Itzá (which dates from around A.D. 600 to 900). There's the northern (new) zone, which shows distinct Toltec influence, and the southern (old) zone, which is mostly Puuc architecture.

El Castillo   As you enter from the tourist center, the beautiful 75-foot El Castillo pyramid will be straight ahead across a large open area. It was built with the Maya calendar in mind. There are 364 stairs plus a platform to equal 365 (days of the year), 52 panels on each side (which represent the 52-year cycle of the Maya calendar), and nine terraces on each side of the stairways (for a total of 18 terraces, which represents the 18-month Maya solar calendar). If this isn't proof enough of the mathematical precision of this temple, come for the spring or fall equinox (March 21 or September 21 between 3 and 5pm). On those days, the seven stairs of the northern stairway and the serpent-head carving at the base are touched with sunlight and become a "serpent" formed by the play of light and shadow. It appears to descend into the earth as the sun hits each stair from the top, ending with the serpent head. To the Maya this was a fertility symbol: The golden sun had entered the earth, meaning it was time to plant the corn.

El Castillo, also called the Pyramid of Kukulkán, was built over an earlier structure. A narrow stairway entered at the western edge of the north staircase leads into the structure, where there is a sacrificial altar-throne—a red jaguar encrusted with jade. The stairway is open at 11am and 3pm and is claustrophobic, usually crowded, humid, and uncomfortable. A visit early in the day is best. No photos of the figure are allowed.

Main Ball Court (Juego de Pelota)   Northwest of El Castillo is Chichén's main ball court, the largest and best preserved anywhere, and only one of nine ball courts built in this city. Carved on both walls of the ball court are scenes showing Maya figures dressed as ball players decked out in heavy protective padding. The carved scene also shows a headless player kneeling with blood shooting from the neck; the player is looked upon by another player holding the head.

Players on two teams tried to knock a hard rubber ball through one or the other of the two stone rings placed high on either wall, using only their elbows, knees, and hips (no hands). According to legend, the losing players paid for defeat with their lives. However, some experts say the victors were the only appropriate sacrifices for the gods. Either way, the game must have been exciting, heightened by the marvelous acoustics of the ball court.

The North Temple   Temples are at both ends of the ball court. The North Temple has sculptured pillars and more sculptures inside, as well as badly ruined murals. The acoustics of the ball court are so good that from the North Temple a person speaking can be heard clearly at the opposite end about 450 feet away.

Temple of Jaguars   Near the southeastern corner of the main ball court is a small temple with serpent columns and carved panels showing warriors and jaguars. Up the flight of steps and inside the temple, a mural was found that chronicles a battle in a Maya village.

Temple of the Skulls (Tzompantli)   To the right of the ball court is the Temple of the Skulls with rows of skulls carved into the stone platform. When a sacrificial victim's head was cut off, it was stuck on a pole and displayed in a tidy row with others. As a symbol of the building's purpose, the architects provided these rows of skulls. Also carved into the stone are pictures of eagles tearing hearts from human victims. The word *Tzompantli* is not Maya but came from central Mexico. Reconstruction using scattered fragments may add a level to this platform and change the look of this structure by the time you visit.

Platform of the Eagles   Next to the Tzompantli, this small platform has reliefs showing eagles and jaguars clutching human hearts in their talons and claws, as well as a head coming out of the mouth of a serpent.

Platform of Venus   East of the Tzompantli and north of El Castillo near the road to the Sacred Cenote is the Platform of Venus. In Maya-Toltec lore, Venus was represented by a feathered monster or a feathered serpent with a human head in its mouth. It's also called the tomb of Chaac-Mool because a Chaac-Mool figure was discovered "buried" within the structure.

Sacred Cenote   Follow the dirt road (actually an ancient sacbe) that heads north from the Platform of Venus, and after five minutes you'll come to the great natural well that may have given Chichén-Itzá (the Well of the Itzáes) its name. This well was used for ceremonial purposes, not for drinking water, and according to legend,

Impressions

The architects of pre-Columbian America were more fortunate than most of those of Europe. Their masterpieces were never condemned to invisibility, but stood magnificently isolated, displaying their three dimensions to all beholders. European cathedrals were built within the walls of cities; the temples of the aboriginal American seem, in most cases, to have stood outside.

—Aldous Huxley, *Beyond the Mexique Bay*, 1934

Chichén-Itzá Archeological Site

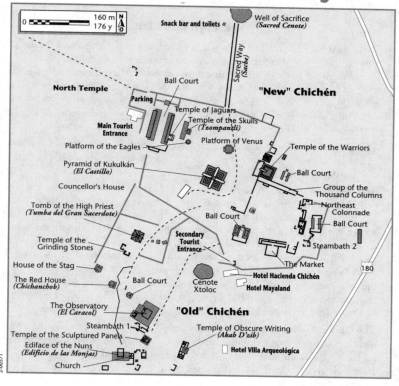

0 160 m / 176 y N

Snack bar and toilets

Well of Sacrifice
(*Sacred Cenote*)

Sacred Way (*Sacbe*)

North Temple

Ball Court

"New" Chichén

Parking

Temple of Jaguars

Main Tourist Entrance

Temple of the Skulls
(*Tzompantli*)

Platform of the Eagles

Platform of Venus

Temple of the Warriors

Pyramid of Kukulkán
(*El Castillo*)

Ball Court

Councellor's House

Group of the
Thousand Columns

Tomb of the High Priest
(*Tumba del Gran Sacerdote*)

Ball Court

Northeast
Colonnade

Ball Court

Temple of the
Grinding Stones

Secondary
Tourist
Entrance

Steambath 2

House of the Stag

The Market

180

The Red House
(*Chichanchob*)

Ball Court

Cenote
Xtoloc

Hotel Hacienda Chichén

Hotel Mayaland

The Observatory
(*El Caracol*)

"Old" Chichén

Steambath 1

Temple of the Sculptured Panels

Temple of Obscure Writing
(*Akab D'zib*)

Ediface of the Nuns
(*Edificio de las Monjas*)

Hotel Villa Arqueológica

Church

2-00571

sacrificial victims were drowned in this pool to honor the rain god Chaac. Anatomical research done early this century by Ernest A. Hooten showed that bones of both children and adults were found in the well. Judging from Hooten's evidence, they may have been outcasts, diseased, or feeble-minded.

Edward Thompson, American consul in Mérida and a Harvard professor, bought the ruins of Chichén early this century, explored the cenote with dredges and divers, and exposed a fortune in gold and jade. Most of the riches wound up in Harvard's Peabody Museum of Archeology and Ethnology. Later excavations in the 1960s brought up more treasure, and studies of the recovered objects show offerings from throughout the Yucatán and even farther away.

Temple of the Warriors (Templo de los Guerreros)   Due east of El Castillo is one of the most impressive structures at Chichén—the Temple of the Warriors—named for the carvings of warriors marching along its walls. It's also called the **Group of the Thousand Columns** for the many columns flanking it. During the recent restoration, hundreds more of the columns were rescued from the rubble and put in place, setting off the temple more magnificently than ever. Climb up the steep stairs at the front to reach a figure of Chaac-Mool and several impressive columns carved in relief to look like enormous feathered serpents. South of the temple was a square building that archaeologists called the Market (mercado). Its central court is surrounded by a colonnade. Beyond the temple and the market in the jungle are mounds of rubble, parts of which are being reconstructed.

The Maya Calendar

To understand Chichén-Itzá fully, you need to know something about the unique way in which the Maya kept time on several simultaneous calendars.

Although not more accurate than our own calendar, the intricate Maya calendar systems begin, according to many scholars, in 3114 B.C.—before Maya culture existed. From that date, the Maya could measure time—and their life cycle—to a point 90 million years in the future! They conceived of world history as a series of cycles moving within cycles.

The Solar Year   The Maya solar year measured 365.24 days. Within that solar year there were 18 "months" of 20 days each, for a total of 360 days, plus a special five-day period.

The Ceremonial Year   A ceremonial calendar, completely different from the solar calendar, ran its "annual" cycle at the same time, but this was not a crude system like the Gregorian calendar, which has saints' days, some fixed feast days, and some movable feasts. It was so intricate that the ordinary Maya depended on the priests to keep track of it. Complex and ingenious, the ceremonial calendar system consisted of 13 "months" of 20 days; but within that cycle of 260 days was another of 20 "weeks" of 13 days. The Maya ceremonial calendar interlaced exactly with the solar calendar. Each date of the solar calendar had a name, and each date of the ceremonial calendar also had a name; therefore, every day in Maya history has two names, which were always quoted together.

The Double Cycle   After 52 solar years and 73 ceremonial "years," during which each day had its unique, unduplicated double name, these calendars ended their respective cycles simultaneously on the very same day, and a brand-new, identical double cycle began. Thus, in the longer scheme of things, a day would be identified by the name of the 52-year cycle, the name of the solar day, and the name of the ceremonial day.

Mystic Numbers   As you can see, several numbers were of great significance to the system. The number 20 was perhaps most important, as calendar calculations were done with a number system with base 20. There were 20 "suns" (days) to a "month," 20 years to a katun, and 20 katuns (20 times 20, or 400 years) to a baktun.

The number 52 was of tremendous importance, for it signified, literally, the "end of time," the end of the double cycle of solar and ceremonial calendars. At the beginning of a new cycle, temples were rebuilt for the "new age," which is why so many Maya temples and pyramids hold within them the structures of earlier, smaller temples and pyramids.

The Maya Concept of Time   The Maya considered time not as "progress" but as the wheel of fate, spinning endlessly, determining one's destiny by the combinations of attributes given to days in the solar and ceremonial calendars. The rains came on schedule, the corn was planted on schedule, and the celestial bodies moved in their great dance under the watchful eye of Maya astronomers and astrologers. *The Blood of Kings* (see "Recommended Books" in Chapter 1) has an especially good chapter on the Maya calendar.

As evidence of the Maya obsession with time, Chichén's most impressive structure, El Castillo, is an enormous "timepiece."

The main Mérida-Cancún highway used to run straight through the ruins of Chichén, and though it has now been diverted, you can still see the great swath it cut. South and west of the old highway's path are more impressive ruined buildings.

Tomb of the High Priest (Tumba del Gran Sacerdote)   Past the refreshment stand to the right of the path is the Tomb of the High Priest, which stood atop a natural limestone cave in which skeletons and offerings were found, giving the temple its name.

This building is being reconstructed, and workers are unearthing other smaller temples in the area. As the work progresses, some buildings may be roped off and others will open to the public for the first time. It's fascinating to watch the archaeologists at work, meticulously numbering each stone as they take apart what appears to be a mound of rocks and then reassembling the stones into a recognizable structure.

House of Metates (Casa de los Metates)   This building, the next one on your right, is named after the concave corn-grinding stones used by the Maya.

Temple of the Deer (Templo del Venado)   Past the House of Metates is this fairly tall though ruined building. The relief of a stag that gave the temple its name is long gone.

Little Holes (Chichan-chob)   This next temple has a roofcomb with little holes, three masks of the rain god Chaac, three rooms, and a good view of the surrounding structures. It's one of the older buildings at Chichén, built in the Puuc style during the Late Classic period.

Observatory (El Caracol)   Construction of the Observatory, a complex building with a circular tower, was carried out over a long period of time. Without a doubt, the additions and modifications reflected the Maya's increasing knowledge of celestial movements and their need for increasingly exact measurements. Through slits in the tower's walls, Maya astronomers could observe the cardinal directions and the approach of the all-important spring and autumn equinoxes, as well as the summer solstice. The temple's name, which means "snail," comes from a spiral staircase, now closed off, within the structure.

On the east side of El Caracol, a path leads north into the bush to the **Cenote Xtoloc,** a natural limestone well that provided the city's daily water supply. If you see any lizards sunning there, they may well be *xtoloc,* the lizard for which the cenote is named.

Temple of Panels (Templo de los Tableros)   Just to the south of El Caracol are the ruins of a **steambath** (*temazcalli*) and the Temple of Panels, named for the carved panels on top. This temple was once covered by a much larger structure, only traces of which remain.

Edifice of the Nuns (Edificio de las Monjas)   If you've visited the Puuc sites of Kabah, Sayil, Labná, or Xlapak, the enormous nunnery here will remind you at once of the "palaces" at the other sites. Built in the Late Classic period, the new edifice was constructed over an older one. Suspecting that this was so, Le Plongeon, an archaeologist working earlier in this century, put dynamite in between the two and blew part of the newer building to smithereens, thereby revealing part of the old. You can still see the results of Le Plongeon's indelicate exploratory methods.

On the eastern side of the Edifice of the Nuns is an annex (Anexo Este) constructed in highly ornate Chenes style with Chaac masks and serpents.

The Church (La Iglesia)   Next to the annex is one of the oldest buildings at Chichén, ridiculously named the Church. Masks of Chaac decorate two upper stories. Look closely and you'll see among the crowd of Chaacs an armadillo, a crab, a snail, and a tortoise. These represent the Maya gods called *bacah*, whose job it was to hold up the sky.

Temple of Obscure Writing (Akab Dzib)   This temple is along a path east of the Edifice of the Nuns. Above a door in one of the rooms are some Maya glyphs which gave the temple its name, since the writings have yet to be deciphered. In other rooms, traces of red handprints are still visible. Reconstructed and expanded over the centuries, this building has parts that are very old; it may well be the oldest building at Chichén.

Old Chichén (Chichén Viejo)   For a look at more of Chichén's oldest buildings, constructed well before the time of Toltec influence, follow signs from the Edifice of the Nuns southwest into the bush to Old Chichén, about half a mile away. Be prepared for this trek with long trousers, insect repellent, and a local guide. The attractions here are the **Temple of the First Inscriptions** (Templo de los Inscripciones Iniciales), with the oldest inscriptions discovered at Chichén, and the restored **Temple of the Lintels** (Templo de los Dinteles), a fine Puuc building.

ACCOMMODATIONS

It's difficult to reach Chichén and Pisté by phone; however, many hotels have reservation services in Mérida or in Mexico City.

EXPENSIVE

Hacienda Chichén-Itzá

Zona Arqueológica, Chichén-Itzá, Yuc. 97751. ☎ **985/6-2513** or 6-2462. For reservations contact Casa del Balam, Calle 60 no. 48, Mérida, Yuc. 97000; ☎ 99/24-8844 or 800/624-8451 in the U.S.; fax 99/24-5011. 18 rms (all with bath). FAN. High season $100 single; $110 double. Low season $60 single; $70 double. Closed off-season.

A romantic hotel a short walk from the back entrance to the ruins, the Hacienda Chichén-Itzá consists of bungalows built years ago for those who were excavating the ruins. Each cottage is named for an early archeologist working at Chichén. There's a pool open to those who drop in for lunch. The dining room is outside under the hacienda portals overlooking the grounds. But any meal is expensive: Breakfast is $7, lunch around $14, and dinner $20.

The hacienda is closed from May through October, though the owners were reconsidering this policy and it may be open year-round. It's often booked solid in the high season; advance reservations are strongly recommended.

✪ Hotel Mayaland

Zona Arqueológica, 97751 Chichén-Itzá, Yuc. ☎ **985/6-2777.** For reservations contact Mayaland Resorts, Av. Colón 502, Mérida, Yuc. 97000; ☎ 99/25-2122 or 800/235-4079 in the U.S.; fax 99/25-7022. 164 rms (all with bath). A/C or FAN TV. High season $130 single or double. Low season $110 single or double. Free guarded parking.

In operation since the 1930s, this is a long-time favorite by the ruins. No other hotel quite captures the feel of a ruins experience with the front doorway framing El Caracol (the observatory) as you walk outside from the lobby. Rooms in the main building, connected by a wide, tiled veranda, have air-conditioning and TV, tiled baths (with tubs), and colonial-style furnishings. Romantic oval Maya huts with beautifully carved furniture, palapa roofs, and mosquito netting are tucked around the wooded grounds. The grounds are gorgeous, with huge trees and blossoming ginger plants. There's a long pool and lounge area, and a restaurant that serves only fair meals at fixed prices, about $20 for a full lunch or dinner. You're better off ordering light meals and snacks by the pool or in the bar. Mayaland has a shuttle service between the hotel and Mérida for about $35 each way.

The Hotel Mayaland is a great bargain if you take advantage of their rental-car deal. If you stay at one of their hotels and rent a car through their office in Mérida or Cancún, your car rental is free with no minimum stay. There is a charge for car insurance, however.

✪ Hotel Villa Arqueológica

Zona Arqueológica, Chichén-Itzá, Yuc. 97751. ☎ **985/6-2830,** or 800/258-2633 in the U.S. 32 rms. A/C. High season $100 single; $110 double. Low season $60 single; $70 double.

Operated by Club Med, the Villa Arqueológica is almost next to the ruins and built around a swimming pool. The very comfortable rooms are like those at Uxmal and Cobá, each with two oversize single beds. There are tennis courts, and the hotel's rather expensive restaurant features French and Yucatecan food (breakfast is $15, lunch and dinner are $25 each).

MODERATE

Pirámide Inn

Carretera Mérida-Valladolid km 117, 97751 Pisté, Yuc. ☎ Caseta Pisté **985/6-2462** (leave a message). Fax 985/6-2671. 44 rms. A/C. $35–$40 single or double.

Less than a mile from the ruins at the edge of Pisté, this hospitable inn has large motel-like rooms equipped with two double beds or one king-size bed; but do check your mattress for its sag factor before accepting the room. Hot water comes on between 5 and 9am and 5 and 9pm. Water is purified in the tap for drinking. There is a pool in the midst of landscaped gardens, which include the remains of a pyramid wall. Try to get a room in the back if street noise bothers you. If you're coming from Valladolid it's on the left, and from Mérida look for it on the right.

Stardust Inn

Calle 15A no. 34A, Carretera Mérida-Valladolid, 97751 Pisté, Yuc. ☎ and fax **985/1-0122.** For reservations contact Calle 81A no. 513, Mérida, Yuc. 97000 ☎ 99/84-0072; 53 rms (all with bath). AC TV. $35 single or double. Free guarded parking.

The two-story Stardust Inn is built around a pool and a shaded courtyard. Each of the comfortable rooms has a tile floor, a shower, nice towels, and one or two double beds or three single beds; check the condition of your mattress before selecting a room. During high season there's a video bar/disco on the first floor; it's open during other times of the year if there are groups. If tranquillity is one of your priorities, ask if the disco is functioning before you rent a room. The very nice air-conditioned restaurant adjacent to the lobby and facing the highway serves all three meals and is open from 7:30am to 9:30pm.

INEXPENSIVE

Hotel Dolores Alba

Km 122 Carretera Mérida-Valladolid, Yuc. No phone. For reservations contact Hotel Dolores Alba, Calle 63 no. 464, 97000 Mérida, Yuc.; ☎ **99/28-5650;** fax 99/28-3163. 18 rms (all with bath). A/C or FAN. $20–$25 double. Free unguarded parking.

You'll be a mile from the back entrance to the ruins and about two miles from Pisté if you stay at the Dolores Alba. The nice rooms are clean with matching furniture, tile floors and showers, and well-screened windows. There's a pool with palapa in front of the restaurant. The restaurant serves good meals at moderate prices.

Breakfast (served between 7 and 9am) runs $2–$4, and main courses at dinner (7–9pm) are around $6–$8. But you should realize that when it comes to dining you have little choice—the nearest alternative restaurant or tienda where you can buy your own supplies is several miles away. Free transportation is provided to the ruins during visiting hours, but you'll have to get back on your own (about a 30-minute walk). A taxi from the ruins to the hotel costs about $5. The Dolores Alba in Mérida, also recommended, is owned by the same family, so either hotel will help you make reservations. The hotel is 1 1/2 miles past the ruins on the road going east to Cancún and Valladolid.

Posada Chac Mool

Carretera Mérida-Valladolid, 97751 Pisté, Yuc. No phone. 8 rms (all with bath). FAN. $10 single; $12 double. Limited free, unguarded parking.

Clean and plain, this no-frills single-story motel opened in 1990. The basically furnished rooms have new mattresses, red tile floors, and well-screened windows. Little tables and chairs outside each room on the covered walkway make an inviting place to enjoy a self-made meal. The motel is located at Calle 15, next to the Restaurant Las Mestizas, and almost opposite Hotel Misión.

Posada El Paso

Calle 15 no. 48F, Carretera Mérida-Valladolid, 97751 Pisté, Yuc. No phone. 13 rms (all with bath). FAN. $5–$7 single; $7–$9 double. Parking on the street in front of the hotel.

If you can handle the traffic noise, this small new hotel may be perfect for you. The buses and trucks roar past on Pisté's main drag, but the rooms are set back a bit from the road. Shower curtains are nonexistent, but the bathrooms are clean and the mattresses adequate.

Posada Novelo

Carretera Mérida-Valladolid, Pisté ☎ and fax **985/1-0122**. 11 rms (all with bath). FAN. $10 single or double. Free parking in front.

Operated by the Stardust Inn next door, this very basic hotel may serve well if your budget is more important than a status address. Rooms, attached in a row and linked by a covered walkway, all have one or two beds, and are sparsely furnished but clean. Hot water is a rarity.

DINING

Reasonably priced meals are available at the restaurant in the visitor's center at the ruins. Hotel restaurants near the ruins are more expensive than the few in Pisté. In Pisté, however, most of the better spots cater to large groups, which converge on them for lunch after 1pm.

Cafetería Ruinas

In the Chichén-Itzá visitors' center. No phone. Breakfast $4; sandwiches $4; main courses $5–$6. Daily 9am–5pm. MEXICAN/ITALIAN.

Though it has the monopoly on food at the ruins, this cafeteria actually does a good job with such basic meals as enchiladas, spaghetti, and baked chicken. Eggs are cooked to order, as are burgers, and their coffee is very good. Sit outside at the tables farthest from the crowd and relax.

La Fiesta

Carretera Mérida-Valladolid, Pisté. No phone. Main courses $4–$5; comida corrida $6. Daily 7am–9pm (comida corrida served 12:30–5pm). REGIONAL/MEXICAN.

With Maya motifs on the wall and colorful decorations, this is one of Pisté's long-established restaurants catering especially to tour groups. Though expensive, the food is very good. You'll be quite satisfied unless you arrive when a tour group is being served, in which case service to individual diners may suffer. Going toward the ruins, La Fiesta is on the west end of town.

Puebla Maya

Carretera Mérida-Valladolid, Pisté. No phone. Fixed-price lunch buffet $7. Lunch only, daily 1–5pm. MEXICAN.

Opposite the Pirámide Inn, the Puebla Maya looks just like its name, a Maya town with small white huts flanking a large open-walled palapa-topped center. Inside, however, you cross an artificial lagoon, planters drip with greenery, and live musicians play to the hundreds of tourists filling the tables. Service through the huge buffet is quick, so if you've been huffing around the ruins all morning, you have time to eat and relax before boarding the bus to wherever you're going. You can even swim in a lovely landscaped pool.

Restaurant Bar "Poxil"

Calle 15 s/n, Carretera Mérida-Valladolid, Pisté. ☎ 1-0123. Breakfast $3; main courses $3.50. Daily 7am–8pm. MEXICAN/REGIONAL.

A *poxil* is a Mayan fruit somewhat akin to a guanabana. Although this place doesn't serve them, what is on the menu is good, though not gourmet, and the price is right. You will find the Poxil near the west entrance to town on the south side of the street.

A SIDE TRIP TO THE GRUTAS (CAVES) DE BALANKANCHE

The Grutas de Balankanche are $3^1/_2$ miles from Chichén-Itzá on the road to Cancún and Puerto Juárez. Expect the taxi to cost about $6. (Taxis are usually on hand when the tours let out.) The entire excursion takes about half an hour, and the walk inside is hot and humid. The natural caves became wartime hideaways. You can still see traces of carving and incense burning, as well as an underground stream that served as the sanctuary's water supply. Outside, take time to meander through the botanical gardens, where most of the plants and trees are labeled with their common and scientific names.

The caves are open daily. Admission is $2.50, free on Sunday. Use of your video camera will cost an additional $4. Children under 6 aren't admitted. Guided tours in English are at 11am and 1 and 3pm, and in Spanish, at 9am, noon and 2 and 4pm. Tours go only if there are a minimum of 6 people and take up to 30 people at a time. Double-check these hours at the main entrance to the Chichén ruins.

6 Valladolid

25 miles E of Chichén-Itzá & Pisté, 100 miles SW of Cancún

The somewhat sleepy town of Valladolid (pronounced *"bye-*ah-doh-*leet"*), 25 miles east of Pisté/Chichén-Itzá, is an inexpensive alternative to staying in Pisté near the ruins of Chichén. You can get an early bus from Mérida, spend the day at the ruins, then travel another hour to Valladolid to overnight.

ESSENTIALS

GETTING THERE & DEPARTING

By Bus Buses leave almost hourly from Mérida, passing through Pisté and Chichén-Itzá on the way to Valladolid and Cancún. There are also regular buses from Cancún and at least six daily buses from Playa del Carmen. Because of the frequency of buses to Mérida and Cancún, advance purchase of tickets isn't usually necessary.

Autotransportes Oriente (☎ 985/6-3449) offers de paso buses to Pisté (the town nearest the Chichén-Itzá ruins) every hour from 2am to midnight; these same buses go on to Mérida. De paso buses on this same line go to Cobá at 4:30am and 1pm. Buses to Tizimin leave every hour from 5am to 10pm. **Expresso de Oriente** buses (☎ 6-3630) go to Mérida six times daily, to Playa del Carmen six times daily, and to Cancún five times daily. **Autobuses del Centro del Estado** offers five daily buses to Tinum and several other small towns on the way to Mérida.

By Car From Valladolid, there are frequent signs directing you via the toll road (*cuota*) to Mérida ($6), Chichén-Itzá, or Cancún ($11). No signs point you to the free (*libre*) road, but don't despair. To take the free road to Pisté/Chichén-Itzá and Mérida, take Calle 39, a one-way street going west on the north side of the Parque Cantón (the main plaza); this becomes the free Highway 180. Calle 41, a one-way east-bound street on the south side of the zócalo, becomes the free highway to Cancún.

Highway 180 links Valladolid with both Cancún and Mérida. It's a good, well-marked road and goes right past the main square in town. If you come from the toll road, the exit road leads to the Parque Cantón (the main plaza).

ORIENTATION

Information There is a small tourism office in the Palacio Municipal which will furnish you with some good information and maps. Señora Tete Mendoza B. is extremely helpful and knows her city and its history.

City Layout All hotels and restaurants are within walking distance of Valladolid's pretty **main square,** the **Parque Francisco Cantón Rosado.** The Valladolid **bus station** is at the corner of Calles 37 and 57, 10 very long blocks from the parque and too far to haul heavy luggage. Taxis are usually in front of the station.

Area Code The telephone area code is 985.

EXPLORING VALLADOLID

Valladolid was founded in 1543 on the shore of a lagoon near the coast. As it lacked good agricultural land, two years later it was moved to its present location on the site of a Maya religious center called Zací (meaning White Hawk). The Franciscans built an impressive monastery here, the **Convento de San Bernardino de Siena** (1552); the town boasts another half-dozen colonial churches, including the Templo de Santa Ana built in the 1500s originally for the exclusive use of the Maya. Two cenotes, one only two blocks east of the Parque Cantón, supplied water during colonial times. A small park, with a restaurant, a small bowl for the performing arts, and three Mayan-style stick-and-thatched-roof houses, has been created around the cenote Zací. These houses are meant to depict a typical Mayan settlement, and inside are some old photographs of Valladolid and a few arts and crafts for sale. **El Parroquia de San Servasio** (1545), the parish church, is on the south side of the main square, and the **Palacio Municipal** (Town Hall) is on the east.

SHOPPING

Embroidered Maya dresses can be purchased at the **Mercado de Artesanías de Valladolid** at the corner of Calles 39 and 44 and from women around the main square. The latter also sell—of all things—Barbie-doll-size Maya dresses! Just ask "¿Vestidos para Barbie?" and out they come.

The **food market** is on Calle 32 between Calles 35 and 37. Though it's open other days, the main market time is Sunday morning, when it's most active.

ACCOMMODATIONS

Hotels (and restaurants) here are less crowded and less expensive than the competition in Chichén.

Hotel El Mesón del Marqués

Calle 39 no. 203, 97780 Valladolid, Yuc. ☎ **985/6-3042** or 6-2073. Fax 985/6-2280. 38 rms (all with bath). A/C FAN TV TEL. $31 single or double; $39 double, suite. Free interior parking; secure.

This comfortable colonial-era mansion-turned-hotel on the north side of the Parque Cantón opposite the church offers rooms in both the original 200-year-old mansion and a new addition built around a pool in back. There is always hot water, and most of the rooms are sheltered from city noise. On the first floor there's a travel agency, gift shop, and restaurant (see "Dining," below).

Hotel María de la Luz

Calle 42 no. 195, 97780 Valladolid, Yuc. ☎ and fax **985/6-2071**. 33 rms (all with bath). A/C FAN TV. $18 single or double. Free parking; secure.

The two stories at the María de la Luz are built around an inner pool. The freshly painted rooms have been refurbished with new tile floors and baths and new mattresses. A couple of rooms have balconies overlooking the square. The wide interior covered walkway to the rooms is a nice place to relax in comfortable chairs. The hotel is on the west side of the Parque Francisco Cantón Rosado (the main square) between Calles 39 and 41.

DINING

The lowest restaurant prices are found in the Bazar Municipal, a little arcade of shops beside Hotel El Mesón del Marqués (see "Accommodations," above) right on the Parque Cantón. The cookshops open at mealtimes, when tables and chairs are set in the courtyard. You won't find many printed menus, let alone one in English, but a quick look around will tell you what's cooking, and you can order with a discreetly pointed finger. Ask the price beforehand so you won't be overcharged.

Casa de los Arcos Restaurant

Calle 39 no. 200A. ☎ **985/6-2467**. Breakfast $3; antojitos $3.50–$4.50; main courses $3.50–$7.50; comida corrida $5. Daily 7am–10pm (comida corrida served 1–4pm). MEXICAN/YUCATECAN.

A lovely, breezy courtyard with a black-and-white tiled floor makes this restaurant especially appealing. Waiters are efficient, the menu is in English and Spanish. The hearty comida corrida might feature a choice of meat and include red beans, tortillas, and coffee. There's also a full menu of beef, chicken, seafood, and a few Mexican specialties, one of which is the delicious longaniza à la Valladolid. To reach the restaurant from the main square (with the Hotel El Mesón del Marqués on your left), take Calle 39 two blocks; the restaurant is on the right across from the Hotel Don Luís.

Hostería del Marqués

Calle 39 no. 203. ☎ **6-2073**. Breakfast $2–$4; Mexican plates $2–$3; main courses $4–$7; sandwiches $2–$3. Daily 7am–11:30pm. MEXICAN/YUCATECAN.

This place is part of the Hotel El Mesón del Marqués facing the main square. Its patrons often spill out of the air-conditioned dining room onto the hotel's open *portales* on the interior courtyard, where tables have fresh flowers and are festively decorated in hot pink and turquoise. It's definitely a popular place, often crowded at lunch. The guacamole is great.

SIDE TRIPS FROM VALLADOLID
CENOTE DZITNUP

The Cenote Dzitnup (also known as Cenote Xkeken), $2^1/_2$ miles west of Valladolid off Highway 180, is worth a visit, especially if you have time for a dip. Descend a short flight of rather perilous stone steps, and at the bottom, inside a beautiful cavern, is a natural pool of water so clear and blue it's like something from a dream. If you decide to take a swim, be sure you don't have creams or other chemicals on your skin, as they damage the habitat for the small fish and other organisms living there. Also, no alcohol, food, or smoking is allowed after you enter the cavern.

Admission is $1. The cenote is open daily from 8am to 5pm.

EKBALAM: NEWLY EXCAVATED MAYA RUINS

About 21 miles northeast of Valladolid is Ekbalam (which in Maya means "star jaguar"), a newly opened archaeological site. Excavations of these ruins, which date from 100 B.C. to A.D. 1200, are ongoing.

To get here from Valladolid, go north on Highway 259 for 11 miles. Watch for the sign pointing right to the village of **Hunuku** and turn right there, following the road for $8^1/_2$ miles. When you reach Hunuku, a small village, ask someone to point to the dirt road that leads about $1^1/_2$ miles to the ruins. Caretaker Felipe Tuz Cohuo or willing young children can point out the highlights (the children have absorbed a lot of information during the years the ruins have been excavated). A tip to the caretaker is greatly appreciated. Pencils or ballpoint pens are good gifts for the children.

To really get a lot out of this site, you should be prepared to climb up the mountainlike pyramids with sides made of loose dirt and even looser rocks. Some of the important parts can also be seen from the pathway, but climbing is much more rewarding.

You can park at the entry sign and walk from there. Located on 2,500 wooded acres, the buildings are grouped closely around a large central area; along 350 feet of the perimeter are the remains of two low walls. The largest building, called **Structure 1** or the **Tower,** is impressive for its dimensions—it's 100 feet high, 517 feet long, and 200 feet wide. From the top you can see the tallest building of Cobá, 30 miles southeast as the crow flies. Scholars believe that Ekbalam was the center of a vast agricultural region. From this lofty vantage point, all around you can see fertile land that still produces corn, cotton, and honey.

Structure 3, also called the **Palace of the Nuns,** has a row of corbel-arched rooms. Though greatly destroyed, this architecture resembles the Puuc style of other Yucatecan sites. A few badly weathered stelae fragments are on display under flimsy thatched coverings. Structures show partial walls, some made of irregular rocks and others of carefully fitted and cut rock. Sacbeob (causeways) fan out in several directions, but so far none is thought to go farther than a mile or so. If you do any climbing at all, seeing the area will take a minimum of two hours.

The site is open daily from 8am to 5pm. Admission is $1.25, free on Sunday. A video camera permit costs $4.

RÍO LAGARTOS WILDLIFE REFUGE: NESTING FLAMINGOS

Some 50 miles north of Valladolid (25 miles north of Tizimin) on Highway 295 is Río Lagartos, a 118,000-acre refuge established in 1979 to protect the largest nesting population of flamingos in North America. Found in the park's dunes, mangrove swamps, and tropical forests are jaguars, ocelots, sea turtles, and at least 212 bird species (141 of which are permanent residents).

You can make the trip in one long day from Valladolid, but you'll have to leave by at least 5am to get to Río Lagartos by 7am, in time to arrange a trip to see the flamingos with one of the local boatmen. There's one poor-quality hotel in Río Lagartos, which I don't recommend. If you prefer to overnight closer to the refuge, then a good choice is **Tizimin** (pop. 50,000), 35 miles north of Valladolid. This pleasant city is the agricultural hub of the region. From Tizimin to Río Lagartos is about a 30-minute drive. Inexpensive hotels and restaurants are on or around Tizimin's main square.

SEEING THE RÍO LAGARTOS REFUGE

Río Lagartos is a small fishing village of around 3,000 people who make their living from the sea and from the occasional tourist who shows up to see the flamingos. Colorfully painted homes face the Malecón (the oceanfront street), and brightly painted boats dock along the same half-moon–shaped port. While Río Lagartos is interesting, if you have time for only one flamingo foray, make it in Celestún (west of Mérida). I've seen more flamingos and other kinds of birds at Celestún.

Plan to arrive in Río Lagartos around 7am and go straight to the dock area. There, boatmen will offer to take you on an hour-long trip to the flamingo lagoons for around $30 for up to six people in a motor-powered wooden boat. Ask around for Filiberto Pat Zem, a reliable boatman who takes the time to give a good tour.

Although thousands of flamingos nest near here from April to August, it is prohibited by law to visit their nesting grounds. Flamingos need mud with particular ingredients (including a high salt content) in order to multiply, and this area's mud does the trick. On your boat tour you'll probably see flamingos wading in the waters next to Mexico's second-largest salt-producing plant—the muddy bottom is plenty salty here. Flamingos use their special bills to suck up the mud, and they have the ability to screen the special contents they need from it. What you see on the boat trip is a mixture of flamingos, frigates, pelicans, herons in several colors, and ducks. Don't allow the boatman to frighten the birds into flight for your photographs; it causes the birds to eventually leave the habitat permanently.

Appendix

A Telephones & Mail

USING THE TELEPHONES

Area codes and city exchanges are being changed all over the country. If you have difficulty reaching a number, ask an operator for assistance. Mexico does not have helpful recordings to inform you of changes or new numbers.

Most **public pay phones** in the country have been converted to Ladatel phones, many of which are both coin- and card-operated. Instructions on the phones tell you how to use them. When your time limit for local calls is about to end (about three minutes), you'll hear three odd-sounding beeps, and then you'll be cut off unless you deposit more coins. Ladatel cards come in denominations of 10, 20, and 30 New Pesos. If you're planning to make many calls, purchase the 30 New Peso card; it takes no time at all to use up a 10-peso card (about $1.65). They're sold at pharmacies, bookstores, and grocery stores near Ladatel phones. You insert the card, dial your number, and start talking, all the while watching a digital counter tick away your money.

Next is the *caseta de larga distancia* (long-distance telephone office), found all over Mexico. Most bus stations and airports now have specially staffed rooms exclusively for making long-distance calls and sending faxes. Often they are efficient and inexpensive, providing the client with a computer printout of the time and charges. In other places, often pharmacies, the clerk will place the call for you, then you step into a private booth to take the call. Whether it's a special long-distance office or a pharmacy, there's usually a service charge of around $3.50 to make the call, which you pay in addition to any call costs if you didn't call collect.

For **long-distance calls** you can access an English-speaking ATT operator by pushing the star button twice, then 09. If that fails, try dialing 09 for an international operator. To call the United States or Canada tell the operator that you want a collect call (*una llamada por cobrar*) or station-to-station (*teléfono a teléfono*), or person-to-person (*persona a persona*). Collect calls are the least expensive of all, but sometimes caseta offices won't make them, so you'll have to pay on the spot.

To make a long-distance call from Mexico to another country, first dial 95 for the United States and Canada, or 98 for anywhere else in the world. Then, dial the area code and the number you are calling.

To call long distance (abbreviated "lada") within Mexico, dial 91, the area code, then the number. Mexico's area codes (claves) may be one, two, or three numbers and are usually listed in the front of telephone directories. In this book the area code is listed under "Fast Facts" for each town. (Area codes, however, are changing throughout the country.)

To place a phone call to Mexico from your home country, dial the international service (011), Mexico's country code (52), then the Mexican area code (for Cancún, for example, that would be 98), then the local number. Keep in mind that calls to Mexico are quite expensive, even if dialed direct from your home phone.

Better hotels, which have more sophisticated tracking equipment, may charge for each local call made from your room. Budget or moderately priced hotels often don't charge, since they can't keep track. To avoid check-out shock, it's best to ask in advance if you'll be charged for local calls. These cost between 50¢ and $1 per call. In addition, if you make a long-distance call from your hotel room, there is usually a hefty service charge added to the cost of the call.

POSTAL GLOSSARY

Airmail Correo aereo	**Post office box**
Customs Aduana	**(abbreviation)** Apdo. postal
General delivery Lista de correos	**Postal service** Correos
Insurance (insured mail) Seguros	**Registered mail** Registrado
Mailbox Buzón	**Rubber stamp** Sello
Money order Giro postale	**Special delivery, express** Entrega
Parcel Paquete	inmediata
Post office Oficina de correos	**Stamp** Estampilla or timbre

B   Basic Vocabulary

Most Mexicans are very patient with foreigners who try to speak their language; it helps a lot to know a few basic phrases.

I've included a list of certain simple phrases for expressing basic needs, followed by some common menu items.

ENGLISH-SPANISH PHRASES

English	Spanish	Pronunciation
Good day	**Buenos días**	*bway-nohss-dee-ahss*
How are you?	**¿Cómo esta usted?**	*koh-moh ess-tah oo-sted*
Very well	**Muy bien**	mwee byen
Thank you	**Gracias**	grah-see-ahss
You're welcome	**De nada**	day *nah-*dah
Good-bye	**Adios**	ah-dyohss
Please	**Por favor**	pohr fah-*bohr*
Yes	**Sí**	see
No	**No**	noh
Excuse me	**Perdóneme**	pehr-doh-ney-may
Give me	**Déme**	day-may

English	Spanish	Pronunciation
Where is . . . ?	¿Dónde esta . . . ?	dohn-day *ess*-tah
the station	la estación	la ess-tah-see-*own*
a hotel	un hotel	oon oh-*tel*
a gas station	una gasolinera	oon-nuh gah-so-lee-nay-rah
a restaurant	un restaurante	oon res-tow-*rahn*-tay
the toilet	el baño	el *bahn*-yoh
a good doctor	un buen médico	oon bwayn *may*-dee-co
the road to	el camino a . . .	el cah-*mee*-noh ah
To the right	A la derecha	ah lah day-*ray*-chuh
To the left	A la izquierda	ah lah ees-ky-*ehr*-dah
Straight ahead	Derecho	day-*ray*-cho
I would like	Quisiera	keyh-see-*air*-ah
I want	Quiero	*kyehr*-oh
to eat	comer	*ko*-mayr
a room	una habitación	oon-nuh ha-bee tah-see-*own*
Do you have?	¿Tiene usted?	tyah-nay oos-*ted*
a book	un libro	oon *lee*-bro
a dictionary	un diccionario	oon deek-see-own-ar-eo
How much is it?	¿Cuanto cuesta?	*kwahn*-to *kwess*-tah
When?	¿Cuando?	*kwahn*-doh
What?	¿Que?	kay
There is (Is there?)	¿Hay . . .	eye
Yesterday	Ayer	ah-*yer*
Today	Hoy	oy
Tomorrow	Mañana	mahn-*yawn*-ah
Good	Bueño	*bway*-no
Bad	Malo	*mah*-lo
Better (best)	(Lo) Mejor	(loh) meh-*hor*
More	Más	mahs
Less	Menos	may-noss
No Smoking	Se prohibe fumar	seh pro-*hee*-beh foo-*mahr*
Postcard	Tarjeta postal	tahr-hay-ta pohs-*tahl*
Insect repellent	Rapellante contra insectos	rah-pey-*yahn*-te cohn-trah een-sehk-tos

MORE USEFUL PHRASES

Do you speak English?	¿Habla usted inglés?
Is there anyone here who speaks English?	¿Hay alguien aquí qué hable inglés?
I speak a little Spanish.	Hablo un poco de español.
I don't understand Spanish very well.	No lo entiendo muy bien el español.
The meal is good.	Me gusta la comida.
What time is it?	¿Qué hora es?
May I see your menu?	¿Puedo ver su menu?
The check please.	La cuenta por favor.
What do I owe you?	¿Cuanto lo debo?
What did you say?	¿Mande? (colloquial expression for American "Eh?")

I want (to see) a room.	Quiero (ver) un cuarto (una habitación) . . .
for two persons.	para dos personas.
with (without) bath.	con (sin) baño.
We are staying here only	Nos quedaremos aqui solamente . . .
one night.	una noche.
one week.	una semana.
We are leaving tomorrow.	Partimos mañana.
Do you accept traveler's checks?	¿Acepta usted cheques de viajero?
Is there a Laundromat near here?	¿Hay una lavandería cerca de aquí?
Please send these clothes to the laundry.	Hágame el favor de mandar esta ropa a la lavandería.

NUMBERS

1	**uno** (*ooh*-noh)
2	**dos** (dohs)
3	**tres** (trayss)
4	**cuatro** (*kwah*-troh)
5	**cinco** (*seen*-koh)
6	**seis** (sayss)
7	**siete** (*syeh*-tay)
8	**ocho** (*oh*-choh)
9	**nueve** (*nway*-bay)
10	**diez** (dee-ess)
11	**once** (*ohn*-say)
12	**doce** (*doh*-say)
13	**trece** (*tray*-say)
14	**catorce** (kah-*tor*-say)
15	**quince** (*keen*-say)
16	**dieciseis** (de-*ess*-ee-sayss)
17	**diecisiete** (de-*ess*-ee-*syeh*-tay)

18	**dieciocho** (dee-*ess*-ee-*oh*-choh)
19	**diecinueve** (dee-*ess*-ee-*nway*-bay)
20	**veinte** (*bayn*-tay)
30	**treinta** (*trayn*-tah)
40	**cuarenta** (kwah-*ren*-tah)
50	**cincuenta** (seen-*kwen*-tah)
60	**sesenta** (say-*sen*-tah)
70	**setenta** (say-*ten*-tah)
80	**ochenta** (oh-*chen*-tah)
90	**noventa** (noh-*ben*-tah)
100	**cien** (see-en)
200	**doscientos** (*dos*-se-en-tos)
500	**quinientos** (*keen*-ee-ehn-tos)
1,000	**mil** (meal)

BUS TERMS

Bus	**Autobus**
Bus or truck	**Camion**
Lane	**Carril**
Nonstop	**Directo**
Baggage (claim area)	**Equipajes**
Intercity	**Foraneo**
Luggage storage area	**Guarda equipaje**
Gates	**Llegadas**
Originates at this station	**Local**
Originates elsewhere; stops if seats available	**De Paso**
First class	**Primera**
Second class	**Segunda**
Nonstop	**Sin Escala**
Baggage claim area	**Recibo de Equipajes**
Waiting room	**Sala de Espera**
Toilets	**Sanitarios**
Ticket window	**Taquilla**

C Menu Glossary

Achiote   Small red seed of the annatto tree.

Achiote preparada   A prepared paste found in Yucatán markets made of ground achiote, wheat and corn flour, cumin, cinnamon, salt, onion, garlic, and oregano. Mixed with juice of a sour orange or vinegar and put on broiled or charcoaled fish (tikin chick) and chicken.

Agua fresca   Fruit-flavored water, usually watermelon, canteloupe, chia seed with lemon, hibiscus flour, or ground melon seed mixture.

Antojito   A Mexican snack, usually masa-based with a variety of toppings such as sausage, cheese, beans, onions; also refers to tostadas, sopes, and garnachas.

Atole   A thick, lightly sweet, warm drink made with finely ground rice or corn and usually flavored with vanilla.

Birria   Lamb or goat meat cooked in a tomato broth, spiced with garlic, chiles, cumin, ginger, oregano, cloves, cinnamon, and thyme and garnished with onions, cilantro, and fresh lime juice to taste; a specialty of Jalisco state.

Botana   A light snack—an antojito.

Buñelos   Round, thin, deep-fried crispy fritters dipped in sugar.

Cabrito   Grilled kid; a northern Mexican delicacy.

Carnitas   Pork that's been deep-cooked (not fried) in lard, then steamed and served with corn tortillas for tacos.

Ceviche   Fresh raw seafood marinated in fresh lime juice and garnished with chopped tomatoes, onions, chiles, and sometimes cilantro and served with crispy, fried whole corn tortillas.

Chiles rellenos   Poblano peppers usually stuffed with cheese, rolled in a batter, and baked; other stuffings include ground beef spiced with raisins.

Choyote   Vegetable pear or merleton, a type of spiny squash, boiled and served as an accompaniment to meat dishes.

Churro   Tube-shaped, breadlike fritter, dipped in sugar and sometimes filled with cajeta or chocolate.

Cochinita pibil   Pig wrapped in banana leaves, flavored with pibil sauce and pit-baked; common in Yucatán.

Corunda   A triangular tamal wrapped in a corn leaf, a Michoacán specialty.

Enchilada   Tortilla dipped in a sauce and usually filled with chicken or white cheese and sometimes topped with tomato sauce and sour cream (enchiladas Suizas—Swiss enchiladas), or covered in a green sauce (enchiladas verdes), or topped with onions, sour cream, and guacamole (enchiladas Potosiños).

Epazote   Leaf of the wormseed plant, used in black beans and with cheese in quesadillas.

Escabeche   A lightly pickled sauce used in Yucatecan chicken stew.

Frijoles charros   Beans flavored with beer, a northern Mexican specialty.

Frijoles refritos   Pinto beans mashed and cooked with lard.

Garnachas   A thickish small circle of fried masa with pinched sides, topped with pork or chicken, onions, and avocado or sometimes chopped potatoes, and tomatoes, typical as a botana in Veracruz and Yucatán.

Gorditas   Thickish fried-corn tortillas, slit and stuffed with choice of cheese, beans, beef, chicken, with or without lettuce, tomato, and onion garnish.

Gusanos de maguey   Maguey worms, considered a delicacy, and delicious when charbroiled to a crisp and served with corn tortillas for tacos.

Horchata   Refreshing drink made of ground rice or melon seeds, ground almonds, and lightly sweetened.

Huevos Mexicanos   Eggs with onions, hot peppers, tomatoes.

Huevos Motulenos   Eggs atop a tortilla, garnished with beans, peas, ham, sausage, and grated cheese, a Yucatecan specialty.

Huevos rancheros   Fried egg on top of a fried corn tortilla covered in a tomato sauce.

Huitlacoche   Sometimes spelled "cuitlacoche," mushroom-flavored black fungus that appears on corn in the rainy season; considered a delicacy.

Machaca   Shredded dried beef scrambled with eggs or as salad topping; a specialty of northern Mexico.

Manchamantel   Translated means "tablecloth stainer," a stew of chicken or pork with chiles, tomatoes, pineapple, bananas, and jícama.

Masa   Ground corn soaked in lime used as basis for tamales, corn tortillas, and soups.

Mixiote   Lamb baked in a chile sauce or chicken with carrots and potatoes both baked in parchment paper made from the maguey leaf.

Mole   Pronounced "*moh*-lay," a sauce made with 20 ingredients including chocolate, peppers, ground tortillas, sesame seeds, cinnamon, tomatoes, onion, garlic, peanuts, pumpkin seeds, cloves, and tomatillos; developed by colonial nuns in Puebla, usually served over chicken or turkey; especially served in Puebla state and Oaxaca with sauces varying from red to black and brown.

Molletes   A bolillo cut in half and topped with refried beans and cheese, then broiled; popular at breakfast.

Pan de Muerto   Sweet or plain bread made around the Days of the Dead (Nov.1–2), in the form of mummies, dolls, or round with bone designs.

Pan dulce   Lightly sweetened bread in many configurations usually served at breakfast or bought at any bakery.

Papadzules   Tortillas are stuffed with hard-boiled eggs and seeds (cucumber or sunflower) in a tomato sauce.

Pavo relleno negro   Stuffed turkey Yucatán-style, filled with chopped pork and beef, cooked in a rich, dark sauce.

Pibil   Pit-baked pork or chicken in a sauce of tomato, onion, mild red pepper, cilantro, and vinegar.

Pipian   Sauce made with ground pumpkin seeds, nuts, and mild peppers.

Poc-chuc   Slices of pork with onion marinated in a tangy sour orange sauce and charcoal broiled; a Yucatecan specialty.

Pollo Calpulalpan   Chicken cooked in pulque, a specialty of Tlaxcala.

Pozole   A soup made with hominy and pork or chicken, in either a tomato-based broth Jalisco-style, or a white broth Nayarit-style, or green chile sauce Guerrero-style, and topped with choice of chopped white onion, lettuce or cabbage, radishes, oregano, red pepper, and cilantro.

Pulque   Drink made of fermented sap of the maguey plant; best in Hidalgo state and around Mexico City.

Quesadilla   Four tortillas stuffed with melted white cheese and lightly fried.

Queso relleno   "Stuffed cheese" is a mild yellow cheese stuffed with minced meat and spices, a Yucatecan specialty.

Rompope   Delicious Mexican eggnog, invented in Puebla, made with eggs, vanilla, sugar, and rum.

Salsa verde   A cooked sauce using the green tomatillo and pureed with mildly hot peppers, onions, garlic, and cilantro; on tables countrywide.

Sopa de calabaza   Soup made of chopped squash or pumpkin blossoms.

Sopa de lima   A tangy soup made with chicken broth and accented with fresh lime; popular in Yucatán.

Sopa seca   Not a soup at all, but a seasoned rice which translated means "dry soup."

Sopa Tarascan   A rib-sticking pinto-bean based soup, flavored with onions, garlic, tomatoes, chiles, and chicken broth and garnished with sour cream, white cheese, avocado chunks, and fried tortilla strips; a specialty of Michoacán state.

Sopa Tlalpeña   A hearty soup made with chunks of chicken, chopped carrots, zucchini, corn, onions, garlic, and cilantro.

Sopa Tlaxcalteca   A hearty tomato-based soup filled with cooked nopal cactus, cheese, cream, and avocado with crispy tortilla strips floating on top.

Sopa tortilla   A traditional chicken broth-based soup, seasoned with chiles, tomatoes, onion, and garlic, bobbing with crisp fried strips of corn tortillas.

Sope   Pronounced "*soh*-pay," a botana similar to a garnacha, except spread with refried beans and topped with crumbled cheese and onions.

Tacos al pastor   Thin slices of flavored pork roasted on a revolving cylinder dripping with onion slices and juice of fresh pineapple slices.

Tamal   Incorrectly called tamale (tamal singular, tamales plural), meat or sweet filling rolled with fresh masa, then wrapped in a corn husk or banana leaf and steamed; many varieties and sizes throughout the country.

Tepache   Drink made of fermented pineapple peelings and brown sugar.

Tikin Xic   Also seen on menus as "tikin chick," char-broiled fish brushed with achiote sauce.

Tinga   A stew made with pork tenderloin, sausage, onions, garlic, tomatoes, chiles, and potatoes; popular on menus in Puebla and Hidalgo states.

Torta   A sandwich, usually on bolillo bread, usually with sliced avocado, onions, tomatoes, with a choice of meat and often cheese.

Torta Ahogado   A specialty of Lake Chapala is made with scooped-out roll, filled with beans and beef strips and seasoned with a tomato or chile sauce.

Tostadas   Crispy fried corn tortillas topped with meat, onions, lettuce, tomatoes, cheese, avocados, and sometimes sour cream.

Venado   Venison (deer) served perhaps as pipian de venado, steamed in banana leaves and served with a sauce of ground squash seeds.

Xtabentun (pronounced "shtah-ben-*toon*")   A Yucatán liquor made of fermented honey and flavored with anise. It comes *seco* (dry) or *crema* (sweet).

Zacahuil   Pork leg tamal, packed in thick masa, wrapped in banana leaves, and pit-baked; sometimes pot-made with tomato and masa; specialty of mid- to upper Veracruz.

Index

FROMMER'S COMPLETE TRAVEL GUIDES

(Comprehensive guides to destinations around the world, with selections in all price ranges—from deluxe to budget)

Acapulco/Ixtapa/Taxco
Alaska
Amsterdam
Arizona
Atlanta
Australia
Austria
Bahamas
Bangkok
Barcelona, Madrid & Seville
Belgium, Holland & Luxembourg
Berlin
Bermuda
Boston
Budapest & the Best of Hungary
California
Canada
Cancún, Cozumel & the Yucatán
Caribbean
Caribbean Cruises & Ports of Call
Caribbean Ports of Call
Carolinas & Georgia
Chicago
Colorado
Costa Rica
Denver, Boulder & Colorado Springs
Dublin
England
Florida
France
Germany
Greece
Hawaii
Hong Kong
Honolulu/Waikiki/Oahu
Ireland
Italy
Jamaica/Barbados
Japan
Las Vegas
London
Los Angeles
Maryland & Delaware
Maui

Mexico
Mexico City
Miami & the Keys
Montana & Wyoming
Montréal & Québec City
Munich & the Bavarian Alps
Nashville & Memphis
Nepal
New England
New Mexico
New Orleans
New York City
Northern New England
Nova Scotia, New Brunswick & Prince
   Edward Island
Paris
Philadelphia & the Amish Country
Portugal
Prague & the Best of the Czech Republic
Puerto Rico
Puerto Vallarta, Manzanillo & Guadalajara
Rome
San Antonio & Austin
San Diego
San Francisco
Santa Fe, Taos & Albuquerque
Scandinavia
Scotland
Seattle & Portland
South Pacific
Spain
Switzerland
Thailand
Tokyo
Toronto
U.S.A.
Utah
Vancouver & Victoria
Vienna
Virgin Islands
Virginia
Walt Disney World & Orlando
Washington, D.C.
Washington & Oregon

FROMMER'S FRUGAL TRAVELER'S GUIDES

(The grown-up guides to budget travel, offering dream vacations at down-to-earth prices)

Australia from $45 a Day
Berlin from $50 a Day
California from $60 a Day
Caribbean from $60 a Day
Costa Rica & Belize from $35 a Day
Eastern Europe from $30 a Day
England from $50 a Day
Europe from $50 a Day
Florida from $50 a Day
Greece from $45 a Day
Hawaii from $60 a Day

India from $40 a Day
Ireland from $45 a Day
Italy from $50 a Day
Israel from $45 a Day
London from $60 a Day
Mexico from $35 a Day
New York from $70 a Day
New Zealand from $45 a Day
Paris from $65 a Day
Washington, D.C. from $50 a Day

FROMMER'S PORTABLE GUIDES

(Pocket-size guides for travelers who want everything in a nutshell)

Charleston & Savannah
Las Vegas

New Orleans
San Francisco

FROMMER'S IRREVERENT GUIDES

(Wickedly honest guides for sophisticated travelers)

Amsterdam
Chicago
London
Manhattan

Miami
New Orleans
Paris
San Francisco

Santa Fe
U.S. Virgin Islands
Walt Disney World
Washington, D.C.

FROMMER'S AMERICA ON WHEELS

(Everything you need for a successful road trip, including full-color road maps and ratings for every hotel)

California & Nevada
Florida
Mid-Atlantic
Midwest & the Great Lakes
New England & New York

Northwest & Great Plains
South Central & Texas
Southeast
Southwest

FROMMER'S BY NIGHT GUIDES

(The series for those who know that life begins after dark)

Amsterdam
Chicago
Las Vegas
London

Los Angeles
Miami
New Orleans

New York
Paris
San Francisco